CULINARY PLEASURES

CULINARY PLEASURES

Cook Books and the Transformation of British Food

NICOLA HUMBLE

ff

faber and faber

First published in 2005
by Faber and Faber Limited
3 Queen Square London WC1N 3AU

Typeset by Faber and Faber Limited
Printed in England by Mackays of Chatham, plc

A CIP record for this book
is available from the British Library

ISBN 0-571-20005-2

2 4 6 8 10 9 7 5 3 1

For Julia, who did bake the best biscuits, and Rachel, who made very good jam tarts.

Contents

List of Illustrations

Introduction

I remember very clearly the first time I read a cook book. It was the Christmas holidays, I was about fourteen, and the book was the magisterial *Constance Spry Cookery Book*, which had sat in fat pink splendour on my parents' bookshelves for as long as I could recall. I had used cook books before, of course, since my sister and I were engaged in a deadly, unspoken competition over who could produce the best biscuits, but I had never read one from cover to cover. Hunched up against the radiator as the light grew dimmer, I was completely captivated. There was narrative – of Constance Spry's setting up of her cookery school in Winkfield Place. There were stories – including one lengthy quotation from a forgotten novel that is forever queasily embedded in my consciousness, about a new wife watched by her husband as she washes the cutlery as gently and carefully as if each piece were a little animal. There were characters, particularly the redoubtable Rosemary Hume, Spry's business partner (the real cook of the team, since Spry's 'proper' career was as a society florist) who appears as R. H. throughout the book, offering small improvements to recipes and refinements of technique. Above all, there was history – the authentic savour of the upper-class culture of the years between the wars, and the valour of Spry's attempts to reintroduce its lost splendours in the years after rationing. These narrative pleasures might seem to be somehow beside the point, the garnish around the edges of the cook book rather than the prime meat of the recipes at its heart. Yet the recipes too turned out to be intensely satisfying: detailed and sternly perfectionist, they offered a full course in classic (that is, pre-war English) cordon bleu cookery. As is the case with much of our childhood reading, they stuck in my mind to the extent that I can still describe in detail Spry's scarily meticulous (but accurate) instructions for the making of choux pastry, and though, as a lifelong vegetarian, I have little experience of handling meat, I could probably follow from memory her method for larding a roast.

Looking back, so many things seem to begin for me with the reading of this book. In some fundamental sense it taught me about active reading, about reading for the ideas at the edge of a narrative as well as those in the centre. It showed me that books can mean more than they intend. It started me looking for the importance embedded in the apparently trivial and unregarded, the things a culture takes for granted.[1] I can date both my career as a literary scholar and the form it has taken from that point. More directly, that reading started a preoccupation with cook books as both texts and objects – as things worthy of study in their own right, not just as the blueprint for a few meals. The result is this book, which sets out to take the cook book seriously and to read it for the many curious and profound lights it throws on the culture of the last century and a half. This is not primarily a history of food, many excellent examples of which already exist; it is rather a cultural history of the cook book, examining it in both its most typical and its most outlandish forms to see what it has to tell us about the hopes and fears, the tastes and aspirations, the fantasies and paranoias, and the changing social roles of its particular historical moment.[2]

Any cook book offers us an abundance of meanings and readings. My mother's copy of Constance Spry, for example, may well have been given to her when she married in the early 1960s, as it was to many tens of thousands of other young women in the decade after its publication in 1956. The contemporary equivalent of Mrs Beeton's *Household Management*, the strapping tome promised advice for every possible culinary eventuality, and in the complexity of its instructions and the assurance of its tone asserted that home-making was both a worthy and a stylish occupation for a woman. It was one of the last cook books to be so sure of that fact. As her most monumental and 'serious' cook book, *The Constance Spry Cookery Book* is the place where my mother keeps her own recipes. Rather like a family bible, it has acquired accretions of text: recipes copied onto the flyleaves (1970s dinner-party classics of cheesecakes and fondues contributed by friends; the recipes she uses each year for her Christmas cake and pudding); cuttings from magazines; and a precious remnant of a letter from my long-dead Lancashire grandmother with instructions for her parkin (made with pinhead oatmeal and black treacle, this tasted disappointingly dry and dusty when we sneaked a newly cooked piece, but left in a tin to mellow it became simultaneously gooey and crunchy, with a dark, rounded taste).

Second-hand cook books are similar treasure troves of their owners' lives, with newspaper cuttings and personal amendments to the printed recipes. Readers actively engage with cook books, testing their claims, altering their instructions to their own taste, adding comments, reminders and personal recollections. Cook books become palimpsests, the original text overlaid with personal meanings and experiences, the spines broken by use and by the mass of extra matter forced between their pages. Some – the most used – also bulge with the literal remnants of the feasts they have conjured up, their stained pages entombing ancient crumbs and morsels.[3] This physical reminder of previous readers is a remarkable thing, one which separates the cook book from most other forms of literature, except perhaps the erotic novel that falls open automatically at its most purple passages. These traces often indicate the intensely personal engagement of readers with their cook books: the horrified 'No!!' inscribed alongside the suggestion to add Oxo-cube gravy to a steak and kidney pie in Ethelind Fearon's 1953 book *The Reluctant Cook* – a passionate aesthetic rejection of the very concept of Oxo cubes this, rather than the considered amendment of someone who has tried the Oxo gravy and decided that on balance it is better omitted. Or the violence with which a chapter on the management of servants has been ripped from a first edition of Marcel Boulestin's *The Conduct of the Kitchen* (1925), the action of someone who has lost all hope of being able to afford or find servants ever again. And then there are the recipes carefully inscribed by hand in the pages left blank by many cook books for this purpose: invariably at odds with the tenor of the book they occupy, they set up counter-textual reverberations, challenging the authority of the cook book, its claims to arbitrate on matters of good taste (of both sorts) and sound technique. So in my second-hand copy of Countess Morphy's monumental *Recipes of All Nations* (1935), which arranges its recipes in geographical sections separated by coloured pages on which readers can write their own recipes, the section on France, full of elegant, innovatory little dishes, is followed by an uncompromising hand-written recipe for Meat Sauce, with ingredients including 1 oz of dripping, 1 tablespoon of tomato sauce, 1 teaspoon of Piquant Sauce and 4 oz of unspecified 'minced cooked meat'. Such recipes can provide an answer to the question that nags away at anyone who works on cook books: did anyone actually cook these dishes? The recipes that people exchange, copy down or amend are those that they are at most interested in and probably at least intend to cook. And these are invariably not the most unusual recipes, nor those that are most intriguing to a food historian. For this reason we need to approach history-through-the-cookbook with some caution, remembering that cook books are not simply clear windows into the kitchens of the past. Rather, they are interventions in the diet of the nation, attempts to popularize new foods, new methods, fresh attitudes. They will always have more to tell us about the fantasies and fears associated with foods than about what people actually had for dinner.

It is questionable whether people really use cook books much at all. How many recipes have you actually cooked from most of the cook books you own? We might consider the story of the 1940s magazine that inadvertently published a recipe with a fatally poisonous combination of ingredients. Having notified the police and desperately tried to recall copies, the editors waited anxiously to hear reports of people taken ill. None came, and they were forced to conclude that not one of their readers had actually tried the recipe. It seems that we may buy cook books and magazines and watch food programmes for altogether different purposes than that of trying to find an exciting new dish for supper. This book is an attempt to find out what those other purposes might be.

CHAPTER ONE

From Mrs Beeton to the Great War

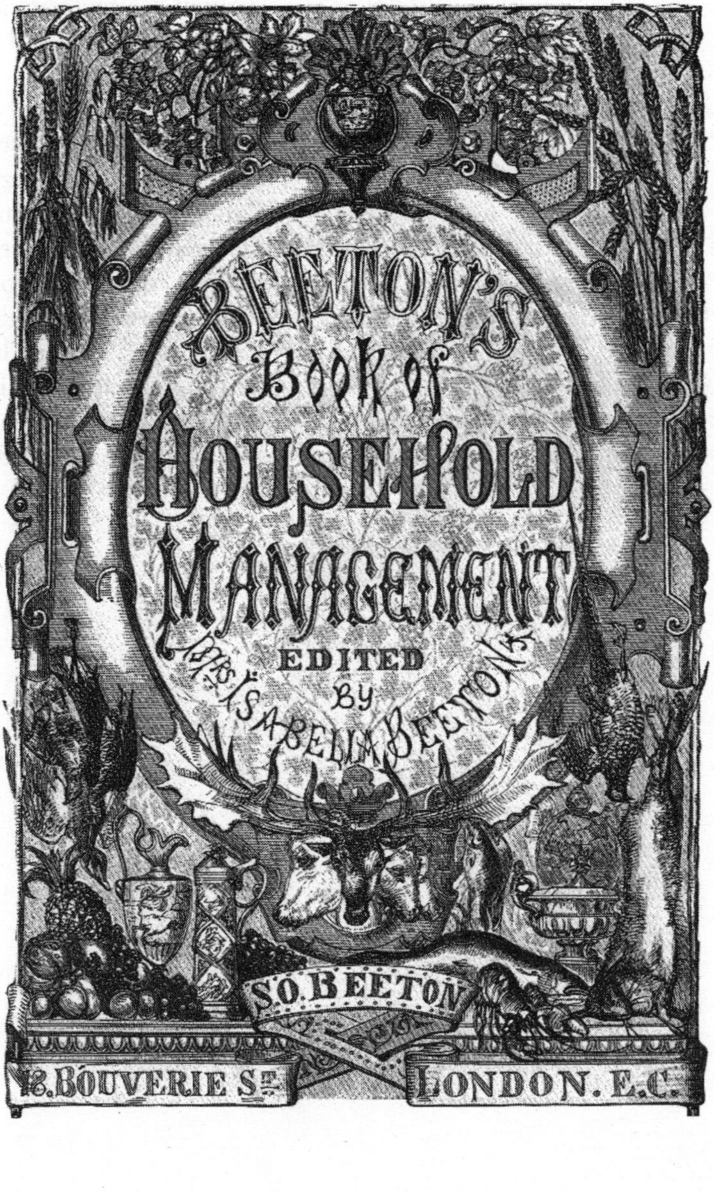

In 1861 the small independent firm S. O. Beeton published what was to become the most famous of all British cook books. Priced at 7s. 6d. and nearly as thick as it was high, *Beeton's Book of Household Management* was a consummate success from the beginning, selling over 60,000 copies in its first year and nearly two million by 1868. But by that time its author was dead: Isabella Beeton died in 1865 of puerperal fever almost certainly caused by the attending doctor's failure to wash his hands before delivering her fourth child. She was twenty-eight.

In no way a typical Victorian woman, Isabella Beeton was a rather unlikely arbiter of middle-class tastes and values. The eldest of a combined step-family of twenty-one children, she spent much of her childhood living in the grandstand on Epsom racecourse (her stepfather was clerk of the course, and she and her older siblings were squeezed out of the family's elegant townhouse by the constant influx of new siblings). She briefly studied pastry-making in Germany, and when she was twenty married the entrepreneurial publisher Sam Beeton, who at the age of twenty-five had already made his fortune when the firm in which he was a partner published the first British edition of Harriet Beecher Stowe's *Uncle Tom's Cabin*. During their engagement Isabella began to contribute to his *Englishwoman's Domestic Magazine*, first translating French novels for serialization, later writing a column on fashion – her great interest – and also the cookery columns that were to form the basis of her monumental work. The magazine, which was the mainstay of the independent firm Sam set up soon after their marriage, was responsible for the introduction of a number of what were to become key features of women's magazines: it had the first problem page – known as 'Cupid's Letter Bag'- a medical column, readers' essay competitions and paper dress patterns.

A fashionable and accomplished young woman, unconventional in her upbringing and opinions; a journalist working in equal partnership with her husband – this Mrs Beeton is a long way from the popular image of an old dragon in black bombazine. And yet it is no accident that we conjure up this mental picture of a sternly didactic Victorian matron: Ward Lock, the publishing firm to whom a grief-stricken and bankrupt Sam sold the rights of *Household Management* after his wife's death, seem to have tacitly created this picture of the author by avoiding, in later editions, any reference to her in the past tense, allowing the reader to imagine her continued existence. The mythology was firmly established by the 1930s, when a brief flurry of excitement was caused by the presentation to the National Portrait Gallery of a portrait of the stylish young girl who had actually written *Household Management*. (It was given by Sir Mayson Beeton, the son whose birth had led to her death.)

Household Management was one of the major publishing coups of the nineteenth century, and in its many subsequent editions over the next hundred years it became the bulwark of the substantial fortune of its publishers. As a cultural object its status is immense: reissued in countless guises, presented to generations of young women as a guide to setting up home, it represents traditional domestic virtues and skills, its solid heft promising authoritative counsel on any culinary conundrum. There is still a strong market for the book today: first editions – not terribly rare given the large size of the original print run – nevertheless change hands for thousands of pounds and facsimile editions regularly make the best-seller lists. Yet the suspicion that very few of the many people who own a copy of Beeton's book do more than occasionally dip into it for a recipe for marmalade is testified to by the misconceptions that abound not only about its author but about the book itself. *Household Management* is popularly seen as extravagant ('take 12 dozen eggs') or as representing a lost rural way of life ('first catch your hare'). To most people the title conjures up British cooking at its most traditional: huge haunches of beef and cannonballs of steamed suet pudding. The beef and puddings are certainly there, but in many ways Beeton's book was strikingly innovatory, introducing the ever-growing and self-consciously respectable Victorian middle class to a wide range of foreign recipes, to the latest manufactured food products and to fashionably different styles of dining. Despite their frequent attribution to her, those lines about eggs and hares were never written by Beeton, a fact that serves to demonstrate the persistent myth-making to which her book has been subject.[1] Although the book does contain a few conspicuously extravagant recipes, if anything it errs on the side of frugality, with many pages devoted to plain family dinners and the use of leftovers (it was these which tended to be removed from later editions, encouraging the view of the book as extravagant). Finally, one of the major factors governing the history of British culinary development is the fact that we had an agrarian and an industrial revolution long before any other European nation: the rural economy in which most people produced their own food was already lost by the time Beeton embarked on her book, and she is almost as nostalgic for that old connection to the land as we are today. World-renowned, yet largely unread, *Beeton's Book of Household Management* exemplifies, even in its extraordinary success, the anomalous place the cook book occupies in our culture. It is among the most commercial of literary forms, yet what we might call its textuality – the ways it addresses its readers, the form and genesis of its recipes, its tone of voice – remains essentially unregarded.

Household Management was largely based on the column on 'Cooking, Pickling and Preserving' Isabella wrote for the *Englishwoman's Domestic Magazine*, and this in turn drew heavily on the contributions of the magazine's readers, who were solicited for their own tips, stratagems and family recipes, which she and her servants would exhaustively test in her kitchen in Pinner. She made no claims for herself as the originator of recipes, and only a handful of the nearly two thousand in the first edition are presented as her own. Her skill was rather in the clear, unambiguous language she developed for the exposition of cooking methods, and her ability to organize an intractable mass of information into bite-sized nuggets. The book is encyclopaedic in its range, and Isabella clearly found it impossible to resist a juicy fact. Each recipe chapter is paired with a preceding one of factual information, covering issues as diverse as history, mythology, religion, agriculture, animal husbandry, science, sociology and so on. These chapters take the work far beyond the conventional scope of a cook book and were envisaged by Sam and Isabella as a unique selling point, emphasized at length in their advertisements:

A new and important feature, which, it is felt, will form an invaluable portion of BEETON'S BOOK OF HOUSEHOLD MANAGEMENT, is the history, description, properties, and uses, of every article directly or indirectly connected with the Household. Thus, if in a recipe for a Christmas plum-pudding, are named the various ingredients of raisins, currants, candied oranges and lemon-peel, sugar, citron, bitter almonds and brandy, BEETON'S BOOK OF HOUSEHOLD MANAGEMENT will give ample information on questions such as these:-

Where are Raisins grown, and how are they dried? – In what Countries do Cur-

rants flourish most, and what Process do they undergo in order to be made suitable for the English market? – How are Candied Orange and Lemon-peel manufactured, and what are the characteristics of the growth of the Orange and Lemon-trees? [. . .] What enters into the manufacture of Brandy, and what are the names of the principal places it comes from? – Do we distill any in this Country? &c.[2]

It is no accident that these questions resemble the schoolroom catechisms put to Victorian girls. In its heterogeneous and sometimes random-seeming mix of disciplines and discourses, *Household Management* belongs to a tradition of female education which, in the absence of professional careers for women, tended to offer learning with no object, exercising the memory rather than the intellect. Nevertheless, although its preoccupation with offering its women readers a plethora of useful facts was not in itself particularly radical, it was unusual in its assumption of the intellectual curiosity of these readers, crediting them as it did with enquiring minds and a desire for self-improvement.

Despite the interest of the encyclopaedic sections of the book, the real success of *Household Management* lies in the presentation and ordering of its recipes. Each dish is approached from the perspective of the novice rather than the expert, with every stage in its construction painstakingly described. The style is matter-of-fact and determinedly impersonal. There are very few anecdotes and asides, no glimpses into her own kitchen or hints as to her preferences. Instead, she tried to put cooking on a logical, scientific basis, devoting a great deal of attention to perfecting her descriptions of methods to make them clear and unambiguous. The form in which she gives recipes – with ingredients, quantities and cooking times listed separately from method – established a new convention that still prevails to this day, but Beeton was not, in fact, its originator. The first cookery writer to employ such an approach was Eliza Acton (1799–1859), whose *Modern Cookery for Private Families* was published in 1845. Beeton copied Acton's method and refined it, by giving the ingredients list logically at the start of the recipe rather than at the end, and also giving the numbers of people each dish would serve and an estimate of its cost. This imitation of Acton's recipe layout is just one example of the huge debt Beeton owed to the earlier writer. She lifted freely and largely from Acton's book, and also from the work of another earlier food writer, Alexis Soyer – in both cases with scant acknowledgement. Despite this borrowing, however, Beeton's book differs markedly from those of her immediate predecessors.

Eliza Acton's *Modern Cookery* was one of the first books to address itself centrally to the culinary needs of the middle classes. Written in response to a publisher's half-joking suggestion that she write a cook book instead of the volume of verse she was trying to sell him, Acton's book was in many ways the antithesis of Beeton's. Where Beeton gives clear, impersonal instructions, Acton (despite her rationalist innovations in the way of recipe layout) offers discussion, explanation and the quirky, confident perspective of the expert. A randomly chosen comparison will serve to illustrate their very different approaches – the first recipe is Beeton's, the second Acton's:

BROILED MUSHROOMS
(A Breakfast, Luncheon, or Supper-Dish)

INGREDIENTS. – Mushroom-flaps, pepper and salt to taste, butter, lemon-juice.

Mode. – Cleanse the mushrooms by wiping them with a piece of flannel and a little salt; cut off a portion of the stalk, and peel the tops: broil them over a clear fire, turning them once, and arrange them on a very hot dish. Put a small piece of butter on each mushroom, season with pepper and salt, and squeeze over them a few drops of lemon-juice. Place the dish before the fire, and when the butter is melted, serve very hot and quickly. Moderate-sized flaps are better suited to this mode of cooking than the buttons: the latter are better in stews.

Time. – 10 minutes for medium-sized mushrooms.

Average cost. – 1d. each for large mushrooms.

Sufficient. – Allow 3 or 4 mushrooms to each person.

Seasonable. – Meadow mushrooms in September and October; cultivated mushrooms may be had at any time.[3]

MUSHROOMS AU BEURRE
Delicious.

Cut the stems from some fine meadow mushroom-buttons, and clean them with a bit of new flannel, and some fine salt; then either wipe them dry with a soft cloth, or rinse them in fresh water, drain them quickly, spread them in a clean cloth, fold it over them, and leave them for ten minutes, or more, to dry. For every pint of them thus prepared, put an ounce and a half of fresh butter into a thick iron saucepan, shake it over the fire until it *just* begins to brown, throw in the mushrooms, continue to shake the saucepan over a clear fire that they may not stick to it or burn, and when they have simmered three or four minutes, strew over them a little salt, some cayenne, and pounded mace; stew them until they are perfectly tender, heap them in a dish, and serve them with their own sauce only, for breakfast, supper or luncheon. Nothing can be finer than the flavour of the mushrooms thus prepared; and the addition of any liquid is far from an improvement to it. They are very good when drained from the butter, and served cold, and in a cool larder may be kept for several days. The butter in which they are stewed is admirable for flavouring gravies, sauces, or potted meats. Small flaps, freed from the fur and skin, may be stewed in the same way; and either these, or the buttons, served under roast poultry or partridges, will give a dish of very superior relish.

Meadow mushrooms, 3 pints; fresh butter, 4½ oz.: 3 to 5 minutes. Salt, 1 small teaspoonful; mace, half as much; cayenne, third of saltspoonful: 10 to 15 minutes. More spices to be added if required – much depending on their quality; but they should not overpower the flavour of the mushrooms.

Obs. – Persons inhabiting parts of the country where mushrooms are abundant, may send them easily, when thus prepared (or when potted by the following receipt), to their friends in cities, or in less productive counties. If poured into jars, with sufficient butter to cover them, they will travel any distance, and can be re-warmed for use.[4]

We can see Acton's influence in Beeton's directions for cleaning and in her suggestions for the meals at which such a dish would be appropriate, but in every other respect the recipes are polar opposites. Where Beeton's is pared down, Acton's is alive with adjectives and opinions – the mushrooms are fine, the flannel is new, the cloth is soft and so on. The prose enthuses and evokes, where Beeton's merely directs. Beeton's functionalist approach leads her occasionally to omit details that might be important: here we are not told, for instance, whether to employ butter during the broiling (grilling) process as well as at the end. Acton, in contrast, considers every eventuality – the precise moment to add the mushrooms, the possible variations in strength and quality of the spices the reader may have. Eliza Acton was the Elizabeth David of her day – a stylish innovator whose elegant prose elevated the culinary activities it described to the status of an art form, and who treated food, its history and preparation as matters of taste and discernment. The reassuringly plodding Isabella Beeton, in contrast, was the Victorian Delia Smith – less stylish, but reaching a far wider range of the population; a popularizer rather than an originator, who for that reason decisively affected the eating habits of the nation.

To continue the analogy, Alexis Soyer (1809–58), the flamboyant chef of the famous Reform Club, was the equivalent of the modern television chef, with a strong media profile and a finger in every available pie. He was the first to establish soup kitchens for the poor, and amidst much publicity took the idea to Ireland during the potato famine. He visited the troops in the Crimea and (like Lloyd Grossman, drafted in to improve NHS meals) reorganized their mess arrangements in the interests of better nutrition. He was also the author of a number of very successful cook books, including *The Gastronomic Regenerator* of 1846, in which he proposed a new and simplified culinary system; and *The Pantropheon* (1853), a scholarly history of food from 'the earliest ages of the world' to the present, from which Isabella Beeton derived many of her heterogeneous food facts.[5] Perhaps most interesting is *The Modern Housewife* of 1850 which, like both Beeton's and Acton's books, was aimed at the middle-class woman. *The Modern Housewife* presents its domestic and culinary advice in the form of letters exchanged between two fictional women friends, Mrs B. ('Hortense') and Mrs L. ('Eloise'). Mrs B., who is acclaimed 'the Model Housekeeper' by all who observe her elegant economy, takes it upon herself to instruct her friend in her secrets:

> Now, believe me, I have always prided myself, whether having to provide for a ceremonious party, or dining by ourselves, upon having everything properly done and served, that so, if any friends should come in by accident or on business, they were generally well pleased with our humble hospitality, and that without extravagance, as my husband is well convinced; for, when we dine with any acquaintance of ours, he is very eager to persuade them to adopt my system of management.[6]

The tone of voice Soyer is aiming at is of practical counsel exchanged lightly between friends, but the disguise is flimsy, and the outline of the rather vainglorious Soyer can clearly be seen. Mrs B. often sounds suspiciously like a famous chef and is given to quoting Soyer's own recipes and recommending his patented devices.[7]

Given such illustrious and renowned culinary predecessors, it might seem hard to account for the spectacular success of Beeton's considerably less stylish and exuberant work. But Beeton recognized something that was not apparent to either of the slightly earlier authors: the changing nature of both the identity and the lives of their potential readership. The middle class for whom they were writing was growing at immense speed: in the twenty years between 1851 and 1871 it tripled in size. The product of the industrial revolution, the members of this new middle class lived very different lives from those of their parents and grandparents. They mostly occupied the new suburbs springing up around London and other large cities, with the men commuting into the towns to work. The divisions between the home and the world outside became more marked, and the ideology of 'separate spheres' – the idea that the woman presided over the domestic sphere, the man over the economic – gained increasing sway. Increased prosperity meant that this new middle class could employ more servants, and this fact became so important that within a generation the keeping of servants had become the defining qualification for membership of the middle class. It was Isabella Beeton's ability to speak to the particular desires, anxieties and snobberies of this mid-Victorian middle class that ensured the success of her book. Her knack of identifying with both the complacencies and ambitions of her middle-class readers is nowhere more entertainingly demonstrated than in her account of that relatively new innovation, the Christmas turkey:

> A noble dish is a turkey, roast or boiled. A Christmas dinner, with the middle classes of this empire, would scarcely be a Christmas dinner without its turkey; and we can hardly imagine an object of greater envy than is presented by a respectable portly paterfamilias carving, at the season devoted to good cheer and genial charity, his own fat turkey, and carving it well.[8]

Typically avoiding genteel circumlocutions, Beeton addresses the issue of class in naked terms, presenting the prosperous middle classes as objects of envy, with no doubt that this is a picture of themselves that her readers will welcome.

The ambiguity in the passage – are we supposed to be envying the possession of the plump turkey or the portly paterfamilias? – points to an aspect of the new middle-class way of life that particularly concerned Isabella Beeton: the fact that the home appeared to be becoming less important to men. With the new emphasis on business that characterized middle-class life, and the drift of the middle class out to the suburbs, many men were taking both their midday and their evening meal in clubs or in the chop-houses that were springing up everywhere. Her husband Sam was a prime example, often catching the last train back from London, and before his marriage tending to eat in town. Isabella, though, insisted on keeping his meal hot for him, and in the preface to *Household Management* advised her female readers to mount a rearguard action:

> Men are now so well served out of doors – at their clubs, well-ordered taverns, and dining houses – that in order to compete with the attractions of these places, a mistress must be thoroughly acquainted with the theory and practice of cookery, as well as be perfectly conversant with all the other arts of making and keeping a comfortable home.[9]

Read as an elaboration of this manifesto, *Household Management* begins to seem less a cook book and more an engine for social change. It is no exaggeration to suggest that Isabella Beeton's preoccupation with getting her husband to spend more time at home was in some part responsible for the new cult of domesticity that was to play such a major role in mid-Victorian life. Her significance in this regard was noted by an academic writing in the context of the women's suffrage campaigns of the early twentieth century who remarked that 'Mrs Beetonism has preserved the family as a social unit, and made social reform a possibility.'[10] With the middle class inheriting something resembling the aristocracy's rituals of living and entertaining, the average mid-Victorian home had become a very complex organization. But because the middle-class home was supposed to be a place of calm and succour, a refuge for its master from the rigours of the working world, none of the labour that went into its daily maintenance could be seen. What Mrs Beeton offered the mistress of the house were the instructions and routines that would enable her to hide the mechanisms of the domestic machine and present the illusion of an elevated ease and leisure.

From its opening sentence, Beeton's book declares its interest in a very distinct ideology of femininity, one which focuses on the traditional womanly skills and the domestic domain but which considerably elevates their status and importance. 'As with the commander of an army, or the leader of any enterprise,' she declares, 'so it is with the mistress of a house.' The activities of running a house, managing servants and bringing up children are presented as challenging, noble and deserving of considerable respect. Beeton sees the lives of her readers in the round, considering every aspect of the business of managing a household and treating it as a profession for which training is required. The Beeton woman is instructed about what time to get up (early), how to manage her finances, how to choose friends and acquaintances and how to act towards them (small disappointments and petty annoyances are inappropriate subjects for conversations; visits of ceremony should last no more than twenty minutes, and the visitor should not remove her shawl or bonnet), how to govern her temper, how to dress, how to shop and how to offer charity. Such detailed information was eagerly received, for life for this newly urbanized middle class was full of pitfalls and confusions: the friendly ease of village or small-town life was replaced by an existence in which neighbours were unknown entities with whom you needed to tread carefully, where shopkeepers could not be trusted, where food was imported from around the world rather than harvested in the local fields, where status and the new exigencies of middle-class existence required the continual presence of servants, and where large numbers of manufactured goods were available, requiring the housewife to choose between numerous different styles of kitchen equipment, foodstuffs, furniture and clothing.

Like most nineteenth-century cook books, *Household Management* was addressed to more than one audience: to the mistress of the house, who would plan the day's meals, and to her cook, who would follow the detailed instructions for individual dishes. Since her book covers the affairs of the household so comprehensively, Beeton could also have expected the husband to consult the legal and perhaps medical sections, and the upper servants to read the chapters on servants' duties in their managerial capacity. She adjusts her tone and language accordingly, employing high-flown quotations in the chapter addressed to the mistress ('The great Lord Chatham thus gave his advice in reference to this subject . . .') and homely saws and proverbs in that for the housekeeper ('short reckonings make long friends').[11] The existence of these two separate chapters is in fact a masterly piece of tact – in most middle-class households the mistress and the housekeeper would have been the same person. Indeed, in many households, including Beeton's own, the mistress would habitually be involved in much of the cooking as well, assisted by kitchen maids. Isabella maintains the polite fiction that middle-class women need not soil their hands with physical work, while actually providing them with copious instructions for how to do such work well.

As well as much tactful elevation of her readers' status, Beeton also offered them fantasy. The elaborate hierarchy of footmen, coachmen, valets and butlers she details is something beyond the wildest imaginings of almost all of her readers. Male servants (except odd-job men and gardeners) were the prerogative of the very wealthy, and many middle-class homes made do with one or two maids-of-all-work (the general servant, of whom Beeton comments that 'she is the only one of her class deserving of commiseration: her life is a solitary one, and, in some places, her work is never done').[12] There is also fantasy in some of the recipes. Three pages are devoted to the elaborate instructions (borrowed from a French chef) for turtle soup, a dish so expensive and complicated that it formed the centrepiece of the annual banquet of the Lord Mayor of London and was quite beyond the scope of a domestic kitchen. First there was the fabulous expense of the giant turtle imported live from the West Indies, then there was the physical difficulty of killing the turtle by hacking off its head, and then the problem of removing its enormous shell. The ambitious cook would then have to embark on a series of preparations lasting at least two days. Beeton's casual opening remark – 'to make the soup with less difficulty, cut off the head of the turtle the preceding day' – suggests that she had not herself seen, let alone despatched, one of these giant beasts. Her readers are also told how to 'dress truffles with champagne', a dish for which Beeton refrains from her usual practice of giving a price, merely remarking that 'truffles are not often bought in this country'.[13] These are fantasy recipes, included not to be cooked but to be drooled over – and the fantasy is not strictly a culinary one, but rather a glittering vision of the luxuries awaiting those who make it to the top of the social ladder. Like the 'Bill of Fare for a Ball Supper for 60 Persons (for Winter)', for the majority of her readers such items were of academic interest only. The point of such rarefied inclusions is to give the upwardly mobile reader something to aspire to and to establish *Household Management* as an arbiter of elegant living.

Leaving aside these dream dishes, it has to be said that most of Mrs Beeton's thousands of recipes are precisely tailored to the needs of the average middle-class household of her day. Modern accusations about her extravagance usually hinge on the quantities of eggs and dairy products she employs, but these are recipes for Victorian households, with hordes of children and servants to feed. It is also the case that middle-class Victorians – with no central heating and leading much more physically active lives than their sedentary descendants – consumed a vast number of calories by modern standards. She provides us with a clear idea of the key features of the middle-class diet of her day in the emphasis she gives to different food products: nearly three hundred pages are devoted to meat, with separate chapters on beef, pork, game and so on; there is one chapter on vegetables and one on fish; and puddings and pastry are allotted a chapter of their own, independent of the other chapters on sweet and dessert dishes and baking. A section on Bills of Fare provides a range of seasonal menus of different levels of extravagance and complexity, with 'plain family dinners' of three simple courses – such as the following suggested for a Friday meal in January: '1. Fried whiting or soles. 2. Boiled rabbit and onion sauce, minced beef, potatoes. 3. Currant dumplings' – and dinners for twelve consisting of multiple courses like this:

DINNER FOR 12 PERSONS (April)[14]

First Course

Soup à la Reine. Julienne Soup.
Turbot and Lobster Sauce. Slices of Salmon à la Genévése.

Entrees

Croquettes of Leveret. Fricandeau de Veau.
Vol-au-Vent. Stewed Mushrooms.

Second Course

Fore-quarter of Lamb. Saddle of Mutton. Boiled Chickens and Asparagus Peas.
Boiled Tongue garnished with Tufts of
Brocoli (*sic*). Vegetables.

Third Course

Ducklings. Larded Guinea-Fowls. Charlotte à la Parisienne. Orange Jelly.
Meringues. Ratafia Ice Pudding. Lobster Salad. Sea-kale.

Desserts and Ices

Typical features demonstrated by this menu are the relegation of fish to the first course with the soup and the strong emphasis on meat, which is the overwhelming ingredient of both the entrée and the second course, and even spills over into the third course in the form of hefty game and poultry savouries. Vegetables are very much an afterthought, and the menu is sprinkled with French culinary terms to denote sophistication. Also notable is its seasonality, with pride of place given to the delicacies of the new season (ducklings, lamb, lobster, asparagus). Despite the increasing importation of goods from around the world, Beeton's book is still firmly grounded in a tradition of seasonal eating.

Household Management is delicately poised between modernity and nostalgia. It tells of kitchens in which meat is still roasted on spits over open fires, but where many of the bottled sauces and condiments we take for granted today were already available. Its medical chapters stress the importance of vaccination, while also recommending leeches for bloodletting. The same tension is observable in its recipes, in which the culinary classics of pre-industrial England rub shoulders with the latest fashionable fripperies and with dishes imported from all over Europe and the Empire. Lengthy instructions on the salting and curing of hams and bacon are addressed to those who maintained the age-old rural tradition of keeping a pig, fed on household scraps, to provide meat for the winter.[15] A similar survivor from a rural economy is the wealth of thrifty ways with offal, with every bit of the animal from head to pettitoes scrupulously employed. The pudding chapter is an encyclopaedic source of treasured regional specialities from apple dumplings to plum pudding by way of Bakewell, Exeter, Manchester, Mansfield, Folkestone. Yet the book that is generally seen as the representative of all that is most traditionally British is in fact generously larded with recipes of foreign extraction. Sitting alongside the raised game pies, boiled suet puddings and spit-roasted haunches of meat (central to an indigenous British cuisine dating back to the Middle Ages) we find innumerable French dishes – some, like blancmange and fritters, adopted from the Norman occupiers and long assimilated, others imported into the British culinary repertoire in the eighteenth century, when French chefs and recipes were the height of fashion. There was little radical in the inclusion of such dishes, but Beeton also gives dishes from less familiar cuisines, notably Italian, German, Belgian, Dutch and Portuguese. A few foreign recipes are quite new, like the 'Soup à la Solferino' (dumplings of egg yolks, cream and flour fried in butter with a hot bouillon poured over), which she got from an English gentleman who had been invited by Italian troops at the famous battle to share their improvised meal.[16] Another significant body of recipes comes from India: mulligatawny, various curries, kedgeree and a number of chutneys are all included, with the assumption that they will already be fairly familiar to the readers. As indeed they were – until the 1870s there was little attempt made to introduce European food into the homes of British officials in India; instead Indian cooks tended to be left to their own devices and produced a series of curries. Those foods particularly enjoyed by the British were passed around as recipes both in India and at home, and in the process of translation and transmission gradually mutated – the development of kedgeree from a vegetarian dish of rice and lentils to one containing smoked fish and eggs is a notable example. It is a remarkable fact (which tells us much about the constituents of national identity in the nineteenth century) that there are roughly as many recipes in the book from India as there are from Wales, Scotland and Ireland put together. Those other nations of the United Kingdom are represented by a few classics like Cock-a-Leekie and Irish Stew and – with unconscious irony on Beeton's part – by a number of those old dishes, such as Welsh Rabbit and Scotch Woodcock, which the English named with insulting implications of the poverty of their neighbours.

The tradition of the encyclopaedic cookery manual established by Mrs Beeton and her forerunners continued to dominate the cookbook market for the rest of the century and beyond, with numerous editions of Beeton's own book heading the field. Continually updated, these books kept pace with the changes in food manufacture and technology, while still maintaining their status as wise advisers, sources of compendious knowledge that addressed every possible culinary (and sometimes domestic) need of their readers. Resembling bibles in their physical bulk, these cook books were rather like medical dictionaries: they were mainly consulted in emergencies, and you only needed one.

The new work that came closest to challenging Beeton's posthumous supremacy in this field was *Mrs A. B. Marshall's Cookery Book* of 1888. An astoundingly enterprising woman, Agnes Marshall ran a cookery school at 30–32 Mortimer Street in London, where she instructed both cooks and mistresses in the preparation of elegant and dainty dishes. From the same premises she ran a kitchen showroom, where 'every kitchen requisite' could be obtained, an agency for cooks, a catering company supplying cooks for specific functions and a mail-order business offering Marshall's own patented kitchen equipment (freezers, refrigerators, moulds, etc.) and foodstuffs. The latter included Marshall's Finest Leaf Gelatine, Marshall's High-Class Baking Powder, Marshall's Harmless Vegetable Colours, Marshall's Coralline Pepper, Marshall's Creme de Riz, Mrs A. B. Marshall's Curry Powder, and Luxette – 'the dainty purée'.[17] All these goods appear frequently in the recipes in Mrs Marshall's cook books, along with many other branded products. The difference from Beeton's book is marked: although Isabella Beeton writes with interest of the first commercial food products, they are still novelties; in the intervening quarter of a century the manufacturing of foodstuffs has become a major business. Mrs Marshall treats such products as luxury items, recommending them as components of many *recherché* and elegant repasts. The introduction to Mrs Marshall's *Cookery Book* boasts that all the recipes are original – either devised by the author or 'the result of practical training and lessons . . . from leading English and Continental authorities'. In this respect she breaks the tradition of assiduous gleaning from the works of others represented not just by Beeton but by the majority of her contemporaries.

Marshall's culinary repertoire is markedly different from Beeton's: where the latter emphasized the substantial in the form of roasts and puddings, the former is interested in much lighter, more elegant fare. 'Daintiness' is very much Agnes Marshall's signature concept and her typical dishes combine delicacy of taste with refinement in both presentation and ingredients: consider Croustades of Lark à la Rothschild, Little Cases of Lobster au Gratin, and Little Bombs of Pheasant à la Royale. With her much-touted dexterity, Mrs Marshall mercilessly tweaks and decorates her individually portioned food, and includes many recipes for food disguised as other food – Little Tongues à la Princess Marie, for example, consist of rabbit, veal or chicken minced with fat and lean pork or ham and moulded in miniature tongue moulds (the moulds were supplied by Marshall's kitchen supplies). There are many confections of aspic, elaborately moulded and embedded with jewel-like morsels. My favourite such dish is the marvellous Little Swans with Luxette, in which swans are moulded of clear aspic, their centres filled with a layer of aspic cream and then with a purée of the ubiquitous Luxette; tiny pieces of truffle form their eyes and beaks, and they swim on a lake of chopped aspic. This is food for show, designed to be extensively admired and then toyed with on the plate. What we find in Mrs Marshall's *Cookery Book* is the beginning of the Edwardian tradition of food for show rather than sustenance. This is the diet of decadence: it is no accident that she is writing as the naughty '90s begin. The opposite of the solid nourishment offered by Isabella Beeton to her earnestly aspiring readership, hers is the food of the confidently, vulgarly wealthy.

The food tastes of Mrs Marshall's primary readership were increasingly shaped by the restaurant culture that had sprung up in the years since 1867, when the Café Royale first opened its doors to reveal its magnificently gilded interior. Eating out for the mid-Victorians had involved the kippers, chops and steaks of the chop-house or the established French classics (lobster thermidor, crème brûlée) that had become the staples of clubland, particularly since the success of Alexis Soyer as chef of the Reform Club in the 1840s. Both modes of dining were the province of men, with women eating out only in private houses. But in the late 1880s it became acceptable, indeed fashionable, for women to dine in the new restaurants, and we can see the influence of this social development very clearly in the switch to lighter, more showy food in Marshall's cook books and those that followed. Restaurants were a French tradition, and the restaurants of the years before the First World War were invariably French affairs. They did much to consolidate the already prevailing sense that good food was French food and to chase away from the fashionable culinary repertoire many of those traditional British dishes that had survived into Beeton's book.

In the work of Auguste Escoffier, the most influential food personality of the late-Victorian and Edwardian period, this tendency came to full fruition. In the introduction to his 1907 *Guide to Modern Cookery*, Escoffier meditates on the changes in British food culture over the past two decades, arguing that ease of travel in the modern world had led to a demand for restaurants, which in turn led to the fashion for post-theatre suppers and thus for lighter food, and so 'ancestral English customs began to give way before the newer methods'.[18] In the story he is careful to tell, the restaurateurs simply supply an already existing demand, rather than creating it, and are at the mercy of the whims of fashion, continually forced into the creation of ever more ingenious novelties. Yet there is considerable pride in his assertion that a revolution has taken place in eating habits and culinary methods, and that he himself was at its centre: 'Circumstances have ordained that I should be one of the movers in this revolution, and that I should manage the kitchens of two establishments which have done most to bring it about.'[19] These establishments are the Savoy – by far the most glamorous venue of its day – where he was the chef from 1889 to 1897, and the Carlton, to which he subsequently moved (after being sacked for fiddling the egg account at the Savoy). His book is very much that of the professional, with foundation methods for stocks, sauces, pastries and so on given most attention. He does not simply present new recipes but offers a complete revision to culinary practice, with more space devoted to technical methods than specific dishes. He also provides in exhaustive detail many, many variations on each type of dish – to enable the satisfaction of that constant public demand for novelty that he attests as a major preoccupation: 'Personally, I have ceased counting the nights spent in the attempt to discover new combinations, when, completely broken with the fatigue of a heavy day, my body ought to have been at rest.'[20] This overriding impulse towards novelty leads him to offer 150 different egg dishes (not including soufflés), and eighty-six varieties of ice-cream bombe, each combination of flavours having its own name (Bombe Zamora is a mould lined with coffee ice and filled with a curaçao ice; Bombe Marquise is an apricot ice filled with a champagne ice, and so on and on). The authority of such invention and the meticulousness with which it is tabulated are Escoffier's key characteristics, and his work remains to this day a much-consulted guide to the principles of French restaurant cuisine, replacing the work of the earlier master, Carême. The logic and structure of the book do not, however, render it particularly useful or practical for a domestic kitchen, making it the first of a long line of chef's books that implicitly reproach the domestic cook with her lack of organization and high seriousness.

While French food was becoming so naturalized as to scarcely seem foreign, other foreign cuisines also became more and more familiar – at least through the pages of recipe books. Mrs Marshall includes an interesting selection of American dishes (a cuisine notably absent from Beeton's geographical meanderings), including Okra or Gumbo Soup, 'American Sauce', and directions for both pigeons and kidneys in the American manner. Lady Clark of Tillypronie (whose *Cookery Book*, posthumously published in 1907, spans the culinary fashions from the mid-century to the height of Edwardian splendour with its collection of recipes garnered in the course of her fifty years as first a diplomat's wife and then chatelaine of a traditional country house) mixes her British and French classics with pastas and sauces from Italy. Both she and Marshall have a number of Anglo-Indian dishes; such dishes had been imported back into Britain by returning members of the Raj and also disseminated more widely by the surprising number of cook books written by memsahibs and retired government officials in the second half of the nineteenth century. With titles like *Culinary Jottings for Madras*; *Simple Menus and Recipes for Camp, Home and Nursery*; *Chow Chow, being Selections from a Journal Kept in India* and the wonderfully named *Camp Food for Camp People*, these are among the most lively cook books of the period. Pretensions to elegance and a desire to keep up standards battle with the exigencies of conditions in India, and the problems of communicating with native cooks, to produce vivid narratives of a cuisine developed under pressure. So Colonel Kenney-Herbert, in his 1878 *Culinary Jottings for Madras*, 'devote[s] a separate chapter to the important subject of the cook-room' and promises to 'expose the besetting sins of our native cooks whenever they occur to me'.[21] By the time Kenney-Herbert was writing, the British in India were eating a curious mixture of curries, British classics and rather garbled versions of the French dishes currently fashionable back home, and he advises his readers to communicate directly to their native cooks the niceties of the latter dishes rather than relying on their butlers as intermediaries:

Between ourselves . . . surely an artist who can actually compose a '*petit pâté à la financière*', a '*kramousky aux huîtres*', or a '*supréme de volaille*', deserves *some* consideration at our hands. The *patois* is easily acquired and you will soon find yourself interpreting the cherished mysteries of Francatelli or Gouffé in the pigeon English of Madras with marvellous fluency. You will even talk of 'putting that troople', 'mashing bones all', 'minching', 'chimmering', &c., &c., without a blush.[22]

But while the British in India battled to import the elegancies of French cuisine to cook rooms where the native cooks crouched on dirt floors and were rumoured to commit such iniquities as holding toast to the fire with their feet, returning Anglo-Indians became powerfully nostalgic for the foods of their imperial sojourn. Classics like kedgeree, mulligatawny (a corruption of the Tamil words for pepper and water), chutneys and relishes, which became an established part of the British culinary repertoire, represent in physical form the processes of exchange, distortion and nostalgia that go to create an imperial cuisine. My own paternal grandfather, who left India as a child of eight in the 1920s, remained overwhelmingly nostalgic for its foods. Bombay duck, that ossified, foul-smelling, sun-dried fish, invariably appeared alongside any dish of 'curry-and-rice' at his table, much to the nose-wrinkling dislike of his grandchildren.[23] It is surprising to anyone born since Indian independence to realize how deeply embedded Anglo-Indian food is in the British culinary inheritance: Worcester sauce was invented in India and brought back to Britain in 1835 by Lord Marcus Sandys, the ex-governor of Bengal; chutneys were imported by the East India Company from the late seventeenth century and so much imitated and elaborated on in this country that an apple chutney now seems like an olde-English recipe. Curries, in particular, were absolutely taken for granted by the middle and upper classes by the turn of the twentieth century, no longer containing even a whiff of exoticism.[24] Yet ubiquitous as such dishes were, they were still the food of the prosperous – the working-class adoption of curry was half a century into the future.

*

So what did nineteenth-century cook books consider the poor should be eating? For self-evident reasons of price, most were addressed to the monied classes, but the culinary requirements of the working classes were not forgotten. In the cook books of the mid-century it was customary to include recipes for food to be given to the poor: Isabella Beeton offers Useful Soup for Benevolent Purposes, interestingly one of the few recipes to which she appends a personal statement:

The above recipe was used in the winter of 1858 by the Editress, who made, each week, in her copper, 8 or 9 gallons of this soup, for distribution amongst the dozen families of the village near which she lives. The cost, as will be seen, was not great; but she has reason to believe that it was much liked, and gave to the members of those families, a dish of warm, comforting food, in place of the cold meat and pieces of bread which form, with too many cottagers, their usual meal, when, with a little more knowledge of the 'cooking art', they might have, for less expense, a warm dish every day.[25]

The note of exasperation admixed with the charity here is typical of middle-class Victorian attitudes to the poor. The 'Lady Bountiful' role was one much adopted by middle-class women and is often reviled in the literature of the period: in Elizabeth Gaskell's *North and South* (1854) the heroine Margaret Hale is rebuked by proud northern factory workers for trying to patronize them with benevolent visits as she had the poor in her rural southern home, while Dickens is similarly scathing in his depiction of the aggressively do-gooding Mrs Pardiggle in *Bleak House* (1853). Soup was considered the best form of food for charitable purposes because of its ease of digestion by the ill and weak, but also – as Beeton's remarks indicate – because of its cheapness. As well as setting up his famous soup kitchen in Dublin during the potato famine (which in five months supplied over a million meals), Alexis Soyer developed a number of recipes for 'Soup for the Poor', which he first published in a letter to *The Times* in February 1847. Here he detailed the experiments he had made with different ingredients to produce an economical and nourishing soup and offered recipes, which included such novel features as the use of vegetable peelings. He later published a booklet, *The Poor Man's Regenerator* (1857), with more soup recipes and others for extremely cheap dishes such as The Poor Man's Potato Pie. A penny from the proceeds on each copy was given to the poor. Concerned, like Beeton, that the poor were unable or unwilling to cook nutritious food for themselves, Soyer had earlier devoted himself to a larger cook book for a working-class readership. *Soyer's Shilling Cookery for the People* appeared in 1854, and in its introduction he notes with disarming honesty that he had known nothing about the needs of the poor when he embarked on the work and so had 'to visit personally the abodes, and learn the manners of those to whom I was to address myself, and thereby get acquainted with their wants'.[26] This course proved very successful: *Shilling Cookery* sold 60,000 copies in the first six weeks, with a quarter of a million in print by 1867. The book is narrated, though in a less elevated style, by the Hortense and Eloise characters from his *Modern Housewife* and takes seriously the physical conditions in which the poor had to prepare food, as well as the issue of economy. Dishes like Simplified Hodge-Podge, Cheese Stirabout (actually polenta) and Good Plain Family Irish Stew concentrate on the use of leftovers and very cheaply available ingredients. A number of recipes are for foods obtainable for nothing, like nettles, field mushrooms and sweet docks, though in other cases – such as the recipe for Farm Custard, involving four egg yolks, sugar, lemon juice and milk, which he recommends to be flavoured with brandy and rum, mixed with cream and served in glasses – he seems to have nodded, perhaps confusing rurality with poverty. Another famous chef who turned his mind to the food of the poor was Charles Elmé Francatelli, 'late maître d'hôtel and chief cook to her gracious majesty Queen Victoria', whose *Plain Cookery Book for the Working Classes* was published in 1861. Largely sensible and moderate, he advises his readers to bake their own bread in order to avoid the adulteration of the commercial article, and rather than applying Soyer's somewhat awkward circumlocutions, addresses them fairly directly and with at least a pretence of equality:

> The thrifty housewife will not require that I should tell her to save the liquor in which the beef has been boiled.[27]

Unembarrassed by the prospect of the straitened circumstances of many of his readers, he strikes a comradely note, remarking on the subject of Roast Fowl and Gravy, 'Let us hope that at Christmas, or some other festive season, you may have to dress a fowl or turkey for your dinner,' and commending 'industrious and intelligent boys who live in the country' on their snaring of small birds before advising them how to clean and cook their catch.[28]

As the century wore on, the living conditions of the working classes became less abject and cook books addressed to them focused more on issues of nutrition than the demands of absolute economy. Mrs Black's *Household Cookery and Laundry Work* of 1882 has stern words on the importance of the principles of nutrition and hygiene in the home: 'by the manner in which [a woman] performs her most important duties, not only the present comfort, but, it may be, the future destinies of the inmates may be influenced, if not moulded'. Consequently, she announces, it is necessary that housework and cooking should be taken seriously and that women of all classes should be trained in 'their natural and certain occupation – the care of the home'.[29] The domestic-science movement in Britain can be traced back to a congress on domestic economy held in Manchester in 1878, where delegates proposed the teaching of the subject in schools, arguing that a basic knowledge of chemistry and biology was relevant to the proper practice of feeding a family and that the new subject should also embrace cleanliness, thrift, health, childcare and needlework, as well as cooking.[30] By the 1890s domestic economy was widely taught in schools and continued to be so in various forms for another hundred years. In this context Mrs Black's yoking together of cooking and laundry work looks less eccentric. She is particularly hot on the principles of nutrition, advising the housewife that there are three essential elements of diet: Nitrogenous, Carbonaceous and Mineral Foods. It is a categorization that roughly approximates to the protein, carbohydrate and vitamin divisions of the modern nutritional system, principles that had become apparent to scientists in the mid-nineteenth century. The question that still concerns nutritionists and scientists – of the appropriate balance of these types of food – begins to preoccupy food writers from about this date, and a scientific discourse on the properties of food becomes an increasingly common element in cook books. In this, as in many other respects, Isabella Beeton anticipates later trends, devoting considerable space to culinary science and showing particular interest in the chemical constituents of meat and their implications for cooking methods.

But the nutritional issue that had vexed the food writers of the mid-nineteenth century was not so much the right foods to eat as the presence of unwanted and hazardous elements in foodstuffs. Food had been adulterated by its providers since at least classical times, for reasons of economy and aesthetics, but the practice had reached scandalous heights in urban areas of Britain in the eighteenth and nineteenth centuries. Tobias Smollett's country squire Matthew Bramble had famously complained of such outrages in the 1771 novel *The Expedition of Humphry Clinker*:

The bread I eat in London, is a deleterious paste, mixed up with chalk, alum, and bone-ashes; insipid to the taste, and destructive to the constitution. The good people are not ignorant of this adulteration; but they prefer it to wholesome bread, because it is whiter than the meal of corn [wheat]: thus they sacrifice their taste and their health, and the lives of their tender infants, to a most absurd gratification of a mis-judging eye; and the miller, or the baker, is obliged to poison them and their families, in order to live by his profession . . . they insist on having the complexion of their pot herbs mended, even at the hazard of their lives. Perhaps you will hardly believe they can be so mad as to boil their greens with a brass halfpence, in order to improve their colour; and yet nothing is more true . . . [Milk is] the produce of faded cabbage leaves and sour draff, lowered with hot water, frothed with bruised snails, carried through the streets in open pails . . . the tallowy rancid mass, called butter, is manufactured with candle-grease and kitchen stuff . . . Now, all these enormities might be remedied with a very little attention to the article of police, or civil regulation; but the wise patriots of London have taken it into their heads, that all regulation is inconsistent with liberty.[31]

In 1855 chemist Arthur Hill Hassall scandalized Britain with the publication of his *Food and Its Adulterations*, which reported that all but the most costly beer, bread, butter, coffee, pepper and tea contained trace amounts of arsenic, copper, lead or mercury. The result was the passing of a series of Acts of Parliament in 1860, 1872 and 1875, the last requiring all processed foods to carry a full list of their contents. Isabella Beeton still complains of the dangerous artificial whitening of bread, the use of red lead to colour cheese and the various – mostly harmless – substances used to stretch beer and milk further, but by the 1880s the complaints of the use of harmful substances in foods had all but disappeared from cook books.

The scientific discourse is an increasingly common element in the cook books of the last decades of the nineteenth century and first decades of the twentieth. Sir Henry Thompson's *Food and Feeding*, first published in the early 1880s, adopts an approach that combines science, anthropology and a public-health impetus with recipes. A brief extract from the list of subjects on his contents page gives a fair picture of his attitudes: 'Improper feeding common among all classes'; 'Importance of perfect mastication of food by the teeth in relation to digestion explained and insisted upon'; 'Food of the middle class generally too solid or stimulating'; 'Soups – Not sufficiently esteemed – Better understood in France'.[32] He engages at length with an issue that was already receiving a great deal of attention: vegetarianism. The vegetarian movement had become active and political in the course of the nineteenth century, with the foundation of the Vegetarian Society in the 1840s, and its ideas are taken seriously by a surprising number of food writers: Thompson rejects a completely vegetarian diet on nutritional and anthropological grounds, but only after devoting a number of chapters to the debate. He does, though, insist that people consume too much meat and that fish and complementary vegetable proteins should be substituted for much of it. And Mrs Marshall, in an interesting passage calling for a change in British attitudes to vegetable cookery, explicitly evokes vegetarianism as a positive model:

> No country produces better vegetables than England both in variety and quality, and yet the weakest part of an English dinner is always in respect to them. It is time that a lesson were taken from continental housewives, and that we in this country should look upon vegetables as separate and distinct foods, and make them into independent and palatable dishes, and not serve them as mere adjuncts to meat. The Vegetarian Society is doing great good in this respect, and through its efforts we may look for some improvement in vegetable cookery.[33]

Even earlier, Francatelli had encouraged his working-class readers to follow the example of the European peasantry and adopt a diet consisting largely of vegetables, wholemeal bread and pulses. That the popularity of vegetarianism increased dramatically in the course of the nineteenth century is clearly related to the increased urbanization of British society in this period. The mass movement of population to the cities and away from the countryside had led, certainly by the 1860s, when Isabella Beeton was writing, to an increasingly sentimental attitude towards the rural way of life in general and animal husbandry in particular. A powerful advocate of the pleasures of meat, Beeton is also strong in her opposition to cruelty to animals – she takes furious sideswipes at the emerging battery farming of hens and the increasing mechanization of veal production. She is particularly attached to pigs, on the subject of whom, as was once remarked, she expresses a 'grandiose pathos', and she castigates the ancient practice of putting rings through their noses to lead them. This dual emphasis leads to curious tensions in her discussions of animal husbandry, where poetic accounts of the beauty and intelligence of particular animals and sentimental pictures of large-eyed cows and noble pigs sit alongside gruesome descriptions of the best methods of slaughter and diagrams of sides of meat marked up for the butcher's cuts. In tension with the modernistic pull towards the industrial, urban world, there is a powerful nostalgia for a time in which a frothy syllabub could be made by milking the cow straight into the mixing bowl, or when every family kept their own pig. In many ways these apparently antithetical positions are two sides of the same coin: the humanitarian opposition to animal cruelty and the sentimentalization of rural life are the responses of an urbanite to a world whose harshness and pragmatism she does not understand.

While other food writers do not concern themselves so directly with issues of food production, there is a thread of anxiety about cruelty running through many nineteenth-century cook books. The question of crimping fish, for example, exercises a number. This practice, which seems to have fallen into abeyance at some point in the last century, involved deeply slashing the flesh of a newly caught fish, before rigor mortis set in. The result was supposed to be the transformation of the texture, as the flesh shrank and compacted, becoming firmer and crisper. Mrs Beeton gives a number of recipes for crimped fish without comment on the method, Mrs Marshall goes to the trouble of asserting that the fish is dead at the time the cuts are made, while Escoffier, making it clear that it is not, calls it a 'barbarous' method and questions its efficacy. All these writers also recommend other practices that modern readers would find barbaric – Marshall tells us to remove the fillets from a living sole, Escoffier recommends the dicing of live lobster – but it does seem that there is a gradual increase in sensitivity towards cruelty to animals in the course of the century, which parallels the increased popularity of vegetarianism.

A few specifically vegetarian cook books were published in the nineteenth century, notably Mrs Brotherton's *A New System of Vegetable Cookery*, first published anonymously in 1821 by 'a member of the Society of Bible Christians'.[34] It was this book, according to Colin Spencer's exhaustive history of vegetarianism, *The Heretic's Feast*, which was to influence vegetarian food for much of the century. By the early years of the twentieth century vegetarian food writing was sufficiently established for Mrs Bowdich to bring out her *New Vegetarian Dishes* (the eighth edition of which was published in 1912). Like earlier proselytizers for the vegetarian way of life, Mrs Bowdich makes large claims for the ethical superiority of those who abstain from meat: 'The thorough-going vegetarian, to whom abstinence from meat is part of his ethical code and his religion – who would as soon think of taking his neighbour's purse as helping himself to a slice of beef – is by nature a man of frugal habits and simple tastes.'[35] But Bowdich also anticipates the direction of later vegetarian food writing in seeking to address not just the confirmed, political vegetarian but those who abstain from meat on 'aesthetic or hygienic' grounds, and even hopes that her tasty dishes will wean away from their bad habits a few of 'our carnivorous friends'.[36] In fact, many such were to alter their dietary habits in the next few years – due not to persuasion but the effects of the First World War, when the protein foods of the vegetarian – pulses and nuts, in particular – were to come into their own.

During the first two years of the First World War there were no significant food shortages, as food imports were largely uninterrupted by hostilities and there was a fortuitous series of bumper harvests. Even bad cereal and potato harvests in 1916 and the loss of significant numbers of ships did not lead to the introduction of rationing measures, with the Board of Agriculture and Fisheries instead concentrating on increasing the amount of land given over to the production of food crops. It was not until the winter of 1917–18, following extensive food shortages and protests by labourers and men at the front about their families' food, that rationing was finally introduced by the newly instituted Ministry of Food – of sugar on 31 December and meat, butter, bacon and ham in the February of the following year. By July jam, margarine and lard were also included, and tea and cheese were rationed locally. Unlike in the Second World War, nuts and citrus fruits were not rationed, and these played a significant part in the recipes suggested by the cook books of the war years. In both wars, the general effect of rationing was to raise the average standard of health of the nation, as price-fixing brought the essential foodstuffs within reach of all. This had certainly not been the case previously: the conscription of 1917–18 involved a medical examination which revealed that only three out of every nine men of fighting age in the country was fit for military service, with two of inferior health and strength, three almost physical wrecks, and one in nine chronic invalids. The situation was no better than during the recruitment campaigns for the Boer War at the beginning of the century, when social investigators had found that the poor tended to subsist on white bread and tea.

Wartime cook books are physically quite unlike those of the pre-war years: instead of the weighty, all-embracing bulk of the past, they are slim and light, invariably rather drab affairs, cheaply produced with thin paper and cluttered typesetting. There is no room for illustrations and little for discussion. Unsurprisingly, thrift is the dominant note, with much concentration on the use of leftovers and the conserving of fuel. Many are compilations of recipes from a number of sources, such as Lady Algernon Percy's *Our Grandmothers' Recipes* of 1916, sold in aid of the Queen's Work for Women Fund, or *The Best Way: A Book of Household Hints and Recipes* (date unknown, but soon after 1916), which proudly headlines itself 'The Cheapest Cookery Book in the World'. It is an indication of the profoundly democratizing effect of the war that these collections, stemming from such different class constituencies – Lady Algernon Percy's contributors are her presumably well-heeled friends, neighbours and fellow committee members; *The Best Way*'s are the readers of downmarket magazines *Women's World* and *Home Companion* – offer virtually identical recipes. What difference there is between them is signalled not in contents but in the voices of the texts and the attitudes they imply. In *Our Grandmothers' Recipes* the contributors of the recipes are named (Mrs Worthington for her Browned Onion Soup) and the recipes given in their own words, full of personal quirks and recommendations ('very good', 'used for many years without fail'). With little attempt at standardization or editing the result is a repetitive hotchpotch (seven potato soups and five lentil) that nonetheless captures something of the spirit of determination with which middle-class women threw themselves into the new culinary situation. The recipes emphasize their thriftiness with monotonous regularity – Cheap Meat Pudding, Cheap Soup, Bone Soup, 'Save All Pudding' (actually a perfectly pleasant-sounding recipe for bread pudding). There is no attempt to tempt with even such unassuming adjectives as 'tasty': all demands of appetite are eschewed in the commitment to being seen to be economical. *The Best Way* is a much more professional effort, effectively edited, with all personality and quirks ruthlessly reigned in. Although it professes to be 'written by practical housewives' (it collects readers' hints from columns in both magazines), there is only one narrative voice, which is studiously distanced and instructive. Yet for all this control, there is much more exuberance in the recipes and less of a sense of conscious privation. There is some slight invitation in names such as Tasty Fish Custard, and a chapter devoted to toffees and sweets admits the possibility of culinary pleasure, if only for children. The difference in tone is accountable, of course, in terms of the previous culinary history of the two class groupings represented in these texts: for Lady Algernon Percy's contributors the food shortages of 1916 represent a significant decline in their culinary expectations, and they resort to that mode of cooking known to their grandmothers as 'food for the poor'; for the lower-middle-class and working-class housewives who proudly sent their tips for shortcuts and contrivances to magazines, those years represented only a worsening of already difficult conditions.

Many of the dishes in *Our Grandmothers' Recipes*, as the title suggests, are Victorian classics, though pared to the bone in terms of both ingredients and attention to method. Hearty puddings – particularly those that make use of leftover bread – replace the fripperies of the previous decades, and Sheep's Head Soup survives here and in other wartime books. The poorer regional specialities – those last vestiges of a peasant culinary tradition that had missed colonization by the Victorian cook-book writers – begin to make their way into print in these years, and Lady Percy gives two versions of Cornish Pasties (one very bad) and one for Fat Brose (an oatmeal porridge with dripping and optional onion).[37] *The Best Way* draws on the same demotic culinary traditions, with recipes for Irish Stew, Hotpot and the like. Even keener on offal than Lady Percy's book, it offers Sheep's Head Pie, Cow-heel Soup and Ox-Cheek Soup, with a deeply unpleasant recipe for Sheep's Head with Oatmeal recommended as a particularly good way of serving oatmeal 'when it is disliked as porridge'.[38] But these books are not just rehashings of the more gruesome Victorian leftovers: both contain a number of recipes for that most distinctive of wartime contrivances, 'mock' foods. Made to imitate those foodstuffs now too difficult or expensive to obtain, mock food was to reach its dubious apotheosis during the Second World War, but examples are also to be found in virtually all the cook books of the First World War.[39] *Our Grandmothers' Recipes* includes Goose Pudding (made with breadcrumbs, sage and onion), Mock Meat Pie (haricot beans, bacon and onion) and Poor Man's Goose (liver with sage and onion, with potatoes sliced over the top). *The Best Way* exuberantly remarks that 'few people know how to make a leg of pork taste like a turkey', and ignoring the obvious riposte that few would want to, proceeds with its arcane instructions (skin and bone it and bake it in a pie crust, which you later discard to reveal a white meat roast).[40] Other suggestions include Mock Goose again – this time with pork, onions, sage and breadcrumbs, Mock Oyster Patties (salsify in cream), Mock Crab Sandwiches (shrimps and herring roes) and Mock Hare (minced beef and pork). (Its substitutions would seem to indicate that *The Best Way* was not taking the privations of the wartime larder quite as seriously as Lady Algernon Percy and her friends – perhaps because the latter were, at the beginning of the war, anticipating shortages that did not in fact immediately materialize.) Unlike the Second World War versions of such recipes, which concentrated on aping the appearance of the imitated dish, the mock recipes of the First World War aim at an approximation of the flavour of the original and blithely ignore issues of textural and visual likeness.

As the war wore on, and rationing and general food shortages really began to bite, the Victorian element increasingly disappeared from cook books, to be replaced by an emphasis on neo-vegetarian dishes. Margaret Blatch's *One Hundred and One Practical Non-Flesh Recipes* of 1917 and Mrs C. S. Peel's *Eat-Less-Meat Book* typify the tendency, which is reflected also in a wide range of less singularly devoted books. Mrs C. S. Peel's own later work, *The Daily Mail Cookery Book* of 1919, continues to recommend vegetarian food as appropriate in the persisting shortages (food rationing continued until 1921). In her chapter on Meatless Dishes she includes Vegetable Cutlets, Brazil Nut Cutlets, Curried Lentils, Baked Beans and Tomatoes, Pease Pudding, Haricot Bean Shape and the very dubious Savoury Oatmeal Porridge Pudding (comprising cold porridge, flour, suet or lard or dripping, dried herbs and sour milk). It is notable that many of the stalwarts of the vegetarian food scene of the 1970s are already present in these wartime books.

The cook books of the later years of the war and the subsequent period of rationing continue to a degree with the mock food of the earlier books, but they are on the whole much more inventive and lively, drawing their culinary influences from around the world and less inclined to cling to the foods of the past or to mourn missing ingredients. A major influence was America: Marion Neil's *The Thrift Cook Book* was one of a number of American books published in Britain that popularized American foodstuffs and culinary practices. It is interesting that nowhere in her book does she give the British reader explanations about the dishes she offers: American culture is assumed to be accessible enough not to require explanation and attractive enough to make its foods desirable to a British audience. So Crab Meat Jambalaya, Shoo Fly Pie, Buttermilk Waffles, Muffins (American style), Rhode Island Johnny Cake, and Maple Sirup (*sic*) are wafted tantalizingly under the noses of the deprived British housewife. Most influentially, the American composed salad with its nuts, cream-cheese balls, fruit and other seemingly extraneous ingredients makes an early appearance here, before going on to dominate the polite British luncheon table in the interwar years. The American influence is also discernible in the work of the English Mrs Peel, who gives recipes for Angel Cake and American Ice Cream and heralds the labour-saving kitchens of the future with a wistful encomium on the American cook's cabinet, with its fold-down work surface and canisters for automatically dispensing flour, sugar and other baking ingredients.

The tone of these later cook books – particularly those published immediately after the war – was understandably much livelier than those written during the first shock of the conflict. Mrs Peel is distinctly peppy about what has been learnt from the war:

> During the years of the Great War many of us became very clever, and learned much which will be of permanent value to us . . . Today as a nation we cook better than we cooked before 1914, and that in spite of the lack of material from which we suffered during the war years.[41]

She perhaps over-optimistically asserts that the habits of economy acquired in those years are here to stay, and particularly extols ingenious fuel-saving stratagems such as one-pot cooking, the use of a multi-tiered steamer, and the haybox. The latter was a box padded with hay or other heat-retaining substance (Mrs Peel suggests newspaper and old carpet), in which a pot of stew, which had been started off cooking on the stove, would be placed to continue a very slow cooking. Much wedded to this device, Mrs Peel feels 'it is improbable that the housewife will discard it' in the post-war years. (In fact, this contraption, so emblematic of the constraints of the war years, seems to have been abandoned almost immediately rationing ended and only rediscovered when war was again declared.[42]) Mrs Peel, a home economist who during the war was a co-director of Woman's Service at the Ministry of Food, writes with some authority and clarity and is particularly precise on vegetable dishes. Her brisk competence is far outclassed, though, by the brazen energy of Marion Neil, who bosses her readers unmercifully – 'Cut your loaf at the table slice by slice as required. Waste not a crumb.' 'Eat plenty of potatoes. They are good fuel.'[43] Neil's exuberance finds particular outlet in the imaginative titles of her recipes, which bring to life in a remarkable way the privations, allegiances, anxieties, losses and passions of the war: Blighty Salad (raw carrots, peanuts, stale cheese, hard-boiled eggs chopped together), Army Broth ('scraps of all kinds can be used'), French Peasant's Soup ('this is one of the numerous inexpensive soups . . . for which we have to thank our Ally across the seas'), Liberty Bond Bread (made from the leftovers of other loaves squeezed together), Utility Pudding, Anzac Pie Crust, Welcome Home Cake and the wonderful, tear-jerking Loved Boy Pudding and Brave Boy Rolls.

These names speak to us across what seems to be a vast expanse of time, and yet one of the more surprising features of the cook books of the Great War is how very familiar many of their dishes are: Cheese and Potato Pie, Macaroni Cheese, Sausage Rolls and Fish Pie were to survive the century pretty much unchanged, while the fashionable food of later periods was to be lost unmourned. In their thrifty simplicities the cook books of the First World War probably got closer than most others to what people actually ate day by day, and what they were to continue to eat for much of the century.

TYPICAL RECIPES 1845–1919

Eliza Acton
Modern Cookery for Private Families (1845)

With its absolute precision of instruction and the elegance of its construction and ingredients (cream, ratafia biscuits, lemon zest) this epitomizes Acton's style as a food writer. In this instance she does not employ her own system of listing the ingredients separately from the method, and this and the wealth of detail in the instructions may make the recipe somewhat difficult to follow. We should note also the archaisms that survive in the language of the recipe – 'stir them to', 'throw to them by degrees' – and contrast them with the very modern-sounding instructions of Beeton's recipe, written less than twenty years later.

THE WELCOME GUEST'S OWN PUDDING (LIGHT AND WHOLESOME)

Author's Receipt

Pour, quite boiling, on four ounces of fine bread crumbs, an exact half-pint of new milk, or of thin cream; lay a plate over the basin and let them remain until cold; then stir to them four ounces of dry crumbs of bread, four of very finely minced beef-kidney suet, a small pinch of salt, three ounces of coarsely crushed ratafias, three ounces of candied citron and orange-rind sliced thin, and the grated rind of one large or of two small lemons. Clear, and whisk four large eggs well, throw to them by degrees four ounces of powdered sugar, and continue to whisk them until it is dissolved, and they are very light; stir them to, and beat them well up with the other ingredients; pour the mixture into a thickly buttered mould, or basin which will contain nearly a quart, and which it should fill to within half an inch of brim; lay first a buttered paper, then a well floured pudding-cloth over the top, tie them tightly and very securely round, gather up and fasten the corners of the cloth, and boil the pudding for two hours at the utmost. Let it stand for a minute or two before it is dished, and serve it with simple wine sauce, or with that which follows; or with pine-apple or any other *clear* fruit sauce.

Boil very gently, for about ten minutes, a full quarter of a pint of water, with the very thin rind of half a fresh lemon, and an ounce and a half of lump sugar; then take out the lemon peel, and stir in a small teaspoonful of arrowroot, smoothly mixed with the strained juice of the lemon (with or without the addition of a little orange juice); take the sauce from the fire, throw in nearly half a glass of pale French brandy, or substitute for this a large wineglassful of sherry, or of any other white wine which may be preferred, but increase a little, in that case, the proportion of arrow-root.

To convert the preceding into Sir Edwin Landseer's pudding, ornament the mould tastefully with small leaves of thin citron rind and split muscatel raisins in a pattern, and strew the intermediate spaces with well cleaned and well dried currants mingled with plenty of candied orange or lemon-rind shred small. Pour gently in the above pudding mixture, when quite cold, after having added one egg-yolk to it, and steam or boil it the same length of time.

Alexis Soyer
Shilling Cookery for the People (1854)

This is one of the most economical recipes from this collection. Soyer's genuine concern to offer the poor affordable and nutritious food is tempered by an irritation at their fecklessness – as indicated in the crack about the disadvantage of nettles being that they are free (and therefore unregarded). The notional letter format allows for political and social as well as culinary points, but the recipe itself is fairly easy to follow and notably free of chef-y pretensions.

NETTLES

Wash them well, drain, put them into plenty of water with a little salt, boil for twenty minutes, or a little longer, drain them, put them on a board and chop them up, and either serve plain, or put them in the pan with a little salt, pepper, and a bit of butter, or a little fat and gravy from a roast; or add to a pound two teaspoonfuls of flour, a gill of skim milk, a teaspoonful of sugar, and serve with or without poached eggs.

This extraordinary spring production, of which few know the

value, is at once pleasing to the sight, easy of digestion, and at a time of the year when greens are not to be obtained, invaluable as a purifier of the blood; the only fault is, as I have told you above, Eloise, they are to be had for nothing; it is a pity that children are not employed to pick them, and sell them in market towns.

Another unused vegetable is mangel wurzel. The young leaf of the mangel wurzel, cleaned and cooked as above, is extremely good.

In all my various visits to cottages during this spring, I have found but one where either of the above vegetables were in use, and that belonging to a gardener, who knew their value.

These nettles are good during five months of the year; for even when large, the tops are tender. They make excellent tea, which is very refreshing and wholesome.

Isabella Beeton
Household Management (1861)

This is a typically brisk set of instructions, in which some of the crucial details are dealt with rather quickly: 'collaring' as a culinary process means to roll up and tie with string, so it is the calf's head itself that should be rolled tightly, not just the cloth in which it is wrapped, a distinction that Beeton's prose leaves rather vague. It is also unclear whether the head should be divided completely or just split to facilitate removal of brains and bones. Beeton follows this recipe with a note on feeding a calf, in which she instructs that 'if the weather is fine and genial, it should be turned into an orchard or small paddock for a few hours each day, to give it an opportunity to acquire a relish for the fresh pasture'. The gruesome contrast between this image and the calf's eventual fate does not appear to strike her – despite her concern with decent animal husbandry she has none of our modern squeamishness about the killing of animals for food.

COLLARED CALF'S HEAD

INGREDIENTS. – A calf's head, 4 tablespoons of minced parsley, 4 blades of pounded mace, ½ teaspoonful of grated nutmeg, white pepper to taste, a few thick slices of ham, the yolks of 6 eggs boiled hard.

Mode. – Scald the head for a few minutes; take it out of the water, and with a blunt knife scrape off all the hair. Clean it nicely, divide the head and remove the brains. Boil it tender enough to take out the bones, which will be in about 2 hours. When the head is boned, flatten it on the table, sprinkle over it a thick layer of parsley, then a layer of ham, and then the yolks of the eggs cut into thin rings and put a seasoning of pounded mace, nutmeg, and white pepper between each layer; roll the head up in a cloth, and tie it up as tight as possible. Boil it for 4 hours, and when it is taken out of the pot, place a heavy weight on the top, the same as for other collars. Let it remain till cold; then remove the cloth and binding, and it will be ready to serve.

Time. – Altogether 6 hours. *Average cost*, 5s. to 7s. each.

Seasonable from March to October.

Mrs A. B. Marshall's Cookery Book (1888)

This is a highly representative example of Mrs Marshall's very complex, extravagant and fiddly dishes. The use of culinary 'franglais' for the title, with the full French underneath, is indicative of the extent to which the French food tradition had come to dominate the English by the 1880s. The recipe is dense with instruction, and it is notable that Marshall does not adopt the clarity of the new recipe layout used by Beeton. The recipe assumes great culinary skill in the reader and also a large domestic or professional kitchen in which all the sauces, stuffings and jellies required will be easily obtainable: this is food for the wealthy.

LARKS À LA RIPON
(Mauviettes à la Ripon)

Take the fresh larks for this dish, pick, cleanse, and bone them, and farce them with beef or veal farce, using a forcing pipe and bag for the purpose. Partly fill the birds with the beef farce, then make a well in the centre with the finger, first dipping it in hot water; place in this well a little piece of pâté de foie gras about the size of a filbert, close up the space by pressing the farce and arrange the legs in the body; cut off the feet and then take little bands of buttered paper and tie one around each bird so as to keep it in a good shape. Put two ounces of butter into a stewpan with half a sliced carrot, two slices of turnip, one large onion sliced, a bunch of herbs (thyme, parsley, and bayleaf), three or four peppercorns; put a buttered paper over the top and place the larks on this; cover each of the birds with a little piece of fat bacon to keep them moist, put the cover on the pan, and fry for about ten minutes, then add about a quarter of a pint of good stock and braise for about fifteen minutes, keeping the birds basted over the top. When cooked take out and put to cool, mask them with brown Chaudfroid sauce; have some dariol [*sic*] moulds lined thinly with aspic jelly and ornamented in any pretty design with cut truffles, tongue, or ham, white of egg, and cooked button mushrooms. Set the garnish with more aspic, and then place a lark in each mould and fill up with the brown chaudfroid, and let these set till cold and firm. Prepare a small border of aspic jelly for dishing the birds on, and a wax figure or rice block for the centre. Make a ragoût of tongue, truffle, white of hard-boiled egg, cooked mushroom, and a little cold sweetbread all cut up in dice shapes and mixed with a little salad oil, a few drops of tarragon vinegar, and a few leaves of picked and chopped tarragon and chervil, and fill the top of the figure and round the centre with it and garnish the dish with chopped aspic jelly, and serve. This can be served for a second course dish in place of game or poultry.

Escoffier
A Guide to Modern Cookery (1907)

A recipe that demonstrates Escoffier's sense of professional food preparation as a highly evolved art. The directions for the waiters are choreographed like a ballet; the notes on the naming and first serving of the dish indicate his sense of himself as a figure of historical stature, whose triumphs should naturally be recorded for posterity. The dish is magnificently extravagant, but has a honed simplicity that contrasts markedly with Mrs Marshall's gussied-up preparations. A pullet or poularde is a young hen, a suprême is one of the two breast fillets, an ortolan is a small bird. Poëling *is an elaborate process someway between roasting and stewing: a layer of* matignon *(finely minced carrot, onion, celery heart, raw lean ham, thyme and bay leaf stewed in butter) is placed in the bottom of a small deep casserole, the poultry well seasoned and placed on top, and then copiously sprinkled with melted butter. It is cooked in a gentle oven and frequently sprinkled with more melted butter. When cooked, the meat is removed and a transparent, highly seasoned brown veal stock is boiled with the vegetables and then strained to produce the accompanying sauce.*

POULARDE SAINTE ALLIANCE

Heat in butter ten fine truffles seasoned with salt and pepper; sprinkle them with a glassful of excellent Madeira, and leave them to cool thus in a thoroughly sealed utensil. Now put these truffles into a fine pullet, and *poële* it just in time for it to be sent to the table.

When the pullet is ready, quickly cook as many ortolans, and toss in butter as many collops of foie gras as there are diners, and send them to the table at the same time as the pullet, together with the latter's *poëling*-liquor, strained and in a sauce-boat.

The waiter in charge should be ready for it with three assistants at hand, and he should have a very hot chafer on the side-board. The moment it arrives he quickly removes the *suprêmes*, cuts them into slices, and sets each one of these upon a collop of foie gras, which assistant No. 1 has placed ready on a plate, together with one of the truffles inserted into the pullet at the start.

Assistant No. 2, to whom the plate is handed forthwith, adds an ortolan and a little juice, and then assistant No. 3 straightaway places the plate before the diner.

The pullet is thus served very quickly, and in such wise as to render it a dish of very exceptional gastronomical quality.

N.B. – The name 'Sainte Alliance' which I give to this dish (a name that Brillat-Savarin employs in his 'Physiology of Taste' in order to identify a certain famous toast) struck me as an admirable title for a preparation in which four such veritable gems of cookery are found united – the *suprêmes* of a fine pullet, foie gras, truffles, and ortolans.

This dish was originally served at the Carlton Hotel in 1905.

WARTIME RECIPES

The sparsity of discussion is as notable as that of ingredients in the recipes from Lady Algernon Percy's collection, while Marion Neil, whose macabrely punning title presumably expresses relief at the end of the war, can again admit the possibility of pleasure, even in the face of butter substitute.

Lady Algernon Percy
Our Grandmothers' Recipes (1916)

MOCK MEAT PIE

Soak a pint of haricot beans in boiling water over-night. Chop up 1 large onion and 2 slices of bacon, place in the bottom of a pie dish with a cup of water. Put the beans on top, sprinkle with pepper and salt, cover with a good crust and bake.

MRS LANGE.

GOOSE PUDDING

Required, ¼ lb. scraps of bread, 1 large or two small onions (previously boiled), ½ oz. of flour, ¼ teaspoonful of powdered sage, 1½ ozs. dripping, 2 tablespoonsful milk, ¼ teaspoonful salt, 1 pinch of pepper.

MISS KNIGHT.

Marion H. Neil
The Thrift Cook Book (c. 1919)

'OVER THE TOP' MUFFINS

2 tablespoons (1 oz.) butter substitute
3 tablespoons (1½ ozs.) sugar or honey
1 large egg, beaten
¾ cup (1½ gills) milk
1 cup (4 ozs.) soy bean flour
1 cup (4 ozs.) flour
4 teaspoons baking powder
½ teaspoon salt

Beat butter substitute with sugar or honey to a cream, add egg and milk. Sift flours, baking powder and salt and mix thoroughly with egg mixture. Divide into twelve greased and floured gem or muffin pans and bake in a hot oven fifteen minutes. These are delicious when served hot with maple sirup (*sic*) or honey.

Sufficient for twelve muffins.

CHAPTER TWO

Fashionable Food and the Invention of the Housewife

Rationing finally ended in 1921, and almost immediately a new sort of cook book began to appear. Elegant, witty and allusive, printed in refined typefaces and laid out with wide margins on thick creamy paper, they resembled slim volumes of verse rather than the hefty close-packed cookery manuals of the years before the war. They were written by society hostesses and famous restaurateurs, and they had a new message: food and its preparation is *stylish*. Typical of this breed of fashionable writer was Agnes, Lady Jekyll, whose *Kitchen Essays*, published in 1922, was derived from a series of articles she had written for *The Times* the previous year. The daughter of an intellectual and artistic family, Agnes Jekyll was a noted hostess among the intelligentsia, and sister-in-law of the celebrated garden designer Gertrude Jekyll, next door to whom Agnes and Sir Herbert lived in Surrey. *Kitchen Essays* is written in a witty and epigrammatic style, with a loose, associative structure lending it a slightly *distrait* charm. Eschewing the all-embracing approach of the nineteenth-century cook book, it offers meditations on subjects as diverse as 'children's bread', 'a little supper after the play', 'food for artists and speakers', 'tray food' and 'their first dinner party'. Recipes or, more often, outline suggestions for dishes are dropped into the meandering discussion, but the main emphasis is not on detailed directions but on encouraging an attitude that sees food as an interesting, life-affirming element of a rich, cultured existence. So, in the chapter headed 'Of Good Taste in Food', she enjoins the reader to take food seriously:

> It is not thought praiseworthy to wear nasty clothes, to have ugly flowers in the garden, dull books on the table, comfortless furniture in the home, and horrid pictures on the walls. Why, then, are God's gifts of food and drink to be spoiled by stupidity and mismanagement? . . . Let us not, then, be too highbrow to learn something both theoretically and practically about food and cookery, or too lazy to take trouble anew every morning; neither let us be so timorous as to sit down under a rule of what a schoolboy friend in a recent examination paper alluded to as 'that practice introduced by the Greeks of a man having only one wife which is called Monotony'.[1]

Another fashionable writer with an evolved philosophy of food was Dorothy Allhusen, an older cousin of the infamous Mitford girls, whose *A Book of Scents and Dishes* appeared in 1926.[2] It balances a respect for the pleasures of the past with a modern interest in foreign cuisines and is eager to evoke the atmosphere associated with particular dishes: the 'scents' of the title refers specifically to a chapter on pot-pourri and soaps, but more broadly to the ephemeral impressions conjured up by foods. Asking 'Why should not a cookery book be interesting?', she meditates on subjects such as the artless personalities of old cook books, the changing history of English meal times and gender tastes in food. The characters and houses of the donors of the recipes (usually titled) are recalled in detail, and the scenes in which foreign meals have been enjoyed are lingeringly evoked. An elegiac note is often struck, a mourning for the great houses and aristocracies of Europe damaged by the tumults of the early part of the century, as with the collection of Bills of Fare with which the book ends:

> The following Russian menus . . . were for the functions Mrs Beresford herself attended at the Winter Palace . . . Since then a terrible cataclysm has overtaken Russia. It seems unlikely that there will ever be a Court in St Petersburg or Moscow again, and I thought, therefore, that these relics of a time that is past might have a melancholy interest for my readers.[3]

Other upper-class ladies also recorded their culinary prescriptions: one of the most stylish is Ruth Lowinsky, the author of a number of much-praised cook books. Lowinsky, who had inherited her father's gold and diamond fortune, was a hostess of note. Now a collector's item, her first book, *Lovely Food* (1931), is an art object, on hand-made paper, with eccentric illustrations by her husband, surrealist painter Thomas Lowinsky (whom she met when they were fellow students at the Slade). Subtitled *A Cookery Notebook* and arranged around menus for particular occasions, *Lovely Food* is consciously minimalist in both its contents and approach, and elegantly mischievous in tone. One menu is offered as 'a slightly more pompous dinner for about ten people who . . . are neither young nor amusing. They think they know all about food, but actually know only what they like,' while another muses suggestively that 'supposing your husband has gone to America on business, this might be the first of a series of little dinners with a chosen friend'.[4]

Taken as a group, these beautifully produced, charming, witty books did much to create a sense of food selection as an art form.

Mostly, they do not go as far as to deal in the actual business of food preparation: they are concerned with introducing new foodstuffs, cunning ideas for table decorations, inventive dishes. Instructions are notably vague, almost certainly the result of the fact that the authors did not themselves know how to cook.[5] What these ladies could do, though, was order food and organize grand entertainments: their books offered the illusion of an entrée into the most privileged dining rooms in the land.

Although their authors profess to be talking to women with lives very similar to their own, these books in fact had a significantly aspirational dimension for the middle-class women who formed their largest readership, encouraging them to regard an interest in food as sophisticated and high status. In this respect they form part of a veritable barrage of domestic literature addressed to the middle-class woman in the years between the wars. This period saw an explosion of food writing, with scores of new books published, as well as the launch of at least sixty new women's magazines in all of which recipes and the management of the home were perennial features.[6] To understand why domestic life, and cookery in particular, became such a dominant topic at this time we need to consider the social changes produced by the First World War. Relief at the ending of the war meant that people began to focus on pleasure. New music, new dance crazes, cocktail parties, the cinema, gramophones, motoring jaunts: technology and American imports provided outlets for a culture giddy with release. Foreign travel became more possible and affordable in the two decades between the wars, resulting in encounters – for the upper middle class at least – with the cooking of Spain, France, Italy, Scandinavia and even Russia. And, of course, the American influence on British culture that began in the war years continued apace in these decades, with a marked casualization of meal structures and entertaining being one of the significant effects.

But although this renewed devotion to pleasure was a major feature of those roaring, glamorous years immediately following the war, something more is needed to account for the singular energy with which cooking and its cultural meaning were repackaged in the interwar years. The key factor in the changed relationship of middle-class women to the domestic sphere was the gradual disappearance of servants. When war was declared, many working-class girls in domestic service left to work in the munitions factories. Having become accustomed to the independence, camaraderie and higher wages of the factories, they were understandably very reluctant to return to life as servants after the war. As the poet Robert Graves commented in *The Long Week-end*, his account of social and cultural life between the wars:

> Any girl who had earned good wages in factories, and had come to like the regular hours, the society of other workers, and the strict but impersonal discipline, was reluctant to put herself under the personal dominion of 'some old cat', who would expect her to work long hours for little money, but show complete subservience and dispense of all former friends and amusements.[7]

The sense of class resentment echoed in Graves's account is significant: in the increasingly democratic climate that followed the war, the working classes were no longer so willing to accept service as their earthly lot. There was also the problem that the upper and middle classes were no longer so able to pay for it. Economic recession and heavily increased taxation in the post-war years necessitated a great deal of belt tightening, and many households had to reduce the number of servants they employed or face the horror of doing without them altogether. What became known as 'the servant problem' – the difficulty of finding servants, of affording them and of keeping them once you had them – was a constant preoccupation in the interwar years. Magazines were full of advice on how to keep servants by treating them well: an article in a series on 'Running a Home' in *Good Housekeeping* of May 1925 advises the reader with two maids that 'the duties of the maids should be made interchangeable as far as possible; in this way each maid has more freedom without inconveniencing the family'.[8] Novels of the period also focused on the servant problem: E. M. Delafield's Provincial Lady is constantly preoccupied with finding new kitchen maids and stopping the cook giving notice, and Miss Marple is continually finding that the rough village girls she has licked into shape as decent maids-of-all-work are lured away by offers of higher wages.

But it is in the cook book that the issue is addressed most directly. Where pre-war cook books had simply assumed the presence of servants in their readers' households, those of the 1920s and 1930s treat servants as considerably more problematic. Thus Lady Jekyll entitles her third chapter 'In the Cook's Absence', neatly encompassing both temporary and permanent absences, without drawing too much attention to the shame of the latter. Similarly double-edged was Catherine

Ives's 1928 book *When the Cook Is Away*. There was an increasing emphasis on the problem of getting servants and on their general inadequacies: their inability to cook palatable vegetables is a common theme, and anecdotes are told about their wilful stupidity in the face of the exotic: mistaking caviare for engine grease, and throwing away the insides of passion fruits and serving the husks. In *Lovely Food* Ruth Lowinsky discusses the difficulty of finding the right sort of cook and of attracting her once you have found her:

Most of us have some drawback from the cook's point of view, such as too large or too small a kitchen – either is an insuperable difficulty – or too large a nursery. How often have I been told 'Well, madam, if you had *one* little boy, I might have tried your place.' I have always pointed out that, had the cook and I met each other earlier, something might have been done, but, with four already in the nursery . . .[9]

There is an increasing sense among the middle classes in particular – sometimes humorously expressed, sometimes not – of the balance of power having shifted to the servants. So a writer in *Woman's Leader* on 1 April 1920 laments that 'there is no freedom with unwilling service, ill performed, higher wages demanded than can be paid, principles of cleanliness and orderliness violated, appearances having to be kept up and rigid rules adhered to for fear "the girl will give notice". It is tyranny.'[10] There is sometimes an attempt to appeal to the servant herself (who is, after, all, assumed to be reading at least the recipes in these books), to suggest that it is in her own interest to acquire new skills and maintain high standards. Thus Doris and June Langley Moore, in *The Pleasure of Your Company*, their 1933 book on the art of hostessing, include a section of 'Instructions to Parlourmaids', where, after four pages of detail on the particular services demanded by modern social life – the serving of cocktails, for instance – they make the following attempt to convince the parlour maid of the usefulness to herself of a good training:

Practice makes perfect, and by the time you are able to serve an elaborate dinner without a blunder, to receive visitors in a manner that spares them all embarrassment, to deliver messages tactfully and accurately, and to remember names . . . you will be fit to work in a very grand and stately house where you will doubtless meet a number of very grand and stately chauffeurs, footmen, valets, and butlers, and gamekeepers, any of whom would be glad to marry a girl with such a splendid array of domestic accomplishments. (That is, if they are not married already. Men so often are).[11]

The uneasy tone here, with its shifts between patronizing assumptions about the class aspirations of the maid, inept persuasion of the likelihood of such being realized and the false chumminess of the final rueful parenthesis, highlights the great difficulty of communication between maid and mistress in these notionally democratic years.[12]

While some cookery writers maintain the illusion that their readers are simply passing their recipes on to their servants, others acknowledge that some, at least, of their readers are now having to undertake the cooking themselves. Their responses to this phenomenon seem to depend on their own social position: so Lady Jekyll devotes a sombre chapter called 'Cottage Hospitality' to the quiet fortitude of those 'dispossessed in yearly increasing numbers' by 'the vicissitudes of fortune', and the Langley Moores talk elegiacally of their ideal reader as 'a rather intelligent person trying to live with grace and dignity'.[13] While these writers see the reduction of genteel incomes as a minor tragedy, others are more bracing. Rachel and Margaret Ryan in their 1934 *Dinners for Beginners: An Economical Cookery Book for the Single-Handed* place themselves with their readers in the category of the newly domestic: 'there are a great many of us in this position today – young married people, single women living without servants, bachelors . . .'[14] Ambrose Heath, the author of over seventy books on food from the 1930s to the 1960s saw his first book, *Good Food* (1932), as appealing to both Lady Jekyll's dispossessed gentlefolk and the Ryans' modern young people. He is careful, in his introduction, to distinguish his two potential audiences from each other: the newly domesticated upper-middle-class woman is offered the balm of delicately chosen phrases – 'those whom our present distress has forced to take, shall we say, a more active interest in the affairs of the kitchen' – while he stands further back from the brash, aspirant young, observing them with a rather distant, sociological judgement: 'There are many ambitious young hostesses today, in flats, in small houses, in suburban villas, who want to know more about Good Food, for their own and their friends' pleasure, and possibly – and who will blame them? – with an eye to social advancement.'[15] This new generation, too young to have experienced the lost glories of pre-war food, want to reproduce the food they have tasted in restaurants. Heath declares them virtually a new class, recognizing food as one of the means by which incursions were made in the interwar years on the boundary wall that separated the upper middle class from the rest.

The youthful suburban class Heath identifies was coming to increasing prominence as he wrote. Reduced incomes, increased taxes and a relative decline in political influence had weakened the aristocracy and the old gentry class immediately after the First World War, leaving the upper middle class in the social and political ascendancy. But by the 1930s that ascendancy was being threatened from below by the rapidly expanding and newly influential lower middle class. These were the people who occupied the new suburbs springing up on the outskirts of every town and along arterial roads, the housing developments reviled by John Betjeman and condemned by Osbert Lancaster in his cartoons of modern architectural styles as 'By-Pass Variegated'.[16] Employed as office workers, technicians, bank clerks, council-school teachers and minor civil servants, the members of this much-expanded lower middle class were essentially modern in their outlook and way of life, embracing the new England of motor cars, the wireless, dance halls and 'the talkies'. Their increasingly visible presence induced an explosion of anxious snobbery on the part of the upper middle classes, who jealously guarded their rank with a plethora of increasingly arcane social distinctions. Middle-class identity consequently became more and more complex in the 1930s, with many people devoting much of their attention to confirming their own class status and simultaneously ruling others out – hence the prevalence of phrases such as 'PLU' (people like us), 'not our sort' and 'not one of us'.[17] Much of the culture of the 1930s was *about* class in one way or another, and cook books are no exception.[18]

This new suburban class was in need of guidance on how to live the new lifestyle: most were first-generation home-owners, and their new houses, with gleaming bathrooms and kitchens and inside lavatories were quite unlike anywhere they had lived before. A literature of home-making for this new market was not slow to develop: many of the most successful women's magazines (notably the new weeklies such as *Woman's Own* – founded in 1932 – and *Woman* – 1937) were directed at the suburban housewife, as were a succession of manuals on 'home-making'. *Every Woman's Book of Home-Making* (1938) and *Keeping House with Elizabeth Craig* (1936) are typical of the genre. They are very concerned to encourage effective money management among those who may be dealing with a salaried income (rather than a weekly wage packet) for the first time.

Many lower-middle-class women could enjoy leisure for the first time, and the manuals are keen that they should not spend all their time beautifying their homes: in this interest *Every Woman's Book of Home-Making* includes chapters on 'Hobbies and Handicrafts', 'Happy Holidays' and 'Making the Most of Your Garden'. The tone in these books is very carefully judged: there is none of the polite third-person distance of more upmarket publications, the approach being instead distinctly chummy. *Every Woman's Book of Home-Making* refers to 'hubby' throughout and employs the casual 'you know' to pull the reader into the discussion. Elizabeth Craig is rather bossier – 'if you want to keep house with me, you must keep house very simply' – but she is accessible rather than high-falutin', her tone being that of an older neighbour or relative ('I've no use for fancy colour schemes in the kitchen').[19] The recipe chapters in these books are concerned with providing standard technical recipes (for roasting, for making pastry) which the cook can then learn to adapt for a variety of dishes rather than a great variety of different recipes.

It is significant that Elizabeth Craig's longest and most detailed chapter is on the role of the hostess. Entertaining was becoming increasingly important at all but the poorest income levels, and class anxieties and aspirations made themselves felt most strongly when the subject of entertaining was addressed. A number of cook books devoted themselves exclusively to this topic, and many others employed it as an organizing principle for their collections of recipes and menus. The naked desire to impress, despite meagre circumstances, is signalled in the subtitle of Winifred Hope Thomson's 1935 *Someone to Dinner: Chef Cooking for Little Kitchens*, while the profound anxiety the activity produced is revealed in her introduction, when she explains how to make use of the 'high-class recipes . . . well within the reach of any plain cook' that she has compiled:

> It is not suggested that any meal should consist entirely of the dishes described here, but if one or two of them are incorporated in the ordinary menu, it is hoped that the hostess will feel she is quite safe from Dr Johnson's criticism: 'This was a good enough dinner, to be sure, but it was not a dinner to *ask* a man to.'[20]

The role of the hostess became increasingly complex, with recommendations to take careful note of the idiosyncratic tastes of friends, relations and other potential guests, and injunctions to study the dishes and devices of those in whose houses you dined. *Vogue* offered the example of its Famous Hostesses, gilded beings whose entertainments were scrutinized month by month throughout the 1930s in the column of that name: 'of course, it would be Mrs Ernest Simpson who first thought of the wonderful combination of seeded white grapes with little cubes of Dutch cheese, stuck through with a wooden toothpick'.[21] For those eager to emulate these exalted figures the key was to be *modern*. The cocktail party loomed large, with cook books providing recipes for *outré* cocktails and the foods associated with them.[22] There are flashes of rather startling modernity, as with Lady Jekyll's suggestion that silver aeroplane cloth 'recently bought by so many when it glutted the market' can be used to make tablecloths and cutlery rolls for picnics.[23] Thomas Lowinsky's illustrations for his wife's book are of similarly modernistic table decorations: surreal and elegant line drawings of objects such as 'two dead branches, one painted red, the other white to resemble coral, in an accumulator jar'.

Lowinsky's book is consciously avant-garde, associating itself with experimental endeavours in film, painting and literature: one of her menus is for 'a dream party of some of the most celebrated people of the day, whom one can never hope to meet, or, if met, be remembered by' – these include Einstein, Charlie Chaplin, Freud, Virginia Woolf, Jean Cocteau and Mussolini.[24] In this respect it is part of a distinctively bohemian element in food writing that emerged in the years between the wars. Bohemianism – the pose of the artist, on the margins of society and self-consciously free of its social and moral rules – held an appeal for many of the middle class in these intensely class-conscious years. Its attractions are explored in many novels of the time, and its gestures of insouciance and devil-may-care assurance became, paradoxically, one of the neatest ways of asserting an haut-bourgeois social status (if the lower middle class is anxiously minding its manners and adopting 'U' tricks of speech,[25] how much classier to host a picnic on the living-room floor or serve your dishes out of the pots they were cooked in instead of the family silver). A number of food writers strike a bohemian pose with reference to avant-garde or shocking literature, so Ambrose Heath gives a recipe for Virginia Woolf's Boeuf en Daube from *To the Lighthouse* and for a dish he calls 'zambaglione', 'a sweet of which many of us heard for the first time in a conciliatory scene in *The Constant Nymph*' (this novel by Margaret Kennedy was a runaway best-seller in the 1920s; the first of what might be termed the 'bohemian novels' of the period, it shocked and titillated its readers with descriptions of adolescent sexuality and noble savagery in the Austrian Tyrol.)[26] Through such literary connections, Heath is making a clear statement about the daring sophistication of his own book. Similar bohemian gestures are made in passing in many of the most elegant books of the period, but bohemia is also the locale of several more curious publications. *Me – in the Kitchen*, the 1935 cook book by novelist Naomi Jacob, challenges the traditional format of the cook book to the extent of refusing to separate recipes typographically, instead weaving them more or less seamlessly into the flow of her prose. Her subject matter is the casual, unaffected, sometimes eccentric diet on which she subsists. She devotes a chapter to the *infra-dig* kipper, but perhaps her ultimate challenge to bourgeois social conventions rests in her prescriptions on the making of the perfect cup of tea: 'Never, never add the milk after the tea has been poured into the cup. It ought to be a punishable offence!'[27] With 'milk in first' one of the key codes used to denote those beyond the social pale, this shoots at the heart of snobbish conventions, insisting on the primacy of considered personal taste over received behavioural diktats. Rather more startling is Moira Meighn's curiously named 1936 book *The Magic Ring for the Needy and Greedy*. Written in praise of the single-ring cooker or primus stove, and addressed to 'educated women whom bitter necessity forces into doing their own housework', it combines often shockingly practical details with a resolutely literary approach to the issues of cooking and eating (quotations from Horace, Congreve and Dr Johnson and historical snippets constantly pepper her discussion). Where other writers touch delicately on the problems faced by the newly servantless, Meighn plunges straight into the more gruesome details, insisting that the servantless woman must streamline her labours by starting the washing-up at the dining table, while her guests finish eating.[28] Chapters are devoted to the needs of the servantless, the hard-up, students and hikers, and those who live in bedsitting rooms. The latter chapter is enlivened by the author's account of her own experiences in such accommodation in the early years of the war:

> A large tin tray on top of [two up-ended Tate cube sugar boxes] supported a single-burner oil-stove and a spirit-gas picnic stove. On this, with the help of a temperamental tin oven, I cooked regular meals for three – often six or eight – grown-ups, and heated water for washing-up as well as for the baby's bottle, sterilizing of bottles, and laundry . . . also the water for baths and for toddy when the nurse, who slept with the baby in an adjacent hutch, woke us during the night to help her fight hordes of rats.[29]

Meighn's domestic distress is temporary, but for many in these years such circumstances were a permanent reality rather than a brief dramatic adventure.[30] Although there had been a massive campaign to improve the nation's housing stock in the years immediately following the First World War (led by Lloyd George's promise of 'Homes Fit for Heroes'), the world economic crisis of the late 1920s and early 1930s hit Britain hard, with the working classes the worst affected. By 1930 unemployment had reached the two million mark. Although the typical working-class diet had improved from that of the pre-war years, it remained nutritionally weak, even in the improved economic conditions from the mid-1930s onwards, as food historian John Burnett comments in *Plenty and Want*:

> A nutritionally adequate diet was probably possible in the 1930s for five sixths of the population, but because of ignorance or prejudice, lack of time or lack of facilities, only half the population was able to receive it . . . Sugar consumption was so high in the poorer social classes partly because of their heavy use of cheap jams and syrups and the quantity that went into endless cups of tea: these, together with white bread, margarine and an occasional kipper, were the hallmarks of the poverty-line diet which George Orwell observed in *The Road to Wigan Pier*.[31]

Historians are inclined to be somewhat testy at such evidence of what seems like wilfully poor nutrition, but Orwell himself gave a rather more sympathetic account of the reasons why people existing in a state of miserable poverty might choose to eat food that is bad for them:

> When you are unemployed, which is to say when you are underfed, harassed, bored and miserable, you don't *want* to eat dull wholesome food. You want something a little bit 'tasty'. There is always some cheaply pleasant thing to tempt you. Let's have three pennorth of chips! Run out and buy us a twopenny ice-cream! Put the kettle on and we'll all have a nice cup of tea! . . . White bread-and-marg. and sugared tea don't nourish you to any extent, but they are *nicer* (at least most people think so) than brown bread-and-dripping and cold water. Unemployment is an endless misery that has got to be constantly palliated, and especially with tea, the Englishman's opium. A cup of tea or even an aspirin is much better as a temporary stimulant than a crust of brown bread.[32]

One reason that the working-class diet remained poor in the interwar years is to do with the routes of transmission of culinary culture: people tend to prepare the food their mothers prepared for them, unless other influences intervene. And most working-class women did not cook from books, as the National Food Enquiry discovered in the mid-1930s, when only 15 per cent of working-class housewives interviewed claimed to use cook books at all.[33] Those who did employ them invariably used those supplied free by food and utility companies: the Gas Board produced many publications, and Borwick's, the makers of baking powder, issued a series of very popular pamphlets on baking, as did flour producers Be-Ro (who boasted over 19 million copies distributed by the time of their 1957 edition).[34] The recipes in these publications tended to be fairly traditional, concentrating on stews, roasts, plainly cooked vegetables, bread, buns, 'family' cakes (the less rich variety), pancakes, scones and so on. One of the liveliest is the pamphlet for Borwick's Baking Powder written by Elizabeth Craig. Declaring 'Let's be houseproud again!', she encourages her readers to return to home-baking instead of indulging in the recent practice of buying cakes and bread from shops. She devises new dishes and gives jolly names to old ones – Mother Hubbard Buns (made with ground rice – presumably because the cupboard was bare of flour), Tango Trifle, Hallowe'en Cake with Black Magic Cream.

A notable feature of the books and pamphlets produced to appeal to a popular audience is that they are among the first cook books to employ detailed pictures of the finished dishes: black-and-white photographs and coloured artist's drawings show the product in enough detail to be of practical assistance to the cook. There are little contrivances designed to make the dishes look appetizing: blazing fires and picturesque china shepherdesses set the scene in Elizabeth Craig's Borwick's pamphlet, while artistically applied steam wafts above the hot food in the photographs in *The Doctors' Cookery Book* of 1935.[35] In contrast, books directed more upmarket very rarely contain images of particular dishes; illustrations are, instead, of designs for table ornaments, witty sketches of people cooking or evocative still lifes of raw ingredients. The main reason that upmarket books avoided the use of photographs of actual dishes is that food photography was not highly developed and the food invariably looked fairly unappetizing. They had also to bear in mind the class implications created by the pictorial styles adopted by different sorts of women's magazines: only the more populist variety used food photography of this sort – *Vogue*, for example, restricted itself to drawings (usually by well-known artists) until the 1950s, though between the wars it did often photograph the great and the good at their dinner tables (food dimly visible in the candlelight).[36] The images that are used in the more upmarket cook books tell us a great deal about their attitudes and aspirations. One of the most interesting books in this respect is Quaglino's *The Complete Hostess* of 1935. The product of one of the most famous restaurants of its day (but actually written by the editor Charles Graves rather than the restaurateur himself), *The Complete Hostess* celebrates the new food culture: 'In England for the last twenty years the public has been taking more interest in food and cooking. It is not just the Upper Four Hundred. Everybody is showing more keenness about it.'[37] The book's 'decorations', by Anna K. Zinkeisen, employ a sharp line and sparse shadings, with highlights and details in a poison green to evoke an atmosphere of fashionable modernity; they also encode very precisely the text's attitudes to women in the kitchen. The cover illustration depicts a fashionable woman (sharply bobbed hair, patrician features) wearing a chef's hat and apron over her smart clothes and juggling half a dozen eggs with an air of distracted competence. The implication is that cooking is a party piece, an entertaining diversion that can be effortlessly undertaken by the woman of fashion. This suggestion is borne out by the frontispiece, which shows a more intellectual-looking woman (wearing glasses and an intense expression) peering at a cook book while she brandishes a wooden spoon. Cutlery and cheese lie on the floor at her feet, but her ingredients are laid out in front of her in an orderly fashion. A very old-fashioned servant (bun, long striped dress and heavy apron) stands disapprovingly in the background. The idea is of a modern woman, eager to learn, approaching cooking as an intellectual challenge. It is notable that she does still have a servant, but one whom she needs to bring up to date. Despite the complexities of his elaborate restaurant specialities, 'Quaglino' is very keen that the modern woman should learn to cook, going so far as to suggest that the high divorce rate is the result of women's neglect of domestic economy.

It is in this period that what came to be known as 'picture cookery' first made its appearance: this is the use of a series of photographs to demonstrate the stages of a recipe and to make clear any particularly technical aspects of its preparation. There are some nice examples in *Aunt Kate's Household Annual* of 1933, a publication slightly more upmarket than the household manuals discussed previously but nonetheless resolutely unstylish. The process of making doughnuts is demonstrated stage by stage, with photographs depicting the actions of a demonstrator visible only from mid-chest to hips, while in a series of pictures entitled 'the chef demonstrates' the art of carving various cuts of meat is portrayed. The pictures are rather blurry, looking more like pencilled renderings of photographs than original images, but the intention to bring the effect of a practical demonstration into the cook book is clear. *Every Woman's Book of Home-Making* also has a series of pictures showing 'how to carve' and some quite effective images demonstrating pastry making. These early experiments give some hints of the potential of the form, which was not to be fully realized until the 1950s (it is used to particularly good effect in *The Constance Spry Cookery Book* [1956] and then later in *Mastering the Art of French Cooking* [1963] by Julia Child, Simone Beck and Louisette Bertolle).

The employment of pictures to break a recipe down into a series of physical actions is a recognition that cooking is a technical skill in which people need training. This awareness of the importance of training was gaining increasing adherence in the interwar years in the form of the domestic-science movement. This movement had continued to gain sway since its late-Victorian beginnings and was now disseminated by large numbers of training colleges set up to teach girls the principles of 'scientific' housework. Involving a commitment to wage war on germs and to apply the efficiencies of time-and-motion studies to housework, the movement was ineffably high-minded, considering that its principles elevated housework to a serious form of employment for intelligent, educated women.[38] Cookery, too, was to be established as a science by the training of young girls in the principles of nutrition and domestic economy.[39] Books written by the movement's adherents discuss food substances as bodily fuels and employ a sociological language to emphasize the importance of good nutrition for the health and future of the entire nation. Such books rigorously avoid the chatty and informal mode, seeking to reduce recipes to the status of scientific formulae.[40] The language and admonitions of the domestic scientists were enthusiastically adopted by the manufacturers and purveyors of new domestic equipment such as gas cookers, vacuum cleaners and refrigerators who promised that these gadgets would transform the home into a high-tech paradise.[41] Some of the most-used cook books of the interwar years were those published to accompany domestic appliances, such as the unfortunately named *Radiation Cook Book* produced by the manufacturers of the Regulo New World Gas Cooker.[42] Much technical attention is devoted to oven use and timings, and it is claimed that each recipe has been subject to careful trial in the Radiation Research and Test Kitchen.

The most famous test kitchens belonged to the Good Housekeeping Institute, set up in 1924 to test recipes and also to 'submit new domestic appliances to exhaustive tests and bring those approved of to the notice of all housewives'.[43] *Good Housekeeping* and other proselytizers of the gospel of domestic science cast housewives as nutritionists, domestic engineers, sanitation experts – above all as *professionals* in the care of the home. Housework was simultaneously a woman's duty (the family must be adequately nourished, the germs must be destroyed) and her indulgence (it merited such shiny new gadgets). The fact that increasing numbers of middle-class women had no choice about adopting this new role was tactfully elided: there is little mention of the servants who would once have carried out these tasks, though very occasionally their ghosts hover, as in the 1930s advertisement for a multi-purpose clothes washer, rinser, wringer, drier, ironer and vacuum cleaner called Atmos – the Mechanical Housemaid. The time-saving methods and devices promised the housewife new leisure, and the advertisers and writers make much of this promise, but at the same time these professionalizing discourses of home care inexorably raised standards throughout the interwar years, so that as more became possible, more was expected. The idea that women should be trained, and that their domestic labour should be modernized, streamlined and treated as serious and respectable work was a result of the changed ideas about women's social roles and capacities produced by the movement for women's suffrage and by the experiences of the First World War, when many women had carried out traditionally male jobs. The irony is that what these worthy ideals ultimately achieved was to wed the housewife that much more firmly to her home.[44]

The need for technical training was also recognized by food writers not devoted to the principles of turning cookery into a science. While many books were dismissively brief in their instructions, others were beginning to recognize that a whole generation of middle-class women was in need of instruction from first principles. Probably the first writer to offer detailed instruction on these lines was X. Marcel Boulestin, who was without doubt the most important single influence on British cooking between the wars. Boulestin was French, an intellectual who had worked as assistant to the writer Colette's Svengali-like husband Willy. He came to London as a penniless young man in 1906, escaping the clutches of his controlling mentor, and worked first as a journalist and then as a society decorator.[45] After the war he stumbled on food writing by accident, publishing his first book, *Simple French Cooking for English Homes*, in 1923. This was followed by cookery articles for most of the major newspapers and journals including *Vogue* and the *Spectator*. In 1925 he opened his first restaurant and a cooking school that was frequented by fashionable ladies. In 1937 he became the first-ever television cook. It was he who introduced the English to the French *cuisine bourgeoise* – the food of the ordinary French household rather than the stuffy *haute cuisine* of banquets and grand hotels. In his 1931 *What Shall We Have To-day?* Boulestin attempts to train his reader in the principles of cookery, advising sensitivity to materials, touching, tasting and experimenting. Cooking, in his description, is an art akin to sculpture – both a sensual and an intellectual experience, requiring imagination as well as skill. Insisting that it is necessary to understand why particular techniques are used, he takes the reader through the classic culinary principles, explaining them with verve and clarity ('the boiling of meat is done with two entirely different aims in view: either you want the goodness, the flavour, to remain in your meat, or you want to extract these from it and impart them to the liquid, which means that either your aim is to eat that piece of meat at its best, or, in the second case, you want to make a soup').[46] His aim is to give the cook (who, in this later book, he begins to acknowledge may sometimes be the mistress) the skills and knowledge to cook instinctively rather than to be led astray by unnecessarily complex or misleading recipes:

> The truth is that one cannot possibly give an exact recipe; it is the part of the cook to take it in and work on it in an intelligent way. Having first tasted what she is doing, she must adapt the recipe to the strength of her gas, the acidity of her vinegar, the size of her vegetables, the quality and freshness of her meat. If she does this, she is safe, safe even from an exact (and bad) recipe, such as the one I saw once, which said, 'put in the tournedos and cook for half an hour', for, if she watches, she will see that after ten minutes the tournedos is ready and she certainly will not give it the generous extra twenty minutes, which would reduce it to the state of burnt india-rubber.[47]

Economical and thoughtful household management is presented as a moral and intellectual as well as a monetary issue: 'No-one, these days, can afford to waste materials, for materials are always more or less costly. Even if money did not count waste is stupid and wicked. It is immoral.'[48]

The sense of a need for cook books to train their readers in technical skills is also reflected in the appearance of a new feature in some interwar cook books: cookery for children. Cooking is presented as fun and entertainment for children, with much concentration on the manufacture of toffees and other treats, but there is also a strong sense of the importance of teaching children to cook. Mrs C. F. Leyel, in her detailed and intriguing *Gentle Art of Cookery* (1925), has a chapter on cooking for children, in which she aims to inculcate in the young an enthusiasm for the kitchen – 'cooking is sheer magic to the child, the purest white magic' – by way of recipes for chocolate fudge, a gingerbread house and ginger beer, and more mysterious concoctions such as white strawberry jam and 'an ostrich egg' (which involves a complex procedure with a dozen hens' eggs and a pig's bladder).[49] In *The Magic Ring* Moira Meighn suggests that all children should be taught to cook before the age of seven and that instead of toy cookers they should be given 'tiny real pots and pans and a workable methylated, or oil-stove, gas or electric ring'.[50] This new emphasis on children as cooks is partly a function of new fashions in child-rearing, and particularly the ideal of raising tough, independent children encouraged by influential child-development experts like John Broadus Watson and Frederick Truby King.[51] It is also, though, a signpost to the fact that the battle to keep servants had already been conceded as lost: it is clear to these writers that the next generation would need to be able to cook for itself.

So if cooking acquired new social and cultural meanings during the interwar years, what about the food itself? How did the types of food and shapes of meals recommended by the new cook books compare with the hefty puddings of the Victorians or the lengthy parade of gussied-up fripperies favoured by wealthy Edwardians? When the shortages and substitutions of the war were behind them, what did people want to eat? Many cook books of the interwar years explicitly distinguish the food they describe from that of the past, drawing attention to the differences between the multi-course meals of the Victorian and Edwardian era and the new spirit of frugality and economy that they felt characterized post-war eating habits. 'If this article had been written 20 years ago, what sumptuous and splendid breakfasts would have been my theme,' remarks Mrs Philip (Alice) Martineau in her lively and popular *Caviar to Candy* (1927).[52] Other writers note the new desirability of shorter menus and simpler foods: 'be simple and avoid pretentious meals', cautioned Boulestin, 'let your dinner be short and good. There is nothing more hateful than a long dinner, in which you get a mouthful of each of the seven courses, and feel hungry immediately afterwards.'[53] Such advice seems to have been followed, and in the houses of the affluent the traditional seven- or eight-course dinner began to be replaced by shorter meals of four or five courses: there would usually be either fish or soup, not both, there would be only one meat course and there was often neither savoury nor dessert. Hors d'oeuvres, which had begun to be popular in Edwardian times, now often replaced the soup course, which was becoming increasingly unfashionable because it was considered to deaden the appetite at the start of the meal.

Reduced income levels among the upper and upper-middle classes in part account for these changes in meal structure.[54] However, the reduction in the quantity, richness and complexity of food offered at the tables of the well-to-do is also a function of a new preoccupation with thinness. A craze for dieting (or 'banting') took hold in the 1920s, produced by the skimpy boyish fashions of the day (and perhaps by more complex factors such as the increasing political, social and physical emancipation of women). Cook books quickly responded, with Lady Jekyll in 1922 offering a chapter 'for the too fat', in which she advises that 'the experience of the war years, with their scarcity of flesh-making foods, shows that weight *can* be reduced by a diminished consumption of dairy produce, sugar, and starchy foods'.[55] Lady Sysonby remarks that puddings are a difficult subject, 'as the craze for thinning cause[s] the immediate waving away of even the most delicious'.[56] For this reason, traditionally English stodgy suet and pastry puddings were also on the way out: what was becoming known as 'the sweet course' now invariably consisted of ices, soufflés or creams, with some books devoting whole chapters to each of these types of light sweets.

Superfluous meals like late-night supper and afternoon tea were being dropped, and the waning favour of the latter resulted in a reduced interest in baking in many of the more upmarket books. In direct contrast, those less fashionable books that were aimed at the middle and lower strata of the middle class sought at this time to revive an interest in baking and to encourage their readers to renounce the shop-bought cake in favour of the home-made article. In such mid-income houses tea remained an important meal – but usually a sort of high tea (including eggs, ham and the like, as well as bread and butter and cake) that formed the main evening meal for children. The association of baking with good motherhood seems to have established itself in the popular imagination at around this date, and by the 1950s had become a key element in the ideological commitment to the home-bound woman.

Vegetables are increasingly important: Lady Sysonby advises her readers to 'get as many vegetables as possible', and Alice Martineau remarks as an indication of how much times had changed that her mother had given her a recipe book on her marriage in which 'there is not a single vegetable dish nor salad'.[57] In a spirit of modernity a number of writers proudly devote extra space to their vegetable recipes; Alice Martineau went one better and wrote her second book, *Cantalope to Cabbage* (1929), entirely on vegetable cookery. In *Caviar to Candy* she bemoans, like so many other writers, the traditional awfulness of British vegetable cookery:

> The intelligent use of vegetables is a gift not vouchsafed to the average cook, who as a rule would not 'demean' herself by touching them (leaving that to the kitchen maid), with the resultant cabbage, or runner beans, and water! (Who does not know their horrid flavours?).[58]

The vegetables she discusses in her first book include jerusalem artichokes, aubergines, cardoons, celeriac, endives, nettles, courgettes and sweet potatoes – a surprisingly modern selection. There was a new consciousness about the health-giving properties of vegetables, and a number of writers emphasize this aspect. Mrs Leyel, reporting that 'doctors are more and more insisting upon the virtues of vegetables', declares that 'the method of stewing vegetables in water and then throwing away the water containing the most valuable properties is not only stupid, it is uneconomical'.[59] Mrs Leyel's is probably the most interesting approach to vegetables of the period. She discusses plants like salsify, seakale and sorrel in the vegetable chapter in *The Gentle Art of Cookery* – familiar items in the pre-industrial British diet, but long unfamiliar to her readers. Recipes in what is by far the longest chapter in the book include a purée of turnip tops, an Italian way of cooking spinach (with sultanas, raisins, anchovies, butter and fried bread – a combination of ingredients that suggest Venice with its Arabic culinary influences), two versions of an artichoke salad, many recipes for beans and lentils (including an authentic dahl – Dàl Bhàt –

rather unusual for this date), and a paprika of cucumbers. She has a taste for sweet vegetable recipes (again an indication of a Middle Eastern influence), offering a dish of potatoes mashed with butter and 'sugar to taste' with crushed macaroons sprinkled on top, and another of spinach dressed with salt, sugar, grated lemon rind and crushed ratafias. She ends the vegetable chapter with some walnut dishes, then gives individual chapters on chestnuts, almonds and mushrooms. A herbalist by trade, Mrs Leyel was to found the famous Culpeper House in Baker Street in 1927, having set up the Society of Herbalists and published *The Magic of Herbs* the previous year. This interest is apparent in the slightly earlier *Gentle Art of Cookery*, not so much in the use of herbs in the recipes, but in the startling originality of her chapter on flower cookery, in which she revives the medieval and Tudor use of flowers for food with recipes such as Eggs Cooked with Marigolds, Nasturtium Salad, Ice Cream of Roses and Marmalade of Violets. Elizabeth David was a great fan of Mrs Leyel's book, which was the first cook book she owned, musing, 'I wonder if I would ever have learned to cook at all if I had been given a routine Mrs Beeton to learn from, instead of the romantic Mrs Leyel with her rather wild, imagination-catching recipes.'[60] Mrs Leyel's appreciation of the culinary as well as the nutritive qualities of pulses and nuts, her adoption of the foods of the Middle and Far East, and her strong sense of the sensual and aesthetic pleasures of vegetable dishes – which are to be served as things in their own right rather than mere adjuncts to meat – all anticipate the direction in which vegetarian food was to develop in the years after the Second World War, though she does not in fact advertise her book as vegetarian.

The new fashion for vegetables helped to establish vegetarianism as increasingly respectable.[61] But though beginning to be socially acceptable, the movement had a long way to go before it would become a major influence on general eating habits. Far more influential in this period was foreign food, in particular the food of America and that of southern Europe. The taste for the latter was inculcated by Marcel Boulestin who, as noted earlier, was the first writer to introduce the British to the recipes of bourgeois France. He insists on the economy, simplicity and charm of ordinary French cooking, and encourages his readers to experiment with new ways of preparing and thinking about food. He offers recipes for Cassoulet, Confits d'Oie (preserved goose) and numerous stews and pates. He suggests that his readers use soup as a main dish rather than a first course – and he means the meaty, chunky soups of the ordinary French household rather than the thin refinement of a consommé. Other very simple dishes include grilled red mullet, mussels with garlic, parsley and breadcrumbs, and *sausages au vin blanc* (baked, then served with a sauce of onions and white wine). A menu for a December Dinner from his 1931 *What Shall We Have To-day?* gives some indication of the radical simplicity of his dishes and his tastes:

Saucisses aux huitres

Fillet de boeuf à l'espagnole

Salsifis à la poulette

Soufflé aux pommes

The hors d'oeuvres is a classic dish from south-west France. It consists simply of cold oysters eaten, mouthful by mouthful, with little hot sausages. The point of the dish is in the contrast of temperatures and flavours: cool salty brine and rich crisp meat. It is a dish to be eaten with the fingers – very far from the polite traditions of the British table, but Boulestin seeks to make it familiar by pointing out that it has similarities with the classic English savoury Angels on Horseback, where oysters are wrapped in bacon. The meat course consists of a casserole of beef, covered in bacon and cooked with stock and Malaga wine, with raisins added near the end of cooking. It is the wine, presumably, that lends the dish its Spanish appellation. The vegetable dish is translated as 'salsify with a sharp white sauce': the sauce is a béchamel enriched with an egg yolk and lemon juice. It is indicative of his serious approach to the overhaul of British culinary attitudes that Boulestin includes unusual vegetables in his menus, while other writers tend to confine theirs to individual recipes, resorting to old favourites like peas when constructing combinations of dishes. The sweet is a soufflé – a fashionable dish, but not so ultra-chic as an ice. It is typical of Boulestin that he should use such a humble fruit as an apple. His books are consciously economical, avoiding, for the most part, sophisticated foodstuffs. He does not, for example, write about caviare, and he encourages his readers to use seasonal foods rather than expensive forced or imported ones. His dishes are charming in their simplicity – gutsy, full of taste, yet clearly also somehow modern – but his wide-ranging influence had also something to do with the *way* he wrote about food. Like Elizabeth David two decades later, he wove a literary fantasy around the foods and the lifestyle he depicts, describing the ancient recipes of the French peasantry in a prose dripping with nostalgia: 'on a summer evening, they sit on low chairs outside the house, just by the door, holding a plateful on their knees. The day's work is over, the last lazy cow back in the stable after a last mouthful at the hedge. The twilight is blue and peaceful, only disturbed occasionally by the guttural song of some frogs in the ditch. The earth smells. But its perfume is not, to them, as sacred as that of the soup . . .'[62] Such sentimental evocations seized the imagination of the public. Foreign recipes became increasingly *de rigueur*, and most writers followed the example set by Boulestin. So Alice Martineau, in her 1927 book *Caviar to Candy* (subtitled *Recipes for Small Households from All Parts of the World*), uses similarly lyrical descriptions of the food she had experienced on her wide travels: 'the pearl-grey caviare of Roumania, and the exquisite wild raspberries of Norway'.[63] As well as the bourgeois and peasant recipes of France first given by Boulestin, she includes a variety of recipes from both eastern and northern Europe and from South America: a Peruvian soup of shrimps and cheese called Chupe is among her more exotic offerings. She is also one of the first writers to include recipes from North America – specifically the composed salads that were all the rage there in the 1920s. This is the era of jellied salads and cream-cheese balls in the States, and Martineau clearly sees these faintly ridiculous dishes, for which she gives a number of detailed recipes, as the height of sophistication:

> It was in Boston that I first came across a salad that has met with much appreciation here, and that is served as a second course at lunch. Fill the scooped-out half of a lettuce, the close white-cabbage kind, or the quarter of a good cos, with grape fruit carefully freed from skin and pips. The lettuce can be dipped in French dressing first or can have a little mayonnaise poured over it before the grape fruit is placed. On the little pyramid of grape fruit should be a small ball of cream cheese, with two halves of walnut – one each side – or some blanched almonds, or pinola nuts, stuck into the cheese.[64]

Martineau treats such dishes so seriously because of the high status American culture and food had acquired in Britain through the offices of noted society hostesses of American birth like Nancy Astor, Emerald Cunard and Wallis Simpson.

The most remarkable British engagement with foreign cooking over the interwar years is that of *Recipes of All Nations* by Countess Morphy. Born Marcelle Azra Forbes in New Orleans, Countess Morphy moved to Britain and authored several cook books in the 1930s and 1940s. *Recipes of All Nations*, which was published in 1935, is an extraordinary work, both for its size (800 pages) and its geographical range. There are individual chapters on many European countries (France, Italy, Spain, Portugal, Austria, Hungary, Germany, Russia, Poland, Norway, Sweden, Denmark, Belgium and Holland), two chapters on the United States (one on the nation as a whole; one, reflecting her roots, on the Creole Cooking of New Orleans), chapters on India, China and Japan, and a final catch-all category of 'Dishes from Many Lands'. It is this last that is possibly the most interesting, containing sections on Sardinia, Corsica, Turkey and the Balkans, Greece, Arabia and Persia, Morocco, Eastern Asia, the French West Indies and South America. There is also a section on Africa (General), which contains what may well be the earliest collection of sub-Saharan recipes published by a major English-language publisher, with dishes from Guinea, the Ivory Coast and the Congo. Throughout the book, the sources of the recipes are left vague, but it seems highly unlikely that the author herself travelled the world collecting all these dishes. The fact that a number of chapters are introduced with heartfelt thanks to different chefs and restaurant proprietors suggests the likeliest source of at least some of her information. Her introduction presents the work both as a study of comparative cookery and a guide for the ordinary British housewife to see how 'her sisters in foreign lands solve the eternal and everlasting problem of daily food'.[65] Her responses to culinary diversity are startlingly expressive of the national and racial attitudes of her day:

> Racial and climatic factors are responsible for the wide divergences in national climate and food, and the study of comparative cookery shows the unbridgeable gulf which exists between peoples. North, South, East, West – learn what they eat and you will realize why they have always clashed. In Europe itself, the abyss between the palates of one nation and another explains the enmity and hostility which exists between human beings whose conception of feeding is completely antithetic. As to the cooking of the older Eastern civilizations – India, China and Japan – they are too remote to be fully understandable.[66]

Food is understood not as a harmonizing force but an engine of cultural division, and the animating energy behind the project is the search for differences, for the tastes and practices that separate cuisines and peoples: the way Austrian cooking differs from German, and Swedish from Norwegian. She is particularly interested in the cuisines of regions that have resisted the culinary influence of others, like Corsica, 'which would certainly never have allowed herself to be dictated to in culinary matters'. Racial characteristics are summed up in sketches of national cuisine: 'Danish cookery is essentially that of a people who require substantial food and who make it tasteful by the use of contrasting ingredients'; while that of Russia 'is full of violent contrasts and discords, and yet it is pleasing and attractive when we get to know it'. Like Elizabeth David (who fondly recalled *Recipes of All Nations* as the first cook book she bought for herself), Countess Morphy favours the foods of warm nations, particularly those of the countries fringing the Mediterranean.[67] Spanish cooking is 'vivid, highly coloured, sometimes Quixotic, brilliant and often enchanting'; that of Italy glows like her art. Understandably, the recipes of countries more familiar and accessible are sounder than those of more distant realms. In her sections on France and Italy she is precise and interesting, often providing recipes for little-known specialities that were to be later ratified as authentic by the likes of Elizabeth David. On Japan she is much shakier, expressing admiration of the harmony and refinement of the food, which is 'arranged and decorated with such artistry and skill that one is tempted to taste even things repulsive to the European palate, such as raw tunny fish or bream', but very unclear on the nature of sushi (which she seems to think is cooked). Her recipes in this section are hardly such at all – more descriptions of what is eaten in Japan. She does, though, refer to dishes and ingredients that were otherwise to take some decades to reach a British readership: Yokan (red bean 'cakes'), tofu, miso and udon noodles. Though she doesn't seem to imagine that her more exotic dishes will actually be cooked by her readers, her work massively expanded the culinary vista, if not the practice, of interwar Britain.[68]

Very few writers were as wholeheartedly adventurous as Countess Morphy. Despite the lip service paid to the notion of foreign food as typifying elegant economy, there is often a hesitancy and timidity in the way in which food writers describe it. Agnes Jekyll, whose *Kitchen Essays* preceded Boulestin's first book by a year, provides two chapters on Italian food: 'Thoughts of Venice from Home' and 'Home Thoughts of Florence and Some Tuscan Recipes'. The titles echo Robert Browning's poem 'Home Thoughts from Abroad', and the Brownings' happy decade-long exile in Florence is conjured up by Jekyll as a paradigm of the experience of the British in Italy when she offers a recipe for 'the *Panetonne* so greatly enjoyed by Mr and Mrs Robert Browning at sunny breakfasts in Casa Guidi'.[69] She imagines that her readers must share the fantasy: 'those who have suffered under the burdens of taxation since the Great War, and experienced the increasing difficulty of adjusting income to expenditure, are apt to think that life is less difficult in the sunny south than under grey English skies'. But Italian food, for the most part, remains for her a thing of fantasy: a lyrical description of the foods of Venice is prefaced by the statement that 'they cannot be transplanted'.[70]

A number of writers seem to share a sense that their readers are not quite ready for full-blown foreignness: so while Quaglino tells us that 'in France, they are very fond of raw vegetables', he is 'afraid that you cannot adopt this system in England. For the climate is different and I do not think you can digest these vegetables so well, especially at night, although they are very healthy and appetizing'.[71] Ambrose Heath reassures his readers, who may have been frightened off by fishy 'tales of Bouillabaisse', that fish soups can be milder tasting, and offers a version 'perhaps more suited to our Northern palates', which consists largely of whiting, spinach and parsley. There is often a sense of daring in the inclusion of foreign recipes, an apology for the garlic, a distancing of the reader from the foreignness of the recipe. Heath, for example, offers a recipe for *Arroz à la Valencia*, which he describes as a famous dish, but also as an 'extraordinary mixture', placing himself with his timid readers in acknowledging that the dish 'sounds very strange to us' (it is, in fact, a classic paella – no longer so strange to the British palate).[72] Perhaps because of the association of the *cuisine bourgeoise* of Europe with the Bloomsbury group and the other intellectuals who were the first to embrace it in Britain, this food was often seen as excitingly bohemian.[73] To cook such exotic, unrestrained and vibrantly flavoured food gave the middle-class housewife an imaginative association with the creative artist, as some compensation for the domestic labour that was now to be her lot. There is thus a tendency for writers to want to outdo each other in the quest for ever more exotic curiosities. Mrs Leyel, who subtly weaves many dishes with an Eastern influence into the main fabric of her *Gentle Art of Cookery*, nonetheless can't resist incorporating the full-blown, wind-swept fantasy of sheikhs and sand in a chapter called 'Dishes from the Arabian Nights', in which she includes some fairly authentic Arabic, Turkish and Persian specialities. The game of foreign flirtation is won hands down, however, by Rachel and Margaret Ryan's otherwise conventionally English *Dinners for Beginners*, which trumps even Countess Morphy's exotica with its final recipe, offered 'in repentance for the lack of exotic novelties in this book', for an east African dish of sun-baked locusts, described as 'a portmanteau meal, the chief ingredients having themselves devoured all other foods available in the district'.[74]

As the traditional local cooking of Europe began to be taken seriously, there was also a sudden recognition that many of our own regional specialities were about to be lost. The English Folk Cookery Association, led by Florence White, sought to recover the traditional recipes of the regions of Britain. The movement was part of a general interest in heritage and folk traditions (songs, rituals and so on) that arose, perhaps in reaction to all things modern, in the 1930s. White's 1932 book *Good Things in England* presented a scholarly, eclectic jumble of recipes dating from the Middle Ages onwards, gleaned from gentlemen's clubs, Oxford and Cambridge colleges, farmhouses, cottages and the Houses of Parliament. It has long been acknowledged as a classic and was responsible for encouraging much later serious research into British food history, but its effects were slow-burning. It was not really until the 1970s that traditional British food was to become actively fashionable.[75] The food-conscious of the interwar years had only just freed themselves from the Victorian tradition of thin soup, roast bird, boiled vegetables, steamed pudding and savoury, and were in no hurry to return to its steamy embrace.

If one thing unites the many and various cook books of the interwar years, it is that they are the product of a culture that was beginning to talk about what it ate. Food had become something to debate and write about, to consider carefully rather than just consume thoughtlessly. Manners had changed, and where food had previously, along with religion and politics, been a forbidden subject for polite diners, it was now more than acceptable to discuss the food your hostess provided. Marcel Boulestin encouraged the trend in the brief list of culinary precepts with which he opened *Simple French Cooking* (1923): 'Do not be afraid to talk about food. Food which is worth eating is worth discussing. And there is the occult power of words which somehow will develop its qualities.'[76] An open enjoyment of food was now in good taste; gusto and even greed were fashionable for women as well as for men.[77] Virtually every cook book of these years includes essays on cooking and eating, on tastes and fashions in food, on skills and techniques, on changes in British eating habits. The cook books of the interwar years helped give food planning and preparation the status of a leisure activity for the upper and middle classes, establishing it as a mode of self-display and self-improvement far too interesting to be left to servants, even if there were any to be had. Anyone reading the cook books of the 1920s and 1930s today will be struck by the degree to which both individual recipes and the types of food discussed seem familiar. There are recipes for polenta and gnocchi, vegetables like avocados, aubergines and artichokes appear regularly, foods that we think of as 1980s clichés, such as raspberry vinegar and chocolate mousse cake, crop up in books published half a century before these dishes appeared on our restaurant menus. To discover why such dishes – and the lively, questing, eclectic food culture that produced them – disappeared for nearly half a century, we need to turn our attention to the Second World War.

TYPICAL RECIPES 1920–38

Lady Jekyll
Kitchen Essays (1922)

This recipe comes from the chapter entitled 'In the Cook's Absence' and is recommended for busy holiday times of the year, 'when cooks, whose mothers so often specialize in sudden and disastrous illnesses, may leave us to face problems we have never really envisaged'. The attitude of rueful, and possibly begrudged, respect for the cook is clear, as is the resentment that she has any sort of independent life. The dish is a simple French onion soup, much complicated by the business of baking the toasts and onions and making a separate stock (the original invariably involves a soup made from the onions with cheese-topped toasts floating in it). The deserted reader is assumed not to be able to cook, but the instructions are rather perfunctory – in particular there is no indication of how to chop the onions, which would make a considerable difference to the finished dish. The evocation of the motor tour, the small French inn, the kindly patronne *and her revelation of her culinary secrets all recall the writing of Elizabeth David. In Agnes Jekyll's work we witness the beginning of food tourism.*

A vision of the pleasant spacious kitchen of a small French inn visited in a recent motor tour came to the rescue. The shining utensils, the charming patronne, all recalled the savour of an excellent brew whose evolution she obligingly encouraged her guest to study. This, if it could be recaptured, should welcome coming guests and cause the artist's temporary absence to be forgiven. It was called *Garbure à la Lionnaise*, and may be accomplished thus:-

> Chop about one pound of onions finely, and place, with 2 ounces of fresh butter, on a moderate fire in a frying pan till browned. Cut 8 or 10 small slices from a long milk roll of bread, lay them in a fireproof glass or shallow earthenware dish, powdering in a little cheese first. On each slice of bread put a little of the cooked onion and a dusting of cheese – preferably half Parmesan and half gruyère. Pour over these a glass of consommé or good stock (thoughtfully left ready by the absent artist). Put the dish into the oven to brown and

if necessary pass a salamander over it just before serving it together with a marmite pot of hot consommé or good stock in the proportion of 1 quart for six people, adding 2 yolks of eggs and half a glass of cream. Serve the garbure and the soup simultaneously but in separate dishes.

Mrs C. F. Leyel and Miss Olga Hartley
The Gentle Art of Cookery (1925)

This comes from the chapter on flower recipes and stands alongside recipes for Cowslip Pudding, Eggs Cooked with Marigolds, and Ice Cream of Roses. Mrs Leyel's taste for flower recipes is in part a scholarly rediscovery of traditional English dishes (the Elizabethans were partial to such scented delicacies) and partly an orientalist taste, as the reference to Yokohama suggests. The style of the salad owes much to the American composed salads so fashionable at this time. This is not as minimalist as the recipes of many of her contemporaries and it provides a number of telling details that they would tend to omit (the intricacies of the washing and blanching processes, for instance), but it assumes some degree of knowledge on the part of the reader and – more tellingly – a confidence of taste, since quantities are not given and the decision about the saffron is for the reader to make.

CHRYSANTHEMUM SALAD

Clean and wash in several waters about twenty chrysanthemum flowers picked from the stalks. Blanch them in acidulated and salted water; drain them and dry them in a cloth.

Mix them well into a salad composed of potatoes, artichoke bottom, shrimps' tails, and capers in vinegar.

Arrange this in a salad bowl, and decorate it with beetroot and hard-boiled egg. A pinch of saffron may be added to this salad for seasoning.

The dark yellow chrysanthemums are best. In Yokohama the flowers already prepared are sold in the greengrocers' shops.

X. Marcel Boulestin
Simple French Cooking for English Homes (1923)

This recipe epitomizes Boulestin's use of the French bourgeois culinary tradition and his simple but clear instructions. Nonetheless, there are some pitfalls in this recipe: he surely means four cloves *rather than* heads *of garlic, and it is not clear why the pork and* confit d'oie *needs to be browned in butter when the latter is dripping in goose fat.*

CASSOULET

Soak a pound of haricot beans for ten hours. Cook them on a slow fire with salt, pepper, and one onion for about two hours. Take half a pound of pork, half a pound of *confit d'oie*, and cut them in several pieces. Brown them in butter with salt, pepper and four heads of garlic chopped with parsley, a glass of white wine; add two tablespoonfuls of pureé of tomatoes and cook one hour. Put in the beans, a few thin pieces of bacon, one pork sausage fried and cut in slices, and let it simmer another hour and a half. Put all this in a fireproof dish, sprinkle with bread crumbs, add a few small pieces of butter and brown in the oven. Serve boiling hot in the same dish.

CONFITS D'OIE
Preserved Goose

Take a well fattened goose. Cut it in pieces, legs, wings, neck, breast, etc. Remove carefully all the fat attached, also the fat inside the bird. Put the meat for twenty-four hours in a jar with coarse salt, thyme and bay leaves. Melt the fat in a large saucepan with a spoonful of water and one pound of pork fat. When well melted, put in the parts of the goose and cook on very slow fire for four hours (drying the pieces well before you put them to cook). Then put them in an earthenware jar and pour the fat over. When cold, cover the jar as for *petit salé* [with a piece of cloth and then a lid or heavy board]. Your *confit* in a few days is ready for use.

When you want a piece take it out and see that none of the others are exposed to the air. It is advisable to melt again part of the fat and pour it afresh over the *confits*. They will keep for months. In Perigord the stock for the year is usually prepared about Christmas time.

Alice Martineau
Caviar to Candy (1927)

Typical of Martineau's eclectic and cosmopolitan vegetable dishes, this is credited to a Madame C. de Langlois in Chile. It is notable that today's fashions in food have not yet reappropriated such South American dishes. This dish is presumably intended to be served as a separate course rather than to accompany a main dish. The recipe is detailed, though there is an assumption of some expertise in the reader (the directions for making stock are very perfunctory).

HUMITOS
(A Chilean way of serving sweet corn)

For this, one requires the ears of corn covered with the outside covering of leaves, and quite fresh.

The corn is stripped from the stalks or grated off them, mixed with a little lard and salt, and fried just a little in a frying-pan, after which a few spoons of well-flavoured stock (fried onions, carrots, herbs, etc.) are added while it is still in the pan.

Take some of the most tender of the green leaves that surround the corn and cut them in strips. Wrap some little heaps of the corn up in these strips, binding them over and round till the corn looks like a packet about four and a half inches by two and a half inches. Split some of the leaves up into much thinner strips and tie up the packets with them. Then place them in a saucepan with some water and boil till cooked. They must not be over-cooked.

Serve one to each person, who undoes the packet and sprinkles a little sugar on the corn before eating it.

The best way of cooking green corn, it is said.

N.B. – Lard means clarified suet.

Rachel and Margaret Ryan
Dinners for Beginners (1934)

A classic, homely American dish, approached with great seriousness by its British interpreters: this epitomizes the mystique American food (and culture) possessed for the British in these years. This recipe is typ-

ical of the exhaustive detail of Dinners for Beginners. *There is no assumption that the readers have any experience of cooking, so the details of how to rub fat into flour and crush strawberries are scrupulously relayed. No other cook book of the period goes into quite such detail. The Ryans are also very particular about expense, always advising their readers about where costs can be reduced (hence the recommendation that cream is unnecessary and the giving of the cost of the dish). It is notable that the recipe employs the rational layout of ingredients followed by method introduced by Acton and Beeton. It is remarkable how few of the Ryans' contemporaries follow suit, given that the convention was well established by this period. In their eagerness to approach food writing in an essayistic, cultured manner, most of the other writers of the interwar years sacrifice clarity to style.*

STRAWBERRY SHORTCAKE (COST: ABOUT 1/6)

6 ozs. flour	2 ozs. butter
1 saltspoonful salt	A little milk
2 ozs. sugar	1½ lbs. strawberries
4 teaspoonfuls baking powder	A little icing sugar

This is an American recipe to which cream can be added if you like, although the dish is then so rich that it is apt to make even the best trenchermen feel a little bloated. The original American recipe contains no egg, although this is almost always included in versions of this sweet given in English cookery books. The latter may be very good sweets, but they are not strawberry shortcake.

Buy a pound and a half of strawberries. They need not be the best, as they are to be crushed. Wash and stalk the strawberries. Select the twelve best specimens for decoration and crush the rest with two or three tablespoons of sugar. There is no need to go through the arduous business of a sieve with such tender fruit, especially as it does not need to be crushed to a *pureé*, but rather to the resemblance of jam. Leave it aside in a cool place, and make the shortcake.

The Shortcake.

Sift together one and a half cups of flour (six ounces) and four – yes, *four* – teaspoonfuls of baking powder, and a saltspoonful of salt. Cut in with a knife a bare two ounces of butter. Cut this up into the smallest pieces you can among the flour, but do not touch it with your hands. Now add a tablespoonful of cold milk and with your hands form the paste into a dough. If you need a little more milk before the paste becomes cohesive, add another tablespoonful – no more. Work as quickly as you can, and handle the dough as little as possible. It should be very stiff and leave the sides of the basin clean.

Flour a rolling-pin and turn the dough on to a floured board. Roll the dough (in one direction only) to fit the pan in which it is to be baked. This should preferably be a baking tin about 8 inches by 4 inches and about 1 inch deep, but a circular one will do, provided it is not too large for the dough.

Remember all this must be done quickly.

Bake the shortcake in a quick oven for twenty minutes. It will rise considerably.

When it is done (it should be golden in colour) take it out of the oven and let it cool *in the pan* for a few minutes. Then turn it out and cut it in two length-wise through the middle with a sharp knife, so that it forms two layers. Spread the lower half with a thick layer of the crushed strawberries and some of the juice – not too much, or the cake will become soggy. Cover with the top half, and decorate with the twelve whole strawberries and a little powdered icing sugar.

Whipped cream may be interposed between the strawberries and the top layer, if you have decided to use it and do not mind the extra expense. Strawberry shortcake is best eaten while the shortcake part of it is still warm, like a fresh cake. But it can be eaten cold with success, in which case it must be left to cool on a cake-rack or the top of a sieve. In each case, the strawberries and the cream, if you are using any, must be very cold.

This mixture (the shortcake) can well be eaten with other fruits or with jam.

Ruth Lowinsky
Lovely Food (1931)

Recipes for iced camembert or camembert ice cream appear in a number of interwar cook books: there are other examples in Nancy Shaw's Food for the Greedy *(she recommends a pint of cream to two cheeses) and Alice Martineau's* Caviar to Candy *(she suggests simply freezing a whole cheese). Typical of Lowinsky's abbreviated recipes, this one fails to indicate whether the rind of the cheese should be discarded (it seems likely that it should).*

ICED CAMEMBERT

Take two Camembert cheeses and mix with a little cream. Pepper and salt. Place in a small round tin which has contained Bath Oliver biscuits. Freeze till hard. Cut into thin slices and serve on broken ice. Serve with hot water biscuits.

CHAPTER THREE

Mock Duck and Making Do

As the shadow of a new conflict fell over Britain, the very meaning of food was dramatically changed. Where people's choice of food had previously involved issues of tradition and habit, social status and style, it was now hedged about with questions of patriotism and morality, the subject of a continual barrage of propaganda. Virtually overnight the language itself altered. As nutrition rather than pleasure became the pre-eminent concern, 'eating' was replaced with 'feeding', with all its animal connotations. The British Restaurants, introduced to provide balanced, inexpensive meals for workers in urban centres, were only saved from being known as 'Communal Feeding Centres' by the personal intervention of Winston Churchill.[1] Food writers devoted much of their attention to information about vitamin conservation and food for health. Cooking was to be women's war work, and culinary experts were alternately chummy and cajoling but unrelenting in their drive to persuade the housewife to accept the responsibility and high seriousness of her newly defined role. In its *ABC of Cookery* (1945) the Ministry of Food was stern about these responsibilities: 'The housewife must know how to plan her family's meals. Her choice of food will largely determine not only their good health but also their good looks!'[2] The Good Housekeeping Institute was concerned to put a brave face on the situation, encouraging women to see 'difficulties . . . as a challenge' – 'Never a dull meal from now until the end of rationing – that should be the aim of every housewife who takes a proper, professional pride in her job.'[3] Following the logic of the domestic-science movement, the Institute saw housework as a serious job and the war as 'an opportunity [the housewife] may never possess again to learn the real art of cooking'. Even more resolutely upbeat is Josephine Terry, who in her 1944 book *Food without Fuss* casts the housewife as star theatrical performer:

> To our delight we housewives of to-day find ourselves in a somewhat exalted position. Each time we serve a meal we stand in the limelight, facing an audience of men and children – with large appetites and small rations.

We know their health and happiness depend on us, up to a point. But what a point! Everyone has become wise about the merits of a good meal, and never before have we received such wholehearted appreciation.

We like it![4]

In case we miss the point, this effusion is matched by a frontispiece picture of the housewife star, young and modern, proudly clutching a casserole dish as she basks in the spotlight. The reality for the wartime housewife was, of course, generally rather different: a never-ending grind of shortages, queues and rationed goods.

Having learnt the necessity of prompt and thorough food control in the First World War, the government introduced rationing in the first few months of the Second. The Ministry of Food was established in September 1939, five days after Britain declared war on Germany. A continuation of the Food (Defence Plans) Department of the Board of Trade set up nearly three years earlier, it was able rapidly to put into action detailed plans for the management of food supplies. By the end of September a National Register had been established and every member of the population supplied with an identity card. Rationing began in January, with bacon, ham, sugar and butter the first foods 'on the ration'; meat followed in March. April 1940 saw probably the defining moment in the story of food and the war: the appointment of Lord Woolton as Minister of Food.[5] Woolton was a Liverpool retailer with a scientific training and a strong social conscience. The chairman of Lewis's department store in Liverpool, he had been involved in the government distribution of supplies in the First World War and had researched the effect of that war on prices and consumer goods. Earlier he had worked in the slums of Liverpool in a charitable capacity, with the shining ambition of discovering the root causes of poverty. With a degree in science and economics from Manchester University, he was interested in discovering scientific solutions for social problems, a bent that enabled him to communicate very effectively with the Ministry's scientific advisers. The chief of these was Sir Jack Drummond, a nutritional biochemist who had been appointed to a university chair at the age of thirty-one for his work on infant feeding and butter and margarine substitutes. The author – with his wife Anne Wilbraham – of the 1939 study *The Englishman's Food* (which surveyed the British diet from the Middle Ages to the present), Drummond combined a rigorous scientific training with a strong personal interest in food and drink, and he soon demonstrated himself to be highly skilled at applying the latest nutritional research to the exigencies of the wartime diet.[6] Woolton's particular gift was communicating complex ideas forcefully to the British public, and together they devoted themselves to apportioning fairly the national food stores, while simultaneously keeping the public onside. Woolton, in his desire to speak personally to the British people, took to broadcasting regularly so that, as he later explained, 'I could reason and explain, sometimes taking the public into confidence as to the reasons why they should take certain action, sometimes explaining government decisions.'[7] Taught by a professional broadcaster how to use his voice, he took his task very seriously, spending an average of eight hours preparing each twelve-and-a-half-minute talk.

Woolton's plan was to ration only those foodstuffs whose supply could be guaranteed, to ensure that everyone received their fair share. Tea, margarine, cooking fats and cheese were rationed in July 1940, and jam, marmalade, treacle and syrup in March of the following year. Sweets came under the ration in July 1942. Eggs had not been rationed, because their supply fluctuated and their sources were difficult to administer, but by 1941 the shortage was so acute that the distribution of eggs was brought under Ministry control, and from June of that year ordinary ration-book holders were allocated one egg as often as supplies permitted, with extra supplies for children, expectant mothers and invalids.[8] Milk was similarly brought under the control of the Ministry from July 1942, with almost half the available milk going to the same special cases as did eggs and the rest shared among the general population. The overriding concern of the Ministry was to ensure that children in particular were adequately fed and that the diseases of malnourishment, such as rickets and scurvy, were eradicated. To this end they issued free condensed orange juice (later supplemented by rose-hip syrup) and cod-liver oil to infants and expectant mothers. They also introduced the National Loaf (and National Flour) of 85 per cent extraction, whose greyish colour made it deeply unpopular despite its healthiness, and launched the campaign encouraging anyone with access to any land at all to Dig for Victory.[9] The keeping of hens and pigs was also encouraged, though sometimes their food proved a problem.[10] Large swathes of Hampstead Heath were given over to allotments, pig bins for waste food occupied street corners, and some ingenious – or desperate – flat-dwellers even experimented with keeping hens in cages suspended outside their windows: 'A standard "layer's cage" had a floor which sloped, so that when the hen laid an egg it would roll gently down out of her reach. This design was particularly useful if you had to lean over a windowbox of tomato plants to collect your eggs!'[11] The gathering of wild food was much promoted, and mammoth communal preserving sessions were organized around the country to preserve fruits and make jams for the winter months.

It was crucial that the country should produce more food, because at the start of war in 1939 over 60 per cent of the nation's food was imported.[12] With shipping difficult and dangerous and many of the exporter countries under occupation, Britain had now to rely on its own resources. It struggled to do so until spring 1941, when the US government passed a Lend–Lease Bill agreeing that America could lend articles of defence to any country deemed vital to the defence of the US. They required no repayment but did expect certain trade concessions after the war.[13] The first shipment of Lend–Lease food arrived at the end of May, and by autumn sufficient stocks had accumulated for the government to begin distributing them. Since these goods were not numerous enough to be available to everyone through the standard method of rationing, a new form of rationing, known as 'points', was introduced. The scheme offered a much-needed element of choice, since people could now 'spend' their points ration on the food of their choice, if available. Food on points included canned fish and meat, dried fruit, condensed milk, biscuits and golden syrup. Many culinary authorities seem to have agreed that the best value on points was represented by the large tins of American pork sausage meat. These 'cost' 16 points – one person's entire monthly allowance at the start of the scheme – but contained pure meat (unlike the British sausage liberally mixed with breadcrumbs and other fillers) and also a large quantity of fat, which was invaluable for cooking. Other goods from America also became a crucial element of the British diet, though not all were liked or appreciated. Dried eggs and soya flour, in particular, proved difficult to cook with, and food writers devoted much of their attention to coming up with ingenious ways to make these ingredients 'work'.

The Ministry of Food was by far the most significant publisher of information about food during the war years. Its advertisements appeared daily in newspapers and magazines, exhorting housewives to save fuel (suggestions included the use of pressure cookers, baking once a week, sharing ovens with neighbours and constructing hay-boxes to finish the cooking of food without heat), to use vitamin-rich foods, to try the new foods from America and to reform their culinary practices in line with wartime conditions. Waste is a major theme: 'Food is a munition of war: don't waste it'; 'Our Sailors don't mind risking their lives to feed you – and your family – but they do mind if you help the U-boats by wasting food.' Much energy was devoted to emphasizing the benefits of fresh vegetables and the useful ways in which they could substitute for fruits and other foods in providing vitamins. The eating of raw vegetables was encouraged to ensure maximum nutritional benefits – 'A new taste thrill!' enthused one Ministry advert: 'Shredded raw cabbage in salads.' Of particular import were carrots and potatoes, soon represented by cartoon characters Doctor Carrot, 'who guards your health', and Potato Pete: 'I'll put pep in your step.' Cheerily prancing across the pages of women's magazines, the duo asserted the seemingly endless versatility of these most common of root vegetables. Carrots could be used to substitute for fruit, and even sugar, in puddings and pies. An example is Mock Apricot Flan, of which the Ministry claimed that 'the carrots really do taste a little like apricots'; the public was clearly not convinced, and later versions of the recipe are called Carrot Flan, which, they were assured, 'has a deliciousness all its own'. The propaganda on behalf of the vegetable was inexhaustible in its ingenuity: 'The Ministry's master-stroke was spreading the belief that carrots enabled one to see better in the dark, thus explaining the sudden success of "Cat's-eyes Cunningham", and other night-fighter aces, which was in fact due to the introduction of radar.'[14] Potatoes were even more vital, and the housewife was advised to substitute them for bread and pastry at every opportunity (they 'feed without fattening and give you *ENERGY*'). Potato Pete brought out his own recipe book, and the Ministry offered a weekly prize to the greengrocer with the best-selling potato display. A radio jingle emphasized the importance of preserving all the vitamin content of the vegetable:

> Those who have the will to win
> Cook potatoes in their skin
> Knowing that the sight of peelings
> Deeply hurts Lord Woolton's feelings.

The Ministry's campaign was so successful that by the end of the war the consumption of potatoes had risen by 60 per cent (the largest increase for any commodity).

The Ministry also published a series of Food Facts columns, which appeared in all the daily papers and in the *Radio Times*. These contained injunctions about food – 'Please make full use of the fruit and vegetables now so plentiful,' 'Never eat more than enough' – alongside health hints and recipes. The housewife was enjoined to 'start now to collect these useful advertisements. Pin them up in your kitchen.' A similar mix of recipes, advice and instruction was provided by the *Kitchen Front* radio programmes, which were broadcast for fifteen minutes daily after the 8 a.m. news. The content varied – one morning a well-known food writer like Ambrose Heath would give recipes and hints, another morning it would be tips on saving fuel or mending kitchen utensils. Comic sketches from 'Gert and Daisy' or 'The Buggins Family' would be interspersed with recipes, and one morning a week the Radio Doctor (Charles Hill, later to be a prominent Conservative politician) would advise on a healthy wartime diet.[15] Sometimes housewives would appear on the programme to give talks on their own recipes.[16] Although the programmes were nominally under the control of the BBC, the Ministry of Food was heavily involved in dictating their content, drafting the scripts, editing those prepared by independent speakers, testing the recipes in their own test kitchens in Portman Square and exercising power of veto over the recipes broadcast. On many occasions they rejected recipes submitted by housewives as not sufficiently interesting or frugal, and one particularly ludicrous situation in January 1943 involved the Ministry insisting that the phrase 'Eat potatoes instead of bread' be inserted into every broadcast for a month, regardless of its relevance to the material under discussion.[17]

The *Kitchen Front* programmes, like much else of the Ministry's food advice, were primarily aimed at the working-class housewife, and this fact accounts for the tone employed in all of its pronouncements, a mixture of cheery informality and stern admonishments from social superiors. Propaganda is naked and unashamed, with little attempt at subtlety, as in the large advertisement 'The Butcher Says . . .', which appeared in newspapers and magazines when the meat ration was reduced and eked out with corned beef:

'That's right, Mrs Smith. We're getting a seventh of our meat now in corned beef – twopence in the 1s. 2d. as you might say. Lord Woolton's watching his stocks – he likes to be sure he's got a bit in hand. I don't mind telling you I was rather afraid the whole ration would be cut down. It's lucky for everyone there is this corned beef to help out with. Cold or hot, you can dish it up in a dozen different ways – and very tasty, too. No, Mrs Smith, I don't want any points coupons, it's all part of the meat ration.'[18]

The Ministry also produced a series of cookery leaflets, which were available free from any Food Office: the first promoted oatmeal, the second cheaper cuts of meat, and the series had reached number 24 by the end of the war. Because of the low income levels of the Ministry's intended audience, it tended to concentrate on providing information that was essentially free, but it did also produce a number of books. *Community Feeding in Wartime* appeared in 1941, *Canteen Catering* in 1942, *Wise Eating in Wartime* in 1943 and *The Manual of Nutrition* and *The ABC of Cookery* in 1945. As the titles suggest, these are fairly serious publications, often aimed at those responsible for mass catering. The latter two are concerned not with recipes as such but with inculcating scientifically based procedures in the kitchen.

A number of books were published as spin-offs from the *Kitchen Front* broadcasts.[19] Ambrose Heath published extracts from his own broadcasts in two volumes: *Kitchen Front Recipes and Hints* (1941) and *More Kitchen Front Recipes* (1941). The first volume preserves the texts of the broadcasts virtually verbatim and is remarkable for its tone, a combination of hesitancy and chumminess interspersed with outright social prescription, as the following example, from a talk broadcast on 9 October 1940, illustrates:

I've been thinking that in all the turmoil just now . . . No. I don't think 'turmoil' is the right word at all; it's much too serious: perhaps 'upset' is the word I'm looking for . . . I've been wondering whether people may not perhaps be getting just a bit too casual about their food. I mean that with all the little difficulties we have to overcome, we may be a little in danger of looking on eating as merely something to keep us going, – 'stoking up', as my father might have called it . . . But what I want to insist on now is that the cook's job, the mother's and the wife's job *is* to make the best of what she has: to carry on, as her husband, perhaps, and her kin are carrying on, *is no mean contribution* towards those days when our homes and kitchens will be normal once again, and we shall have learned from our present discomforts how simple those things really are which we once found difficult – and how comparatively simple, now, if we could only realise it.[20]

Heath is both tentative and bossy as a result of his clear unease with what he assumes to be a working-class audience: his address is a long way from the charming, sophisticated whimsy that characterized his *Good Food* of 1932. Heath published a great deal during the war years (a staggering total of twenty-one books during the war, and a further twenty-three up to the end of austerity in 1954), yet it is significant that in later life he remarked of the beginning of the war that 'the following years were lean ones for my sort of writer', expressing a sense that his own culinary tastes and practices were unsuitable for wartime use.[21] The sense of teeth-gritted discomfort with his role as Ministry stooge is clear in the marked adjustments he makes to his pre-war culinary style, in particular in his scrupulous avoidance of foreign names for dishes. Heath, as discussed in the last chapter, had been one of the first writers to popularize the foods of continental Europe for the middle-class reader, and yet in his first wartime book he sticks rigorously to British food – or rather, to what *appears* to be British food. In fact, he makes use of a number of foreign recipes, but they are all hidden under the guise of prosaic wartime names. So in both *Good Food* and *Kitchen Front Recipes and Hints* he gives a recipe for Clafoutis, but in the former it is presented as a sophisticated piece of exotica, while in the latter it is a hint for ways of eking out the sugar ration by serving a pudding of bits of fruit in Yorkshire pudding batter: the same dish, very different meanings.[22] In the second volume, *More Kitchen Front Recipes*, the prose style is tightened up (he notes in the foreword that 'I have met a criticism of diffuseness in the previous book by keeping, in this, strictly to business, and this has entailed the addition of quite a large number of recipes'), while the tone is relaxed, and a very few card-carrying foreign dishes are allowed to creep back in.[23] These include a Minestrone, a Dutch Autumn Salad and a Creole Soup. Possibly the most interesting is a dish called Lobscouse, which Heath describes as 'a Danish Stew of Beef'; he footnotes the recipe with an account of the massive volume of correspondence the recipe drew forth after its broadcast, concluding somewhat oddly that since listeners had contributed 'so many different versions of the same dish . . . I have thought it best to reproduce here only the one which started it'.[24] Recipes of the same name appeared in other wartime publications, sometimes glossed as a traditional sailor's dish. The reason for this confusion, and for Heath's much-exercised correspondents, is that the dish is not quite as foreign as he supposed – or at least not recently so. According to the *Oxford Companion to Food*, the name Lobscouse is given in the north-west of England to a group of dishes that originally had their origins in the Baltic ports and were recorded in this country as early as the 1820s. Mainly denoting meat stews rather similar to the one given by Heath, it can also refer to fish stews. Although originally German and Danish in origin, Lobscouse had a long enough history in Liverpool, in particular, for it to have lent its name to the city's inhabitants: it is the etymological source of the term 'scouser'. As far as Heath's work is concerned, the episode serves to indicate that he had by now developed a clearer sense of his listeners – people with a keen, indeed powerful, interest in food traditions, to whom the odd foreign dish would not prove an insuperable obstacle. It is also a demonstration of the extent to which the British culinary tradition has always taken foreign dishes to its heart.[25]

Many food writers proved extremely co-operative at selling the Ministry of Food's line on nutrition, new foods, new cooking methods and the minimizing of waste. One particularly zealous exponent of Lord Woolton's ways was Irene Veal, who in 1944 published *Recipes of the 1940s*, which she dedicated 'to Lord Woolton, who taught British Women to Cook Wisely'. The book is written with one eye on the historians of the future and seeks to justify the food policies of the wartime administration. Veal celebrates rationing and the centralized control of food distribution, claiming that 'Never before have the British people been so *wisely* fed or so equally wisely food conscious, or British women, generally speaking, so *sensibly* interested in cooking'. She goes further and argues that they should continue to operate indefinitely after the end of hostilities: 'A great many people are hoping that some form of control, and very definite control at that, will continue to be exercised for very many years'. Alongside her rampant paternalism, Veal demonstrates an upbeat jollity in the face of difficulties that sometimes verges on the hysterical: 'The British housewife . . . being introduced to the excellent qualities of the dried egg . . . is evermore realising its infinite possibilities'.[26] Having explored the nation's wartime culinary practices by way of the dishes served by a number of major institutions – the BBC, the various armed forces, the Bank of England and a number of hospitals (Veal is very much in favour of 'communal feeding') – as well as recipes from restaurants and ordinary homes, she ends with a rousing peroration:

> Yet the English people took it all smiling, used their own inventiveness as never before in cooking and culinary achievements, and regarded the lot as part of their war effort – just as Lord Woolton intends they should do![27]

Astoundingly sycophantic though Veal's remarks on Lord Woolton are, they are by no means atypical in their sentiments. One of Woolton's major achievements was the great affection he seems to have aroused in a large section of the British public. It is expressed by one Dorchester housewife quoted in Norman Longmate's memoir of the home front: 'Lord Woolton was always so sympathetic and if he could not give us more butter he added an extra ounce to the margarine. We all trusted and loved him.'[28] And this affection apparently prevailed despite the deep unpopularity of the dish to which Woolton lent his name: Woolton Pie was a combination of root vegetables (usually potatoes and carrots, sometimes swedes, parsnips and turnips) under a pastry crust. Sometimes moistened with a white sauce, sometimes not, it seems to have been universally disliked, and it is notable that there are few recipes for it included in even the most pro-Ministry cook books. Another of Longmate's interviewees summed up the general feeling: 'I just can't believe that such a wonderful man could have given his name to such a dish'.[29]

The war-economy standards in book production meant that the cook books of the war years are small, drab affairs compared with those of the 1920s and 1930s. Type is cramped, there are few decorations and the paper is cheap and rough. Books continued to be published, as there was a continual and pressing need for new recipes to cope with the changing food supply, but in fact the cook book *per se* was not the main form in which recipes were distributed in the war years. As well as the government's proliferation of culinary advice and recipes in many different media, manufacturers of foodstuffs and kitchen equipment issued advertisements and leaflets designed to keep their products before the public's eye, even if conditions meant they were physically unavailable. So we get the curious spectacle of manufacturers advising people to use *less* of their product or to be patient if they can't obtain it. Heinz took a full page (rare in this time of acute paper restrictions) to assure the public that they were still manufacturing their products: 'It may be difficult to secure them, because the demand is large and retail output restricted, but Heinz 57 Varieties remain unchanged in purity, flavour and excellence.' 'Sorry it's scarce,' apologized the makers of Camp coffee essence, assuring would-be purchasers that 'your greengrocer is doing his best to distribute his limited supplies of "Camp" fairly among his customers'. Recipe leaflets were another way of ensuring continued brand loyalty among customers. Some of the most-used culinary guides were the leaflets produced by companies like Stork (margarine), Brown and Polson (cornflour and custard), and Be-Ro (flour).[30] The flour manufacturers McDougalls also published a recipe book, and went one better by offering a Wartime Recipe Service, run by Miss Janet Johnstone, the author of the cook book, who promised to answer readers' queries about cookery problems. Home Economists, usually on secondment to the Ministry of Food, toured the country giving demonstrations and supplying recipes for the new foods.[31] Recipe columns abounded in newspapers and magazines and were evidently much used, judging by the number one finds carefully clipped out and preserved between the pages of wartime cook books. This cutting loose (often literally) of the recipe is a significant development in the food writing of the Second World War, and it may help explain some of the long-standing culinary effects of the conflict. The recipe ceased to be embedded in a signifying discourse and instead became free-floating, without any historical or national roots. Only significant as a way of using the available foods as efficiently as possible, the instructions for individual dishes began to lose their cultural meaning. So historical specialities like Glamorgan Sausages are recast as Semolina Cheese Sausages (in Mrs Arthur Webb's 1939 *War-Time Cookery*), foreign dishes are altered and renamed, and the telling details that make all the difference are lost in the desire for succinctness in the press and ease in the kitchen. The food of Britain in the war years was an improvised cuisine, and its results may well have included a coarsening of the national palate and a lingering suspicion of British food among those with culinary pretensions which has only recently shown signs of abating.

Even in cook books themselves, that sense, found in pre-war books, of a unified or developing cuisine is largely missing. Recipes are included because of their cheapness or their ingenious use of easily available ingredients, not because they represent a particular style of cooking or are unusual or interesting – or even because they taste good. One surprisingly dominant note in most wartime books is experiment. 'NEW RECIPES ARE NEEDED TODAY,' proclaims the back cover of *Good Eating*, a selection of recipes from readers of the *Daily Telegraph*. 'Homes are now experimental kitchens from which dishes are being launched, many to retain a lasting place in our national fare.' Readers are cast as scientists or encouraged in creative improvisation by many food writers. Ambrose Heath tells the story of his moments of inspiration as an encouragement to his readers to do likewise: 'Sometimes we may long for sausage rolls, but cannot get sausages! This happened to me once, and this is what, on the spur of the moment, I did.' To demonstrate that creative cooking is open to all, he shares the results of his readers' experiments as well as his own: 'A listener has discovered that fried raw carrot is pleasant with bacon for breakfast when you can't get tomatoes.'[32] (It is notable just how often wartime culinary secrets turn out to involve carrots – or parsnips.) It was not just food writers who made use of the public's experiments: 'The Ministry of Food wants your cooking secrets,' announced the advertisements. Josephine Terry's *Food without Fuss* is devoted to the notion of experimental cooking; full of zeal, it positively celebrates the sacrifices the wartime housewife has had to make:

> We have had no time to indulge in looking for trouble and we have been forced to throw overboard one beloved tradition after the other. Now we see that many of them were unsuited to modern life anyway.[33]

She offers strong encouragement to persuade readers to experiment with their cooking, letting them into the secrets of her own great discoveries, such as the combination of parsnips and cheese, of which she wonders why 'none of the famous old French – or Scotch for that matter – cooking geniuses ever thought of it', modestly acknowledging that 'I probably would not have ventured this mixture myself had it not been for the force of circumstances'.[34] On the subject of stale bread she virtually conducts a seminar on the possibilities of improvisation:

> Whenever we look through our stocks, as we often have to do with a frown, we come across bits and pieces of stale bread . . .
>
> So let us take all our crusts and crumb, put them on a wooden board – and think.
>
> There is flour and yeast, a promising flavouring. As it is stale bread, it is dry and therefore has the ability to soak up moisture and swell.
>
> You will be surprised what you can do quickly, and with a minimum of basins and spoons, if you just concentrate for a moment. You will produce some bright idea for the kind of moisture and ingredients to be added to these bits, and the shape and way to cook them.[35]

Having encouraged her readers to devote their mental energies to the process of invention, she then supplies some possibilities, wheaten porridge, carrot bread, savoury pie and quick chocolate pudding amongst them. Massive ingenuity and boundless optimism are the hallmarks of Terry's approach, but the results often sound deeply unappealing. On the subject of 'No Trouble Tea Fancies' she explains gleefully how 'you can make three different kinds of fancy cakes for generous helpings for six to eight persons out of a plain small sponge round (bought at the bakers or grocers) – or in high emergency even a plain teacake will do. You will be far more successful if your sponge or teacake is stale!'[36] Since the fancy cakes involve much ingenious cutting of the already small cake into thinner layers, triangles and stars, and then the applying of various ersatz fillings, peanut butter and icing made from milk powder, we can be fairly confident that the visual effect was a great deal more important than the taste.

In fact, this was true of a whole class of food eagerly recommended by wartime cook books – mock food. The phenomenon of mock food in the First World War was discussed in Chapter One, but there are decided differences in the fantasy foods of the two conflicts. In the First World War the aim was to produce food that tasted like the unobtainable article, regardless of appearance, while during the Second World War visual resemblance became more important, with taste a more minor consideration. These ersatz foods appear in virtually all Second World War cook books. In *Good Eating*, a collection of dishes supplied by readers of the *Daily Telegraph*, there are four different recipes for mock cream (involving, in various combinations, milk, cornflour, dried milk, margarine, evaporated milk and gelatine).[37] Ambrose Heath, in *More Kitchen Front Recipes*, offers the monstrous Mock Fish – ground rice cut into the shape of fish fillets – and Mock Toad-in-the-Hole – which replaces the egg in the batter with bicarbonate of soda and vinegar.[38] Josephine Terry gave her readers Mock Whipped Cream, Cake Icing ('this looks and tastes so much like the real thing that your guests will suspect black-market sugar sooner than a substitute'), Mock Chops (grated raw potatoes, soya flour and onions, shaped and fried) and the rather interesting Mock Goslings (potato pastry wrapped around apple slices and baked, served with vegetables and gravy).[39] So keen was she on the subject that she devoted a whole chapter to Make-Believe Dishes, in which she suggested many ingenious substitutes for ingredients: cheese in Flaky Pastry instead of butter, raw grated turnip instead of pepper, sweets made from dried milk powder instead of sugar and butter. Of these last she comments, laying bare the purely representational impulse behind the artifice, that 'these sweets *look* so real that they can hardly be called a substitute' (emphasis added).[40] The *Punch* humorist 'Fougasse' recognized the absurdities of the fantasy-food principle in his contribution to *A Kitchen Goes to War*, a 1940 collection of recipes from famous people put together by publisher John Miles; offering instructions for Danish Frikadeller (a sort of pork rissole), he asserts that 'this is a recipe for a most economical dish which, when complete, is indistinguishable from chicken (or caviare or pâté de foie gras or crêpes suzette, or anything else you specially fancy)'.[41]

A pattern emerges of the sort of dishes for which mock versions were provided: they were, on the whole, high-status foods of significant symbolic value, notably roast birds or joints, luxurious sweet dishes, cakes and treats. They were dishes whose ritual importance was such that their appearance at the centre of a meal or festive occasion was of more importance than what they tasted like. In essence their replacements were to allow the eater to *imagine* himself eating the things he desired. The most significant example of this phenomenon is the cardboard wedding cake: in July 1940 Lord Woolton issued an order prohibiting the use of sugar for decorating cakes. In response, large hollow cardboard 'cakes' were produced, decorated in what looked like magnificent royal icing. These would be placed over the usually much smaller fruit cake and appear resplendent in many a photograph of a wartime wedding reception. Upmarket restaurants also played the game of make-believe; restricted, under Ministry orders, to a five-shilling price limit on meals and only one main dish per customer, establishments like the Ritz and the Ivy served ersatz dishes, while covering their overheads by charging heavily for wine ('a custom,' as Christopher Driver notes, 'that long survived the war in almost all British catering establishments'):

> Clearly it was not a time when people would visit restaurants for the food, except to save domestic rations, but they were quite prepared to spend as freely on a game of conspiratorial make-believe with their friend Mario as they would have been to pay for *filet béarnaise* and *crème Nesselrode*. As Gallati [Mario – manager of the Ivy] remembers, they seldom complained about anything, and the knowledge that you could still get lunch or dinner at the Ivy in interesting company, at some slight risk of a flying bomb, was a minor but indisputable prop to the morale of the upper middle classes.[42]

Fantasy feasts became more important as the war wore endlessly on. In the absence of turkeys for the Christmas of 1943 'Gert and Daisy' suggested serving a boned leg of mutton and imagining that it was the missing bird:

GERT: Have bread sauce with it and stuff it with the whatnot – no, shut up, Daisy. I suppose you could imagine your leg of mutton was a turkey. Often me and Bert used to eat whelks and kid ourselves they were oysters . . . Of course, you know, there's just as much goodness in the joint. I mean, that's if you use your imagination.[43]

Despite the highly improvisational nature of wartime cookery, cook books shared a fairly high degree of consensus. As far as they are concerned, the most popular dish of the war years would seem to be something usually called 'surprise potatoes': large baked potatoes stuffed with something – often a sausage. The recipe is given in most books, including a version in *A Kitchen Goes to War* contributed by Agatha Christie: hers is called Mystery Potatoes, and the stuffing is cream and anchovies (both were largely unobtainable during the war, so perhaps that is the mystery). The dish is a classic example of the sort of food the Ministry was continually recommending, where a little bit of protein is bulked up with a large amount of vegetable matter.

Food writers were very keen to encourage their readers to grow their own food, and a number provide recipes for unusual vegetables that were relatively easy to produce: Ambrose Heath suggests celeriac, kohlrabi, salsify, seakale beet and sugar peas (mange tout). Other typical recipes were those that encouraged the reader to make use of wild food: dishes like Passion Dock Pudding (dock leaves, oatmeal and egg, boiled) and Nettle Broth were suggested, and Ambrose Heath waxed lyrical on the subject:

A poached egg on a bed of dandelion or nettle purée covered with a cheese sauce is an almost perfect meal, containing every one of the foods which we are being told to eat, body-building, protective and energizing . . . and very good eating too![44]

The American influence of the years between the wars continued to be felt, with a number of American salads given in most books (a good way to serve the portions of raw vegetables the Ministry of Food insisted one must eat). The import of American Lend-Lease foods, and the very visible presence of American servicemen from early in 1942, led writers to turn their attention to the way these foods were used in their country of origin. Josephine Terry, in particular, eagerly embraces American dishes, suggesting such exotica as Virginian Hot Pan and Thanksgiving Slices. She also gives one of the earliest examples in a British cook book of the hamburger, which she constructs from American tinned sausage meat, fried and served in a halved muffin: she calls it an After-Cinema Treat, a name that signals the very beginning of the American influence on the casualization of British eating habits. Although European foods were less in evidence during the war years, certain cuisines do seem to have aroused some interest. There is a significant minority of dishes from eastern Europe, particularly Poland, undoubtedly a result of the presence of the dashing Polish pilots in the British Air Force.[45] It seems that it was necessary for foreign nationals actually to be present on British soil in significantly large numbers for the war-induced insularity and patriotism of our cuisine to be broached.

The shape and pattern of eating during the war seems to have been founded on a determination to preserve as much as possible of familiar and comfortable culinary rituals. So small joints or their ersatz equivalents were served with accompanying vegetables and gravy, if only on Sundays. Tea regained the focus it had lost – at least for the fashionable – in the interwar years, with many pages of most cook books devoted to biscuits, cakes and preserves. These may not have been the best uses for the meagre rations of meat, fat and sugar, but for many people they were clearly the most comforting.

The combination of limited ingredients and a licence to experiment meant that the cook books of the Second World War contained some of the most unpleasant food of the last 150 years. High on the list must come Josephine Terry's nauseating Fish Spread, which mixes the oil from canned fish with oatmeal as a sandwich spread. Also vile are her Lemonettes, biscuits made from household milk powder, with large amounts of baking powder and bicarbonate of soda, lemon flavouring and one tablespoon each of flour and sugar. The *Daily Telegraph*'s *Good Eating* supplies some monstrous concoctions: Curried Fish and Cabbage, and Mushroom Shortcake rank high, but the worst of all must be the repellent recipe for Winter Breakfast Spread:

> A good way to use up surplus fats is to render down and clarify in usual manner, mixing different varieties. Take a meat cube, crush into powder with a fork, and just as the fat, which has been poured into a bowl, is beginning to set, stir in crushed cube and beat well in. When cold this makes a tasty and appetising breakfast spread, saving butter or margarine.[46]

Such dishes are condemned as 'famine food' by one of the very few cook books of the war years not to toe the Ministry's line. Constance Spry's *Come into the Garden, Cook* (1942) is remarkable for the stand it takes against some of the most firmly established culinary pieties of its day. (She seriously flouts convention, for example, by suggesting that eggs and fat should be saved up and splurged on a treat like a chestnut cake rather than eked out over many meals.) From its opening peroration, her book sets itself up in direct opposition to current thinking:

> Here we are in the middle of the war, rationed and restricted as never before, with economy and belt-tightening the order of the day, and yet I want to cry out about food.
>
> It would be safe enough if I meant to paint a dim picture, to accentuate difficulties, to concentrate on left-overs and the best use of roots. But I don't mean to do that at all; I want to emphasize that we have better ingredients than almost any other country and that we frequently treat them abominably.[47]

A well-known society florist, Spry was venturing into cookery writing for the first time. Her book focuses on garden produce as a source of interesting, stylish dishes, elaborating on the theme that many other wartime food writers had dealt with only in passing. Where she is startlingly original is in her refusal to accept that wartime food needs to be improvised, worthy and rushed. Above all, she restores a sense of culture to food writing. She discusses the origins and associations of dishes, evokes a sense of appetite and insists on the importance of proper method in the kitchen. Her book was greeted with profound relief by the critics, even those, like Ambrose Heath, who had themselves followed the government line. 'I hail her book,' he writes in *The Queen*, 'as the first effort, so far, towards facing the problems of the middle class kitchen . . . with some sort of constructive imagination.' Spry herself acknowledges that she is writing for a middle-class, in fact, upper-middle-class readership: 'I am thinking . . . of women who, perhaps, for the first time in their lives, will go into the kitchen and cook, and bring to bear on cooking the intelligence and judgement which hitherto they may have reserved for other occupations'.[48] She sees this class as the key to the major culinary transformation she is convinced the nation desperately needs: 'The truth is we need a food revolution, we need to be flung out of our old, indifferent, wasteful habits. But such a revolution, if it is to have lasting effects, should, I believe, start from the top.' The well-off, she declares, should 'start a fashion rather than preach a sermon' and take up cooking as an enjoyable, absorbing hobby.[49] The magazines that determine lower-middle-class culture will follow suit, and the new attitudes will inexorably spread. It sounds like wishful thinking – and rather snobbish thinking at that – and yet, of course, this is precisely what was to happen with the profound food revolution Elizabeth David's works kick-started less than a decade later.

Unlike almost all of her contemporaries, Spry wants to keep alive a sense of French cooking as the classic culinary system, on which variations can be built. She recommends vegetables be served as a main dish, but because of their innate goodness, not as a wartime exigency:

> Vegetable cookery of the highest order, as the French know it, for instance, had nothing to do with the complicated dishes to be found in some books under the heading of vegetarian cookery; nothing whatever to do with the lentil cutlet, vegetable turkey, or mock anything at all.[50]

Her writing seeks to promote appetite, not to say salivation, and she plays an interesting variation on the game of fantasizing about foods by imagining what she would choose to cook with the most common vegetables if they were rarities. So carrots – 'the unfortunate carrot is suffering, like certain film stars, from too much publicity. Really it is a tortuous path from fresh, crisp raw carrot to carrot flan, and I, for one, don't want to travel it' – she chooses grated raw as part of a coleslaw or as a cream of carrot soup. Cabbage she would have as *soupe aux choux* ('I suppose it is affected to keep on calling it by its French name, but "cabbage soup" sounds disrespectful') or bubble and squeak.[51] Marrows, she says firmly, should be harvested when small and are best fried. Her taste is unerring, and her innovations intriguing rather than alarming – for example, the suggestion of fritters of parsnip purée topped with walnuts. (The same dish is given in Jane Grigson's 1971 *Good Things*, though Spry is not acknowledged as the source). She tends to supply dishes with their heritage and to establish an atmosphere around their consumption. So she discusses the sun-dried tomatoes made by her friend in Tunis at the beginning of the war and recalls with a touching sense of daring the loaf of garlic bread she partook of at a smart dinner in Oregon. She is not scared to discuss unobtainable food – neither tomatoes nor garlic were easily available in wartime Britain – partly because she intends the book to continue to be of use after the end of rationing but also because she seems to take a perverse pleasure in evoking an appetite for lost delights. Or perhaps not so perverse – by awakening appetites she reintroduces the sense of food as pleasure: a literary pleasure if not a physical one. She is scrupulous about her sources, including a chapter on her favourite cook books, which – unsurprisingly – include many of the most elegant of the interwar books. She is particularly complimentary about the work of Rosemary Hume, with whom she was later to collaborate so extensively.

The originality of Spry's approach in the wartime context is dual: as well as restoring a surrounding discourse to the recipe, she also devotes intense attention to method. On the subject of mashed potatoes she insists, 'whatever you do, do not let the method slip back, for it is this that really makes for perfection'.[52] Many of the dishes she describes are included in other wartime cook books, but Spry's are different. Partly it is the intelligent enthusiasm with which she discusses the food (a long way from Josephine Terry's hectic gaiety) and partly it is the minute attention to detail, the insistence on the importance of getting it right. On her version of a casserole of vegetables, an absolutely ubiquitous wartime dish, she writes, 'The principle of the dish is that each vegetable shall be cooked individually, and that the sauce shall be the best and creamiest béchamel you can make.'[53] This example also shows all the ways in which Spry was not a 'proper' wartime food writer: very few women had the time to cook seven or eight varieties of vegetables separately, not to mention the ruinous waste of fuel involved, when all could easily be cooked together.

Although she was a pioneer, Spry was not the only writer to challenge the conventions of wartime food writing. Another maverick was novelist Sheila Kaye-Smith, whose *Kitchen Fugue* was published in 1945. Originally setting out to write 'a Mug's Cookery Book, designed for those . . . who start not from zero but from frozen depths of ignorance which no thermometer records', Kaye-Smith ended up producing a series of essays on food, with a cookery chapter sandwiched in the middle.[54] Her culinary attitudes resemble Spry's, and she is even less inclined to pull her punches. She too prefers to adapt pre-war recipes to limited ingredients rather than start with a wartime recipe, and she is particularly trenchant on the worst excesses of these: 'I dislike war-time recipes – they always seem to me either defeatist, making the worst of a bad job with starchy messes, or else unwarrantably optimistic as to the results, say, of substituting vinegar for brandy in mince-pies.'[55] Like Spry she includes an essay on her culinary influences, seeing cooking as essentially part of a literary culture. She condemns general primers of cookery as useless, and although she has good words for Mrs Beeton (for her scrupulous attention to detail and the whimsical byways opened up by a perusal of her mighty index), her favoured food writers are French and American (specifically Boulestin and a brochure produced by the Frigidaire Company called *The Silent Hostess*). She goes out on a shaky limb by recommending these two cuisines as much superior to the English for the purposes of wartime cooking – the French because its methods conserve vitamins, and the American because it is economical with time and fuel. More radically, she suggests that if people would give up their habitual tea time they could use the saved rations to cook French dishes:

If we are going to attempt even an emergency version of French cooking we must divert our dairy rations from the tea-table. We shall have to cut down on cake-making, to do with less milk in coffee and even in tea, to forgo the convenience of a bread-and-cheese lunch, and spread our carpet of jam without the luxurious underfelt of butter or margarine. It is a question of choice – which would we rather have? A French dinner or an English tea? I personally have chosen the dinner, but I know a great many who would prefer the tea.[56]

Even Constance Spry didn't go this far (in fact, she is lyrical in her praise of the English tea, spending many pages on an account of the extravagant collations of her Edwardian childhood). Kaye-Smith demolishes a few more shibboleths in the course of her curious book, perhaps most audaciously in her comments on vitamin conservation:

The trouble is, of course, that at the present time there are many people cooking to whom food means nothing except nourishment – an idea which I fear has been encouraged in certain official quarters. I am all on the side of those who do not mind losing a vitamin or two if thereby they enhance the pleasantness of a meal.[57]

Not content with casually dismissing the Ministry of Food's dearest-held principles, Kaye-Smith threatens to spread disaffection with a conclusion that is a powerful lament for missing foods. A long way from Constance Spry's delicately sketched memories of pre-war delights, this is definite complaint, and borders on the unpatriotic:

I want to make something that is really clever and delicious, not merely a creditable imitation. I am tired of margarine and 'the top of the milk'. I want to make omelets and cakes with real butter, to put a spoonful of real cream into each egg 'en cocotte'. I want to pour a good slosh of maraschino into the fruit salad and to cook strawberries in wine. I am tired of miniature 'joints' almost too small to carve and, if one is not to lose all their precious scrap of dripping, involving synthetic gravy. I want to cook a sirloin, with potatoes 'under the roast' from the start instead of being parboiled first to be ready at the same time as a pound of animal mystery. I want to make a cake black with fruit and iced with real almond icing instead of a concoction of almond essence and soya flour. I want to make breakfast rolls and waffles dripping with golden syrup . . . Or I could enjoy . . . that most delicious of all meals – a loaf of crusty home-made bread, real farmhouse butter, and a slice of ham.[58]

It's a good thing the war was almost over.

Constance Spry and Sheila Kaye-Smith are unusual not only for their attitudes but because they speak from a privileged position, and speak to others like themselves. This precise class focus is very unusual in the war years, when virtually all food pronouncements were focused on the needs of the widest possible section of the population. If, as Spry complains, this had the effect of significantly reducing culinary standards for the middle classes, it also dramatically improved the diet of the average working-class family. Very many who had survived the Depression years on nothing more than 'bread and scrape' and strong tea could now in a time of full employment afford and obtain good, filling food, which the Ministry taught them to prepare nutritiously. This democratization of food habits and access to food was one of the proudest achievements of the Ministry of Food. It is agreed by virtually all historical authorities that the nation as a whole was better fed during the war years than at any time previously – or, according to some, since:

> At the end of the war, the British were surprised to learn that they had never been healthier in their lives.
>
> 'The vital statistics during the war years,' reported the nation's Chief Medical Officer in 1946, 'have been phenomenally good' . . . The nation's children were sturdier and taller. Their teeth were better, too . . . By the end of the war . . . there were fewer anaemic women and children, although the meat ration for years had been a few ounces a week at most.[59]

This is one of the major paradoxes that bedevils any study of the effect of the Second World War on the British diet. The war put paid to the internationalist, elegant cuisine that was developing for the wealthy in the interwar years, but it also transformed the diet, culinary expectations and health of the vast majority of the population. The fact is, of course, that the industrial and urban poor had been very badly fed in this country for a very long time as a result of a concatenation of factors including poor wages, little time and the loss of contact with indigenous culinary traditions that was one of the results of the industrial revolution. The war vastly improved this situation, but it did so by sweeping away many of the class distinctions around food and cooking. When commentators bewail the poverty of the British food of the recent past, they need to bear in mind the considerably worse diet it was replacing for much of the population. For the middle classes also, particularly those many women who first learnt to cook in the war years, improvisation, the need for energy conservation and severe time restrictions created very different results than they and their families had previously enjoyed. Perhaps the most we can say is that while no one may have eaten well during the war years, everyone ate properly.

The question of the long-term effect the war had on the nation's diet is an interesting one. Many wartime food products continued to be used for many years afterwards. Anyone who grew up, as I did, in the 1960s and 70s will remember spam as a component of school dinners; we baby boomers also continued to be offered free condensed orange juice as infants (it came from 'the Clinic' and was accompanied by malt extract in the winter months). Camp coffee and rose-hip syrup appeared in my parents' kitchen cupboards until well into the 1970s. The kitchens at the boarding school I attended in the latter part of that decade used dried egg to make vast trays of uniquely rubbery scrambled eggs and were still employing wartime recipes for dishes like bean cobbler. Probably the furthest reaching, and most devastating, effect of the war on the standards of British cooking was in its encouragement of an increased reliance on manufactured food products. The nutritional scientists whose wartime work kept the population from starvation continued to advise industry after the war on more and more ways of preserving, dehydrating, packaging and generally denaturing food. The canned meat and fish that had been such a novelty to wartime housewives, the pressure cookers they used to save fuel and time, the domestic freezers that they had desperately envied their American counterparts – all these were to become central to the food practices of the 1960s and 1970s. The use of ersatz and substitute ingredients did not end with the war but became a major part of the industrial production of food. The focus on maximizing crop yields during the war years led to the deleterious practices of industrialized, chemicalized farming, whose results we still struggle to overcome. It was not so much the shortages of the Kitchen Front as its successes that were to haunt the future.

TYPICAL RECIPES 1939–45

Ambrose Heath
More Kitchen Front Recipes (1941)

This is absolutely representative of the mock food of the Second World War: the aim is to produce something that looks *like fried fillets of fish; the taste and texture is much more of an approximation. The method, incidentally, is much like that for firm polenta.*

FISH, MOCK

Bring half a pint of milk to the boil, and when it is boiling, shower in two ounces of ground rice, and add a teaspoonful of chopped onion or leek, a piece of margarine the size of a small walnut, and a seasoning of anchovy essence. Let this simmer gently for twenty minutes, then take the pan off the fire, and stir in a well-beaten egg. Mix well together, and then spread the mixture out in a flat dish: it should be about half an inch thick. When it is cold, cut it into pieces the size and shape of fish fillets, brush these with milk, roll them in breadcrumbs, and fry until golden-brown. Serve parsley sauce with them.

Daily Telegraph
Good Eating (date unknown)

Contributed by a reader, this is a twist on the ubiquitous potato-stuffed-with-sausage theme. The brevity of style (no articles, no pronouns) and the minimal list of ingredients signify the need to be frugal with both foodstuffs and paper. The fact that the quantity of ingredients is for a single serving indicates the newly provisional quality the war had given to meals, with many more people eating alone and at unusual times (after a night's fire-watching, for instance). There is no longer any consensus in recipes about how many people you are likely to be serving and an increasing tendency to give recipes in a form that can be easily multiplied for different numbers.

SAVOURY APPLES

1 cooking apple
Cloves
1 large sausage or 3 small ones for each person

Take cooking apples of even size. Wipe, do not peel, core carefully. Stick clove into wall of each cavity and push in pork sausage, well pricked.

Put sausage-apples into baking dish with a little water in the base, bake slowly 20 minutes. Dish up just before apples begin to pulp and serve with any vegetables and gravy. Braised onions are good.

More sausages can be cooked around sausage-apples; in this case melted cooking fat should take place of water.

E. J. Champion, Pembroke Road, Seven Kings.

John Miles (Ed.)
A Kitchen Goes to War (1940)

The lively, personable style of these recipes, contributed by celebrities, jollies the reader along with a sense that we're all in the same boat and everyone's doing their bit.

EVA TURNER sends a cake that has had adventures:

AN EXCELLENT CAKE FOR THE TROOPS[1]
(It needs no eggs and makes a good-sized cake)

6 oz. margarine
6 oz. brown sugar, or granulated can be used
2 oz. chopped peel (optional)
¾ lb. mixed fruit
¾ lb. flour
1½ teaspoonsful bi-carbonate of soda
Nearly ½ pint milk

METHOD: Cream the margarine and sugar. Warm the milk and pour it on to the soda. Add the prepared fruit, the milk, and the flour. Mix well. Bake in a moderate oven for about 2 hours in a 7-inch cake tin, or in slabs, for about 1 hour.

[1]A slab of this cake was sent to the Front, travelled around France, chasing the owner, missed him and came back. Other things in the

parcel were spoilt, but this cake was good after 10 weeks. It finally went out again and was much appreciated.

STELLA GIBBONS: 'It is Extremely Filling,' says Miss Gibbons. 'It's cheap, and men love it.'

SAVOURY RICE

METHOD: Fry a clove of garlic in margarine until it is brown. Then put into the pan a breakfast-cupful of cooked rice that has been washed before cooking (more rice can be used if you want more, of course) and keep on stirring it until it has absorbed the fat. Then put in curry powder to taste, the pulp and seeds of three tomatoes, and a third of a cupful of currants and sultanas (well washed, of course). A dash of salt, pepper and lemon-juice improves it. (You need to be careful and choice with the seasoning, or there is a risk of the dish being merely rich and sticky.)

If the average housewife is scared of garlic she can use onion.

The dish goes well with a plain salad of lettuce leaves dressed sharply with vinegar and salt (but you might as well say a plain salad of gold leaf with the price lettuces can be during wartime).

Josephine Terry
Food without Fuss (1944)

The constantly inventive Ms Terry gives not one but three versions of her fish pastry recipe. The very detailed explanations about opening and cleaning out the tin are typical of her excessively solicitous style. Note also the numbers she claims this dish will serve – a case of the loaves and fishes?

SAVOURY FISH PASTRY

The following recipes all require the same initial preparation.

Necessaries: flour, tinned fish.

A small tin of sardines in oil will make enough for six persons. A large tin of pilchards would therefore be enough for one cold snack meal and a hot dish or the latter left to cool and used for a 'Carry Lunch'.

(*Note:* If you have lost the key to your tin, open it bottom side up with an ordinary tin opener)

Take out the sardines or pilchards carefully with as little of the oily sauce clinging to them as possible. Keep the oily sauce in the tin.

Now make a pastry: (flour, baking powder, salt, no fat at all!)

Sift one well rounded cup (6 oz.) flour together with two level teaspoonfuls baking powder and ½ level teaspoonfuls of salt.

Add to this amount either all the oil from a small tin of sardines, or two to three tablespoonfuls of oily sauce from the pilchards. To make sure that no oil is left in the tin, clean the tin with a little of the flour. Stir quickly, tossing it to mix well. Add enough cold water (about half a teacupful) to make a tender dough, as for scones. Be quick in doing this: the dough should look flaky. Turn on to a slightly floured wooden board and roll out to not quite ¼ inch thick. Roll out into an oblong.

FISH IN WRAPPERS

Cut this oblong into long pieces, about 1 inch wider than your fishes are long. Cut these pieces into squares and the squares once more into triangles. Pull these triangles slightly lengthwise. Place on to half the amount of triangles either a whole sardine, or half a pilchard. Cover with the other triangles. Seal the edges well. Bake in a moderately hot oven for about 20 minutes.

BAKED FISH ROLL

Place the fishes in the centre of the pastry oblong – lengthwise. Leave at least 1½ inches of pastry all the way round. Gather the edges together and seal well. Bake in a moderately hot oven for about half an hour.

FISH CRISPS

Instead of separating the fish from the oil or sauce, mash it all together and add to the sifted flour mixture. Now, make a pastry as described above. Roll out about ½ inch thick. Cut into sticks about 3 inches long and bake for 15–20 minutes.

Sheila Kaye-Smith
Kitchen Fugue (1945)

Kaye-Smith differs from almost all her contemporaries (with the notable exception of Constance Spry) in her continued emphasis on French styles of cooking. She combines this emphasis – notable here in the insistence on soup as a nutritious and worthwhile culinary habit – with an address to those assumed to be absolutely ignorant in the kitchen – represented here by the parodic figure of Mrs Mugg. Hence the many jokingly couched warnings about possible dire failure. Despite outlining the many tricks and dodges necessary to save fuel and ingredients, she insists on the difference between this makeshift version and the genuine article; like Constance Spry, she is anxious that culinary knowledge and discrimination should not be entirely lost, whatever the exigencies of the moment.

I serve soup every day. It is filling, nourishing, and a most practical and appetizing way of using up the remains of earlier meals. Say that you have some cottage pie left over – not enough to serve again, even if that would not be too depressing. Mash it up and put it in a saucepan with a little stock – add perhaps an onion or a carrot or a bit of what you fancy. Simmer for half an hour and then push through a sieve. Add some curry powder now and a little milk and you will have a very pleasant soup that has given you scarcely any trouble and used up nothing precious.

Of course, if you have an electric or gas cooker you must forget all you ever heard about soup simmering for hours. Believe me, the most delicious soup can be begun and finished in an hour or less. On the other hand, if your soup really must cook long and slowly, as in the case of my chicken bones, it is not difficult to arrange for it to share with some other dish any hot plate that may be in use. The slower it cooks the better. I started my chicken soup the day before I wanted it, moving my saucepan about the top of the stove to any cooking space where there was room, then I left it overnight and started on it again the next day. I am not saying that the method is ideal, but in this case it certainly produced the most delicious soup with scarcely any extra consumption of fuel. By a similar contrivance you can cook soup in the oven.

I am assuming to-day that Mrs Mugg wants to use only raw materials, and we decide to embark on a diminished variety of *potage bonne femme*. The first thing to do is to have all the ingredients and utensils ready. Tragedies may be precipitated by having to search for milk or peel an onion at the critical moment. So put the following articles on the kitchen table before you do anything else.

Utensils Required. – 1. A saucepan big enough to hold a quart and yet be only half full. You want to make soup for four people, and half a pint is plenty for each and allows for reduction in cooking. If the saucepan is full there is some danger that you, being a mug, will let it boil over and make a mess, so it is wisest to fill it only half. 2. A grater. 3. A wooden spoon. Never use a metal spoon for soup, or indeed for most things. 4. A teacup.

Ingredients. – 1. Two large potatoes. 2. Three medium-sized onions. 3. A small stick of celery (if obtainable, but the soup tastes very good without it). 4. A pint of water and a pint of milk. Or you can use Household Milk. Remember that a breakfast-cup roughly measures half a pint and a teacup a quarter of a pint or a gill. 5. Small piece of margarine. 6. A tablespoon of flour. 7. Pepper and salt.

Procedure. – Grate up your potatoes and onions on the large side of the grater. This is a good way out of the usual dainty dicing, which takes more time, more trouble, and more fuel. Melt your margarine in the saucepan. (A more experienced cook would do this while she was grating the vegetables, but you had better do one thing at a time.) When the margarine is making the sizzling noise which shows it is ready for cooking, put in the vegetables and put on the saucepan lid. Make sure that the heat is very low. (The pre-war recipe requires a large piece of margarine, if not butter, and the tossing of the vegetables in this for twenty minutes, tossing and turning them continually with a wooden spoon to ensure that they do not brown. My expedient involves their cooking partly in their own steam and not for more than ten minutes, or they will brown. Shake the saucepan from time to time in case they stick to the bottom, and you may peep in occasionally, if you feel nervous, just to make sure that nothing untoward is happening.) Pour your water – hot or cold – over the vegetables, add seasoning and turn up the heat a little, but do not let them cook fast. Simmer – that is, let them cook with a slight movement of the fluid, not the bubble and bounce of boiling – until the vegetables are quite soft, which, as they are grated, will not take much longer than twenty minutes.

Now this would be the time to put the whole thing through a sieve, if you want to follow the normal English custom. But personally I prefer this kind of soup unsieved. Certain sorts you must sieve – pea-soup, for instance, and soup made of left-overs – but I think this continental kind of soup tastes better if you eat it the continental way, that is with the vegetable shreds floating in it. If you sieve, do not add the seasoning until afterwards, as the flavour of it will probably remain on the wrong side of the sieve. On the other hand, if you are making a soup with, say, a flavouring of bacon-rind, you must put this in at the start and though it will not actually go through the sieve the flavour of it can be *pushed* through if you crush it well against the wires. Bacon-rind is a great improver of the flavour of many soups, especially potato soup.

Having now decided whether to sieve or not to sieve, your next step is to thicken the soup with a little flour. Put this in a cup and add just enough milk to make a paste. Stir until it is quite smooth and then add a little more milk and stir again. Be sure there are no lumps, and do not pour it in all at once or over a hot fire, but add it gradually with the saucepan over a low heat. Then add the rest of the milk, turn up the heat and stir with a wooden spoon till the soup is thick and boiling. Do not on any account leave it to take care of itself at this stage – it needs watching and stirring, that is if you want a soup which is both smooth and thick.

This is as near as you can get in these days to a genuine *potage bonne femme*, but you can vary the recipe by adding bacon-rind to the vegetables (at the start) or two tablespoons of grated cheese (at the finish – after it has ceased to boil). Or you can substitute leeks for the onions.

CHAPTER FOUR

Austerity and the Food Revolution

The war ended, but food control did not. The British public, exhausted by war, endured another nine lean years until the last controls were finally lifted in 1954. This long period of post-war shortages and rationing was commonly known as 'austerity', and, understandably, it was met by the British public with less good grace than they had shown during the war years. In many ways the food situation was worse than it had been during the war. Many parts of the war-slashed world were threatened with starvation, and stocks that Britain might have imported were diverted to nations facing famine. The American Lend–Lease scheme stopped abruptly in 1945, with the supply diverted to countries previously occupied by Germany and Japan. For the British, therefore, queues and shortages continued, with rationing not only not ending but actually getting worse. The bacon, poultry and egg rations were reduced in 1946, the government threatened to withdraw dried eggs, and – most shocking of all – it began to interfere with bread supplies. In April 1946 the National Loaf was reduced in size, and in July bread, cake, flour and oatmeal were rationed – something that had been very carefully avoided throughout the war years. The reason was not discreditable – the government had agreed to donate part of the nation's wheat crop to a starving Germany as the price of America supplying the bulk of what was needed. But this generosity was successfully spun by the Conservative opposition as incompetence, adding to the general public resentment at the new administration's handling of matters of food. The new Labour Ministers of Food, first Sir Ben Smith and then, from spring 1946, John Strachey, proved to lack Lord Woolton's common touch and were much less popular. Ideologically committed to building on the very effective nutritional measures of the war years, they saw no particular reason why food control should not continue indefinitely; the British public was soon to put them straight.

Worse was to come: a bad potato crop over the bitterly cold winter of 1947–8 led to the imposition of a restricted allowance of 3 lbs a week, and milk was also in short supply. Rations were lower than at any point during the war, and the loss of canned meat and fish from America was strongly felt. The government's solution was dramatic: it began to import whale meat. A staple food in Norway and Japan, whale is by no means inedible, but it apparently requires careful preparation if it is not to taste rank and oily.[1] Ministry officials conducted numerous experiments with the new meat, and concluded that '[while] it is not very satisfactory grilled or cooked as a joint, most people cannot distinguish it from beef steak when it is finely cut before cooking or mixed with strong flavours'.[2] Some cooks managed to make the meat palatable – this presumably included those working at one London branch of the Lyons Corner Houses, which reported selling 600 whale-meat steaks a day in September 1947 (almost certainly disguising the meat's origin). But many people refused to touch it, and by 1950 4,000 tons of unwanted whale meat lay abandoned at the docks.[3] When whale meat failed to hit the spot, the government's next attempt to supply the protein deficit was snoek, a fish like a barracuda, which the Ministry's home economists tried in vain to make tempting. This much-vilified fish was emblematic of the hardships and resentments of the post-war years for Susan Cooper in her classic essay 'Snoek Piquante':

> In October 1947, with the butter and meat rations newly cut, the bacon ration halved, restaurants' food supplies dwindling, and potato rationing on the way, the hungry British first heard the word 'snoek'. Ten million tins of it from South Africa were to replace Portuguese sardines, whose import was restricted by exchange troubles; the new fish, said Mr Strachey, would go on points. 'I have never met a snoek,' he added with the Ministerial waggishness that always holds a faint sense of doom, 'so I cannot tell you much about it.' . . .
>
> Wholesalers did not welcome snoek; they had already imported a number of tins, off points, and these had not been a success. 'People didn't like it,' said one. 'Tasteless and unpalatable,' said another. 'Abominable stuff.' The Minister, however, had not only spent £857,000 on snoek, but had eaten it: at a picnic, in sandwiches. It was, he said with rash honesty, 'good, palatable, but rather dull.'[4]

With its ridiculous name, snoek became the butt of endless jokes and attacks in the press; housewives rejected it *en masse*, and even the Minister gave up on it, declaring it 'one of the dullest fish I have ever eaten'.[5] It came off points at the end of 1949 and was tacitly forgotten, except that 'eighteen months later, quiet among the junketings of the Festival of Britain, a mysterious quantity of tinned fish came onto the market, labelled: "Selected fish food for cats and kittens." It cost tenpence a tin, and its origins were left muffled in tact. One of the distributors admitted that it might be either snoek or barracuda. "Cats", he said, "are very fond of both."'[6] The story of snoek and the British indicates the difference between the food control of the war years and that of the period of austerity: when patriotism and the national interest were no longer at stake, when fear was no more a constant element in life, the British public rebelled. For those members of the government keen to continue food control well into the future, it was a key lesson in what the public would stand.

Public disaffection was felt not just in grumblings and the refusal of disliked new foods but in the active protests of women. This period saw what may well have been the first organized action on the part of domestic labour, as housewives joined forces in a mass campaign against government actions. In their thousands they joined the non-partisan Housewives League, and with mass meetings and protests resisted the government's attempts to cut off supplies of dried egg in 1946. After being faced with a demonstration several hundred strong, the then Minister of Food, Ben Smith, caved in, and the once-hated but now staple dried eggs were returned to stores. The organization received financial support from women all over the country and began to publish its campaigning journal, *Housewives Today*. Bread rationing produced even more serious protests: together with the long-established Townswomen's Guilds and Women's Institutes, the British League of Housewives presented Parliament with a petition of 600,000 signatures.[7] This time the Ministry decided to sit it out, and when the expected shortages did not materialize the protests died down. Bread was finally removed from the ration in the summer of 1948, with the whole episode having served mainly to severely damage the government:

> It was no wonder that by the time bread rationing was abandoned in July 1948, 750 Food Officers were dealing full time with bread alone, and in retrospect, 'the most that could be said was that consumption had not gone up'. Politically the chief beneficiary of bread rationing was the young Edward Heath, who reduced Labour's majority from 11,000 to 1,000 at the 'bread-rationing' by-election in Bexley, and won the (re-distributed) seat at the 1950 General Election.[8]

Jam came off the ration in December 1948, but there was then a four-year wait before tea was de-rationed, in the autumn of 1952. Sweets, cream, eggs and sugar were removed in the course of 1953, and in the early summer of 1954 rationing at last ended, with butter, cheese, margarine and cooking fats, and finally meat released from government control.

The cook books of the austerity years reflect the prevailing mood. No longer prepared to pass on the wartime messages of patriotism and desperate ingenuity, food writers instead started to rebel. The pieties of the war are routinely challenged: 'the authors do not believe that the whole art of cooking consists in cleverly making do', announced the blurb of *Quick Dinners for Beginners* (1950), Rachel and Margaret Ryan's follow-up to their 1934 success, 'any more than they believe that dried eggs and milk give as good results as fresh eggs and cream.'[9] The ever-positive Ambrose Heath of the war years had resumed his earlier role as critical connoisseur by the early 1950s when he published his *Kitchen Table Talk* (a selection of his articles published in the *Manchester Guardian* between 1951 and 1953). Present-day supplies of cod he describes as tasting like 'wet sacking', and sausages are roundly condemned: 'to-day this "stuffed cylindrical case" (as a dictionary describes it) is too often in the nature of a Job's comforter, for its contents are as indeterminate and often as insipid as the everlasting fish fillet – perhaps, alas! a sign of the times'.[10] Austerity cook books are often surprisingly lively as they attempt to gee up their readers and drag them out of a slough of depression and lowered expectations. They are also much less inclined than wartime books to treat the reader with kid gloves. In his entertaining *Off the Beeton Track* of 1946 Peter Pirbright challenges his reader to reform her attitude:

> How well we know that beaming smile on the face of the shopkeeper, the waitress or, alas, the housewife, when they announce gleefully: 'No (whatever it may be) to-day'. This curious pleasure in emphasising the difficulties of life, enlarging them, and using them to spread a general atmosphere of depression, is one of the phenomena that has caused us the greatest amount of discomfort during the last few years. Shortages should never be an excuse for a good cook to produce a beastly meal. If one can't have one thing, there is always something else; use imagination and don't blame wars, or any other inevitable circumstances. Blame yourself if you don't succeed.[11]

Published very shortly after the end of the war, Pirbright's book is a significant departure from the drab, worthy cook books of the Kitchen Front years. Physically it is very striking, with a generous collection of witty, brightly coloured lithographs by Victor Ross. These contrast the drab, bad English cookery of the past with the dazzling new culinary possibilities of the future. One sequence shows a wrinkled old crone hurling a pleading cabbage into boiling water, from which it is saved by a modern housewife who dives in to rescue it, dries it tenderly and serves it up proudly with a crown on its head. Another has a female creature made of vegetables tenderly composing a salad of fresh young greens while old vegetables fruitlessly plead to be included, looking rather like sinners in a Dantesque hell. A pig and a sheep are ostracized at a party until they reappear with some vegetables and are suddenly transformed – the pig into the life and soul, the sheep into a dancing houri in a skirt of spaghetti and bra of cauliflower. These are surreal images, executed with a rather charming naivety and enthusiasm. Social criticism rather than whimsy is signalled by the more realistically rendered double-page spread which demonstrates the troubled recent past of British food. Five images, each with a differently coloured background, circle the page: the opulent Edwardian dinner, all show rather than substance, is represented by the table with its elaborate place settings (eight glasses, six knives) awaiting the grand company; the gentleman's club by men dining alone in isolated splendour, each with his newspaper propped before him, paying no attention to his food; the fast-food restaurant is a scene of chaos – jostling crowds, elbows knocking off hats and cigarettes stubbed out on plates; in an artist's studio bohemians cheerfully cook fried eggs on a smoking heating-stove, surrounded by cats and rubbish; while the worst image shows two downtrodden clerkly types resignedly receiving burnt porridge prepared by their slatternly landlady in her dirty kitchen. There is no caption, but the message is clear: upper-class British food is stuffy and cramped with ceremony; the rest is rushed and slovenly, and it is this situation that *Off the Beeton Track* is setting out to reform. The pun of the title is beguiling, and Pirbright certainly accuses Beeton and her ilk of perpetuating the heinous crimes of the English against vegetables, but most of the culinary atrocities of which he complains are of more recent origin. Canned, pre-prepared and generally denatured food comes in for most attack, an attitude captured in one more visual allegory in the frontispiece, which shows two intrepid chef-travellers striking away off the 'Beeton' track into the green and pleasant land of fresh vegetables, fish, pork and goat's milk, while the wounded soldiers of the kitchen front – tinned soup, ready-made sauce, aged potatoes and an exhausted cow ridden into the ground by a fat butcher – limp greyly down the road. Pirbright is firm in his opposition to convenience foods, insisting that 'you will always be able to concoct a soup yourself which is infinitely better than most of the liquids you pour out of tins'. 'It's just laziness to pour something out of a bottle if you want a sauce,' he later opines, 'and what's more, it's a pointless waste. Why not make that little extra effort?'[12] His is one of the earliest voices raised in outcry against the post-war boom in industrially produced food, but his final question, and his genuine inability to see its obvious answer, reveals why this campaign was doomed to failure. Women would not make that little extra effort, at least on a daily basis, because they did not have the time. And it is this fact that was to determine the direction of our food history for the next half century.

The naive surreality of the book's illustrations are complemented by the lively optimism of its text. The writing bubbles with a sort of hectic enthusiasm, particularly in the alphabet (complete with charming lithographed illustration for each letter) that does service for an introduction. This spans the gamut from general prescriptions and encouragement – 'A stands for Adventure, the Spirit of. That is what you need if you want to make anything of this book' – to notes on suggested ingredients (vanilla pods and yoghourt [*sic*] are some of his more surprising recommendations).[13] Pirbright acknowledges the dreary reality of food shortages but refuses to allow it to daunt him:

> Now you are going to ask me: but is this, of all times, the right moment to use big words about adventure in cooking? After all, we have to make do with the few things we can get? Well, the answer is that we have never had such a good chance and such a good excuse as now for aiming at the greatest possible variety of dishes. You see, the whole point of this book is that it shouldn't be in the least bit extravagant, as far as the required ingredients go. It's only extravagant in its demands on your imagination, your courage, and your Spirit of Adventure.[14]

The demands the book makes on its readers include using cider in cooking, making soup from peapods, eating eels and at least trying to like garlic. His note on the latter is a perfect period piece, capturing exactly both the suspicion with which the English public faced garlic and the sense of daring with which food writers recommended it:

> G stands for Garlic. Can I hear the shrill voices of indignation? Yes, I say garlic, and I mean garlic. If you know it and hate it, don't use it. But if you don't know it, please try it, just for once – not masses of garlic, just a tiny bit, half a clove, well crushed. Or, when you prepare a salad, rub the salad bowl with garlic beforehand. You know, the contempt for garlic in this country is somehow connected with the vague notion of wicked dagoes, loose living and general frivolity. Garlic is almost

considered a moral issue. Be that as it may, I have recommended garlic very often indeed in these pages. Take it or leave it. I personally take it, and love it, and I'm not really as wicked as all that.[15]

The tone is comic, but such assertive defence of the pungent orb is striking at this date. Garlic was to be at the centre of the food revolution spawned by Elizabeth David, and it is notable that she writes in somewhat similar terms of the English attitude to garlic in her 1955 book *Summer Cooking*, though absolutely refusing to stoop to the sort of persuasive tactics with which Pirbright seeks to cajole the reluctant reader: 'The grotesque prudishness and archness with which garlic is treated in this country has led to the superstition that rubbing the bowl with it before putting the salad in gives sufficient flavour. It rather depends on whether you are going to eat the bowl or the salad.'[16]

As both writers understand, garlic represented the last-ditch defence of the British against the onslaught of the food of other nations, and Pirbright is no less revolutionary than David in his desire to replace the traditional dishes of this country with exciting new foods from Abroad: 'Enough of the safe precincts of Roast, 2 Veg. and Milk Pudding; sail forth into uncharted seas, be an explorer!'[17] Pirbright's recipes include many more foreign dishes than had been typical in wartime cook books, while consolidating the taste for the foods of eastern and northern Europe that we saw beginning in the books published later in the conflict with recipes from Poland, Hungary and even Moravia. There are a number of recipes for Goulash, and the detailed instructions on obtaining the authentic result suggests that the dish had already attained sufficient popularity for bastardized versions to be common: 'First of all I want to make one important point: you cannot, as some people seem to think, make Goulash without paprika. *If you can't get paprika at your grocer's, go and try another one*. Do make an effort – you'll see it's well worth your while.'[18] Pirbright is particularly fond of paprika, using it in a wide variety of dishes (Paprika Cheese, Paprika Chicken, Paprika Fish, Paprika Lamb . . .) and also of yoghurt, which is substituted for the traditional sour cream of eastern European cooking. Another favourite flavouring is sweet-and-sour sauce, which he presents with fish, pork and kidneys, among others; it is not clear if the original source is Chinese cooking or – more likely – Scandinavia and central Europe, where 'sweet–sour combinations are basic to the cookery'.[19] *Off the Beeton Track* shows a distinct taste for Scandinavian foods – dill is used almost as much as paprika – and is very quick off the mark in rehabilitating German food for a British readership, with a recipe for Fat Pork and Sauerkraut and another for a typically German potato salad with pickled cucumbers. Pirbright's culinary reach gets as far as Turkey (Turkish Lamb, Skewered Lamb or Mutton), but he also includes a number of traditionally English – not to say Beeton-esque – recipes (Boiled Mutton with Cabbage, Mutton Pudding). He is very keen on the use of offal – '*don't let the word frighten you too much*,' he pleads – a taste which harks back to ancient British culinary practice; but he follows through his project of breaking with the Victorian past by including not a single recipe for a traditional suet pudding (an omission he confesses has him 'shaking in [his] shoes' at his own trepidation).[20] But Pirbright is simply capturing the zeitgeist here: within a very few years suet puddings would have disappeared from British cook books (only to be enthusiastically revived in the late 1970s with the rediscovery by Jane Grigson and others of traditional British food). Other new trends appear in the book which are very much heralds of the food of the 1950s and beyond. Meatballs are ubiquitous, and there is a recipe for hamburgers, but perhaps most significant are the detailed instructions he gives for cooking and eating spaghetti authentically (including a full explanation of what is meant by '*al dente*' and how to achieve it), which anticipates the massive popularity of Italian food in the Britain of the next decade:

> First of all, try and get full-length spaghetti or macaroni – not broken-up ones. They are far nicer – the little ones are really meant for soup. When you eat spaghetti or macaroni, for goodness' sake don't use a knife, but keep to fork and spoon. Dig your fork bravely into the nest of spaghetti or macaroni on your plate and twirl it, using the spoon to push. *Don't be afraid that they'll suddenly start flying round your head* and tie up your ears in knots. You might be a little bit messy at the beginning but you'll soon learn.[21]

Pirbright's book represents the moment of the decisive break with the culinary attitudes and practices of the war, and many of the trends we find in *Off the Beeton Track* are shared by other, later, austerity cook books. Rachel and Margaret Ryan's *Quick Dinners for Beginners* (1950) features a number of Italian recipes among its rather brief selection (brief because each recipe is outlined in exhaustive, meticulous detail in the manner established in their previous book). Zabaione, Macaroni Cheese, Risotto (in fact a pilaff, as most pre-

Elizabeth David British recipes for risotto tended to be) and Spaghetti with a meat sauce are carefully elaborated. These are not the exotica that we might have found in the elegant books of the 1920s and 1930s – there is no polenta, no cuttlefish stew – but they are notably precisely the types of Italian dishes that were to become solid favourites with the British public over the next decade. American dishes are firmly established as classics: Hamburgers are given pride of place at the beginning of the Ryans' chapter on meat dishes, with Baked Meat Loaf, Corned Beef Hash, Harvard Beets (diced beetroot glazed in a sweetened arrowroot and vinegar sauce) and Fish Chowder all proudly tagged with the recommendation '*American recipe*'. The increasing influence of America on British cooking is signalled also in the introductory note on weights and measures, in which they detail the difficulties they have had obtaining the cup measures for American recipes: 'in a desperate search for accuracy we have consulted innumerable tables purporting to give equivalent measurements of cups in ounces, and scarcely two of them agree'.[22] American food has ceased to belong to the category of amusing exotica that it occupied in the pre-war decades and has now become an authoritative culinary system to the rules of which British cooks must adapt themselves. Ambrose Heath also takes American cooking seriously, suggesting that 'it is to the American kitchen that we may best look to recipes' for the newly available canned tuna and offering a number of versions of tuna loaf and tuna pie in illustration of this claim. These are dishes that, with our particular angle on the American culture of the 1950s, it is hard to see as anything other than kitsch, so it is intriguing to see the apparent respect with which Heath treats concoctions like the following:

> . . . simplest of all, mix a small tin of tuna with a breakfastcupful of white sauce, and the same amount of crushed chip potatoes, sprinkle the top with more crushed chips, and heat well through in the oven.[23]

Hamburgers appear yet again, once more the first dish in the meat chapter, with Heath's comment that 'we all know by now the round of fresh minced beef', suggesting that the dish had achieved a really rather remarkable ubiquity by the early 1950s (and this familiarity seems to pre-date the commercial introduction of hamburgers into the country – 'Wimpies', the earliest British attempt to imitate the American commercial hamburger, were first sold at the Ideal Home Exhibition in 1953, with the first Wimpy bar set up in 1955).[24] A clue to the powerful hold American food had over the British imagination in these years is provided by Heath's comments at the beginning of a section entitled simply Cream Pie:

> American novels are always exciting when it comes to food. Ham and eggs for breakfast possess a nostalgic value high above others; we delightedly inhale the seductive fumes of coffee made as if by second nature at any time of the day or night; and as for Cream Pie, what two words in the English language could be more evocative of the pleasures of the ordinary table.[25]

Virtually alone among nations in the period immediately after the Second World War, America luxuriated in plenty, enjoying 'an orgy of eating . . . which the rest of the world . . . could only sit back in amazement and watch'.[26] However strange its recipes, however far its reliance on convenience foods was from the classic techniques of high-status French cooking, American dishes had the glamour of abundance, and were desired for that reason.

Just as Heath resumed in *Kitchen Table Talk* the judicious, gourmet tone of his pre-war *Good Food*, he also returned to the wide geographical reach of his earlier work, including many of the French bourgeois classics popularized in the interwar years, but also, like Pirbright, many central and northern European dishes – Goulashes, a Swiss Beer Sauce, Wiener Schnitzel, Hungarian Potato Soup and an Anchovy Sauce described as middle-European among them. He gives a number of Italian dishes, more than either Pirbright or the Ryans, and includes gnocchi and an interesting clove-flavoured beef stew called Il Garofolato. He speaks lyrically of the dolmádés of Greece (though advising the British reader to substitute cabbage for the hard-to-obtain vine leaves) and has a section advising on the use of the 'exotic vegetables' – primarily aubergines and sweet peppers – that were beginning to enter the British market.

The authors of all three books share a concern for proper method and for judgement to be exercised in cookery. In reaction to the culinary compromises of the war, the tolerance of ersatz ingredients and shoddy methods, austerity cook books show a renewed interest in notions of authenticity, of cookery as a skill to be carefully honed. So Ambrose Heath seeks to encourage in his readers the development of independent judgement, offering alternative methods of preparation or cooking for many of his dishes, and in some cases refusing to give precise quantities of flavourings: 'The direction about the rosemary leaf is vague, but whether it is a large leaf or a small sprig you must discover for yourself just how much you like, for rosemary is so pungent that a very little will make all the difference.'[27] Rachel and Margaret Ryan intend their scrupulously detailed instructions not to close off the reader's independence of thought but to liberate her in the kitchen by explaining the reasons behind culinary processes:

To be a really fine cook you must have the sense of confidence that comes from knowing exactly what you are doing and why you are doing it. Most young housewives have never been to classes in domestic economy – a few hints from Mum and a vast torrent of recipes pouring forth from magazines and papers and a loving Government are the confusing and sometimes misleading background to their first efforts. How simple most recipes are to read! and how treacherous that simplicity may prove to be![28]

They insist on reinvigorating the spirit of culinary discrimination that had been erased by the war effort on the Kitchen Front, stating bracingly that 'there is no point in lowering one's standards just for the sake of lowering them'.[29] Most strikingly, *Off the Beeton Track* crucially anticipates the dominant culinary mood of the future in its insistence that food preparation can actually be enjoyable, a notion that the hardships and necessities of the war had driven quite out of mind. In a note on taste Pirbright emphasizes the importance of testing a dish as you cook it, with a final coda that seems to promise to liberate the housewife for all sorts of pleasures, culinary and otherwise (and remember, this is the era of the Kinsey Report):[30]

A number of housewives seem to think that to taste food while they are preparing it, is rather wicked, since some people might get the idea that they are doing it out of greediness . . . But it's impossible to know whether your stew wants just another pinch of salt, or pepper, whether your spaghetti is done and a thousand other things that matter. If you do enjoy yourself – what of it?[31]

This account of the cookery writers of the austerity years has so far ignored the most important. In 1950 – bang! – Elizabeth David burst onto the culinary scene like a firework, like the rising sun, like the clear note of the church bell on a Greek island.[32] With the publication of her first work, *Mediterranean Food*, she liberated the post-war British from their hell of shortages and spam, ushering aubergines, olive oil and avocados into the shops and single-handedly revolutionizing our food habits and tastes . . . Or that's how the story goes, for Elizabeth David has been subject to a degree of myth-making comparable only with that accorded to Isabella Beeton. Katharine Whitehorn declared that 'she completely opened up the insularity of British cooking. Food was just grey and awful and lifeless and across those awful grey mud flats, Elizabeth David burst like a sunrise, gilding pale Spam with heavenly alchemy,' while Auberon Waugh declared her the single person responsible for most improving British life this century.[33] I'm the first to acknowledge Elizabeth David's great contributions to food writing – but one does wonder if these judgements can really be true.

Elizabeth David, as she herself would have freely admitted, was hardly the first writer to introduce the British to the food of southern Europe.[34] She was also not alone in denouncing the inadequacies of the British cooking of the past and present, a subject that has been a perennial theme among British culinary authorities since the start of the industrial revolution. As to her immediate effect on post-war Britain – well, her book was rapturously received by reviewers in 1950, but the small first edition can only have touched the lives of a relatively few people. It was the paperback Penguin edition of 1955 that really had an effect – and by that date rationing was over, and most of the ingredients David discussed (chick peas, olive oil, pine nuts, tahina, salami, mozzarella and so on) were available to those prepared to hunt for them. The most excessive claims made for Elizabeth David are those that accord her responsibility for the import and distribution of exotic foodstuffs, but the food shops around Soho were already supplying such delicacies to the Italian cafés and restaurants that had begun to spring up in the area immediately after the war (run by immigrants now released from wartime farm labour). As Elizabeth David herself notes in the first edition of *Mediterranean Food*, 'so odd has the system of export and import become that the ingredients of many Mediterranean dishes are not only easier to come by in London than the materials of plain English cooking but sometimes more plentiful than they are abroad'.[35] She removes this remark in the revised post-rationing edition of 1955, instead suggesting, as many of her admirers have subsequently agreed, that her book had initially functioned mainly as a sort of fantasy literature:

> This book first appeared in 1950, when almost every essential ingredient of good cooking was either rationed or unobtainable. To produce the simplest meal consisting of even two or three genuine dishes required the utmost ingenuity and devotion. But even if people could not very often make the dishes here described, it was stimulating to think about them; to escape from the deadly boredom of queuing and the frustration of buying the weekly rations; to read about real food cooked with wine and olive oil, eggs, butter and cream, and dishes richly flavoured with onions, garlic, herbs, and brightly coloured Southern vegetables.[36]

She is right, of course, and this brief passage admirably demonstrates the two chief factors in her phenomenal success: her writing and her timing. Her finely wrought, highly evocative style brought the glories of the food of the south alive for a significant group of food writers and enthusiasts at a moment when their imaginations had been ground to a pap by the dreary realities of seemingly unending food shortages. She then reached a wider (though still pretty exclusively middle-class) public at the very moment when food controls had at last been lifted, offering them a vision of vibrant new flavours, exotic destinations, and food as an integral part of a cultured, informed and well-lived life.

Elizabeth David's style is a striking combination of the lyrical and the tightly controlled. The lyricism is in her descriptions of places and atmospheres, the conjuring up of markets overflowing with produce, of simple meals taken in mountain inns or beach-side tavernas. The control is in the precision of her judgements, the meticulousness of her research and the tightness of her writing, where each word seems carefully considered and necessary. It is also in the evasion of intimate revelation: even when recounting journeys she has taken and places she has lived, she always steers away from the particularly personal. And yet her writing is full of personality, anecdote and opinion, even from the first driven by a sense of its own rightness, not given to persuasion or concession. Artemis Cooper makes a similar point at the start of her enthralling biography of David, *Writing at the Kitchen Table*:

> There was also something compelling about her writing. On the surface, it seemed admirably spare, straightforward and to the point. But behind those crisp sentences, one can feel the pressure of her loves and hates, her enthusiasm and her passion. The reader becomes acutely aware of these emotions, although they are never mentioned.[37]

It is perhaps this contrast between the strong sense of self in her writings and the simultaneous evasion of autobiographical revelation that has fuelled the cult of personality that has long existed around Elizabeth David. There is something tantalizing, almost teasing, about the evasions because she reveals so much, and no more. Admirers speculated excitedly about her, friends protected her privacy with scrupulous silence, and David herself avoided public appearances and refused to comment on personal issues: 'Everything I want to say is in my books,' she insisted.[38]

Some of the facts of Elizabeth David's life remain obscure, but this much is established. She was born in Sussex in 1913, the second of the four daughters of Rupert Gwynne, a Conservative MP, and his wife Stella, who was the daughter of Viscount Ridley. Elizabeth grew up at Wootton, a seventeenth-century manor house set in the Downs. Her father died when she was ten years old, and soon after Elizabeth was sent away to boarding school. At the age of sixteen she was removed from school (apparently because of her mother's horror at the sight of her wielding a lacrosse stick) and sent to France, where she took art lessons, studied French literature and history at the Sorbonne and lodged with a bourgeois family, whom she was to immortalize in *French Provincial Cooking* as the Robertots, describing the fine food at their table and the great greed with which they consumed it. It was only later that she was to realize that it was this first experience of good middle-class French food, rather than the art training or the culture, that was the really significant legacy of her time in France. Her eighteen months in France were followed by six months in Germany learning the language (interestingly, she remarked later that the food was delicious but that she would never want to write about it).[39] She was then presented at court as a débutante and did the Season in what seems to have been a very half-hearted and resentful manner. Having realized that she had little talent as a painter, she now turned to another artistic form and determined to become an actress. In the face of her mother's strong opposition she joined a repertory theatre in Oxford as an assistant stage manager, playing occasional small parts. She soon concluded that she was a 'hopeless' actress, but she enjoyed stage management and became adept at hunting out obscure objects for props and persuading their owners to lend them. Having moved to a London company she met another actor, Charles Gibson Cowan, with whom she soon began an affair. Gibson Cowan was handsome and raffish, Jewish (his father had changed their name from Cohen) and working-class. He represented everything her family disapproved of, and Elizabeth was deeply attracted to him, despite the fact that he was married with a small child.

From the mid- to late 1930s Elizabeth lived a life that looks surprisingly liberated to us today – she travelled independently (to Malta and Egypt), worked in the fitting room at Worth's fashion house and conducted a number of flirtations. She and Charles both believed in open relationships, and he at least had several other affairs during the time they were together. In 1938 they pooled their resources and borrowed money from Elizabeth's family to buy a boat in which to sail to Greece. The plan was to live cheaply there while Charles tried to establish himself as a writer. They set off in July 1939. Their experiences on the trip were later retold by Charles in *The Voyage of the Evelyn Hope* (1946) – though how accurately is open to question.[40] They had got as far as Marseille when they found out that Germany had invaded Poland. Instead of returning home, they remained in the south of France for eight months, during which period Elizabeth made what was almost certainly the most influential friendship of her life, with the writer and traveller Norman Douglas. An exile from England because of his sexual relationships with young boys, Douglas was an extraordinary character: gracious, witty, arrogant and learned, with an ability to pass his learning on to his acolytes with great charm. One of his many loyal friends, Compton Mackenzie, described him as 'crisp as a pippin, ruddy and comfortable as a plum, spicy as a peach, shameless as a fig'.[41] He was seventy-two to her twenty-six, and in later life Elizabeth admitted that she had been in love with him. He taught her much about travel, food and culture, and his maxims on life struck a deep chord with her. As Artemis Cooper puts it, 'Much of what he taught her she already knew, on an instinctive level: what Norman did was to express, develop and refine the principles which she wanted to guide her life. Look for what is true and authentic; see things as they are; be constantly vigilant against the pretentious and the sham; above all, please yourself and take the consequences.'[42]

In late May Elizabeth and Charles continued their journey; on reaching the Sicilian port of Messina they were informed by Italian officials that Italy and Britain were now at war. They were suspected of being spies, their boat was impounded and they were interned for nearly three weeks before being sent under guard to Yugoslavia. They then travelled to Athens, where they were stranded, snubbed by the hidebound British community because of their unorthodox relationship and without the means to return home. Charles eventually found a job teaching on the small island of Syros, and there they spent eight months, until the German bombardment of the island in late April forced them to leave for Crete.[43] It is here that their respective accounts part company. Charles devoted the last section of his book to a dramatic account of their escape from Crete: he has them being caught on the edge of the great battle, stumbling dangerously over mountains strewn with corpses and desperately scrambling aboard the last of the Royal Navy warships. It's a wonderful story and makes for a dramatic ending to his book, but Elizabeth's account was much more prosaic: they left the island on a civilian convoy six days before the massive invasion by German paratroopers. The embarkation permit cited by Artemis Cooper would seem to bear out Elizabeth's account, as would her furious reaction when she finally read the last chapters of Charles's book some years later.[44] They travelled to Egypt, where Elizabeth was to remain until the end of the war. She and Charles soon drifted apart, and she spent the next four years working first in Alexandria as a cypher clerk, then setting up a reference library for the Ministry of Information in Cairo. She had a number of romantic relationships during this period, and in 1944 married Lieutenant Colonel Tony David, an officer in the Indian Army. Although it was clearly a love match on his side, Elizabeth seems to have been more motivated by a desire for security and an awareness of her age (nearly thirty-one). They travelled to India in mid-1945, where Elizabeth found herself very unhappy: she loathed the culture of the British Raj in its dying days, hated the food (still, as it had been at the turn of the century, a combination of Edwardian neo-French fantasies, poor British 'club' food and searingly hot curries) and became ill because of the climate. A little over a year later she returned to England – alone.

The England in which she found herself at the end of the summer of 1946 was very much changed from the one she had left six years earlier. For one who had missed the gradual deprivations and communal spirit of the war, austerity came as a great shock: however meagre her food had been during her Mediterranean junketing, it had always had some spirit, some life, unlike the brown pap that was now accepted by her fellow countrymen. As she later commented: 'Everyone else had hoards of things like powdered soups and packets of dehydrated egg to which they were conditioned. I started off untrammelled; an empty cupboard was an advantage.'[45] Stuck in a flat without heat during the bitterly cold winter of 1946–7, she decamped to a hotel in Ross-on-Wye in the company of her current lover, George Lassalle. There, horrified by the terrible food she was served in the Trust House establishment – 'it was worse than unpardonable, even for those days of desperation . . . produced with a kind of bleak triumph which amounted to a hatred of humanity and humanity's needs' – she began to write about the food of the Mediterranean:

> I sat down and . . . started to work out an agonized craving for the sun and a furious revolt against that terrible, cheerless, heartless food by writing down descriptions of Mediterranean and Middle Eastern cooking. Even to write words like apricot, olives and butter, rice and lemons, oil and almonds, produced assuagement.[46]

The resulting book was rejected by several publishers before finding a home with the small firm of John Lehmann Ltd, whose reader (Julia Strachey, niece of Lytton) reportedly championed it because she was so impressed by the audacity of a recipe for Turkish Stuffing for a Whole Roast Sheep at a time when the meat ration was a few ounces a week. Lehmann commissioned John Minton to produce lively, joyful pen-and-ink illustrations to capture the atmosphere of the warm south conjured up by Elizabeth's words and published the book in June 1950. By this time Elizabeth was already a published food writer, having started writing food pieces for *Harper's Bazaar* the previous year. Her journalism, which shared the same qualities of pungency and clarity as her books, was to give her name some currency among the upper middle classes, but it is on a relatively small number of books that her reputation as the greatest of British food writers rests (notably the five published in the 1950s and 1960s: *Mediterranean Food* [1950], *French Country Cooking* [1951], *Italian Food* [1954], *Summer Cooking* [1955] and *French Provincial Cooking* [1965]).

Elizabeth David's success is to some extent surprising. Her work was scholarly from the first – though her earlier books have none of the atmosphere of dusty burrowing in recondite sources that was increasingly to characterize her writing. They are rich with literary quotation, often from non-English sources, full of historical notes and digressions, and demonstrate an entirely unconcessive approach to their reader – there is none of the careful persuasion and gentle coaxing of other cookery writers. This, after all, is the writer who on the first page of her first book remarks that 'anyone who has lived for long in Greece will be familiar with the sound of air gruesomely whistling through sheep's lungs frying in oil'. Obscure and scary ingredients are introduced with no apology, with not the faintest acknowledgement that they might prove a problem for the insular post-war British; so in *Mediterranean Food* there is a recipe for melokhia, an Arab soup made with a sort of mallow of the same name, one for frog's legs, a whole chapter on snails, and what were to become infamous instructions for tying a live lobster to a spit and roasting it (David later claimed she had included this simply as a curiosity and had not tried it herself). Food shortages are mostly grandly ignored, though in the first editions of both *Mediterranean Food* and *French Country Cooking* she suggests a few substitutes for unobtainable ingredients (which she hastily removed in the post-rationing editions). The lofty tone of voice that was to characterize her work is discernible even in her first books: in her comments on Cassoulet Toulousain in *Mediterranean Food*, for example, with their graceful movement from implied sniff, through trenchant correction, to devastating put-down:

> Cassoulet . . . [has recently] achieved some popularity in this country, no doubt because it seems an attractive solution to the entertaining of a fairly large number of people with little fuss or expense. A genuine cassoulet is not, however, a cheap dish. Neither are the materials always easy to find . . . it should be remembered that tinned beans and sausages served in an earthenware casserole do not, alas, constitute a cassoulet.[47]

In fact, though, this textual voice, so unapologetic, so absolutely assured in its tastes and judgements, constitutes a significant element in the appeal of Elizabeth David's writing. And – it has to be said – the appeal is one of class. There is a bracing quality in David's work which stiffens the sinews and resolve of her readers; like the strong-minded headmistress of a girls'-school story she expects much of them, and they rise to the challenge. Rebellious though her behaviour and life choices were, she retained the authoritative attitudes of her class (and, especially in later life, expected to be treated with due deference, as a number of journalists discovered to their cost). Paul Levy (himself the victim of a number of put-downs from Mrs David) recognized this quality in her work when trying to analyze her unique appeal:

> In part, I feel it is the appeal – and the natural authority – of a particular kind of good-humoured, slightly bossy upper-middle-class Englishwoman, the sort of woman whose speaking voice is instantly recognisable in her prose; the sort of woman who gets things right. Above all, a woman possessed of wit and taste.[48]

Her confidence in her own judgement is the primary engine of her work; although wedded to notions of authenticity and tradition, she will override them if they conflict with her taste: she doesn't like the strength of flavour imparted by the prawn shells to Zuppe di Pesce, so she leaves them out; she adds cheese to Gratin Dauphinois, though noting that many people (and, she omits to say, almost all authorities) feel it should not be included.[49] As Michael Bateman states, 'She alone among cookery writers can be so aloof as to say of some classic dish, of French onion soup, for example, that she doesn't like it, and therefore won't give the recipe.'[50]

Aside from her bossiness, another factor in her early success is that Elizabeth David's was food writing that appealed to men.[51] Not many were in the kitchen as yet, though that was coming, but she hooked male editors, reviewers and opinion-formers. For these men, here were cook books of a different order – ones they could take seriously. Their masculine appeal lies in the combination of fine writing, a cultivated appreciation of art, culture and wine, and the travel narratives, with their unabashed response to rumbustious peasant life.[52] This is something David has in common with the American M. F. K. Fisher, whose elegant, evocative stories of her adventures and philosophies, interspersed with accounts of food and its meanings, were praised by W. H. Auden, who declared, 'I do not know of anyone in the United States today who writes better prose.'[53] It is no accident that David and Fisher are rivals for the position of greatest food writer of the twentieth century. Both are to some extent the inheritors not only of the essentially feminine tradition of the recipe book but also that of the gentleman gourmet-traveller. It is notable that it is writings of this sort (or their more muscular modern equivalents) that David tends to quote in her early books – her picture of the Mediterranean is built up via accounts from Osbert Sitwell, Henry James (*A Little Tour in France*), D. H. Lawrence (*Sea and Sardinia*), Norman Douglas and Lawrence Durrell (whose wonderful lines about the taste of black olives – 'A taste older than meat, older than wine. A taste as old as cold water' – are left to substitute entirely for any word of hers on the subject).[54] The proportion of quotation to her own text is greater in this first book than any other she was to write; at times it reads more as an anthology of evocative writings on the Mediterranean than a cook book. And this was by no means an impediment to its success: it was above all in its evocativeness that *Mediterranean Food* captured the attention of its first audience. Elizabeth David's own prose could, of course, share this quality with those she quoted: there are a few passages of hers in the book as lyrical as anything else that has been written about the Mediterranean – her account, for instance, of the simple hors d'oeuvres of different countries: in Greece 'you can sit at a table on the sand with your feet almost in the Aegean as you drink your *Ouzou*; boys with baskets of little clams or *kidónia* (sea quinces) pass up and down the beach and open them for you at your table . . .'[55] Or her description of the abundant produce of those southern regions: 'the brilliance of the market stalls piled high with pimentos, aubergines, tomatoes, olives, melons and limes; the great heaps of shiny fish, silver, vermillion or tiger-striped, and those long needle fish whose bones so mysteriously turn out to be green'.[56] Here, as in her other descriptive passages, the effect is essentially painterly – she evokes the colours, the setting, the landscape, with the people present only as components of the picturesque scene. In this respect she differs markedly from M. F. K. Fisher, whose writings are very rarely pictorial, being much more concerned with character and interiority, with emotions and ideas brought into association with food. Fisher brings the sensibility of a novelist to her food writing, while David brings her trainings as both painter and librarian. John Minton's illustrations for David's first two books very effectively echo these qualities: bounteous dishes and raw ingredients are pictured with backgrounds of Mediterranean seascapes and ruins and French farmhouse kitchens and yards; contented families cluster around groaning tables; lovers offer each other choice morsels. The cover of *Mediterranean Food*, with its bright blue, sun-streaked sea, its tables overflowing with casually heaped abundant raw materials, effectively sold the book before it had even been opened. It was this vision of elsewhere, of a world where the sun shone and the food was not brown, that warmed the souls of the ration-sick British. It is perhaps curious that it is the food of the Mediterranean that so seized the chilled British imagination at this moment. But it is the vision her book imparts of lands of languor and warmth that proved so seductive – to the extent that the nascent taste for the foods of northern and eastern Europe was, in the following decades, to be completely subsumed in a rush of garlic to the nation's head.[57]

The food Elizabeth David wrote of in her early books was essentially peasant food, simple and unrefined, but imbued with centuries of tradition and with the hearty, pungent flavours of garlic and anchovies, of olive oil and goose fat and wine. Typical dishes are Bouillabaisse, Moules Marinière, Stewed Octopus, Boeuf en Daube and Risotto. Although it took some time for her dishes, as opposed to her inspiration, to filter through to the general population, a surprising number of the dishes in *Mediterranean Food*, obscure exotica at the time of the book's publication, were to be deli and dinner-party favourites within fifteen years – foods like Spanakopittá, Ratatouille,

Dolmádés, Baba Ganouch (David calls it Salad of Aubergines), Taramasalata (Taramá) and Hummus bi Tahina. The foods of France were, of course, better known in Britain, but *French Country Cooking* can be said to have popularized (in the case of the first, perhaps unfortunately, as she herself would later feel) Quiche Lorraine, Chicken roasted with lemon (though David uses just a piece of lemon peel rather than the whole lemon that is now invariably stuffed up the beast's fundament) and St Emilion au Chocolat, a rich confection of chocolate, butter and macaroons that was to become a bistro classic throughout the 1960s.

Her recipes in both the early books are often rather sparse, suggestive rather than exhaustive, with less of the scholarly obsessiveness and meticulous attention to detail that characterizes her later work. Where she differs, even at this stage, from those earlier writers on the foods of southern Europe is in the close attention she pays to regionality. Even the briefest of recipes is a potted history lesson: 'the origin of Pistou is Genoese, but it has become naturalised in Nice and the surrounding country'; 'Majorca once belonged to the Catalan province which included the town of Perpignan, where the castle of the Kings of Majorca is still to be seen. This traditional soup [Mayorquina] probably dates from those days. It has all the characteristics of the combined French and Spanish cooking of this region.'[58]

Elizabeth David's greatest fans would have us believe that the British public fell on her cassoulets and daubes with relieved delight the moment rationing ended. In fact, it didn't happen quite like that. It was not really until a decade later that the food revolution she pioneered could be said to have taken place. David certainly did influence the eating habits of a generation, as is so often claimed, but it was the generation of the mid-1960s who cooked her cassoulets, splashed about the olive oil and treasured their unwashed omelette pans – not that of fifteen years earlier. As Christina Hardyment points out, it required the nationwide spread of the delicatessen in the late 1950s and early 1960s and 'the revolution in food processing and retailing that has now made garlic as easily available in Stranraer as in Soho' before David's food gospel could be more than an inspiration and a fantasy to most Britons.[59]

With her status as culinary Mother Superior set in stone for almost forty years, it is very difficult for us to see Elizabeth David in the context of her contemporaries. But the transformative, inspirational effect she had on British eating habits and attitudes to food is best understood if we realize that her concerns were not hers alone and that her books sprouted so vigorously because the ground on which they fell had been to some extent prepared by others. She began her career as very much an austerity writer, animated by the same resentments and longings as writers like Pirbright and Heath, and by Constance Spry and Sheila Kaye-Smith during the war, desperate to break free of the restraints and petty subterfuges of wartime cookery but hampered by food restrictions and shortages. She shared with them a strong interest in foreign food, a concern for authenticity, a scrupulosity about method and techniques, and a sense of food preparation as an enjoyable, highly skilled occupation. She was more high-minded than they, and so demands to be taken more seriously, and her writings were based on a more intimate knowledge of the cuisines and countries of which she wrote, but she was not a lone voice crying out for good food. The food revolution of the post-war years would probably have happened without Elizabeth David, though in her absence it would have happened very differently.

Rationing finally ended in 1954, but austerity had been tailing off for some time. As Susan Cooper remarked: 'Wars end tidily in the history books, with the signing of a document. But there was no single finishing line for the shortages of food, clothes and fuel, and all the aspects of austerity which gave a dull grey tinge to post-war life. They slackened, gradually.'[60] As shortages diminished throughout the 1950s, an increasing number of books were published that were clearly post-austerity in spirit, if not in fact. By 1955, with food at last abundant, the trickle of new cook books had become a flood. It is at this point in the history of the British cook book that it becomes impossible to do justice to more than a small selection of the many cook books published.

One of the most striking features of the culture of the 1950s is its reinvention of the role of housewife as desirable, exciting and glamorous. Magazines, advertisements and television showed the housewife as young, attractive and fulfilled, glorying in her husband, her children and – above all – her home. Hers was a marvellous new home, one of the 300,000 built every year throughout the 1950s, with many labour-saving features (simple clean lines, with no picture rails or elaborate mouldings to catch dust, and appliances galore). Particularly splendid was its kitchen, for the kitchen was at the centre of the 1950s domestic dream, the place where the young wife bound her husband to her with her culinary skills, where she supported his business career by producing impressive dinners for his boss and clients, where the mother prepared for the family bonding ritual that was the daily evening meal. The kitchen was no longer just a room – now it had deep psychological significance: 'A woman's place? Yes it is!' enthused an editorial in *Woman's Own*. 'For it is the heart and centre of the meaning of home. The place where, day after day, you make with your hands the gift of love.'[61] The dream kitchen of the 1950s was fitted, like that in 'the Home of the Future' which attracted such crowds at the 1951 Festival of Britain. The sink was stainless steel, rather than the deep fire-clay Belfast sink of the past, and had an integral draining board, not an unhygienic and awkward wooden board. Fitted cupboards and baseboards eliminated dust-collecting corners and spaces, while the new gas and electric cookers offered clean, controllable heat.[62] The introduction of Formica made work surfaces easily cleanable – no more heavy labour scrubbing bare wood tables. 'Labour-saving' was the manufacturer's key selling point, and much attention was paid to reducing the time the housewife spent on her feet and the distance that she had to walk. The large kitchen tables of the past were replaced with small Formica or enamel-topped work tables, and external larders were abolished in most new houses with the expectation that all households would have a refrigerator in which perishable goods would be stored.

It was in the 1950s that the modern 'science' of kitchen design was developed, based on the time-and-motion studies of the interwar years. Conventions like the ideal height of work surfaces, the necessity of placing the sink under the window and particularly the sanctity of the 'working triangle' (fridge, sink and cooker as the apexes of a triangle) were established in this decade and have held sway ever since. The housewife was expected, indeed encouraged, to involve herself fully in the designing of her kitchen, and it was supposed to be tailored precisely to her needs and tastes. Appliances were produced in a dazzling variety of colours, not just the dull grey and white of the past, so that housewives could choose a colour to match their decor.[63] The kitchen and its contents became fashion items and therefore would inevitably go out of fashion and be replaced, a process that manufacturers guaranteed by building obsolescence into their machines.

The nation was enjoying an unprecedented economic boom, goods were at last available now that the post-war export drive had ceased, and women's new economic role was as eager consumers. As Betty Friedan memorably put it in *The Feminine Mystique* (1963), 'Why is it never said that the really crucial function, the really important role that women serve as housewives is to buy more things for the house?'[64] The 1950s mark the start of the consumer culture, in which advertisers, magazines, newspapers, radio, television and books persuaded us, with various degrees of subtlety, that perfect happiness was just around the corner, attainable with only one more purchase. Buying became an act expressive of style and taste. We were to exercise our consumer choices, to say something about ourselves through what we bought; the 1950s housewife was persuaded that her choices of soap powder and cookers, her tastes in curtains and biscuits, would help the manufacturers to improve their products and usher in an even bigger and brighter future. Through her buying power she was aiding the scientists, contributing to national advances from the ever-increasing comfort of her own home.

From a distance, it all looks rather ridiculous – and indeed it is precisely the images and icons of 1950s consumer culture that epitomize our idea of kitsch. And yet the wholesale embracing of the home makes perfect sense from the perspective of the early 1950s: that generation of young women who had worked during the war, living in hostels or lodgings, could at last have their own homes. As Christina Hardyment pertinently remarked:

> To understand the general enthusiasm for home-making at all levels of society, we have to bear in mind how deprived women had been both of normal home life and of any opportunity to express their own individual domestic creativity during and after the war years.[65]

The new fashion for matrimony had also, of course, something to do with the loss of so many young men during the war: they were in short supply and therefore more desirable. Women of all classes joyfully and consciously embraced domesticity, almost as a holiday from the rigours of the past, freely entering into the fantasy that was the 1950s home. Domesticity, matrimony and maternity were seen not as a rejection of the old-style feminism of the suffragettes but as an intensely satisfying way of life. Part-time work for women was easily available (though not well paid), and many planned to return to employment when their children were older.[66] In the meantime, they threw themselves into their new roles with gusto.

For those young women who had at last acquired a husband and a hearth, the temptation to play house for a while must have been overwhelming. And playing it was: the essential unreality of the image of the new glamorous housewife is epitomized by that icon of 1950s femininity, the hostess apron. A tiny little frilly fig leaf of a garment worn over the stylish clothes of every coiffed model in every advertisement, it signalled the impossible mix of identities women were expected to embrace: the perfect cook, yet always immaculate and unflustered, the ideal mother but also the sex kitten, the hostess but also the maid. Another iconic image of this era's domestic life is the serving hatch between kitchen and dining room, to allow for the easy passing of dishes back and forth between the two. Originally introduced in big houses in the 1930s to compensate for the reduced numbers of servants, it was a standard feature in new post-war suburban houses. It allowed the housewife to communicate with her family or guests from the kitchen while coping with difficult and messy tasks unobserved, and yet it also symbolized her apartness, her immurement in an eternally domestic space, watching the rest of life through a window. And then there is the significant paradox at the heart of the 1950s dream: that the fantasy of the kitchen as the centre of a woman's life is utterly bound up with the acquisition of appliances that promise to free her from it.

By the end of the decade it had become clear to many that the dream of domestic bliss had turned sour. Doctors reported that many of their female patients were depressed, as the loneliness of life in the new towns and suburbs, far from family support structures, began to hit home: 'An unlooked-for result of the modernization of household work and cooking was the increasingly private nature of the household at all income levels. Fewer servants and fewer co-operative support systems between housewives led to a generation of women closeted behind net curtains.'[67] It was what Betty Friedan was to identify as 'the problem that has no name' – the neurotic discontent of women offered what they thought they wanted and then unable to reconcile themselves to the gap between the ideal of domestic bliss and the reality.

It is possible to find small pockets of resistance to the new cult of the domestic – a talk entitled 'Meek Wives' on *Woman's Hour* in 1953, for example, in which Antonia Ridge attacked contemporary male attitudes to women as exemplified by advertisements suggesting husbands should 'buy her a mangle for Christmas'; or another piece on the same programme by a father of twins, suggesting that men, 'the sex who excel in cooking and dress-making', should learn to care for their children.[68] But these are rare; there is a surprising consensus in favour of the new domesticity, with liberals and conservatives, feminists and anti-feminists united in what social historian Elizabeth Wilson has described as 'the achievement of a deceptive harmony out of a variety of noisy voices'.[69] The reasons behind the widespread support for this pro-domestic ideology are various. One factor was the extent of marital infidelity during the war (a third of illegitimate children in the last two years of the war were born to married women) and the resulting dramatic increase in divorce, which led to a fear that the institution of marriage was doomed. Another significant influence was the new 'permissive' theories of childcare advanced by John Bowlby and Donald Winnicott, which reached a wide public through their popularization in women's magazines and Winnicott's radio broadcasts. Rejecting the behaviourist model of the pre-war years, they argued that an infant's early bond with its mother is crucial and should on no account be broken by her absence. Instead of the infant being trained to accommodate the needs of its parents, the mother had now to be willing to adapt herself to every need or desire of the child. What it all added up to was a housewife firmly wedded to her home.

Cookery writers were no different: it seems to have been virtually impossible to have addressed the issue of food in the 1950s without at least paying lip service to the monolithic cultural edifice that was the housewife. Even Elizabeth David, happily bucking the trend in her childless independence, strikingly remakes her rackety bohemian past into something resembling the correctly housewifely in the formulation she employed on the dust jackets or author descriptions of all of her books: 'Mrs David has lived and kept house in France, Italy, Greece, Egypt, and India, learning the local dishes and cooking them in her own kitchens.' Doris Grant, the doughty campaigner for real bread, addressed her 1954 polemic against food adulteration to *Dear Housewives*, pushing every manipulative button in an effort to persuade her readers to reject convenience foods: 'If wives could give their husbands the right kind of food, many homes would be happier ones, and there would be fewer broken marriages. If mothers could feed their children on natural, unprocessed foods, difficult children would become manageable and good'; '*if you love your family . . .*

become your own cake-baker'.[70] Strikingly, she celebrates the power of the housewife at a time when most others are extolling her looks and quiet virtues, singing the praises of the British Housewives' League and declaring, 'What important people we housewives are – we shape the destiny of a nation on the kitchen stove!'[71] Yet despite her radical challenge to contemporary values, she works firmly within the confines of the new domesticity: housewives may have more power than they realize, but they must exercise it within the four walls of home.

Even books that sell themselves on their opposition to the domestic ideology end up complying with it – like Ethelind Fearon's *The Reluctant Cook* (1953), which offers to free the reader from drudgery in the kitchen: 'by the elimination of unwanted effort [you will] have so much time and energy to spare that you can take up golf or archery'.[72] Fearon speaks in a jokily cajoling style to readers who find cooking a chore. She offers to teach them 'not how to *dodge* cooking', but 'how to dodge the *obstacles*, and so simplify the job that you will *like* doing it and not want to dodge it'. What this mainly involves is completely refitting the kitchen, cutting the wooden kitchen table in half and adding a plastic top, and 'if very ambitious', obtaining 'one of those exquisite units of sink and two draining boards with cupboards below for saucepans and things'.[73] The illustrations by Alex Jardine show a glamourpuss in the current style (hourglass figure, full skirts, high heels and upswept chignon) relaxing with cocktail and cigarette (in long black holder) while her cooking takes care of itself. But it is striking that she retains the essential hostess apron and is always depicted in the home – indeed, in the kitchen, though she has ingeniously supplied the room with a sofa on which to decoratively recline. The book only pretends its opposition to the happy-housewife propaganda; in fact, it is deeply in thrall to the labour-saving magazine culture. Its language and horribly 'bright' suggestions are straight out of the mid-market woman's magazine of the day:

> Why *black* cups? Oh, just an idea! I always use them, standing on yellow plates, with a yellow and black tablecloth (just sheeting, home appliqué in amusing patterns) and napkins to match. By the side of each plate is a minute black pitcher containing my usual mixture of salt/pepper/nutmeg and a ditto yellow one with powdered sugar. It saves passing to and fro, which interrupts good conversation, [and] looks extremely chic . . . Perhaps it is just spoof, but we're after a reputation at negligible cost, aren't we?[74]

So much of 1950s culture is in this passage: the desire to be original and amusing, the curious mixture of the carefree and the immensely, meticulously care*ful* (think of the endless hours spent on the jolly appliqué), the devotion to entertaining and the establishing of a reputation as a good hostess, the suburban sophistication, the *competitiveness*. Fearon's recipes are not even simple or labour-saving. She is particularly attached to the soufflé, devoting a whole chapter of her fairly slight book to them. Her recipes avoid the excesses of convenience culture and are actually quite sound and attractive, but they are hardly likely to make cooking easier or more appealing to a truly reluctant cook.

In fact, Fearon's is one of the earlier examples of the bandwagon cook book, written not out of any particular conviction but to make some money (it followed her best-seller of the previous year, *The Reluctant Gardener*). As food came off the ration there was suddenly a huge market for cook books of all varieties, and publishers and writers were quick to exploit it. The war had broken the tradition of culinary instruction from mother to daughter, resulting in a whole generation of women who had learnt to cook wartime food from the instructions of the Ministry of Food and were entirely at a loss when it came to anything other than improvisational fuel foods. So, at every level of the market, cook books sprang up to supply the instructional deficit. For the well-heeled the bible was the monumental *Constance Spry Cookery Book* by Constance Spry and Rosemary Hume.

Published in 1956, and nearly 1,250 pages long, the book had been almost a decade in the making and was the result of the authors' collaboration on two enterprises: the Cordon Bleu Cookery School in London and the boarding school Winkfield Place, which instructed girls in the domestic arts. Before the war Constance Spry had run a school of floristry, an offshoot of the florist's shop she had opened in Burlington Gardens in 1931. In the foreword of the book she recalled that as her students drifted away to join the war effort, one suggested that after the war she should include cookery lessons in the curriculum, 'adding thoughtfully "I think we shall need it"; showing in this constructive suggestion a prophetic vision'.[75] Post-war she followed up the idea, approaching Rosemary Hume, whose Au Petit Cordon Bleu restaurant and school had also folded during the war, to establish a joint venture. The resulting schools attracted upper-crust girls preparing to run a home without the staff of servants their mothers would have thought essential. The curriculum was a combination of French classics and English tradition, though the latter dishes were very often dignified with a French name (Pommes en Robe de Chambre rather than Baked Potatoes, Crabe Gratiné Diable rather than Devilled Crab). The association of the term 'Cordon Bleu' with a training in classic French cooking derives from the internationally renowned Ecole du Cordon Bleu founded in Paris in 1880 by Mlle Martha Distel. It was adopted by a number of English enterprises, though the schools run by Hume and later Spry were the best known.

Despite its success, the book was rather anomalous, representing as it did an attempt to revive the splendours of pre-war upper-class cooking for the post-war generation. The authors were very much creatures of that pre-war world – Spry, who was born in 1886, was seventy the year the book was published, Hume forty-nine – and many of their most interesting passages concern the details of a world already lost: the carefully planned railway picnics and shooting lunches, the elegance of Edwardian 'at-home' teas from a child's perspective. Yet both were life-long educators, and there is a concerted attempt to see things from the point of view of the younger generation. The book begins with a chapter on the Cocktail Party, because 'I had an idea that perhaps a light-hearted approach might present a more immediate appeal'.[76] Despite this attempt at frivolity, the book lacked the glamour of many of its competitors, especially those produced by the emerging breed of TV chefs and culinary entertainers, and within a decade it was already looking rather old hat. It is notable, for instance, that regardless of their major influence, the book and its authors fail to feature in Michael Bateman's 1966 book *Cooking People*, in which he surveys the major post-war food writers. Hume and Spry were anathema for the 'foodies' of the 1980s according to their (only slightly) tongue-in-cheek chroniclers Paul Levy and Ann Barr: their influence was considered disastrous – 'cuisine dodo'.[77] And only recently the distinguished food writer Colin Spencer devoted a couple of pages of his *British Food – An Extraordinary Thousand Years of History* (2002) to lambasting the book for its snobbery.[78] I feel a need to defend the *Constance Spry Cookery Book* against this half century of calumny. Yes, it can be stuffy and unnecessarily grand; yes, it is prone to tweaking its foreign recipes into something blander to suit unadventurous British tastes (though it is always explained where and how this has been done); and yes, it is dry and serious rather than lively and lyrical. But it is solid, detailed and its recipes really work – something that can be said of surprisingly few cook books.[79] Rather like Mrs Beeton's similarly enormous tome, it has much to tell us about the attitudes and aspirations of the class to whom it is addressed, and reveals considerable personality and charm in its more digressive moments. As well as this, something rather interesting seems to me to be bubbling beneath its somewhat dry surface – there are tensions at play, and sometimes wisps of steam appear.

The Cordon Bleu curriculum owes much to Escoffier and other Edwardian interpreters of French food for the upper-class English market. The bulk of the dishes Hume and Spry include derive from this tradition, though they avoid some of the presentational excesses of the past. Like Escoffier they have reams of recipes for eggs (fifteen omelets, twenty soufflés and fifty-seven general egg dishes), including some immensely pompous concoctions, like Oeufs au Miroir Foie Gras, and some extremely fussy ones, such as Oeufs Mollets Duchesse (Cold), which involves short-crust pastry, two sauces (one containing mushrooms and shallots, the other mayonnaise, horseradish and cream) and a garnish. The section on petits fours resembles in its obsessive attention to detail the work of that arch fiddler Mrs Marshall – tiny confections including Madeleines, Chocolatines, Mirlitons, Sacristans and many others are constructed in complex processes involving pralines and caramels, spun sugars and fondants. This section reveals the fundamental problem with the principles of the British schools of Cordon Bleu: their aim, at this date at least, was not to train chefs but to educate girls in the domestic arts, to equip them for running their own homes. Yet many of the techniques and dishes they taught were in their original form the province of professionals; French housewives did not prepare such elaborate specialities, they bought them from the patisserie; many of the other dishes nicely brought-up girls laboured over in Cordon Bleu establishments were really restaurant classics and highly unsuitable for a domestic setting in which the cook had also to be hostess. This fact may well account for the somewhat equivocal reputation that attached itself to the label over the next few decades – one commentator remarked that the phrase tended to be 'as much a risk as an invitation'.[80]

Another group of dishes Spry and Hume include are those introduced by the experimental, simplifying, fashionable food writers of the interwar years, and it is these writers who, as in her *Come into the*

Garden, Cook, Spry singles out for praise in her section on cook books – Mrs Leyel, Boulestin, Ambrose Heath, Lady Sysonby, Lady Jekyll and Ruth Lowinsky, who was a friend of Spry's and whom she quotes from at length in this book as in the last. It is also notable that this is the first English book I have found that makes reference to Irma Rombauer's *The Joy of Cooking* (1931), which, despite its classic status in its homeland, never really found a major market in this country. Spry has particular praise for its cakes and includes a whole section on American cakes, with their thick frostings and gooey consistency, mostly borrowed from Mrs Rombauer and her predecessor Fannie Farmer.[81]

A third category contains those foreign recipes whose popularity really belonged to the post-war period, and it is these that the authors are inclined to fiddle around with, evidently feeling them to be less authoritatively established than those derived from the great culinary names and therefore more available for reworking. There is none of Elizabeth David's scrupulous respect for the authenticity of peasant food; note, for example, the cavalier attitude expressed in the recipe for Puchero:

> This is a rich bean stew of Spanish origin. The version given here is an anglicized one; no doubt the real thing has other, and different ingredients. The one I have is made with red or brown beans, and the saveloy obviously replaces some type of smoked sausage. Beef or mutton may be used instead of pork.[82]

They are inclined to be shakier on the methodology of these dishes: the directions for risotto, which insist that it must not be stirred once it is boiling or it will become sticky, suggest that they were unfamiliar with the authentic dish.

A final category embraces recipes that are their own inventions or that they have revived from ancient texts. Most dishes of this sort are collected in the chapter called 'Winkfield' (as they were designed to be tried out at the school), which is probably the most interesting in the book. Highly discursive, it describes parties catered for by the students, including the Coronation banquet for which Rosemary Hume devised the famous recipe for Coronation Chicken (usually wrongly attributed to Constance Spry). Poulet Reine Elizabeth, as the dish was called on the menu for the banquet (reproduced in the book), involved the poaching of two young roasting chickens, which then cooled in the poaching liquid, were jointed and coated with a mildly curried mayonnaise sauce, finished with whipped cream and apricot purée. It was served with a rice salad. Spry describes the sauce as 'delicate and nut-like', adding that she doubts whether many of the three hundred-odd guests at the coronation luncheon detected the flavour of the curry.[83] Elsewhere in the 'Winkfield' chapter she gives an account of the luncheon, which was an overflow affair for the 350 foreign guests who could not be accommodated at the Palace after the ceremony and was held in the Great Hall of Westminster School. Students and staff of Winkfield and the London Cordon Bleu School prepared and served the meal, which was kept simple since the waitresses were amateurs.[84] The Coronation seems to have been something of a family affair for the Cordon Bleu ladies, since Constance did the flowers: she advised the Minister of Works, was herself responsible for the Abbey annexe and parts of the royal route, and she and her staff personally planted in Parliament Square the plants sent from all over the Commonwealth. Also in the 'Winkfield' chapter are some of the most modern recipes in the book – Goose Pâté, Aubergine Caviar, Tartelettes of Smoked Cod's Roe and Salad Niçoise.

Despite some of the faults implied in the above summary, *The Constance Spry Cookery Book* attained its great success because of its effectiveness as a manual of instruction. The reader is steered past pitfalls and given the explanations needed to make her an independent cook rather than a slavish follower of recipes. They give explanations you won't find elsewhere – for example, that pastry can be fitted more easily into small moulds by laying a single sheet of pastry over the top of all of the moulds, and then pressing it down into each with a small ball of paste. This we learn from one of the many sequences of picture cookery: it is in this book that picture cookery at last attains its possibilities. The photographs are very clear, the important stages are clearly demonstrated and the right techniques have been chosen for demonstration. The photographic guides include a number of essays on carving, 'the correct method of mixing egg whites into a soufflé mixture', the making of brioche (very clear instructions for a complex process) and elaborate instructions for the icing of petits four (we may not wish to do it, but it is interesting to observe that one sticks each cake to the palette knife with a dab of fondant icing before holding it over the bowl of icing and dousing it in one movement, otherwise one might be inclined to smear stickily). The breaking into stages of the picture cookery is also employed in the prose. Dishes like soufflés and curries are deconstructed into their constituent parts to enable the reader to construct her own recipes from first principles. Possible reasons for failure are scrupulously itemized, so that next time you will know how to avoid your cake falling, your pheasants rapidly decomposing, your jam failing to set.

The authors' skill at providing explanations and instructions stems from their particular backgrounds and expertise: Hume was a professional cook in the *haute cuisine* mould (she trained at the original Cordon Bleu school in Paris), while Spry was an enthusiastic amateur. Both were highly experienced lecturers, and they see the book primarily as a teaching manual, referring continually to their students and their capabilities and mistakes. The reader is cast as another student, warned that certain dishes may be beyond her capabilities ('RH says do not start a novice on this one'; 'not a dish for the inexperienced cook'), but encouraged to develop her skills and take the whole thing seriously.[85] The book is not co-authored in the conventional sense; instead Spry supplies the narrative and Hume most of the recipes. Spry makes this clear, speaking in the first person throughout, but giving RH's comments and additions with a respect accorded to holy writ. Spry sees it as her role to ask questions on the reader's behalf:

> In preparing a book of this kind it is not a bad idea to have a stooge, and that is the part that vis-à-vis Rosemary I have tried to play; if I have done so properly I believe that the plan will have served to make clear a lot of things that professionals, in their knowledge and experience, take for granted, matters which cookery books do not always mention, and things that you aren't born knowing. I really wanted to call this book *The Reason Why*.[86]

The authors clearly concur on many points, but because their attitudes and approaches to food are not identical, the result is sometimes a curious mismatch. If we look at their earlier independent cook books, we can see how they differ as food writers: Rosemary Hume's *Au Petit Cordon Bleu* of 1936, co-written with Dione Lucas, was a competent training manual, breaking down complex recipes into easy stages, but it lacked personality; Constance Spry's *Come into the Garden, Cook* (1942), on the other hand, was bursting with character, invention and high spirits.[87] There is a sense sometimes of Spry being pulled by Hume's attitudes, and by the curricula of their schools, in a direction she would not naturally have chosen. On the subject of presentation, for instance (to which they devote a chapter), very sensible remarks on avoiding the prissy in decoration and making use of the dishes in which the food is cooked ('cauliflower au gratin does not look its best in silver, but calls for a brown fireproof dish') are followed by a long section on 'dishing-up' – that is, removing foods from the cooking dishes and presenting them (rapidly cooling the while) on platters, which Spry makes clear was initiated by her partner: '"Do you think", said RH to me, "that we might have a little section of this book devoted to the process of dishing?"'[88]

From her comments on food it is evident that Spry's personal taste tends to the simple rather than the elaborate – the book comes alive with her enthusiasm when she describes simple picnics, one-pot meals and fresh vegetable dishes served alone. On the subject of parties she ends an account of some grand and elaborate occasions with a mention of 'the sort of party which appeals equally to the cook-hostess and to the shy guest – a kitchen party':

But I am really thinking of such items as the rustic gazpacho, the salade niçoise, a good terrine, and a dish of wafers of smoked ham with black olives and gherkins.[89]

The aesthetic here is very modern, very close to that of Elizabeth David, in fact, and rather at odds with the prissiness and elaboration of many of the other recipes in the book. Colin Spencer makes a similar point about the potential divergence of the two authors' culinary attitudes, suggesting that Spry 'sold-out . . . at this vital moment in our culinary history' by '[taking] the easy route of agreeing with her colleague that French cuisine was superlative'.[90] While I would not go as far as Spencer (it seems to me that their use of French terms, to which he is objecting here, is a convention – admittedly rather outmoded – rather than a statement), I do concur that there is a tension in the book between two attitudes to cooking: what, with retrospect, we can see as the old model and the new. *The Constance Spry Cookery Book* represents a very specific sort of compromise between fashion and tradition, a concern to embrace the new but not at the expense of the way things have been done in the past. The sense of *comme il faut* is strong, though sometimes with an apologetic nod to the democratic sensibilities of the young:

If what I have just said sounds ridiculous and snobbish to you, and meaningless into the bargain, I will excuse myself by saying that as tea-time was in its glory in the old, conventional days, it is forgivable to report what was then *de rigueur*. This expression, which applies to far fewer things to-day than it did long ago, may be boring, as conventions can be. But when too many conventions disappear a certain grace goes with them.[91]

This sounds like the last gasp of a certain sort of social dinosaur, a much-bejewelled Edwardian dowager, but in fact Spry's class position is more complex and more interesting than this. Class was as much a factor in the identity and success of Spry's book as it was in those of Elizabeth David, but to assume that Spry's is the posher book is fundamentally to misunderstand the conventions of class at this date. Where David's is the careless, bohemia-embracing assurance of the gentry class, Spry's is the careful, etiquette-minded preoccupation with taste and protocol of the *arriviste*. Spry's family offers a perfect demonstration of the fluidity of the British class system. Her father began his career as a railway clerk, educated himself at evening classes and soon became a tutor, then headmaster, at the Workers' Educational College. He then moved to Ireland as an assistant secretary to the Department of Agriculture and Technical Instruction. Constance, his eldest child, followed him into educational and socially responsible work; in her teens she worked with Lady Aberdeen in her campaign to reduce tuberculosis among Irish children (an experience that makes sense of the impassioned pages she writes on the subject of milk and its modern-day cleanliness compared to the horrors of the past). During the war she was the principal of a school in the East End. The praise her friends and family heaped on her flower arrangements led to a change of direction and the opening of a flower shop; she rapidly gained an international reputation as *the* society florist, doing the flowers for the weddings of both the Duke of Gloucester and Princess Elizabeth. This background makes one look again at those long set-piece descriptions of Edwardian splendour: the elaborate teas with elegant lady visitors, the grand luncheon at the house of relations before a concert – 'after all these years I recall the food and think of it when I pass the great block of flats which had replaced the imposing Victorian house near the concert hall'.[92] Are these fantasies? It is clearly the case that Spry works very hard to establish the image of an elevated social background in her book. We can certainly accuse her of snobbery, but she is a more interesting variety of snob than the crusty dowager – and also more a creature of her time.[93]

Snobbery was very much the order of the day in the late 1950s; everyone was eager to elevate their social position, and food seemed to be one of the best ways to do so. Entertaining, which had been a subject simply omitted from cook books during the years of war and rationing, took on a new importance, not just for the upper levels of society but in the suburban home, where social success and status depended significantly on the drama and style of your dinner party. Magazines were full of suggestions for glamorous entertaining, the more elaborate the better: soufflés, rich gateaux and shellfish were rampant. Fire was especially good – flaming kebabs, crêpes suzette; as Marguerite Patten remembered 'we flambéd meat, we flambéd fruit salad – it was one of the great show-off dishes, a way of creating a great impression'.[94] It was not enough for the food to create a good impression; the hostess had also to be groomed, soignée and elegant: many cook books addressed themselves to the problem of serving spectacular food with unruffled calm so that, as Viola Johnstone's *The Hostess Cooks* (1955) puts it, 'when the guests arrive, neither her make-up nor her equanimity will be disturbed'.[95]

The sense of the art and glamour of entertaining was encouraged by television cooks who turned food preparation into a form of theatre. Tubby, bearded Philip Harben was the first when television broadcasts began again after the war (he is often given credit for being the first-ever TV cook, but that honour actually belongs to Marcel Boulestin), but the most glamorous was the highly eccentric Fanny Cradock, who burst onto the screen in 1954 in full evening dress, dripping jewels and mink stole, caked in heavy make-up like a pantomime dame. Fanny's act (and it was an act, since by many accounts she was actually a rather poor cook) involved cooking elaborate, expensive food in front of a theatre audience while bossing around her dinner-jacketed husband Johnnie in 'a comedy of Cordon Bleu manners'.[96] The Cradock double-act remained extremely popular for two decades, until an increasingly unstable Fanny was sacked by the BBC after furiously insulting a Devon housewife who had just won a cooking competition. The food Fanny demonstrated was bizarrely grand, upping the stakes in the arena of domestic entertaining still further as people strove to replicate her dishes. The Cradocks also published books and articles on food and wine, travel and restaurant criticism throughout the 1950s and beyond, under the pen name 'Bon Viveur'. Their books, like their television performances, are astoundingly snobbish – full of name-dropping, champagne and truffles – and also very funny. Throughout their writing career they engaged in an elaborate process of personal myth-making, where famous people and fêted chefs sing the praises of Bon Viveur or set for them fiendish gastronomic tests which they pass with flying colours.

The Cradocks' food, with its many sauces, its towering arrangements and intricate garnishes is very like that described by semiologist Roland Barthes in a famous essay entitled 'Ornamental Cookery', written in the mid-1950s. He is actually discussing the food described and photographed in the French journal *Elle*, but the phenomenon is identical:

> Golden partridges studded with cherries, a faintly pink chicken chaudfroid, a mould of crayfish surrounded by their red shells, a frothy charlotte prettified with glacé fruit designs.[97]

Barthes, arguing that the readership of the magazine is working class, sees the excessive attention devoted to the presentation of this food as a fantasy of smartness, of petit-bourgeois gentility: 'hence a cookery which is based on coatings and alibis, and is for ever trying to extenuate and even to disguise the primary nature of foodstuffs, the brutality of meat or the abruptness of sea-food'.[98] He sees it as dreamlike cookery, presented not to be cooked (most of the magazine's readers could not afford a pheasant) but to be marvelled at. Barthes later retreated from the intellectual positions taken in his essays *Mythologies*, from which this piece derives, considering their reasoning overschematic. In the case of the Cradocks, his model accounts for some features of their extraordinary career, but not all. To judge by retrospective accounts, it would seem that many suburban British housewives *did* attempt to cook some at least of the sort of glamorous dishes photographed in magazines and flamboyantly demonstrated by Fanny Cradock, but such dishes fitted into an area of their lives that if not actually belonging to the realm of fantasy was pretty close to it. Entertaining in these years existed as a sort of media-inspired dream world, divorced from the practices of everyday life, where ordinary people acted out a simulacrum of elegant living.

The Cradocks are part of the rise in the late 1950s of the culture of the gourmet. The word, much in vogue at the time, denotes an informed appreciation of 'the finer things in life', those being expensive French or French-style restaurant food and 'fine wines', his knowledge of which the gourmet is immensely proud. Chief gourmet was André Simon, founder in 1933 of the Wine and Food Society, and already in his late seventies by the mid-1950s. The author of over seventy books, mainly on wine, Simon represented the acme of French sophistication to the monied connoisseurs who sought to assimilate his expertise. His prose is measured and stately, but his attitudes are as unrepentantly epicurean as the Cradocks: his work, like theirs, is filled with lists of perfect meals, course by course, with the wine matched to each course lovingly recorded. His opinions are trenchant: 'There are people who never grow up: they drink milk or water like babes all their life. Gourmets, however, drink wine. It is not mere affectation but the recognition that the best food can never be so good as with the best wine for partner'; 'to shut one's eyes to beauty or one's nostrils to truffles is sheer puritanical heresy'.[99] The gourmet may have been a stuffy, snobbish Edwardian throwback, but his moment had come. Men in the late 1950s wanted to be connoisseurs, dinner-jacketed, elegant and worldly-wise, like James Bond (whose first appearance in print was in 1953) dining in the Casino Royale.

Glamorous food and gourmet food were, naturally, foreign. For the gourmet, French food ruled supreme, but the specialities of other nations also had cachet – the trick was to know what was good. This is Philip Harben, laying down the law about international gastronomy: 'American food is terrible. They are tone deaf about food. Germany is very limited. The Swiss have two dishes, sausages in potato cake, and *fondue*. But *fondue* is magnificent. It's beautiful. Danish *smoerrebroed* is good, but I was told by an official at the Embassy there that the food they eat before their meals is marvellous, and what they have as their meals is nothing.'[100] For the suburban hostess originality was more important than excellence, and magazines and cook books trawled the globe for new specialities. There was an explosion of international cook books, typified by *The International Cookery Book* (1953), edited by the inexhaustible Ambrose Heath, in which the recipes of at least ten contributors are arranged, not nation by nation, but according to type, so a Czechoslovakian recipe for Baked Spinach jostles a West Indian one for Bean Pie. The geographical regions represented also include Scandinavia, the USA, Russia, Austria, Holland, Greece, Hungary, China, Italy, Spain and France. It is significant, though, that the last three nations are very under-represented and that the emphasis is very much on the cuisines of eastern and northern Europe (*lots* of noodles, dumplings and pancakes), with Czechoslovakia the most predominant. The recipes are hardly the most authentic (the Green Pea Soup from China includes a sprig of mint and a teaspoonful of Marmite), but the collection gives a neat picture of the pre-Mediterraneanized tastes of the Britain of the earlier 1950s. Other 1950s cook books were more specific in their focus. Worth a mention is *American Cooking for English Kitchens* (1957), edited by Grace Hogarth, with recipes supplied by American women living in Britain, mostly members of the Vassar Club of London. Recognizing the true ground of the appeal of American cooking to British cooks, they dispose of soups, appetizers, main dishes and vegetables in the first four chapters, then devote the next five to hot and cold desserts, ice cream, cookies and cup cakes, cake and frosting, and bread and muffins. Guides to oriental cooking written by natives rather than British interpreters began to appear: Savitri Chowdhary's *Indian Cooking* was published in 1954, with recipes for Chapatis and Parathas, Raita and Pakorhas, and strict injunctions never to use curry powder.[101]

In 1954 Elizabeth David expanded on her earlier investigations into the food of southern Europe with the highly authoritative *Italian Food* (of which more in the next chapter), but her discursive, educated, scrupulous approach to food and its culture was to be rivalled by two other books published in the mid- to late 1950s. The first was the *Alice B. Toklas Cook Book*, which appeared in its English edition in 1954. Toklas was the lover and housekeeper of American modernist writer Gertrude Stein, and her cook book tells the story of their domestic life in France during a period covering both world wars, with interludes in America. Fascinating and deeply eccentric, it arranges its recipes according to the exigencies of whim and reminiscence, rather than any sort of culinary logic. She begins the book with a fine essay on the particular qualities that define the French as cooks: 'to cook as the French do one must respect the quality and flavour of the ingredients. Exaggeration is not admissible. Flavours are not all amalgamative.'[102] Other chapters include 'Dishes for Artists' (with an account of how she coped with Picasso's strict diet when he dined with them), an essay on 'Murder in the Kitchen', which recounts grisly adventures with beasts she had to slay herself, and one on detection, which turns the tracking down of an authentic recipe for gazpacho into a story of international culinary exchange and theft. Further reminiscences concern food encountered on their journeys in an old truck (whimsically entitled Aunt Pauline) during the First World War and the food eaten during the German occupation in the 1940s. Food for Toklas, like Elizabeth David and M. F. K. Fisher, cannot be divorced from the circumstances in which it is prepared, discussed or encountered. Her recipes are always embedded in a context – treasures collected over a long and curious life, discovered on a journey or given by friends. It is in the chapter on the latter category that we find the recipe for Haschich Fudge that made the book infamous. It is not actually a fudge at all but an oriental confection of chopped nuts, dates and figs mixed with spices and the pulverized cannabis and rolled into small balls. This one recipe, given to Toklas by beat poet Brian Gysen, gave her cook book a far longer textual life than would otherwise have been likely and ensured that the book, which she saw as a simple *jeu d'esprit*, rivals in fame the works of her fêted companion.

The second important work was *Plat du Jour, or Foreign Food* (1957) by Patience Gray and Primrose Boyd, a charming guide to the domestic culinary traditions of (mainly) France, Italy and Spain, very much in the Elizabeth David mould. In fact, the authors pip the illustrious Mrs David to the post in their account of the French *cuisine bourgeoise*, territory she was not to make her own until three years later. They approach food with the same strong sense of history and regionality as David, quoting antique culinary authorities and noting the precise regional origins of their dishes. They are given to very strong, clear judgements: 'cloves can be quite disgusting if used to excess. Cinnamon, on the other hand, is not used enough in meat dishes.'[103] Like Elizabeth David they employ a resolutely unornate language that elicits trust through its honed simplicities, and like her they have a gift for bringing alive the atmosphere of a dish, evoking appetite and enthusiasm through a description of its preparation or consumption: of Garbure they comment, 'The soup is sufficiently solid to be eaten with a fork. When nothing remains but the broth a little red wine is poured in, and the soup bowl is emptied at a draught.'[104] Their tone is a little gentler than David's, though – a bit less strict. You don't feel so much on your mettle reading Gray and Boyd, are less concerned as to what they might make of your slips from the counsel of perfection. Unusually for its period, the book has a chapter on wild mushrooms, with information about identifying them. It also includes a chapter on 'Vins Ordinaires', which stands as a sharp counterpoint to the gourmet approach to wine, which the authors gently satirize: 'Some people have a rather formidable attitude towards wine, giving one to believe that only a few chosen spirits are equipped with the necessary palate, sensitivity, and imagination to appreciate properly its great qualities.'[105] In suggesting that it can be enjoyed without fuss, simply as a quaffable accompaniment to an everyday meal, *Plats du Jour* anticipates the demotic spread of wine in the 1960s and 1970s. For the Britain of the late 1950s, freed from over a decade and a half of food shortages and culinary restrictions, good food was foreign food. Although a classic history of English food – Dorothy Hartley's monumental 1954 book *Food in England* – was published in these years, it failed to make a significant contribution to national attitudes to food. It was not until two decades later, in the company of Jane Grigson, that we were ready to rediscover the glories of the food of pre-industrial Britain.

TYPICAL RECIPES 1946–59

Peter Pirbright
Off the Beeton Track (1946)

This recipe is typical of the appropriation of the foods of central Europe in the years immediately after the war. The taste for Polish food, in particular, seems to have been encouraged by the large numbers of Polish airmen in Britain during the war. Pirbright's recipe is curiously transitional: it has the preoccupation with authenticity that was soon to be found in the work of Elizabeth David and others, but it continues the wartime spirit of thrift with its numerous suggestions for the use of leftovers and its blithe encouragement of experiment.

GOULASH

Stewing beef	paprika
1 clove garlic	marjoram
caraway seed	salt
vinegar	plain flour
meat extract	
2 dessertspoons lard or dripping	(potatoes, black coffee, tomatoes, Yoghourt)
3 large onions	

First of all I want to make one important point: you cannot, as some people seem to think, make Goulash without paprika. If you can't get paprika at your grocer's, go and try another one. Do make an effort – you'll see it's well worth your while. And don't let them sell you Cayenne pepper instead – it's much too hot. Another thing: don't hurry your Goulash. Give it at least 3 hours. The longer you cook it over a very moderate fire, the better it will be.

Use an iron saucepan or a thick aluminium one. Remove the gristle and cut the meat into one- or two-inch dice. Cut 3 large onions into rings. Melt 2 dessertspoonfuls of lard or dripping in the saucepan, add the onions and a crushed clove of garlic, cook gently for about 10 minutes. Then add a heaped dessertspoonful paprika, ½ teaspoonsful of caraway seed and a pinch of marjoram. Then add the meat. Stir and cook until the meat is well browned. Salt after 20 minutes. Cover and simmer for 3 to 4 hours, adding hot water by the spoonful from time to time. Instead of water you can also use peeled, sliced tomatoes; this improves the flavour and the colour. If you want a lot of gravy, add more water. If you want the Goulash to be strongly flavoured, add stock or dissolved meat extract instead of plain water, and a tablespoon of strong black coffee. Just before serving add a dash of vinegar and sprinkle with flour. Bring to the boil. If you want the Goulash rich, stir in 2 or 3 tablespoons of Yoghourt before serving.

There are many ways in which you can use up any of the Goulash you don't eat at once. First of all you can heat it up, which even improves the flavour. Then you can add a certain amount of stock or meat extract dissolved in plain water or vegetable water to obtain a delicious soup. If you have not added any Yoghourt to the sauce you can add a large amount (2 or 3 lb.) of chopped leeks to what remains of the Goulash and cook for an hour. This will give you a rich and very satisfying dish. Again, you can add a certain amount of stock and throw in some quartered raw potatoes which you cook gently in the sauce.

You can also use the rest of the Goulash as a sauce with Spaghetti, Macaroni, Rice, Noodles, or Dumplings of any kind.

By the way, this whole rigmarole applies equally to quite a number of the braised beef recipes given here. Try some experiments!

Elizabeth David
A Book of Mediterranean Food (1950)

These recipes from her first book already demonstrate Elizabeth David's distinctive style and attitudes: the firm assertion of her tastes; the confident claims of historical and regional authenticity; the precision of method. The recipe for Aïoli dispenses entirely with the cajolings and apologies with which other food writers of the period introduce garlic-rich dishes, but it is a mild affair compared with the version she offers a decade later in French Provincial Cooking, *where she specifies two cloves of garlic per person – roughly eight times what she suggests here.*

BOURRIDE

For anyone who likes garlic this is perhaps the best fish dish of Provence, to my taste much superior to the Bouillabaisse or any of the Italian *Zuppe di Pesce*.

Bourride is usually made with a variety of large Mediterranean fish, such as *loup de mer* (bass), *daurade* (sea bream), *baudroie* (angler or frog fish), *mulet* (grey mullet), but is successful with almost any white fish, and one variety alone will do. Grey mullet, a despised fish, but very good when properly treated, is excellent for a bourride, or whiting, rock salmon, gurnard, John Dory, even fresh sardines will do.

Whatever fish is used is poached in a *court bouillon* previously prepared from an onion, bayleaf, lemon peel, fennel, the heads of the fish, salt and pepper all simmered together in water, with the addition of a little white wine or vinegar, for about fifteen minutes. Leave this to cool, and strain before putting in the fish and bringing them gently to the boil, and then just simmering until they are done.

Have ready an aïoli made from at least 2 yolks of eggs and about ½ pint of olive oil. Have also ready at least two slices of French bread for each person, either toasted or baked in the oven (the second method is easier to manage, with two or three other operations going on at the same time). When the fish is all but ready put half the prepared aïoli into the top half of a double pan; stir into it the beaten yolks of 4 eggs, then a ladleful of the strained court bouillon in which the fish are cooking. Cook over very gentle heat, whisking all the time until the sauce is thick and frothy. Pour this sauce over the prepared toast in the heated serving dish, arrange the strained fish on the top, and serve quickly, with the reserved half of the aïoli separately.

AÏOLI

Aïoli is really a mayonnaise made with garlic, and sometimes breadcrumbs are added.

It is served usually with salt cod, or with boiled beef, accompanied by boiled carrots, potatoes boiled in their skins, artichokes, French beans, hard-boiled eggs and sometimes with snails which have been cooked in water with onions and fennel, or with baby octopus plainly boiled, with pimentos; in fact with any variety of vegetables, but always cooked *à l'eau*. It is one of the most famous and best of all Provençal dishes. The aïoli sauce itself is often called *beurre de Provence*.

Start by pounding 2 or 3 cloves of garlic, then put in the yolks of eggs, seasonings, and add olive oil drop by drop, proceeding exactly as for mayonnaise. Add lemon juice instead of vinegar.

The Alice B. Toklas Cook Book (1954)

Toklas so fully embeds her recipes in prose that the effect is almost that of fiction. These recipes come from a chapter entitled 'Food in French Homes', in which she details particular meals she and Gertrude Stein ate in the households of French friends, with a view to defining the particular qualities of French food and attitudes to eating, and how they differ from the American. Her description of her impoverished friend's domestic arrangements interestingly anticipates those of Elizabeth David, whose habit of living in the kitchen has been hailed as revolutionary in its influence. The food itself is typical of the elegant, restrained dishes Toklas favours.

An old friend of ours, living alone for some years now in conditions requiring the strictest economy, has finally accepted a modern conception of working in her home. It has become a pleasure and no longer a drudgery. For a long time she brought the food that she cooked from the kitchen to a well-set table in the dining-room, course by course. She now eats not only in the kitchen but in what she calls the Anglo-Saxon manner. The meat course is served with the vegetables and potatoes or salad. She moved a fine seventeenth-century cupboard into the kitchen, in which she keeps all that is necessary to serve a meal for four people – she does not have more than four guests as many times as that in a year. In her kitchen, where she now reads, sews and writes letters in either of two fine winged arm-chairs, I have eaten a

BRAISED GROUSE

Clean the grouse, empty the cavity, and wash it with a little milk. Pour the milk out. Put the grouse in a bowl and pour over it 1 cup milk. Leave it in the milk for at least an hour, turning it from time to time. Then dry and skewer the grouse so that the wings and legs remain neatly in place when served. Remove the rind if there is any from a slice of fat bacon large enough to cover the grouse. Tie the bacon securely around the grouse. Melt 1 tablespoon butter in a heavy saucepan or iron pot. Brown the grouse uncovered on all sides over medium flame for $\frac{1}{4}$ hour. Skim off some of the fat, add salt and pepper, 1 cup cream, and simmer covered for 20 minutes. Then add the juice of $\frac{1}{2}$ lemon. After this do not allow to boil. Place grouse on serving dish and pour over it the sauce. It is a delicious way to prepare grouse, and had lost none of its savour because my friend had shot it. She goes off intrepidly on her bicycle for miles to shoot a bird or catch a fish. These economies and pleasures permit her to keep a small but excellent wine cellar.

She made an original but luscious *purée* to eat with the grouse.

PURÉE OF CELERY ROOT (CELERIAC) AND POTATOES

Wash and peel a celery root weighing 1 lb., remove all fibres, cut in large cubes. Boil in salted water until the tines of a fork enter into it easily. Wash $\frac{3}{4}$ lb. unpeeled potatoes and steam. Use the same test for them as for the celery root. Peel and mash 4 potatoes with the celery root and 1 hard-boiled egg, put through a strainer with the potato masher. Add 3 tablespoons butter, $\frac{1}{2}$ teaspoon salt, a pinch of pepper, and heat over asbestos mat until hot, stirring from the bottom so that it does not burn.

This purée makes an equally novel salad. Instead of heating in butter add $\frac{1}{3}$ cup cream, place in a mound on a flat plate, cover with a thick mayonnaise in which 1 teaspoon lemon juice has been mixed, and surround the mound with hearts of lettuce.

Ethelind Fearon
The Reluctant Cook (1953)

Fearon's breathless prose leaves no natural place to start a quotation – one recipe simply flows into the next. This recipe is remarkable for all the things that it doesn't tell the reader, particularly given the book's apparent remit. There is no explanation about how to soften the chocolate, how to stop the custard curdling or the gelatine lumping, while the French rock clearly needs crushing to a powder rather than simply being 'broken'. The final vague aside about the making of praline adds insult to injury with its throwaway 'of course'. This is elaborate dinner-party food whose entire rationale is to impress – hence the remarks about dinner guests and the fact that as much space is given to the final decorative gussying-up as to any of the technically delicate stages of the recipe.

And another really superb example which I learned in France is called *Soufflé Praliné au Chocolat*, but, in spite of its name, no more complicated to make than apple tart and custard, which involves three separate operations (four if you count peeling the apples) and a whole kitchen-full of apparatus to wash up.

And apple tart is no great treat when you've finished, because the pastry may have behaved badly, or the custard curdled, or you been thinking about something else and put Epsom salts instead of sugar, or the guests had apple pie in their own homes for lunch.

But I bet they didn't have one of these. You need

3 eggs	Juice of ½ lemon
4 oz. cooking chocolate	1½ gills cream
1 oz. gelatine	½ gill water (hot)
2 oz. French almond rock	½ " " (cold)
1 oz. sugar	

Prepare and paper a soufflé mould and brush with water. Beat yolks and sugar over hot, but not boiling, water until pale in colour. Add lemon and go on beating until a custard is formed. Remove from heat, add softened chocolate, gelatine dissolved in ½ gill of warm water, and the broken French almond rock. When they show signs of setting, fold in the cold water and lightly whipped cream or ice-cream, and finally the stiffly whipped whites of egg.

Decorate when cold with crystallised violets or roses and 'leaves' of pistachios. You can make your own French almond rock by putting chopped almonds in brittle toffee, of course.

The Constance Spry Cookery Book (1956)

These linked recipes come from the book's opening chapter on 'The Cocktail Party', but the modernity of the subject is tempered by the meticulous attention to detail and tradition of the recipes. The reference to the lost grandeur of Edwardian dining is a note often struck elsewhere in the book, where it is usually, as here, balanced by concessions to modern tastes and habits of eating. The proliferation of alternatives is also typical of Spry and Hume's approach: they follow the logic of the cooking school, where one basic recipe leads to many different offshoots and possibilities. In fact, the list of fillings given here is not all – the recipe as quoted is followed by another set of cream-based fillings. The instructions for choux pastry are the best I know of – succinct but precisely detailed, particularly point (2), which provides crucial information omitted from the directions of most other food writers.

SAVOURY ÉCLAIRS OR CHOUX

Prepare a choux paste with $\frac{1}{4}$ pint water, 2 oz. butter, $2\frac{1}{2}$ oz. flour, seasoning, and 2 eggs (for method see below). Lightly grease a baking sheet and put the mixture on it in small teaspoons. Sprinkle with chopped almonds or grated cheese and bake until crisp, or you may mix savoury ingredients in the paste:

Choux paste as above, season with salt (no sugar), mix with a little chopped lean ham or, more delicious, smoked ham and shredded browned almonds, and fry in deep fat.

Or you may fill cooked choux paste:

Bake the paste plain as choux, or pipe into little éclairs, split and fill with a cheese cream or other savoury mixture. Or you may like to incorporate a little cheese with the mixture to give added interest.

In Edwardian days these savoury éclairs and choux were called carolines when shaped like éclairs, and duchesses when formed like choux à la crème; they were finished off, after being filled, by a coating of chaudfroid sauce or by a light brushing of aspic jelly just on the point of setting, and they were then sprinkled with finely chopped pistachios or other salted nuts. This finish is not often carried out to-day and is indeed a job for experts. The addition of sauce or aspic, of course, makes these savouries suitable for the dinner table rather than the cocktail party. Some of the fillings used for them, however, will serve our purpose.

Chicken. Cold chicken, shredded and pounded in a mortar, mixed with an equal quantity of butter and seasoned with salt, freshly ground black pepper, a squeeze of lemon juice, and a few drops of tabasco. Finely chopped herbs, such as tarragon, chervil, and parsley, can be worked into the mixture to taste.

Ham. Lean ham, with a very little fat added, shredded and pounded with enough hot chutney to flavour, a drop or two of Worcestershire sauce, some French mustard, and an equal quantity of butter.

Tongue, shredded and pounded with a tablespoon of Cumberland sauce, salt and pepper, a touch of made mustard, and an equal quantity of butter. Chopped orange or lemon rind added to taste.

Salmon. Fresh or smoked salmon, pounded and mixed with horseradish sauce, seasoned with salt, pepper, and lemon juice.

Sardine. Boned and skinned sardines pounded with lemon juice, plenty of freshly ground black pepper, a little salt, and a teaspoon or more of Worcestershire sauce.

N.B. Instead of butter, a small quantity of good béchamel or demi-glace sauce, according to the other elements chosen, may be used with these purées.

CHOUX PASTE

1. The flour must be sifted and dried, and it is convenient if it is put onto a piece of paper so that it is easier to shoot it all into the boiling water at once.
2. The beating of the mixture should be not more than is just enough to bring the paste away from the sides of the pan, a condition which indicates that the flour is cooked. If beating is continued beyond this point the paste will fail to rise properly and become cake-like in consistency, and this is a common fault in the making of choux paste.
3. Thorough beating must be given when the eggs are added.
4. For baking choux paste the oven should be hot, average temperature 430°F., and the paste should on no account be taken from the oven until it is quite firm to the touch. If this rule is not observed, the pastry will fall immediately it is taken from the oven. Choux pastry should always be well baked and freshly made.

1½ gills water	3¾ oz. plain flour
3 oz. butter	3 eggs

Bring the butter and water to the boil together. When bubbling draw aside and immediately add the flour all at once. Beat until smooth and the paste will leave the sides of the pan. Leave to cool. Whisk the eggs lightly and add by degrees, beating thoroughly. If the eggs are exceptionally large retain the last spoonful until you have ascertained whether it is required, or whether you may get too wet a mixture. When finished the paste should be smooth and shiny-looking.

CHAPTER FIVE

The Schizophrenic Food Culture

Photograph of Isabella Beeton at the age of twenty-one. Her fourth son, Sir Mayson Beeton, presented this picture to the National Portrait Gallery in 1932, where it initiated a revived interest in the 'real' Mrs Beeton, who many by that date had assumed to be simply a publisher's fiction.

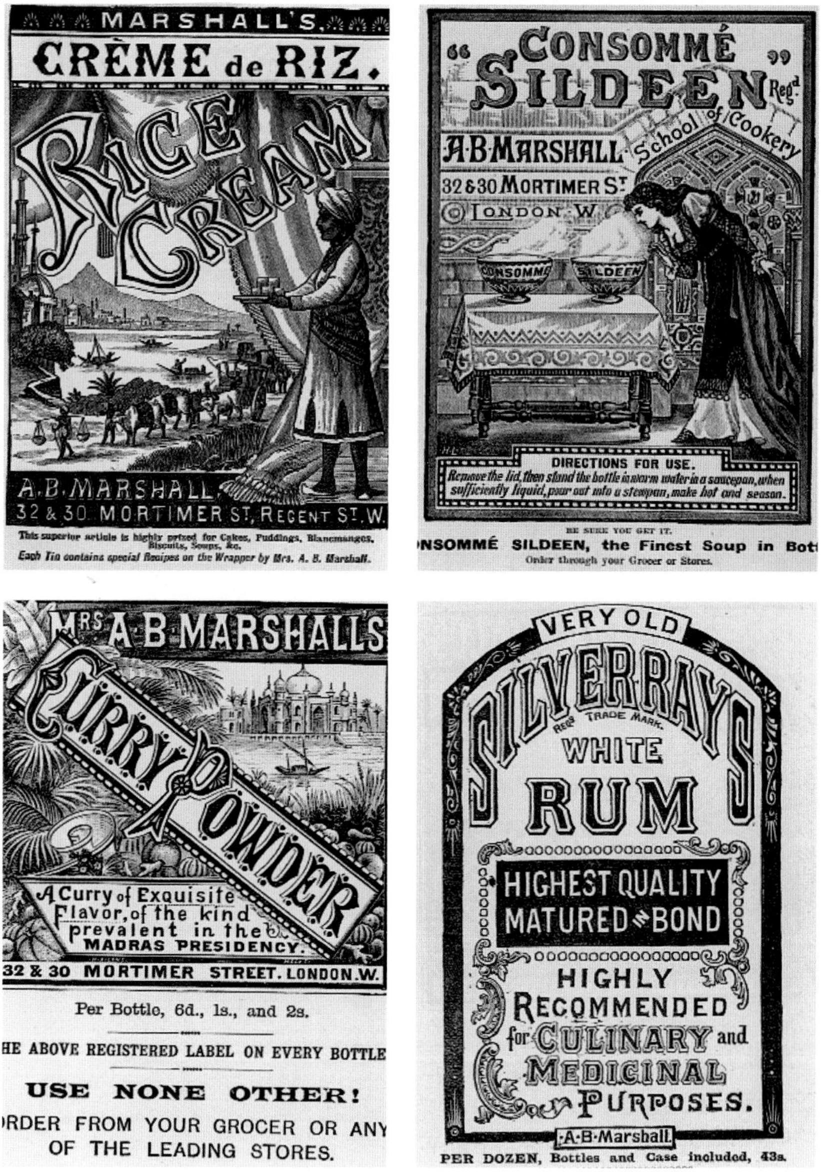

Advertisements for Marshall's products appended to *Mrs A. B. Marshall's Cookery Book* of 1888. A highly astute businesswoman, Mrs Marshall wasted no opportunity to advertise her many goods and services.

Serve all dishes as attractively as you can. The above suggestions for garnishing will be found useful for the following recipes:—

1. Beefsteak pie (p. 26).
2. Chicken rissoles (p. 37).
3. Egg omelet (p. 155).
4. Mince collops with poached eggs (p. 157).
5. Creole eggs (p. 154).
6. Claret jelly (p. 71).

The Art of Garnishing from *Aunt Kate's Household Annual* (1933). The suggestions are both prissily effortful and oddly unappealing.

A vegetable cook from Peter Pirbright's *Off the Beeton Track* (1946), lithograph by Victor Ross. The whimsical surreality of Ross's illustrations contribute significantly to the book's argument and its appeal.

Antipasti and Fish from Elizabeth David's *Italian Food* (1954), drawings by Renato Guttuso. David commissioned the drawings herself from Guttuso, a Sicilian painter who was considered one of the most important working in Italy at the time. Her publisher, John Lehmann, was less enthusiastic, put off by the artist's communism and commitment to social realism.

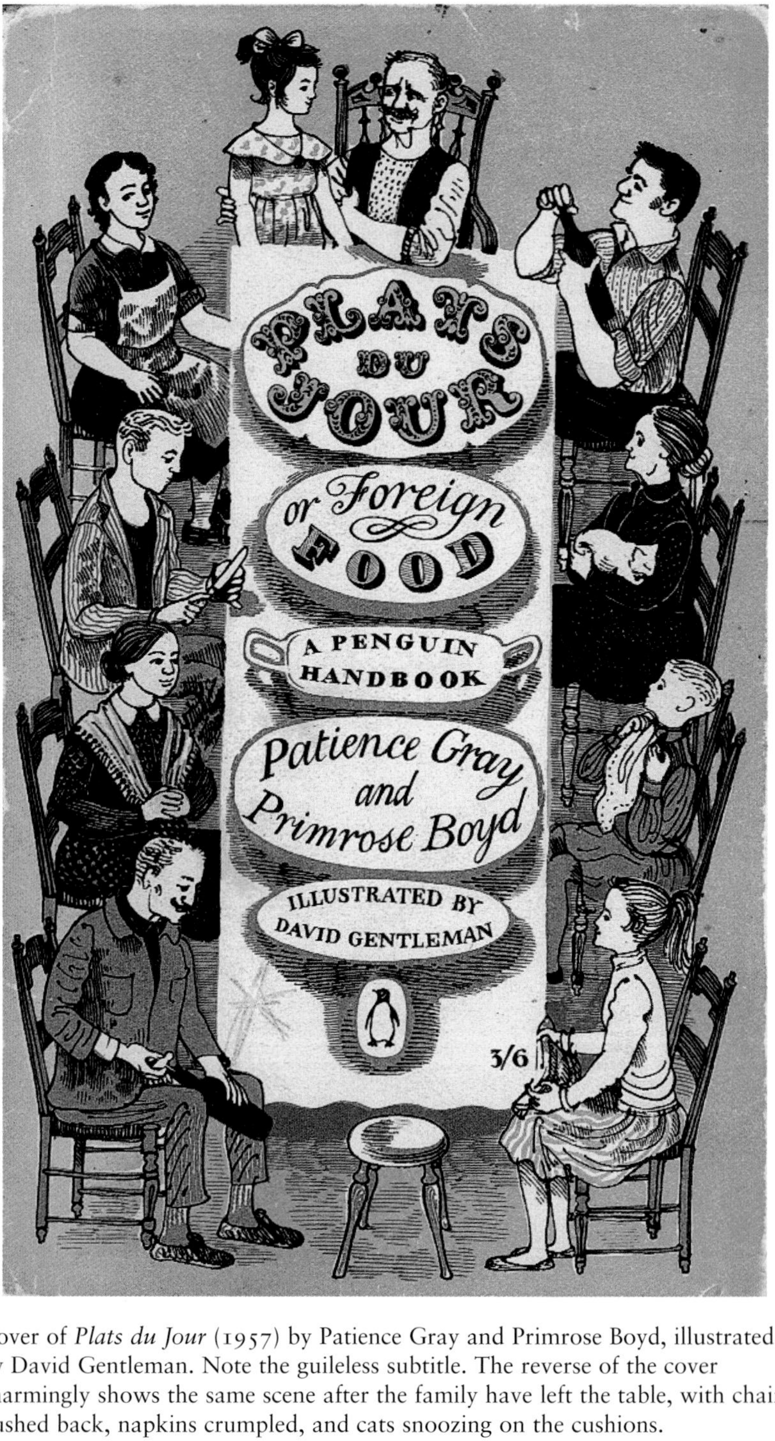

Cover of *Plats du Jour* (1957) by Patience Gray and Primrose Boyd, illustrated by David Gentleman. Note the guileless subtitle. The reverse of the cover charmingly shows the same scene after the family have left the table, with chairs pushed back, napkins crumpled, and cats snoozing on the cushions.

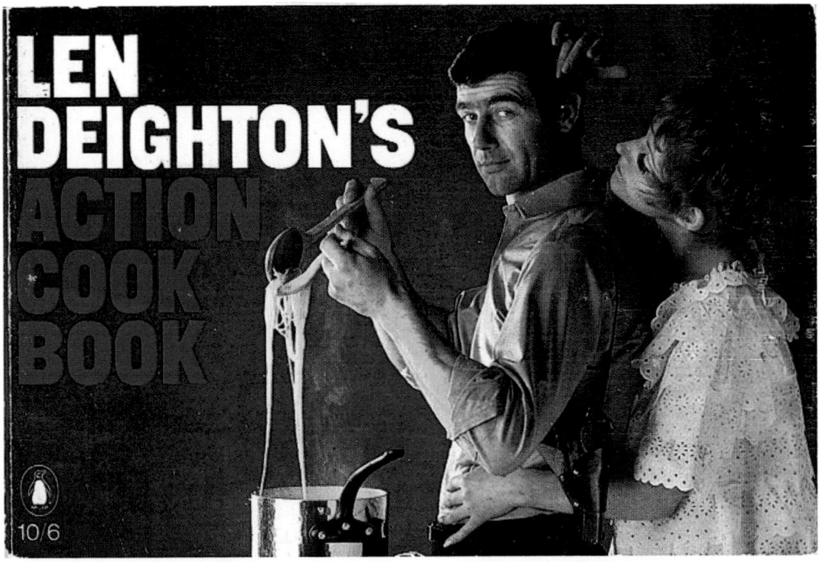

Three covers from the 1960s: the glumly comic image that fronts Peg Bracken's *I Hate to Cook Book* (1960) sets the tone for her exploration of women's domestic dissatisfactions. Raymond Hawkey's design for Len Deighton's *Action Cook Book* (1965) makes clear the rewards on offer for the male cook, while George Molnar's drawing for Ted Moloney and Deke Coleman's *Oh, for a French Wife!* (1965) connects food and sex even more explicitly.

Food photography in the 1980s and 1990s became ever more seductive in its focus on the detail of the ingredients. Georgia Glynn Smith's photograph of fennel for Nigel Slater's *Real Cooking* (1997) renders the glistening vegetable with positively gynaecological intensity.

The flood of new cook books in the years immediately after austerity became a tidal wave in the two decades that followed. Niche marketing was of increasing import, with books catering to more and more precise situations and categories of readers: consider *The Executive Cook Book* (1965) ('the executive is not only a busy man but a hungry one, and his meals need careful thought and preparation'), or *The Liberated Cook's Book* (1975) ('I've always boasted that from stocks in the cupboard I could produce a presentable and interesting three-course dinner after stepping straight off the plane without a chance to shop') and *The Something Went Wrong What Do I Do Now Cookery Book* (1973) ('What to do about salty soup, burned stew, fallen cakes, overcooked cauliflower, runny eggs, and hundreds of other kitchen catastrophes').[1] These were the decades of the novelty cook book. There were cook books as menu planners, with pages divided horizontally to allow starters, main courses and puddings to be mixed and matched (the pioneer, in 1964, was Arabella Boxer's *First Slice Your Cook Book*), cook books as cartoons (Len Deighton's *Action Cook Book* of 1965, a cook strip which appeared first of all in the *Observer*, is the most famous, though Ambrose Heath had already done it during the war with the Patsy series for the *Daily Mirror*) and cook books as cards (*Robert Carrier's Cookery Cards*, which appeared from the mid-1960s onwards 'with protective wipe-clean surfaces to ensure immunity in the kitchen, and each card small enough to use as a shopping list'). There seems to have been a market for anything and everything written about food, and cook books started to look like a licence to print money. So who was buying all these books – and why?

Two apparently distinct and seemingly unquenchable thirsts for culinary instruction had been created. One was simple cookery for absolute beginners (bachelors, young people living in bedsits) and the very busy (working women); the other was impressive food, which came in two forms: highly sophisticated and elaborate, or 'authentic' (that is, peasant or bourgeois food rather than the refined specialities of chefs). One of the striking features of post-austerity culinary culture was that these two categories – the basic and the impressive – appealed, to a surprising extent, to the same buyers. The description Katharine Whitehorn, the original bedsitter cook, gives of her own practices is fairly typical:

> I think the food here tends to be on two very distinct levels. There's proper food which I suppose is more French than anything else, which is what I basically love to do if I've got time . . . When I do it, it's good. The stock leads to the soup and so on. It's all a cycle, the materials are good and fresh and it's fine. Then one tends to go with a terrific bump down to 'short order' stuff. The important thing is to keep in one's own mind the distinction, when it's a hamburger night and when it's a proper food night.[2]

And so we settled into the schizophrenic habits of eating under which, as a nation, we still operate today: convenience foods for every day with the family (then tins, stock cubes, frozen veg.; now frozen ready-meals and takeaways); exotic, impressive meals 'from scratch' at the weekend, and particularly when entertaining. Because both schools of cookery were essentially new to most people, there was an ever widening market for cook books. And as more convenience foods and more gadgets came on the market, ever more exotic cuisines were colonized, and higher and higher standards of both glamour and authenticity were established by food writers, then more books were needed to explain, to popularize, to simplify and to enlighten.

Elizabeth David's cook books represented the ideal. The books she wrote at the height of her career, *Italian Food* (1954) and *French Provincial Cooking* (1960), promised to remake the British attitude to food, to encourage a respect for raw materials, for tradition, for the taking of pains to achieve the proper results. And while the British of the austerity years could only dream about her recipes, by the early 1960s they were making them in their thousands. Specialist food shops and delicatessens were opening in every reasonably sized town, and the new supermarkets supplied many of the imported ingredients her recipes required; all over the country dinner parties and kitchen suppers were courtesy of Mrs David. But the revolution did not happen quite as she would have liked. Good food for her was not something you ate on high days and holidays but every day, calmly but with attention. Her ideal was 'sober, well-balanced, middle-class French cookery, carried out with care and skill, with due regard to the quality of the materials, but without extravagance or pretension'.[3] The trouble was that to cook like this you needed to be able to buy your carefully chosen ingredients fresh every day and to have the time to wait while your daube simmered, your stock reduced, your soufflé rose to a wobbly peak of perfection. For the increasing number of working women or those who looked after their young children alone, such cooking was a luxury demanding the one commodity in increasingly short supply: time. Cooking the Elizabeth David way became a leisure activity, a relaxing, absorbing occupation for the weekend, when you could plan your time around it, enjoy pottering knowledgeably in specialist shops, then get down to some serious simmering, chopping, tasting and reflecting.[4]

Elizabeth David's first two books reached what was probably the peak of their direct influence in the mid-1960s, when the dishes they introduced were becoming staples on dinner tables and in bistros across the land (though her oeuvre is so frequently reworked by other cookery writers that she never seems to be out of date). Her later books were rather different: fuller, more discursive, viewing food and its culture more and more with the eye of the scholar. There is an increasingly obsessive concern to ferret out historical connections, to record variants of a dish, to work out origins. In her later books the scholarly was to be the dominant impulse (there are no recipes at all in the posthumously published *Harvest of the Cold Months* (1994), a social history of ice and ice cream), but in the major works of the middle period of her career she achieved a perfect balance between the evocative and the erudite. In both *Italian Food* and *French Provincial Cooking* the scholarship is fully at the service of the cook, used to determine the absolutely right method, the best ingredients, the authentic tastes.[5] Consider, in this respect, her notes on the variations of Quiche Lorraine:

> The one universally known as the *quiche Lorraine* contains smoked bacon, cream and eggs. Parisian, and English, cooks often add Gruyère cheese, but Lorrainers will tell you that this is not the true *quiche Lorraine*, whose history goes back at least as far as the sixteenth century.
>
> There is, however, a time-honoured version containing a proportion of fresh white cream cheese as well as the cream, and it is perhaps this recipe which has caused the confusion. No doubt it is all largely a matter of taste, and for myself I find that whereas the combination of the mild flavour of white cream cheese with the smoked bacon of Alsace and Lorraine (which much resembles our own at its best) is quite attractive, that of Gruyère with the same smoked bacon tends to be rather coarse and heavy.[6]

She then deals tactfully with the historical conundrum by giving the recipe for the version with no cheese at all, with the cream-cheese alternative as a separate recipe under a different name (Quiche au Fromage Blanc). Her recipes in these later books are a considerable contrast to the often sketchy instructions of the first books: they are full and highly detailed, while never narrowly prescriptive (in both books she quotes Marcel Boulestin's assertion that 'the dangerous person in the kitchen is the one who goes rigidly by weights, measurements, thermometers, and scales'). Recipes for technically challenging dishes like soufflés and mayonnaise she breaks into numbered stages, and she often gives two or three closely printed pages of instruction for a simple recipe. But the writing, even of basic instructions, is so lively that her recipes are intensely readable in a way that can be said of very few other cookery writers. This is what she says about how to tell if your gougère is cooked:

Although the gougère begins to smell cooked after the first 20 minutes, do not be taken in; it will have swelled up and turned golden brown, but it is not ready. If you can resist, do not open the oven, because of the risk of the mixture collapsing. If you feel you have to look, open and shut the oven door very gently. To test when the gougère is done press lightly with a finger in the centre of the cake; it should be firm to the touch. If it is too soft it will fall the instant you take it from the oven into a sad flat pancake.[7]

Her descriptive writing has filled out also: the evocations of place that were so painterly in the earlier books have become richer, more narrative. They are stories with an air of romance – of strange inns and brasseries stumbled upon on journeys to somewhere else, of taciturn waiters bearing magical foods. One narrative, in *French Provincial Cooking*, is of an ordinary *café routier* (café attached to a filling station) where Elizabeth David and her travelling companion requested bread, butter and sausage as a mid-morning snack:

Seeing that we were English, the old lady in charge tried to give us a ham sandwich, and when we politely but firmly declined this treat she went in search of the *patron* to ask what she should give us.

He was an intelligent and alert young man who understood at once what we wanted. In a few minutes he returned and set before us a big rectangular platter in the centre of which were thick slices of home-made pork and liver pâté, and on either side fine slices of the local raw ham and sausage; these were flanked by black olives, green olives, freshly washed radishes still retaining some of their green leaves, and butter . . .

We came back the next night for a specially ordered dinner of Provençal dishes . . . The young man was a cook of rare quality, and the dinner he prepared to order put to shame the world-famous Provençal three-star establishment where we had dined a day or two previously. But had it not been for the appearance of the delicious hors-d'oeuvre, which was so exactly the right food at the right moment, we should have had our drink and paid our bill and gone on our way not knowing . . .[8]

Another, in *Italian Food*, tells of her serendipitous stumbling upon a dish of stuffed, fried olives, which in the brief description she invests with the associations of romance quest (the fabled object, the chance encounter, the rustic wedding):

OLIVE RIPIENE

A dish of which I long doubted the existence, but arriving very late for luncheon in the town of Ascoli, of which these stuffed olives are a speciality, I was lucky enough to find a wedding feast still in progress in the very excellent little restaurant, and these stuffed olives had been made for the occasion.[9]

The reader is cast by such narratives as a fellow scholar-adventurer, travelling with David on her quest, the ultimate aim of which is much more than the educated palate of the gourmet: it is a knowledge of the fullest part food can play in the experience of being human. For Elizabeth David food is a serious business, perhaps the most serious, and she requires her readers to take it seriously too. Her recipes in these later books have to be worked for, buried as they often are in disquisitions on regional variations in dishes and accounts of the ways locals eat particular foods: the fleshy nugget of instruction has to be teased out from the intricate shell of her prose. The following example is for Jambon à la Corsoise (Ham with Tomato and Garlic Sauce) from *French Provincial Cooking*:

This is a dish I remember from my first visit to Corsica, which now seems a very long time ago. In the little town of Piana of the red rocks, I took a room in the house of a very humble family. There were a large number of children in their teens. Their mother was a great big brawny woman with a robust sense of humour. Amid a tremendous clatter we would all sit down to meals at one big table. Madame's cooking was of the same nature as her own: rough, generous, full of character and colour. There were great dishes of ham and tomatoes, eggs and olives, plenty of salads and oil, huge hunks of bread and great bowls of bursting ripe figs. In all the years since then I have never quite forgotten the very special savour of that food. The ham dish was made with thick slices of the Corsican version of *prosciutto*, or raw ham, fried and served on top of a tomato sauce freshly cooked in oil and well spiced with garlic, pepper and herbs. Nowadays I sometimes make it with gammon rashers, but cooked in a baking tin, just covered in water, in the oven, then drained and just barely browned in olive oil. Served on a big round earthenware dish, surrounded by the tomato sauce, flavoured with plenty of dried basil as well as garlic, and with some croûtons of bread fried in oil, this makes a splendid quickly cooked dish for lunch or supper.[10]

While her first two books, particularly *Mediterranean Food*, were primarily travel memoirs, recalling sights, sounds and tastes that seem already lost, so powerful is the nostalgia with which they are viewed, the later books, especially *French Provincial Cooking*, are guides for travellers, full of advice about where to go and how to eat well when you get there. As such, they perhaps lack the atmosphere of mystery and longing of her first book, but they serve a tremendous practical purpose. It is no exaggeration to say that Elizabeth David is pretty much solely responsible for the yearly exodus of well-heeled Britons to Provence: the headily evocative passages in *French Provincial Cooking* seem almost calculated to drive her fellow countrymen thither:

> Provence is a country to which I am always returning, next week, next year, any day now, as soon as I can get on a train. Here, in London it is an effort of will to believe in the existence of such a place at all. But now and again the vision of golden tiles on a round southern roof, or of some warm, stony, herb-scented hill-side will rise out of my kitchen pots with the smell of a piece of orange peel scenting a beef stew. The picture flickers into focus again.[11]

The lengthy initial chapter of *French Provincial Cooking* discusses each of the regions of France in turn, calculatedly whetting the appetite of the food-minded tourist. The introduction in particular is addressed rather more to the needs of the traveller, planning to eat these foods *in situ*, than to the cook hoping to reproduce them in England.

All of the qualities outlined above apply more fully to *French Provincial Cooking* than to *Italian Food*, which is something of a transitional work. It also represented much more of a voyage of discovery for its writer, who found the research for the book somewhat arduous:

> My command of the Italian language is decidedly the wrong side of adequate. The amount of money I had to spend was not boundless. Neither is my eating capacity. The Italians are on the whole abstemious drinkers but big eaters. Sometimes I was asked to plough through a five-course meal and then start all over again with some dish for which I had particularly asked. My kind hosts would be astonished, and cease to believe that I was a serious person, when I could do no more than taste a spoonful. There were times when I was close to despair at the proverbial Italian disregard for their own and other people's time.[12]

Despite – or perhaps because of – such difficulties, Elizabeth David often declared *Italian Food* to be her own favourite among her books. It is a work of major importance, being the first British cook book to represent the highly regional nature of Italian food (the product, as it is, of separate city states only united in the mid-nineteenth century). It was also to have the longest lasting influence of any of her works if we judge by current culinary fashions: French food is long gone as a culinary destination for most home cooks (though still a staple in the restaurant trade), while Italian food was grasped so closely to our national bosoms that we would be hard pressed to tell it from our own. The reason, of course, is that Italian food – or at least, the Italian food that most of us cook almost daily – is quick and easy, while French food is manifestly not. So polenta, pizza, risotto and endless varieties of pasta with pesto, with olive oil and garlic, with tomato sauce, baked with cheese and meat sauces, are everyday suppers throughout much of Britain, while Provençal daubes, escargots and boeuf à la bourguignonne belong to the lost world of the 1970s dinner party.

Between the publication of *French Provincial Food* and her next cook book there was a ten-year gap, during which time Elizabeth David founded a kitchen shop with friends (of which more later) and wrote numerous pieces of campaigning food journalism for publications including *Vogue*, *House and Garden*, the *Daily Express*, the *Sunday Times* and the *Spectator*. In 1970 *Spices, Salt and Aromatics in the English Kitchen* was published. A slim book, it was envisaged as the first in a series on English Cooking Ancient and Modern. David's interest in the history of English food had been developing for some time, and while occupied with the shop she had written a series of little booklets on the subject – on spices and condiments (the basis of the book), the baking of an English loaf, potted meats and syllabubs. *Spices, Salt and Aromatics* is concerned to rethink the traditional English use of spices. Where previous historians had attributed this habit to the need to disguise bad meat or as a conspicuous sign of wealth, she argued that there is much evidence that the English just liked the taste of spicy food: 'quite simply . . . the English have a natural taste for highly seasoned food – as do most northern people – and since trade with the Near East and southern Europe brought us early in the evolution of our cookery considerable opportunities for indulging the taste, we took to spiced food with an enthusiasm which seems to have been almost equal to that shown by the Romans at the height of their preoccupation with the luxuries of living'.[13] She prefaces the book with an essay on Mrs Leyel, first published in the *Spec-*

tator seven years earlier, in which she states that the 'excursions into far Arabia' of the *Gentle Art of Cookery* 'make it quintessentially a book about one particular facet of English food and English tastes'.[14] This broadening of our conception of English tastes – and of Englishness itself – is at the heart of David's project. In this work she allows her historicizing impulse to run unfettered, digressing into weird and wonderful culinary byways: of Cassia, for instance (a form of cinnamon), we learn that Sir Kenelm Digby, 'by way of being something of an alchemist, was fond of putting it into his mead and metheglin', and that there is another variant of the plant, used as a laxative, the English vernacular name of which is Pudding Stick.[15] Since she begins her note on this spice by indicating that it is inferior in delicacy and subtlety to cinnamon, it is pretty clear that none of this information is really of relevance to the cook. We are now in the territory of food history rather than cookery writing. The writing remains incisive and evocative and has lost none of its slightly sardonic, opinionated edge: cayenne pepper, we are told, adds zest to cheese sauces, 'the beloved English cheese straws' and 'some people think – I do not – to oysters'.[16] And on paprika, that ineffable taste of the 1950s engagement with the foods of central and eastern Europe, she is nothing less than barbed: 'Unending arguments as to which is best for what kind of goulash or other central European speciality are a Hungarian pastime; don't ever ask a Hungarian food expert to tell you about paprika unless you are prepared to hear more about the subject than you want to know. In other words, this is not the place for me to write about paprika, nor indeed do I use it very much in my cooking.'[17] The opening chapters in which she discusses spices, salt and herbs one by one are so full of matter that it is difficult to select just a few examples. Here are her remarks on rosemary, for instance:

> With sage, this herb figures in my kitchen as a decoration only – with their grey-green and reddish leaves both herbs are beautiful in a jug of country flowers but in cooking I don't want either. Many Italians stuff joints of lamb and pork almost to bursting with rosemary, and the result is perfectly awful. The meat is drowned in the acrid taste of the herb and the spiky little leaves get stuck between your teeth. Once, in an out-of-doors Capri café I saw an old woman basting her fish – it was grilling over an open charcoal fire – with a branch of rosemary dipped in olive oil. That's about as much of rosemary as, personally, I want.[18]

And then there are her many notes on taste, which evoke sensations utterly familiar but which you had never before called to consciousness: 'The peppery taste which is so overwhelming in many of the foods of commerce – English sausages in particular – is due to the inferior and mixed peppers used. These produce a hot and prickly sensation in the mouth without the true aromatic smell and taste of good pepper.'[19] The recipe section of the book, which amounts to a bit over two thirds of the whole, concentrates on dishes in which the flavourings are an essential rather than subsidiary element. Sauces include a cinnamon butter (without sugar) described as 'excellent with white fish', and an anchovy-based cream sauce called Granville Sauce derived from one of David's favourite historical cook books, Lady Llanover's *Good Cookery* of 1867. Other interesting dishes are Greek, Moroccan, Italian and Malay recipes for kebabs, included as a corrective to the American-influenced 'craze for the so-called barbecue which hit the British Isles in the late fifties', Pig's Head-Cheese (or brawn) and a number of recipes from Colonel Kenney-Herbert, whose *Culinary Jottings for Madras* and other works she much admires.[20] There is a very detailed recipe for Spiced Beef for Christmas, which treats a round of beef much like a ham, rubbing the raw meat with brown sugar and a spice mixture including allspice, juniper and black peppercorns daily for about two weeks and then baking very slowly. Harrods had been selling beef spiced to Elizabeth David's recipe since 1958 (she first published it that year in an article on Christmas cooking in *Vogue*). She comments of the recipe (which she derives from an ancient Sussex one) that 'the beef will carve thinly and evenly, and has a rich, mellow, spicy flavour which does seem to convey to us some sort of idea of the food eaten by our forbears'.[21]

The concern with determining exactly what our ancestors ate continues in her next book, *English Bread and Yeast Cookery* (1977), which was originally intended as volume two in the English Cooking Ancient and Modern series but which far outgrew the limits that implied. It is a monumental book, deeply and exhaustively historical, tracing the development of English bread back to its ancient origins and studying the process from the harvesting of the grain to the emergence of the finished loaf. It was a very timely book, appearing at the height of the popularity of the health-food movement, when many people were so fundamentally dissatisfied with the bread available commercially that they were willing to try baking their own as a regular commitment rather than an occasional experiment. Elizabeth David's book certainly contained the information to enable them to do so, but it had to be diligently sifted from the many chapters of historical, scientific and anthropological enquiry into subjects such as the anatomical structure of a grain of wheat and the history of bread consumption, of grains and their cultivation, of milling and of different sorts of flours and meal. Advice is given about the possibilities of buying grain direct from the miller or grinding your own grain, of distinguishing the different sorts of flour available commercially. The book does not proselytize the benefits of 100 per cent wholemeal flour and bread as so many wholefood campaigners were doing at the time. David is as saddened as they by the bleaching and extracting processes of commercial milling, but her position is not dogmatic:

> Now, I do not think, as do wholehearted wholefood campaigners, that all the ills of this country stem from the eating of white bread and the lack of bran in roller-milled flour. I do think that there should be far more choice, and, above all, that every responsible person should know what he is choosing.[22]

She feels that wheatmeal flours of 81 to 85 per cent extraction make the best bread and that, most importantly, they retain the germ, 'that part of the wheat which is its life'.[23] She finds it curious that campaigns about better bread focus on the bran (the husk of the wheat seed) but show little interest in the germ (its heart). She is particularly scathing about the commercial millers' long-standing practice of extracting the germ and selling it (more profitably) as animal food or to be expensively packaged and sold as a health food.[24] She is sometimes equally scathing about the ways of the health-food lobby, expressing her exasperation at the 'nanny-type' injunctions of the assistants in health-food shops and mocking the stoneground pastry ('the very words', she remarks, 'are sufficiently leaden') served in Cranks restaurants.[25]

In contrast with the simplicity of the Doris Grant no-knead basic wholemeal loaf (the recipe for which David gives, with approval, as the best method for producing an eatable 100 per cent wholemeal loaf) most of Elizabeth David's bread recipes are quite complex. An intrinsic part of her project is the study of the whys and wherefores of ancient and traditional methods of bread-making, and so she quotes many historical recipes and incorporates arcane practices into her own recipes. So we have Mrs Rundall's recipe for a natural yeast from 1807, and one for a ginger yeast from Lady Clark of Tillypronie. Then there is the archaic baker's recipe for using 6 oz of yeast to 280 lb of flour (the less yeast one can use, the better the taste and texture of the bread, David says, and the better its keeping qualities); it is an elaborate process which involves three spongings, taking seventeen hours in all. Following this example, David suggests that we should habitually use less yeast (about half the recommended quantities) and leave our bread doughs to rise slowly: 'To me it seems both convenient and practical to give bread doughs a long fermentation. Rather like meat steeping in a marinade it is looking after itself while you are asleep or busy with other jobs. What could be less troublesome?'[26] Her chapters on yeast cakes and crumpets and muffins are among the most engaging, with recipes for pikelets and Sally Lunn, eccles cakes and galettes, and glimpses into the farmhouse kitchens of the past where their manufacture was a weekly occurrence.

Because bread-making is an absorbing craft, those interested will be fascinated by the level of detail David provides – her notes on salt, on yeasts, on liquids, on provings and spongings lay the ground for many years of happy experimentation. The book was received with great enthusiasm by reviewers and won the Glenfiddich prize in 1978. Yet there were some who were disappointed by Elizabeth David's shift in direction. She was known as the prophet of the cooking of southern Europe, and her new forays deep into English culinary history were not what her fans expected. Arabella Boxer's feelings may well have been typical of many:

> Gradually, as . . . her scholarly inclination started to assert itself, she began to rely on research for her material, and as her love for such pursuits grew, she lost me. I missed the romance and pleasure of her early books, and having by this time become a food writer myself, I was heartily sick of reading or writing recipes. The intricate niceties of comparing twenty-five similar receipts for muffins and crumpets failed to interest me, and I felt sad.[27]

This may have been the response of many readers to the most intensely historicizing aspects of David's later work, but there was emerging a group of food writers for whom the prospect of comparing twenty-five similar receipts was infinitely beguiling. These were the 'scholar cooks' (as Paul Levy and Ann Barr's not entirely sympathetic *Foodie Handbook* designates them): writers like Claudia Roden, Alan Davidson and, above all, Jane Grigson.[28] Elizabeth David's writing offered a lead – and a market – for those who were to follow: a serious interest in the history of food and the origins of recipes was now acceptable. To some extent David acted as a mentor for this younger generation of writers. When Alan Davidson, a career diplomat on a posting in Tunis, published a booklet on the identification of the seafish of Tunisia, it found its way to David.[29] She wrote enthusiastically about it in a *Spectator* piece in 1963 and encouraged him to turn it into a book. Some years later he approached her to ask if she would sell an enlarged, privately printed version in her shop. She did much more, giving him an introduction to Jill Norman at Penguin, who published *Mediterranean Seafood* in 1972. The book, and those on the identification and cooking of fish that followed it – notably *North Atlantic Seafood* (1979) – have remained the key authorities on the subject. Davidson himself became probably the most significant mentor of food scholarship in this country, through the publishing company Prospect Books that he and his wife Jane set up to publish works on food history, anthropology and 'food ways' that mainstream publishers would not touch (the company is now run by Tom Jaine), the food history journal *Petit Propros Culinaire* and the annual Oxford Food Symposia, co-founded with Dr Theodore Zeldin. Most recently he edited the *Oxford Companion to Food*, an astonishing 900-odd pages, which manages to be both absolutely authoritative and quirkily entertaining.[30]

Jane Grigson was also the beneficiary of Elizabeth David's support; she read Grigson's first book, *Charcuterie and French Pork Cookery* (1967), in typescript and was so impressed that she recommended her for the *Observer* food column that was to establish her reputation (and from which a number of her books originated).[31] Grigson began her career as a food writer by accident, having agreed to do the research for a book on French charcuterie for a friend who, in the end, was unable to write it. So she wrote it instead, investing the subject of the pig and all his products with a wit, scholarship and lightness of touch that was instantly engaging:

> It could be said that European civilization – and Chinese civilization too – has been founded on the pig. Easily domesticated, omnivorous household and village scavenger, clearer of scrub and undergrowth, devourer of forest acorns, yet content with a sty – and delightful when cooked or cured, from his snout to his tail.[32]

Although she and Elizabeth David shared very similar attitudes to their subject, and often wrote on similar areas, there were distinct differences in their approach. Jane Grigson's works have none of the haughtiness that can emanate from David's writing, and they wear their scholarship very lightly. Where David will quote a source at length, giving a meticulous background and context for the quotation, Grigson will refer to her historical and literary evidence almost casually, in passing, as one cultured person to another. Here, for example, are her remarks on kippers from the 1971 *Good Things*:

> Over the centuries we have developed various ways of curing and keeping the herring, that splendid northern fish which Shakespeare's contemporary Thomas Nashe – loyal to his East Anglia – grandly and comically called the 'Semper Augustus of the sea's finny freeholders'. Our best and longest known forms are the red herring, the bloater, and the kipper – in that order of seniority.[33]

Like David, she involves the reader in her culinary quests, describing serendipitous moments in libraries and restaurants, drawing us into her thought processes and sharing her triumphs. This is her account of her tracking down of a recipe for 'the Charter', mentioned in the diary of Parson Woodforde, 'the Norfolk clerical glutton', in the 1780s:

> Was it sweet or savoury? Savoury, I think (on another occasion the dog ate the Charter which had been put to cool in the cellar). It bothered me for a couple of years until I found this *Charter Pie (Cornish Recipe)* in a Victorian recipe book compiled by Lady Sarah Lindsay. It's a winner of a dish, well worth the expensive ingredients, and quite up to Parson Woodforde's exacting standards.[34]

The Charter, incidentally, turns out to be a chicken pie with a sauce of cream and parsley, though Grigson continues to worry away at the historical conundrum, expressing her doubt about this solution in 1974's *English Food*.[35]

Jane Grigson was brought up in the north-east, in Sunderland, an area where there remained a strong culinary tradition, particularly of baking. Her initial inspiration as a food writer came, however, from the French village of Trôo, in the Loire valley, where she and her husband, the poet and critic Geoffrey Grigson, had bought a house in the early 1960s. Built into a cave in the rock, as many houses are in that area, it was remarkably primitive, with no running water, drains or electricity. For twenty years the family divided their time between France and their English home in Wiltshire, spending three months of each year in Trôo. Her food writing, too, was divided between France and England. She followed the book on charcuterie with *Good Things* (1971), which derived from her *Observer* column. The work on the column formed the basis of her culinary education, as her daughter Sophie recalls: 'All she knew about was pork at that point, and I can remember her saying she was suddenly faced with writing her first article. She and my father sat down and said "My god, what do we do?" And they decided to approach the article from the point of view of putting strawberries within a cultural context of art, literature, historical importance and development, and that really was the basis for all her writing.'[36]

Good Things is a charming book, very much in the tradition of those pre-war writers who revolutionized stuffy upper-class cooking with suggestions for simple, appetizing dishes on a domestic scale (and its title encapsulates perfectly the sense of comfortable yet informed chat, of recipes shared between friends, that epitomizes her work). It is divided into five categories – fish, meat and game, vegetables, fruit, dessert and fruit liqueurs – and draws its recipes mainly from the French and English culinary traditions. Its aim is not the exhaustive coverage of a whole food culture but the revival of interest in food that is good and seasonal. That this food often has a long and interesting pedigree adds to the fascination of the book, but these are not just historical curiosities: all of Grigson's recipes work. They are meticulously tested and clearly and simply written, never forgetting the significant detail but not overloaded with information. Chat and instruction are graphically separated, so that the following of a Jane Grigson recipe does not offer the same challenge to the concentration as one of Elizabeth David's.

Grigson's recipes and recommendations had a significant effect on middle-class tastes and food habits in the 1970s; just a brief selection of dishes from *Good Things* clearly evokes that period: Walnut Bread, Jambon Persillé, Curried Parsnip Soup, Gooseberry and Elderflower Jelly. There is also a strong whiff of the 1970s cult of self-sufficiency about the book. She is much more wholefood-y than Elizabeth David, interested in food you can pick yourself and how to use up seasonal gluts: her clutch of walnut recipes in *Good Things* derives from a need to find a use for the sackfuls she acquires from her neighbour's harvest:

> We bring them home by the kilo, every autumn, from our neighbour's tree in France. After the hard work of the vintage is over, he finds walnut picking a pleasant job. The tree grows at the foot of a steep slope, and one suddenly sees his head, and the heads of nephews, cousins, and friends, popping out of the leaves like Jacks in the Green. Down below wife and children bash at the branches with sticks, and the nuts come raining to the ground. We munch steadily for days, walnuts with the new wine, walnuts with new bread, walnuts fried with apples to go with *boudins noirs*.[37]

The book includes a section on edible woodland mushrooms, including advice on how to recognize a handful of the most useful, prefaced by the regret that 'thousands and thousands of the best edible mushrooms go to waste in the woods – on this side of the Channel – every good mushroom season'.[38] There is a definite bias towards food that can be grown, picked, shot or fished rather than bought in a shop: a lot of game recipes, brown trout, and fruit and vegetables liable to be found in the English rural garden (apples, quinces, and gooseberries, peas, parsnips and carrots). In *Jane Grigson's Vegetable Book* (1978) she argued that every house could grow at least some of their own vegetables:

> Marmande and plum tomatoes in pots, herbs in window boxes, courgettes and squashes trailed round the doors. Inside, there could be aubergine, pepper, chilli and basil plants on the windowsill, jars of sprouting seeds, dishes of mustard and cress, with mushroom buckets and blanching chicory in the dark of broom and airing cupboards. In my most optimistic moments, I see every town ringed with small gardens, nurseries, allotments, greenhouses, orchards, as it was in the past, as assertions of delight and human scale.[39]

Her focus on individual ingredients in *Good Food* was elaborated on in a series of later books which concentrated on a single type of ingredient: *Fish Cookery* (1973), *The Mushroom Feast* (1975), *Jane Grigson's Vegetable Book* (1978) and *Jane Grigson's Fruit Book* (1982). The latter two, in particular, take an encyclopaedic approach to their subject, mixing vivid historical, horticultural and literary anecdotes with a rich selection of recipes. She was awarded both the major prizes for food writing – the Glenfiddich Writer of the Year Award and the André Simon Memorial Fund Book Award for her *Vegetable Book* – and then scooped both prizes again four years later for the *Fruit Book*. Neither book looks likely to be superseded soon. Probably her most influential book, however, was the 1974 *English Food*, which she described as an anthology. Here she sought to reintroduce the English to their pre-industrial culinary heritage, to 'renew and develop the old tradition of Hannah Glasse, Elizabeth Raffald, Maria Rundell and Eliza Acton'.[40] From the first sentences she takes issue with the old chestnut of terrible English food:

> The English are a very adaptive people. English cooking – both historically and in the mouth – is a great deal more varied and delectable than our masochistic temper in this matter allows.[41]

Curiously, given the title, she includes a fair number of Welsh dishes – because she likes them, she says, and also because 'they are linked closely with much English food, while retaining a rustic elegance which we have tended to lose'.[42] So we have Wyau Ynys Mon or Anglesey Eggs (hardboiled eggs in a cheese sauce on a bed of mashed potatoes and leeks), Cacen-cri (Griddle Cakes), Pice ar y Maen (Welsh cakes on the stone) and a number of recipes using Laverbread, a traditional puréed seaweed which Grigson describes as tasting of the sea, with a hint of oysters.[43] English dishes like Cornish Pasties, Jugged Hare, Banbury Cakes and Trifle form the bulk of the collection, but because the aim is to develop rather than just record our traditional food, she offers some surprising adaptations and additions. French methods are allowed to inform English dishes (as with a leek pie altered according to the practice of a French friend), and she gives the unorthodox method for Yorkshire Pudding with which a Chinese chef won a cooking contest in Leeds. She includes a number of recipes from French chef Guy Mouilleron, who elaborates on traditional English dishes: the results include a Jellied Eel Mousse with Watercress Sauce (the result of his image of 'the silver eel, nosing its way through the thready stems of watercress in a stream') and Leg of Lamb stuffed with Crab, a combination of ingredients apparently used in England in the eighteenth century.[44] A number of our dishes are reclaimed from other nations who have made them their own: so Oyster Loaves, as she notes, a speciality of New Orleans since the nineteenth century, are firmly named as in fact an eighteenth-century English dish, and a very French dish of stuffed goose or turkey neck is discovered to be identical to the practice of fifteenth-century English court cooks with their *Poddyng of Capoun necke*. The book is more than a record of the good things we have eaten in the past; it is an active intervention in current eating habits, as when she provides a list of the many varieties of fish teeming off our shores which we fail to eat. Top of the list is monkfish – 'much of the English catch goes to France, at a high price'.[45] That this is no longer entirely the case is due to a change in our tastes and attitudes inspired, at least in part, by Jane Grigson. A number of the dishes she writes about in *English Food* have become established classics, reworked continually by other food writers and chefs: these include Glamorgan Sausages (a Welsh speciality of grated Caerphilly, white breadcrumbs, chopped leek and eggs formed into sausages and fried), Brown Bread Ice Cream and – most famously – Sussex Pond Pudding (a casing of suet pastry filled with brown sugar, cubes of butter and a whole lemon: when cooked 'the butter and sugar melt to a rich sauce, which is sharpened with the juice from the lemon').[46]

Jane Grigson was not, of course, the first food writer to try to revive interest in traditional English food. Florence White, in her *Good Things in England* of 1932, had attempted to record the traditional dishes still being produced in mostly rural kitchens throughout the country, before they were lost in the rush of modernity. Her enterprise was part of the folk-history movement, and many of her recipes were derived from correspondents who contributed their inherited specialities; White adds historical notes, often tracing the recipe back to an early printed version, and offering fascinating comments on connections and derivations. The book is necessarily piecemeal and sometimes repetitive, but it preserves dishes from sources as diverse as Oxford and Cambridge colleges, old court recipe books, gentlemen's clubs and farmhouses and cottages. It is a wonderful hotchpotch of the elegant and the utterly basic, spanning five or six centuries, and in its preservation of the voices of its correspondents gives a strong sense of cookery as a part of living history. One curiosity is 'Donkey', an old Fifeshire recipe for a steamed pudding of oatmeal, suet and onion, to be served with cold meat, to which White appends the laconic 'curious, but very good'.[47] Then there is the recipe for Eel Pie from Richmond, recorded in 1873 by *Times* journalist Aeneas Dallas, who was even then regretting its disappearance. From the seventeenth century there is Queen Henrietta Maria's Morning Broth; from the eighteenth a Hedgehog Tipsy Cake (a sort of trifle moulded in the form of a hedgehog). Hawkshead Whigs (small cakes) from 1826 are 'exactly similar to those eaten by Wordsworth as a boy'.[48] Everything you would expect to find is here – eels and parkin, griddle cakes and ham – and much that you might not – Gingerbread Husbands, Cowslip Tarts, and Manchets for the Queen's Maides (1526).

In 1954 Dorothy Hartley, a medieval historian who had been one of Florence White's contributors, published her own huge and stately *Food in England*. Clearly the work of a historian, Hartley's book is more analytical and factual than White's, and as a result rather less charming. But it is highly authoritative, and many of its historical essays stray into areas unvisited by other histories of food: she is particularly interested in the culinary history of sailing voyages, informing us that medieval sailors ate laver and so were remarkably free of scurvy, and asserting that it is 'to the early sailing ships we owe our knowledge of potted and dried meats'.[49] The book is highly illustrated, with a number of images of ancient foodways and many drawings showing the selection and use of different raw ingredients and the construction of dishes. These include a demonstration of how to pull a cannonball of pease pudding apart with two forks to serve, how to select pea pods with peas just ready for eating, and detailed drawings of traditional shapes for pastries, including the Checky Pig – a variation on the pasty that includes strips of pastry folded in to resemble the ears and tail of a fanciful pig of 'most lovable design'.[50]

And then there were the books on farmhouse cookery, which appeared in a steady trickle throughout the century, the best known being Alison Uttley's *Recipes from an Old Farmhouse* of 1966, a surprise best-seller that combined nostalgic memories of Uttley's late-Victorian rural childhood, sweetly-pretty line drawings and recipes.[51] Heralding the fashions for rural self-sufficiency and the old-fashioned ways that were to dominate the next decade (think of Laura Ashley, *The Country Diary of an Edwardian Lady*, Holly-hobby dolls), Uttley's book appeared just at the moment when the culture of the 1960s turned away from its preoccupation with modernity, precisely capturing the zeitgeist. Her writing is charming but also often surprisingly perceptive: Elizabeth David declared that her description of her childhood perception of bread dough as 'a lively white cushion, growing bigger and bigger' would be hard to better.[52]

These were interesting, much-respected books, so why is it that Grigson's was the first account of traditional English food to have a transformative effect on our eating habits? One answer is cultural: her book appeared at a time when there was a general reaction against the modern and artificial and a longing to return to our rural roots. Another is accessibility: you had to be a truly dedicated devotee of traditional cooking to search through White's ephemera or Hartley's intense historical essays to find the dishes that you really wanted to cook, while Grigson's book is remarkably reader-friendly, with tested recipes clearly laid out and in modern form. Primarily, what her book does that its predecessors did not is to select. *These* are the dishes worth retaining or rediscovering, she says, and then explains why. So we don't get the full range of fifty-odd traditional suet puddings; we get one – the one that Grigson has decided is the best. Much of what she revives was not long gone, if it had gone at all – I doubt that black pudding or faggots had ever stopped being eaten, especially in the north – but the major contribution of her book was to make such food fashionable again.

The wholefood and associated health-food movements that influenced Jane Grigson had been developing for some time. In the 1950s food-reformer-to-the-stars Gayelord Hauser led Hollywood and smart London and Paris to raw carrot juice, brewer's yeast, wheatgerm and yoghurt, promising them transformed lives, renewed energy and glowing skin in gospels like *Look Younger, Live Longer* (1951). Although a wholefood diet did not necessitate vegetarianism, the two movements were clearly fellow travellers, with a similar raft of concerns about animal welfare, health and the environment. It was reading Hauser that encouraged David and Kay Cantor to found in 1961 the famous Cranks restaurant in Carnaby Street, which defined vegetarian eating for a generation with its organic produce, free-range eggs, Doris Grant wholemeal bread and wholemeal pastry; its stoneware dishes and stripped-pine tables. The hippy culture of the late 1960s and 1970s embraced with enthusiasm vegetarianism and macrobiotic eating (based on Zen Buddhist principles this concentrates mainly on brown rice and vegetables, avoiding dairy products, refined foods and sugar as well as animal products). At the same time there was a move towards self-sufficiency among a significant group of the middle classes, who turned their backs on the consumer culture to run smallholdings and attempt to produce their own food without chemicals or cruelty. The impetus behind the movement was an increasing awareness of the realities of agribusiness. Works like Rachel Carson's *Silent Spring* (1963) and Ruth Harrison's *Animal Machines* (1964) exposed respectively the massive devastation wreaked by the use of DDT and other herbicides, and the routinely inhumane treatment meted out to animals like veal calves and battery hens. This was the moment when cook books began to be overtly political. Books like Frances Moore Lappé's 1971 *Diet for a Small Planet*, with its wonderfully self-explanatory subtitle – *How to Enjoy a Rich Protein Harvest by Getting Off the Top of the Food Chain* – and Sharon Cadwallader and Judi Ohr's *Whole Earth Cookbook* (1973) were American, the product of the revolution in lifestyles and politics spreading out from California. For the authors of both books the choice of diet is a highly politicized act, one that has the potential fundamentally to improve the world's resources and the health of individuals. There was a tendency to look to the foods and practices of non-industrialized nations, a move to simplify our food to staples, a reaction against excess and plenty. In this vein Huguette Couffignal's *The People's Cookbook* (1977) (*La Cuisine des Pauvres*, in its original French) collected the foods of the world's poor – locust dishes from North Africa, Eskimo specialities such as seal liver and decomposed auks, guinea pig roasted in a hot tomato and pepper sauce in South America.

While most cook books did not go this far, many in the 1970s expressed a desire to get off the treadmill, to reject the rampant consumerism of the post-war period. Wild food, untainted and, furthermore, free seemed very attractive. A major influence was Richard Mabey's *Food for Free: A Guide to the Edible Wild Plants of Britain* (1972). Poised somewhere between a tract and a field guide, the book encouraged the consumption of puffballs, ground elder, lichens and seaweed, and led to a cult of mushroom gathering and sloe-gin making. Another impetus behind the self-sufficiency movement was recession: high inflation and unemployment in the 1970s left many living on a shoestring. One cook book that promised to meet their needs was Jocasta Innes's *The Pauper's Cookbook* (1971), which told you 'how to live it up in your own squalid tenement without recourse to poaching, rustling, guddling, scrumping or shop-lifting'. Her thrifty ways with cheap ingredients avoid convenience foods but include lots of vegetable- and egg-based dishes, meats like tongue and rabbit, and some advice on the gathering and use of wild food – dandelion salad, sloe jelly, cowslip pancakes called paigle fry, and fried limpets stand out.

By the end of the 1970s vegetarianism was losing its cranky image, and vegetarian cook books were more and more catering to a mainstream audience. Books like *The Home Book of Vegetarian Cooking* by N. B. and R. B. Highton, published by Faber & Faber in 1964, and Patty Fisher's *Vegetarian Cookery*, published by Hamlyn in 1969 as part of their very populist 500 Recipes series, are significant not for their content but because they indicate the extent to which vegetarianism was becoming accepted: publishers now needed vegetarian books in their cookery lists. The first really inspirational vegetarian cook book was published in 1967, the work of a twenty-two-year-old called Rose Elliot, who had left school at sixteen to start cooking at the retreat centre run by her parents in Sussex. *Simply Delicious* received rave reviews on *Woman's Hour* and from Katie Stewart in *The Times*, and Elliot was launched on her path to become the most successful of British vegetarian food writers. She followed it with the memorably titled *Not Just a Load of Old Lentils* (1972) and *The Bean Book* (1979). What distinguished her approach from what Derek Cooper has called the Marxist–lentillist school was that she was less preoccupied with cutting out items from the diet than with providing a balance in what was eaten.[53] Cream, sugar and butter were not outlawed, and she saw no reason why vegetarianism should equate with puritanism. Other writers agreed: as the foods of the Mediterranean, the Middle and the Far East became more familiar, people realized that many ancient and sophisticated cuisines contained little or no meat. New horizons beckoned beyond the homity pie and nut roast, and vegetarianism poised on the brink of fashion.

The foods of the Middle East that gave such a fillip to the vegetarian repertoire also had a much wider appeal. Their chief popularizer was Claudia Roden, another of the second generation of scholar cooks, who in 1968 published *A Book of Middle Eastern Food*.[54] Exiled from her native Egypt (her family were Sephardic Jews, among the many banished by Nasser in 1956), she recalled with great affection the traditional dishes of the region. She was inspired to set about collecting them in an organized manner by a single sentence in Elizabeth David's *Book of Mediterranean Food*, in which 'she intimated that there were many more dishes in the Near East which needed to be discovered: that was the spark that fired me'.[55] Roden's first book resembles David's own in having a scholarly bent but not developing it in a systematic manner. It embraces the foods of Egypt, Turkey, Syria, Israel, Lebanon, Greece, Iran, Iraq, Saudi Arabia, the Yemen, Tunisia, Algeria, Morocco and the Sudan, the cooking of which, she states, 'is inextricably linked'.[56] Her purpose is not to deal in an entirely comprehensive way with the cooking of these various countries and its myriad points of connection but to 'make a complete and comprehensible picture of what was originally my "family's food"'.[57] For her exiled and widely dispersed family, food became a way of holding on to their memories and their sense of identity: when family members got together, 'after asking how everybody was in the different countries and hearing all the gossip, people would start saying "I found this recipe", and recipes came to seem almost the most important thing we had lost'.[58] Her book is the virtually palpable record of the pain of a community cut off from its past, writing and rewriting its cultural self in the dishes it cooked. It is also an act of rescue, recording for posterity the essentially oral culinary traditions of her extended family of Egyptian – once Syrian – Jews.

Middle Eastern food, as Roden demonstrates, is 'elaborate but easy . . . every vegetable is stuffed, everything is wrapped up in leaves and there is a long slow cooking – in those societies where women did not work, they spent a lot of time cooking together and enjoying the company – but there are also many simple, quick and easy things and there aren't the French sauces or the trickiness of a soufflé. You can't fail.'[59] Roden's main scholarly impulse is anthropological rather than historical – she collects variations, but does not often attempt to track them down to their origins – an immensely challenging task when dealing with the multiple diasporas and cultural exchanges of the region. The main sense of cultural 'atmosphere' is provided by the little stories, poems and proverbs with which the recipes are interspersed.

The book captured the public imagination and had a strong influence on popular eating habits. As she noted sixteen years later:

> The smoke of roasting lamb wafts into the streets of London and many a suburban kitchen is filled with the smells of Cairo, Fez and Baghdad. Health food shops and delicatessens sell burghul, halva, tahina and couscous, while packets of pitta bread quickly disappear from supermarket shelves.[60]

Though the spread of Turkish restaurants was partly responsible, Roden's work played a considerable role in popularizing the foods of the Middle East in Britain.[61]

If modern British familiarity with the foods of the Middle East is largely attributable to a book, the case was very different with the two foreign cuisines that most firmly established themselves in our consciousness in this period. For both Indian and Chinese food the main agent of assimilation was not cook books but restaurants. There had been Chinese restaurants in this country for many years, particularly in the areas around the docks in Liverpool, Limehouse and Cardiff, where generations of Chinese seamen had jumped ship, but the boom began in the mid-1950s, with the immigration of large numbers from Hong Kong and the New Territories. Chinese restaurants multiplied rapidly until the early 1970s, when harsher immigration laws and the introduction of VAT slowed their growth and led to many restaurants being transformed into fish-and-chip shops or takeaways. By 1970 there were 4,000 Chinese catering establishments (compared with 2,000 Indian food businesses and about 500 French). Research conducted five years earlier found that of the British public who regularly ate out, 31 per cent had eaten Chinese food.[62] Indian restaurants, though not as widely dispersed around the country, were equally successful. They were mainly run by Bangladeshis: in fact, remarkably, until the 1990s, almost all the owners of Indian restaurants in this country were family and neighbours from one small area, Sylhet, in the north of the country, where traditionally 'whole villages once monopolised cooking and galley work in the British Merchant Navy'.[63]

The food served in both Chinese and Indian restaurants was very standardized until the 1970s. Chinese food was based on the styles of Canton, Hong Kong and Shanghai (finely chopped vegetables, fish and pork, stir-fried or rapidly steamed, and served with rice or noodles), though in the 1970s this was supplemented with Pekinese cooking from the north of China with its wheat-based menus (dim sum dumplings, steamed buns, pancakes as wrappers, crispy fried duck). In Indian restaurants, a mode of cooking was developed that bore no relationship to traditional culinary practices: 'batch' cooking kept prices low and created an impression of variety, as a basic recipe could be transformed into a wide range of different dishes by adding flavourings at the last minute. Conventional names, largely unrelated to the origin of the dishes, were used as codes to the British customer: dhansak was sweet, korma was creamy, madras was 'hotter than it ever was in India' and 'the notorious vindaloo, a macho challenge to a generation of lager louts, was laced with up to twenty times as much chilli powder as was customary even in Goa, where it originated as a dish made from wine (vin) and garlic (aieul)'.[64] In the late 1960s some enterprising establishments began to produce more authentic food: they imported clay tandoor ovens to cook Punjabi tandoori recipes – mild, marinated meat seared on skewers in a very hot oven, which is eaten as street food in Pakistan. The success of Indian restaurants in the 1960s and 1970s was very largely the result of their appeal to a generation of young people living away from home for the first time: students benefiting from the massive expansion of the universities in the late 1960s, and the bedsit dwellers in the big cities. Prices were cheap, the food was excitingly exotic (but cunningly adapted to British palates), and perhaps most crucially, the restaurants were open long after other establishments had shut their doors.

Cook books lagged well behind the oriental restaurant explosion: the best-known Indian cook book of the 1960s was E. P. Veerasawmy's *Indian Cookery* (1963), which harks back to the sort of Anglo-Indian food recorded by Colonel Kenney-Herbert in his 1878 *Culinary Jottings for Madras*. Mulligatawny, Kedgeree and Bombay

Duck all find a place in *Indian Cookery*, which makes repeated concessions to the tastes of the Anglo-Indians and Europeans in India. Veerasawmy does, however, seek to correct some western misapprehensions about Indian food, and he supplies dishes with their regional identity and some history – 'Madras is famous for its Vuddays which are seldom made at home. They are made in the Bazaars and hawked round the town just as Muffins and Crumpets were in England.'[65] Despite its very partial and somewhat confused picture of the cooking of the Indian subcontinent, it is interesting to note the large number of editions the book ran into (seven in paperback just between 1972 and 1979) and the fact that it is still in print today.

In 1976 both the Indian-restaurant and memories-of-the-Raj styles of Indian cooking were fundamentally challenged by the first book of a well-known Indian actress. The book seems to have come about by accident: the *New York Times* published a feature on Madhur Jaffrey to publicize her new film, *Shakespeare Wallah*, describing her as the actress who loved to cook. Since Indian food was relatively unknown in America, a publisher approached her to put together a collection of recipes, and the book was published in New York in 1973. When it appeared three years later in Britain it was a phenomenal success. Pulling no punches, Jaffrey condemned the travesties of real Indian food served in many of the new restaurants in Britain:

> Upon visiting the restaurants, I found most of them to be second-class establishments that had managed to underplay their own regional uniqueness as well as to underestimate the curiosity and palate of contemporary Britons. Instead of specializing in foods from particular states or districts, they served a generalized Indian food from no area whatsoever; a restaurant calling itself 'Delhi' had no *karhi*, that thick soupy dish with its bobbing flotilla of gram flour dumplings; another, advertising food from the Punjab, was minus those delicious Punjabi mainstays corn bread and mustard greens; at another called 'Bombay', where were the spongy cakelike *dhhoklas* or those delicious sweet breads called *puran-poli*? And at all those new Bangalee restaurants I saw no roe fritters, or fish smothered with crushed mustard seeds and cooked gently in mustard oil or *bhapa doi*, that creamy, steamed yogurt.[66]

Having whetted the curiosity and appetites of her readers, Jaffrey offers a brief sketch of the practices, flavour combinations and techniques of Indian cooking, rooted in her own personal history. She was born in Delhi, a city where there is a heady mix of cultural and culinary traditions: the Muslim Persian and Arabic tastes adopted by the great Moghul emperors, and the Hindu vegetarian tradition that long pre-dated their arrival. In her potted history Jaffrey accounts for the intertwining of these cultures into what she calls 'Delhi cuisine':

India has a way of influencing, if not overpowering, everything it comes in contact with. Very soon the mighty Moghuls were chewing the betel leaf, crying in ecstasy over the mango, adding more spices to their Persian meats, and relishing the vegetarian dishes prepared for them by their Hindu wives and mistresses.'[67]

Her own family was the product of this mixed tradition: the men, who could trace their service as courtiers in the Moghul courts back to the fifteenth and sixteenth centuries, learned Persian, spoke Urdu and ate meat. On her mother's side of the family, though, while the men spoke Persian and Arabic, the women kept alive the Hindu traditions of the *Ramagana* and the *Mahabharata*, and the family diet was mostly vegetarian.[68] In an *Invitation to Indian Cooking* Jaffrey concentrates on the food of Delhi and the adjacent sections of Uttar Pradesh, grounding her culinary account, much like Claudia Roden, in 'the smells and tastes which *I* grew up with as a child'.[69] Coming from a fairly wealthy family, Jaffrey had not learned to cook as a child (there were servants to do that, including one, the *masalchi*, whose sole task it was to grind on a heavy stone the unique combination of spices required for each dish), and it was only when homesick at drama college in the Britain of the late 1950s that she began to cook, guided by airmail letters of instruction from her mother back in India. Her style as a food writer is relaxed, friendly and reassuring. Jane Grigson referred to her as 'the Elizabeth David of India', but actually her writing more resembles that of Grigson herself. Issues of history, regionality and tradition are dealt with lightly, and a healthy balance is struck between the desire for authenticity and the need to create usable recipes. She rails against curry powder, declaring that no Indian cooks use it: 'If "curry" is an oversimplified name for an ancient cuisine, then "curry powder" attempts to oversimplify (and destroy) the cuisine itself'.[70] But she willingly provides substitutes for hard-to-obtain ingredients: using cod instead of freshwater *rahu*, and advising on how to make English lamb taste like Indian 'mutton' – actually goat.

The food to which Jaffrey introduced her British readers is a world away from fiery vindaloos and mass-produced biryanis. Even the list of ingredients is exciting: smelly asafetida resin (break chips from a lump with a hammer, she advises), fresh kari leaves (possibly the source from which misguided Europeans derived the word curry), tart tamarind paste, and vark – the whisper-thin sheets of real silver with which Indian banquet food is gilded. We are advised how to grind our own garam masala, how to test the strength of chillis and what to do with coriander leaves (Jaffrey was responsible for a Delia-like rush on the latter when she used them in the 1978 television series based on the book). Recipes include Whole Pea Pods with Cumin, Aloo-Ki-Tikiya (potato patties as sold from street-barrows), many kebabs and barbecued dishes, and many recipes for simple dhals and breads. She also gives instructions for a number of those dishes popularized by restaurants – biryani, Tandoori chicken – as they would be prepared in India. Although she is eager to correct western misapprehensions about Indian food, she is no purist. She expresses some suspicion of the new fashion for culinary authenticity, the idea that certain dishes should be kept 'pure': 'The most exciting thing for me is the intellectual exercise of linking foods. The first thing you learn, as you travel, is that nothing is authentic. People are absorbing recipes from each other at such a fast rate, and that has always been the case.'[71]

What Jaffrey did for Indian food, Kenneth Lo did for Chinese. His *Chinese Food*, which was published in 1972, came about as a result of a chance meeting at a party with the assistant food editor at Penguin. Lo had already written a number of books on particular aspects of Chinese cooking, but it was this book that began to transform British attitudes to the eating and cooking of Chinese food. Lo was a talented and energetic figure, very well placed to act as ambassador for his native food. He had spent his childhood moving back and forth between China and London, where his father was Chinese consul. Lo had a degree in physics from Yenching University in Peking and one in English literature from Cambridge. He worked variously as a diplomat, a fine-art publisher, a journalist, a lecturer and a professional tennis player before turning to food writing. He had been involved in the Chinese food community in Britain since its inception: before the Second World War, in his capacity as a welfare and industrial relations officer attached to the Chinese Consulate in Liverpool, he had organized restaurants for the many disabled Chinese seamen. In the 1950s, with this experience behind him, he helped many friends to set up catering businesses in London. He inspected Chinese restaurants for the *Good Food Guide* for several years in the 1960s before becoming their Chinese consultant. He was one of the founders of the Chinese Gourmet Club of London, which assisted its members in finding the best restaurants and to choose the best dishes when they had found them. It is interesting to note that Penguin marketed *Chinese Food* as mainly a guide to the food you will find in restaurants and only secondarily as a recipe book:

> Most patrons of Chinese restaurants, one suspects, have to be content with 'Meal A (for two persons)' . . . and usually are, even when they're three. Largely to help them go *à la carte* (or to cook Chinese at home) this handbook has been prepared by a well-known expert on Chinese food.[72]

There had been previous respected guides to Chinese cooking, notably Frank Oliver's 1955 book *Chinese Cooking*, but they were invariably written not by Chinese but by Europeans who had spent time in China.[73] Kenneth Lo introduces his British readers to Chinese cookery from first principles, outlining the basic cooking techniques – including stir-frying, red-cooking (meat or fish pre-fried and then simmered in a stock with soy sauces and herbs), clear-simmering, steaming, deep-frying, dry-frying, crystal-boiling (heating food in water until it boils, then finishing the cooking only in the retained heat) and hot-plunging (plunging morsels of fish or meat briefly into boiling stock). The latter method is typified by the Mongolian hot-pot, where guests cook their own pieces of lamb at the table in a broth kept warm over a charcoal burner and end by drinking the now richly flavoured broth. Lo brings alive the foods of his native land, investing them with magic and fascination: 'Yellow River Carp is a famous dish which is brought to the table audibly crackling from the contact of sweet and sour sauce poured over the sizzling hot, deep-fried fish'; 'translated literally wuntun means swallowing a cloud; indeed, well made wuntuns floating in clear soup resemble clouds'.[74] The names alone are wonderful: crispy meatballs are called Lion's Heads, while a dish of chicken and scallops fried with wine sediment paste is known as Fried Dragon and Phoenix (the seafood represents the dragon, the chicken the phoenix).

The main body of the book is divided into two sections: Chinese Food Abroad, which accounts for the sort of food served in the majority of Chinese restaurants (stir-fried for speed of cooking, relatively unvaried and unadventurous so as not to provoke anxiety in the neophyte customer), and Chinese Cooking in China, which provides recipes grouped in menus according to the four main geographical divisions of China and by the seasons. Lo is not as critical as Jaffrey is of the food served in restaurants in Britain, partly because of his connections with the trade, but also because he finds them to be producing food that is simplified and rather bland but not travesties of the original Chinese dishes. This must be to do with the fact that stir-frying and steaming allow them to produce fresh food on demand: Chinese restaurateurs did not need, unlike Indian ones, to resort to inauthentic methods to produce food that is cheap and quickly available. Of the usual dishes found in Chinese restaurants abroad he remarks that they 'do not deserve the disdain and distaste with which [they] are sometimes regarded by would-be connoisseurs. Only a few are without pedigree, and although they have all suffered a slight sea change, they are still recognizable, and, if properly prepared, wholesome and tasty; they can still make a hungry mouth water'.[75] For Chinese food abroad to become more adventurous, he states, the customer needs educating. But 'Chinese chefs and restaurateurs are not in the West to educate, they are here to make a living', so Lo takes on the role himself.[76] His purpose in the restaurant chapter is to steer the reader towards combinations of dishes that will broaden their minds and educate their palates. When he turns to Chinese food as it is cooked in its native land there is an immediate sensation of broadening horizons, as the western reader realizes what he has been missing:

> What connoisseurs miss most [when away from China] are the tip-out meat puddings, earthen-pot Chinese casseroles, long-simmered red-cooked dishes and steamed multiphase-seasoned poultry, which are all typical and characteristic of a good Chinese meal: or the jellied or drunken or smoked meats, and the exquisitely marinated thin-sliced vegetables, which are by no means only great banquet dishes.[77]

In autumn on the East River (in the south of the country) one might eat Carp Wrapped in Lotus Leaf, Liver and Kidney Buried in Salt, and Eight Treasures Chicken; in Peking in the winter Fried Pig's Liver with Tree-Fungi, and Kao Li Frosted Bean Paste Balls (sweetened bean paste meringue balls).

Although the book opened up a window on a cuisine and a country shrouded in mystery (particularly since the Revolution), most readers probably didn't venture very far into the exotic reaches of authentic Chinese cooking: my second-hand copy of the book is pristine, except for a few grains of ossified rice that fell from the page with the fried rice recipe. As much of the fascination for his first readers must have been due to the light he sheds on the many mysteries of the Chinatown on their doorsteps and its inhabitants. So we learn that the shiny lacquered ducks hanging in the windows of Chinese shops and restaurants are not Peking Duck, as many of us assume, but Cantonese Roast Duck (which is roasted upright because it is filled with liquid, and then glazed with honey, soy sauce and vinegar or water); that Spring Rolls are so called because the fresh vegetables that should make up their filling are usually only available in that brief season; and that the classic Chinese breakfast is Thousand-Year-Old Eggs (really just pickled eggs), Meat Wool (dehydrated meat stir-fried) and congee (a rice gruel) – a collation that sounds fantastically exotic to British ears, but is actually very little different to our own meal of eggs, bacon and porridge.

The other cuisine to have a major influence on Britain in the 1960s and 1970s was, as in previous decades, that of America. But America had its own food revolution in the 1960s, and the serious food writers it was now exporting were no longer interested in down-home American dishes but in mastering the foods of other nations. That domination rather than discipleship was the cultural imperative seems to be indicated by the title of the first work by the woman who was to become one of America's most fêted culinary stars.[78] *Mastering the Art of French Cooking* by Julia Child and her co-authors Simone Beck and Louisette Bertolle first appeared in America in 1961 and was published in this country two years later. The three had founded a cookery school, L'École des Trois Gourmandes, in Paris in 1951, and the book draws on this experience to provide immensely detailed instructions for the core principles of French cooking (the basic soufflé recipe takes eight pages, with diagrams). Although the book is nearly 800 pages long in paperback, the authors found they were forced to omit many things they considered essential, particularly patisseries and elaborate breads, so a second volume followed, with recipes for tarts, French bread (twelve pages long, this one), croissants and brioche. More than the book, it was Mrs Child's television cookery show, *The French Chef*, that turned her into a household name and kick-started the food revolution in America. Six feet tall, middle-aged, hefty and physically clumsy, Julia Child was far from being a natural television star, but in fact it was precisely these qualities that so endeared her to her audience:

At first some viewers assumed that Julia, as she would soon fondly be known, was parodying the traditional cooking show. But even when they realised the show was entirely serious, viewers watched her shenanigans with enthusiasm. Mrs Child huffed, puffed, and galumphed across the screen, her high-pitched voice cracking like an adolescent schoolboy's, and she was famous for dropping things and demonstrating cuts of meat using her own body. All of this enchanted viewers and assured them that if this seemingly average American woman could cook French food, then so could they.[79]

Comic though she seemed, Child was responsible for introducing authentic French food into the average American kitchen, and if in practice some of her techniques were a bit unorthodox, her written instructions were sound and largely obedient to the French culinary authorities. (Elizabeth David, always a stickler where other food writers were concerned, described volume one of *Mastering the Art of French Cooking* as 'a very remarkable work indeed', going on to remark that 'the techniques explained, and more authentically and fully explained than in any previous cookery book in the English language, are applicable to all French cooking of whatever category'.[80]) Child's books sold pretty well in this country – the Penguin edition of her first book had gone into eight editions by the mid-1970s – but her television show was a flop, with the British public 'complain[ing] about that "mad, drunken American woman" on their television screens'.[81]

Other fêted American culinary stars were to translate much less well to Britain. Though her books are widely available in this country, even the marvellous M. F. K. Fisher has remained very much a minority taste. This seems to me a great shame, since Fisher at her best transforms food writing into a form of prose poetry, full of anecdotes and evocations, with tantalizing hints about her rather chaotic love life and a highly philosophical sense of food as central to a well-lived life. I can't resist just one example – this is Fisher on Cauliflower Cheese, turning the prosaic into profundity:

There in Dijon, the cauliflowers were small and very succulent, grown in that ancient soil. I separated the flowerets and dropped them in boiling water for just a few minutes. Then I drained them and put them in a wide shallow casserole, and covered them with heavy cream and a thick sprinkling of freshly grated Gruyère, the nice rubbery kind that didn't come from Switzerland at all, but from the Jura. It was called *râpé* in the market, and was grated while you watched, in a soft cloudy pile, onto your piece of paper.

I put some fresh pepper over the top, and in a way I can't remember now the little tin oven heated the whole thing and melted the cheese and browned it. As soon as that happened we ate it.

The cream and cheese had come together into a perfect sauce, and the little flowerets were tender and fresh. We cleaned our plates with bits of crispy bread crust and drank the wine, and Al and Lawrence planned to write books about Aristotle and Robinson Jeffers and probably themselves, and I planned a few things too.

As I say, once back in California, after so many of those casseroles, I found I could never make one. The vegetable was watery, and there was no cream thick enough or unpasteurized and fresh. The cheese was dry and oily, not soft and light. I had to make a sauce with flour in it. I could concoct a good dish, still . . . but it was never so *innocent*, so simple . . . and then where was the crisp bread, where the honest wine? And where were our young uncomplicated hungers, too?[82]

But now we move from the sublime to the ridiculous, because our other major culinary import from America in these decades was the culture of convenience foods. These foods had become a significant part of the British food scene in the years immediately following the war:

When the terror, the flames and the bomb smoke had cleared, when the lights had gone up on London and the food controls were lifted early in the 1950s, a strange phenomenon was to be seen. Under cover of the black-out, science had reached in and made off with the seasons. The shops were filled, no matter whether it was spring, summer, autumn or winter, with the same millions of canned, frozen and dehydrated vegetables, soups, meats and ice-creams.[83]

By the 1960s they were an accepted part of life for most people, embraced with an enthusiasm that may seem strange to us now. Many food writers catering for the 'quick, cheap and easy' market leapt on these ingredients with alacrity, relying on cans for their main ingredients, turning soup mixes into sauces, substituting dehydrated onion flakes for the real thing and never serving a fresh vegetable if a frozen one would do. Their chief constituency was single people catering for themselves and busy women despairing at producing yet another meal for their families. There is an easy acceptance in these decades that convenience foods are the perfect diet for children; in fact, Erin Pizzey in her *Slut's Cook Book* (published in 1981, but very much of a piece with the convenience-culture books of the previous decades) sternly insists on the *superiority* of such foods for children:

Don't force your children to eat your carefully prepared home-made stews when what they really want is fish fingers and beans (which are just as nutritious anyway) . . . Remember that kids get addicted to hamburgers for years of their lives. They don't like them home-made; they like them from the take-away, so don't whine – get them a take-away when you can afford it.[84]

One of the earliest and most influential books to concern itself with the use of convenience foods was Katharine Whitehorn's *Kitchen in the Corner* of 1961, which was republished by Penguin two years later in its better known guise of *Cooking in a Bedsitter*. Its author was a young journalist, and though she had written nothing on food before and little since, the book earned her a considerable reputation. The daughter of a schoolmaster, Whitehorn spent two years at Roedean (from which she ran away) and read English at Cambridge. After university she worked as a publisher's reader in London for two years, teaching English to foreigners in the evenings and living in a bedsitter. She then spent a year in Finland and another in America, where she lived in a shared postgraduate hostel. The book that emerged from these experiences spoke of a way of life that was commonplace to many young men and women of her generation but absolutely alien to their parents. In the past students and those in the big city for their first jobs would have tended to live in lodgings, where the landlady provided (usually dreadful) meals and the issue of cooking for oneself simply did not arise. Whitehorn's was the first generation to enjoy the independence of the bedsitter, free to cook what they liked and to entertain friends and romantic prospects in their rooms. Her humorous approach to the practical difficulties of catering for oneself on a gas ring won her a large readership – this was clearly the work of someone who had been there:

> Cooking a decent meal in a bedsitter is not just a matter of finding something that can be cooked over a single gas ring. It is a problem of finding somewhere to put down the fork while you take the lid off the saucepan, and then finding somewhere else to put the lid. It is finding a place to keep the butter where it will not get mixed up with your razor or your hairpins. It is having your hands covered with flour, and a pot boiling over on to your landlady's carpet, and no water to mop up any of it nearer than the bathroom at the other end of the landing. It is cooking at floor level, in a hurry, with nowhere to put the salad but the washing-up bowl, which in any case is full of socks.[85]

She manages to invest the whole rather sordid experience with a rakish bohemian charm. Furthermore, she writes as someone who clearly loves food and has a certain skill in handling it. She relies, like all convenience cooks, on tins and packets and frozen foods (she is particularly devoted to packet mashed potato and recommends frozen fish as preferable to fresh – less mess, and you simply defrost it by holding it under the cold tap), but she also suggests home-made mayonnaise, zabaglione and gnocchi. A number of her contrivances produce very good food (I should know – I cooked out of the book for a year on an electric ring illegally smuggled into my not-very-fireproof fourteenth-century college room). Frying Pan Pizza, Shrimp Wriggle and La Truffado (potatoes sautéed with melted cheese) are fine dishes, quick and easy but free of any taint of the ersatz. Many of her recipes derive from other cook books, but it is writers like Elizabeth David and Mrs Leyel who are her inspiration. The epilogue to her book is the account of a man who 'has wholly solved the problem of eating well in a bedsitter': he has mushrooms growing in his wardrobe, a vanilla bean on the bookcase and 'curd cheese draining into a small shaving bowl through a sock'.[86] Asked how he managed to eat so well in a bedsitter, he indignantly retorts that it is not a bedsitter – he is sleeping in the kitchen. One gets the distinct impression that Whitehorn would like her readers to emulate him.

Much more wholeheartedly devoted to the culture of convenience foods was a book published ten years later: *How to Cheat at Cooking* (1971) was the first work of a food journalist who had gained some reputation in middle England as a result of her recipe column in the *Daily Mirror* magazine. Delia Smith was thirty-three when the book was first published, recently married to Michael Wynn Jones, the deputy editor of the magazine. From its first sentence her book made it very clear who its audience was *not*: 'If you're one of those dedicated cooks who's a keen early-morning mushroom gatherer and wouldn't dream of concocting a salad without using the "just-picked" variety, then this book is not for you.' There is none of the care for method and ingredients that Delia was to develop later in her career: this book was about cheating with convenience foods and 'at the same time convinc[ing] everyone that they're strictly *homemade*'.[87] She begins with a Cheat's Charter: '1. There are more important things in life than cooking . . . 2. If something tastes good, it is good . . . 4. Never do for yourself what you can get someone else to do for you . . . 5. Exploit your supermarket' and so on.[88] The book attempts a witty insouciance, but in fact tries much too hard. It is uneasily poised between the casual and the anxiously snobbish, recommending for entertaining dishes like fish fingers baked with tinned tomatoes and tinned mushrooms, and banana instant whip with crumbled digestives, but insisting that the reader serves packet soup from a soup tureen and recommending that she bedeck her kitchen with 'serious-looking accoutrements' to create the appearance of culinary skills. The book is very manifestly the product of someone who has recently married 'up' and is anxious to expunge her lowly origins. The 'cheating' in which she gaily invites her readers to join often seems to be as much about disguising one's social background as one's lack of cooking ability. At times the gaucherie is almost painful, as in the naively affected remarks on drinks before dinner: 'Vermouth is a pretty safe bet. I'd be surprised if at least one guest didn't ask "what is it?" so choose an example that will give you a chance to drop the name of your wine-merchant (don't say off-licence).'[89] Cheese too can find the housewife poised on a knife edge between social success and disaster: 'Guests can be easily impressed and intrigued by your unusual selection of cheese (experiment yourself with the stock of your usual delicatessen, but make certain you get to know the history of the ones you like because you're certain to be asked).'[90] Not all the recipes are bad and not all rely on convenience foods, but there is a tendency to introduce them even when they serve no purpose and to insist on cheating for cheating's sake: on the subject of starters she observes that 'luckily there are now plenty . . . that can be bought and served with no effort at all. These are all fine up to a point, but you can't fool anyone with them. I mean, people just don't smoke salmon nowadays.'[91]

The rise and rise of the convenience culture did not go unresisted. Elizabeth David devoted a significant proportion of her journalism to castigating and humiliating the manufacturers of processed foods, whose PR companies continued despite this to send her their products. In a piece called 'Lucky Dip', published in the *Spectator* on 29 June 1962, she is in typically acerbic vein:

> The fact is that the emergency in which I find myself obliged to offer a tin of say Walls' Chicken and Veal Pie to that nomadic and marauding tribe known to every reader of magazine cookery as Unexpected Guests, although a recurring dream of mine, is one that has never yet actually come about; and I am thankful for it, because in my dream I can see that these people are beginning to turn ugly as soon as they see me reaching for the tin-opener . . . True, I did once offer the filling of one of these pies (chicken, veal, flour, edible fats, seasoning, milk powder, flavouring, phosphate. Preheat oven to a hot condition. Remove lid of can) to my cat, and whether it was the chicken and veal or the flavouring or the phosphate, or was it just that I hadn't got the oven to the sufficiently hot condition, she took to it no more than she did to that pair of frankfurters which arrived in the post one early morning after they'd spent a long weekend at the offices of the magazine for which I was then writing, and were thoughtfully packed with a tube of mustard. Come to think of it, it was the mustard they were pushing, not the sausages.[92]

Furious, the manufacturers of the pie complained to the editor of the magazine, who passed the letter on to Elizabeth, remarking, 'if their pies are anything like their ice cream I'd shoot the lot of them'. Artemis Cooper quotes the letter she drafted, with evident enjoyment, to the manufacturers:

> The Editor of the *Spectator* tells me that your board takes serious exception to my cat's reported attitude to a . . . pie. Of course, my cat was serious too, but in recording her lack of enthusiasm I did not intend to imply, nor do I think would any intelligent *Spectator* reader infer, that the pie in question would have been rejected by a human being – or indeed, by all other cats. Standards differ . . .
>
> The Editor also tells me that you have been so kind as to invite me to see over the factory. I have already had this pleasure. I found the experience most instructive and impressions are still vivid in my mind, so I will not put your directors to all the trouble again.[93]

She was impatient with the idea that convenience foods served a social purpose for busy women: in the privileged position of being able to work from home within arm's reach of her cooker she seemed not to be able to envisage the very different situation in which most working women found themselves. (When Derek Cooper interviewed her for the *Food Programme* on Radio 4 he asked, when discussing the time it took to make bread, 'What about women who work all day?': her response was a brusque 'That's their problem.'[94]) Yet even Elizabeth David did not reject all packaged and processed foods, remarking in another essay that her basic stores always include tinned tomatoes, and elsewhere speaking well of tinned vine leaves, sardines and tuna (or 'tunny fish', as she calls it).[95] It is no accident that these are precisely the products that even the most precious foodie would today feel happy about having in his cupboard – though he might well indulge in little snobberies about the particular brands. This is in part a function of David's pervasive influence and partly the result of our massive inferiority complex about British foods – these products are acceptable because they are not produced here. The younger generation of 'serious' food writers tended to be somewhat more relaxed about convenience foods, particularly the frozen variety. Jane Grigson embraced the variety offered by frozen foods, seeing it as an affectation to reject the plenty provided by technology: 'I reflect that we have been trying to beat winter starvation for centuries and centuries. I think we should be grateful, not guilty, when we buy frozen peas – particularly in December – reflecting that a hundred years ago one subsisted for six or seven months of the year on root and dried vegetables.'[96]

If Elizabeth David was not able to see the implications of convenience foods for women's lives, many other writers were: throughout the 1960s and 1970s there was a concerted attempt by both food writers and manufacturers to offer these foods as a route to women's liberation. One of the earliest books to link women's social role to convenience cooking was Peg Bracken's amusingly skittish *I Hate to Cook Book*, first published in her native America in 1960 and here a year later. Its assumed reader is a giddy young housewife, modern enough to be bored with domestic tasks but nevertheless condemned to perform them: 'This book is for those of us who hate to [cook], who have learned, through hard experience, that some activities become no less painful through repetition: childbearing, paying taxes, cooking.' With recipes like Stayabed Stew ('This is for those days when you're *en negligée, en* bed, with a murder story and a box of chocolates, or possibly a good case of flu'), Hushkabobs ('so called because the family isn't supposed to know it's just that old Sunday roast still following them around') and an ersatz Chinese dish of noodles and pork called Gung Ho, it is an unrelentingly lively read.[97] But beneath the frothy surface run darker currents. There is, for instance, the suspicion of other women: Good Cooks Who Like to Cook are required to 'stay away from our husbands', and the menus for Luncheon for the Girls can all be made in advance so that you can stay in the living room with your friends – 'after all, if they're your best friends you want to be with them; and if they're your second-best friends, you don't dare not'.[98] The book's tone and illustrations are jaunty, but the language it employs in relation to its apparently frivolous subject is extreme:

> Never doubt it, there's a long, long trail a-winding, when you hate to cook. And never compute the number of meals you have to cook and set before the shining little faces of your loved ones in the course of a lifetime. This only staggers the imagination and raises the blood pressure. The way to face the future is to take it as Alcoholics Anonymous does: one day at a time.[99]

Underlying the jollity is a whiff of desperation, of Valium and secret martinis. The product of that immediately pre-feminist moment of the 1960s, Bracken's book spoke to the Sylvia Plath generation, those whose confusions Betty Friedan was to outline three years later in *The Feminine Mystique*. It was a generation of women – particularly in America, but also in Britain – marked by a pervasive sense of discontent with the gender roles established for them in the 1950s, but without the political analysis that would enable them to formulate a response. So Bracken's solution to the fact that many women hate to cook is not to question whether they should have to do so but to suggest ways in which they can lie and cheat and get other women to do it for them:

POTLUCK SUPPERS
OR HOW TO BRING THE WATER FOR THE LEMONADE

Do you see that shaft of sunny sunshine cutting across the kitchen murk? This, friends, is the Potluck Supper – quite the best invention since the restaurant . . . Think of the advantages here! First, you need to cook only one thing. Second, having cooked and brought your one thing, you don't actually owe anyone a dinner, and you needn't invite them to your house unless you feel like it . . .

First, however, a word of advice on how to handle yourself when a Potluck is being planned. *Beware of the entrée*. The entrée is usually the most trouble as well as the most expensive. So never volunteer for it. Instead, volunteer someone else. 'Ethel, *would* you make that marvellous goulash of yours?' you can say. The other ladies will probably join in – it would be rude not to, especially if they've ever tasted Ethel's goulash – and while Ethel is modestly dusting her manicure on her lapel, you can murmur something about bringing a couple of your delectable

LEFT BANK FRENCH LOAVES

2 loaves French bread
8 oz butter
1 packet onion-soup mix

You split the loaves in half, the long way. Then cream the onion-soup mix and butter together. Spread this on the cut side of the two bottom halves, put the tops back on, wrap the loaves in aluminium foil, and throw them in the back seat of the car. When you get to the party, you can ask your hostess nicely to put them in a 350° oven for twenty minutes. Open the foil a bit to keep them crisp.[100]

In direct contrast is another book, published fifteen years later, the product of a world changed by the feminist movement of the 1970s. When Shirley Conran, in her 1975 book *Superwoman*, tells women to cut down on the time and energy they spend on domestic tasks her tone is not giggly and sly but direct and assertive. 'Life's too short to stuff a mushroom,' she famously declared. Like many other British food writers in the 1970s she is particularly enamoured of the freezer, advising the keeping of a freezer book with contents diligently listed and ticked off, and batch cooking to fill it up. There are tips for prettying-up store cupboard foods – 'The principle is simple: use available fresh windowdressing to disguise the unappetizing look, feel or taste of stored foods' – and a fourteen-day plan of meals so that the jaded cook doesn't have to *think* about food.[101] But like Germaine Greer's *The Female Eunuch* (1970), the book is shocking to a reader thirty-odd years on not because of its radicalism but because of those elements of the status quo it takes for granted.[102] Conran's meant-to-be-encouraging suggestions of how to pare your weekly cleaning down to a bare minimum looks to us today like a major spring clean (on a Monday morning one is supposed to defrost the fridge, scrub out the dustbins and clean the oven, as well as cleaning the kitchen in general and doing household paperwork), and she talks wistfully of that fabulous beast 'the husband who doesn't mind the occasional snack meal in a crisis – or even cooks it'.[103] In fact, as Carole Wright, the author of another feminist cook book, remarked, women would only be free from the drudgery of continual cooking when men started to enter the kitchen in significant numbers: 'Women's Lib, I feel, should encourage the production of cook books for men and bolster their egos as chefs . . . I was recently told by a domestic science teacher that there will be no emancipation of women until boys are instructed in home economy and taught that cookery can be interesting and rewarding.'[104]

Actually, increasing numbers of men were making incursions into the kitchen in these decades. The age-old assumption that it was a woman's place was being repeatedly challenged as women moved in ever greater numbers into the workplace, as feminism impacted on marital relationships, as more and more men and women lived alone. Male cooks and chefs like 'Galloping Gourmet' Graham Kerr were flamboyant figures on our television screens, and cook books began to address themselves specifically to men. Such books shared a certain uniformity of tone – a bluff plain speaking, a brisk impatience with fripperies, a certain loucheness that linked culinary skill with sexual success. *Oh, for a French Wife!* by Ted Moloney and Deke Coleman is typical. The book had been published in their native Australia in 1952 and was reproduced for a British readership in 1964, complete with vulgar cartoons by George Monar of naked, large-breasted, messy-haired women and fully-dressed, exhausted-looking men. Philosophical and scientific reflections on culinary processes are mixed with simple man-minded recipes – Beef Casserole, French Fried Onions, Sweet-and-Sour Pork. The prissy and mimsy is outlawed, everything is to be big and manly: chicken must not be carved into slices (the juice runs out) but hewn into quarters or eighths; barbecues (a very important feature of masculine cooking) should be massive affairs, big enough to take a spit with 'whole sucking-pigs and baby lambs . . . specially fed on milk'.[105] Cartoons seem to be an obligatory feature of cook books for men – they appear again in Donald Kilbourn's *Pots and Pans: Man's Answer to Women's Lib* (1974) (drawn this time by Larry, ubiquitous in *Punch* and other journals throughout the 1960s and 1970s). The idea seems to be that male readers need their culinary instruction diluted with a spirit of chummy levity, a sense of all boys together, not taking this business too seriously. Kilbourn sells his male readers on their new role with the same combination of science, raw macho appeal and hail-fellow-well-met humour employed by Moloney and Coleman:

> Cooking is basically a production job that is concerned with converting raw materials into a finished product. It is not cissy. Far from it. It is also fun . . . This book, then, is for men. There is, I promise you, no tarty stuff about rolling pastry and baking cakes or upside-down, inside-out, back-to-front puddings. There are no abominations along the lines of 'glazed gooseberry chicken with fried eggs and ice-cream' to titillate our already punch-drunk taste buds.[106]

Not cissy, no tarty stuff, nothing back-to-front, no abominations, no titillation: the sexual anxiety here is palpable. It is no accident that in his first sentence Kilbourn references his wife, mother-in-law and daughter – firmly establishing his heterosexual credentials from the outset. The book is very much concerned with reclaiming cooking from the unscientific, dabbling little woman: the man of the house is advised to retrieve the cooker manual from where his wife 'with feminine conceit' is using it as a fly swat and study it as if it were the manual of a new car. He must gird his loins and approach the jargon of his new activity with stalwart courage – 'don't be alarmed, or you will play into THEIR hands'.[107] Len Deighton's famous cook-strips were also directed at a male readership: the cover of the first collection – *Len Deighton's Action Cook Book* (1965) – has a James Bond-alike deftly testing spaghetti, one sardonic eyebrow raised at the reader, while a flimsily dressed, false-eyelashed popsy admiringly fondles his hair. The cook-strips themselves take the cartoon theme one crucial stage further by presenting the whole recipe in visual form. The idea is that everything can be understood from the strip, and the cook-strips stood alone in their original incarnation in the *Observer*, though in volume form he accompanies each with a page of discussion on variants, sources and refinements of technique. Unlike many of the other books produced specifically for men, Deighton's are pretty good – he acknowledges his sources, is usually sound on both technique and issues of authenticity, and manages to convey a startling amount of information in each strip. This is not picture cookery in the established sense – the drawings are not detailed enough to demonstrate techniques; rather than representing verbs and adverbs (blanch, sauté, simmer and so on) the pictures stand in for the nouns of the culinary process, showing ingredients, types of cooking pot and utensils. Fancy typescripts convey energy and enthusiasm, while the pared-to-the-bone effect has a clear masculine appeal. In *Où Est Le Garlic: Len Deighton's French Cook Book* (1965) he applies the same process to the technicalities of French cookery, with some success: the drawings here are slightly more clear-edged and in a larger scale, so that it is possible to demonstrate some techniques graphically – the strip on omelettes manages an effective diagram of the process of pulling cooked egg to the middle of the pan to allow the uncooked egg to run to the edges.

If many writers of cook books for men were falling over themselves to establish the macho heterosexuality of themselves and their readers, others dabbled unashamedly in a world of high-camp spectacular. The Galloping Gourmet, with his lounge suits and cravats, his flamboyant presentation and beautiful assistant, looks pretty camp to us today, though his act was very much in the tradition of male television entertainers and was almost certainly read straight by its mainstream audience. More spectacular still was Robert Carrier, described (probably in all innocence) by *Home* magazine as 'London's gayest gourmet' and wonderfully depicted by Michael Bateman in his *Cooking People* as holding court in his stage-set of a house ('gilt chandeliers dripping with crystal', dining room done up in trompe d'oeil as an Italian castle garden, bathroom as a Moorish palace, and two kitchens – one for entertaining, the other a show kitchen for testing and photography), flanked by his Greek valet and his Jamaican 'boy'.[108] An American, Carrier spent the war in France, working in broadcasting and journalism, associating with avant-garde figures like Jean Cocteau and André Gide. In 1952 he moved to England, where he worked in PR (in which capacity he had a famous run-in with Elizabeth David, who wrote an uncomplimentary article on Bramley apples that enraged Carrier, who, as their representative, had given her significant help with her research).[109] Cookery writing came about by accident when he entertained the editor of *Harper's Bazaar* to an elaborate but effortlessly relaxed meal, and she commissioned him to write a series for the magazine. His first article contained the recipes for the meal that had so impressed Eileen Dixon, including a dish in which the lobster is sliced alive:

> Some people say I ought to be in Belsen, but the flavour is extraordinary. The shells are made into lobster butter, with a reduction of wine and aromatics, onion and so on. You use about one-third of a pound of butter, heat it up, and the fat at the top is the beurre. You make a sauce with this butter, fish stock, tomato, brandy and cream. This goes over the quenelles, made of pounded pike. You have the puff-pastry ready, which goes into the oven for ten minutes when you're ready. At the last minute you poach the lobsters in court bouillon (I had four lobsters), then sauté in butter, and flambé in brandy.[110]

This was to set the tone for his future culinary writing: decadent, highly elaborate, pretentious 'gourmet' cooking, big on snob appeal. His first 'book' was a box of cooking cards, the first to appear in England, though others had already done the same thing in America and France. More boxes followed, while Carrier moved from *Harpers and Queen* to *Vogue* and the *Sunday Times*. For the new colour magazine of the latter he wrote a series that was accompanied by spectacular large-scale colour photographs of his dishes, and it was this that really established his reputation. His *Great Dishes of the World* (1963), which derived from this *Sunday Times* series, is an enormous tome, with full-page glossy illustrations presenting images which alternate between a neo-minimalist fine-art aesthetic – pure white eggs balanced on a simple pottery stand in front of a hessian-draped background – and extravagant advertisements for conspicuous consumption – splendid dishes on silver platters photographed in some of the world's most exclusive restaurants. In these images, which dominate the book (the recipe text is cramped and functional), Carrier positions himself simultaneously as wealthy gourmet and restrained aesthete. The recipe selection is similarly schizophrenic, with elaborate French restaurant specialities like Caneton de Colette ('pressed duck with a sauce made rich with mashed duck livers, cognac, port, butter and allspice' – the illustration shows the duck flanked by an elaborate brass duck press against a background of old panelling and oil paintings in the restaurant famed for the dish) jostling with peasant food like onion soup and bizarre convenience food concoctions like Fish Fingers in Foil.

Carrier's reputation, it seems to me, rests pretty squarely on his image. With his homes in London and St Tropez, his cosmopolitan gloss and his Thunderbird sports car, he epitomized glamour and sophistication to his readers, who bought his books in such numbers that in the mid-1960s he was the highest-paid cookery writer in the country.[111] The first of the colour-supplement food writers, and one of the first to appreciate the effects of high-quality food photography, Carrier was the forerunner of a breed of cookery writers who were to dominate the cook-book markets in the next decades: self-publicists who realized that their most important product was not their writing or their food but themselves.[112]

TYPICAL RECIPES 1960–79

Katharine Whitehorn
Cooking in a Bedsitter (1961, as *Kitchen in the Corner*)

From a section entitled 'Cooking to Stay Alive', this is one of the most basic of Whitehorn's recipes. It makes use of convenience foods, yet it still shows some small attentions and refinements – the onions are to be gently softened, the cheese is to be melted. The witticism of the title (and the fact that she doesn't deaden the joke by explaining it) are typical of her lightness of touch.

TOUCAN MUSH

Your two cans contain (1) peeled tomatoes, (2) broad beans. And you need also:

1 onion	fat for frying
1 tablespoon grated cheese	

Fry the onion till golden and soft; add the two cans without their liquid; cook 10 mins.; sprinkle grated cheese, cook 3 mins. more until cheese begins to melt. (20 mins.)

Robert Carrier
Great Dishes of the World (1963)

The introductory material establishes the gourmet approach: exotic food embraced with bravura, and a preference for cooking as a public performance. The elaborate explanations make clear the extent to which Chinese food was still unfamiliar to a British readership in the early 1960s. The detailed discussion of the illustration accompanying the recipes indicates the importance of this feature in Carrier's book – the expensive full-colour photographic portraits did much of the work of establishing Great Dishes *as the last word on elegant living. In fact, the pictures were often at odds with the recipes, containing details (in this case, the fried pastry) not given in the text, and in some cases representing dishes for which no recipe is given at all. The recipes repro-*

duced here are absolutely of their time – deep-fried titbits accompanied by a sticky, glutinous sauce. In its unashamed use of commercial ingredients the sweet-and-sour sauce belongs firmly to the convenience-food decades, and it is notable that Carrier offers no apology – for him there is clearly no conflict between the ideal of high-glamour gourmet cooking and the reality of tinned pineapple chunks.

CHINESE PORK AND LOBSTER BALLS IN SWEET AND SOUR SAUCE

Just how far back good cooking actually goes in China is hard to determine, but the Chinese were early discoverers of fire, and have been farmers for well over four thousand years. In the course of their long history they have evolved a high sense of harmony in the delicate blending of tastes and textures.

Some cooks believe that Chinese food is too exotic to be attempted in the home kitchen, but nothing could be further from the truth, for no special utensils are needed and the few extras – soy sauce, bean sprouts, bamboo shoots and water chestnuts – can now be bought, bottled or tinned, throughout the country.

Chinese dishes are inexpensive, quick to prepare and fun to cook. Using an electric frying pan, or a more traditional chafing dish, you can even cook Chinese food right in the living room in front of your guests. A Chinese dinner served in true Oriental fashion assures a gay evening. And for those who like an authentic atmosphere, Chinese serving dishes and chopsticks are inexpensive and easily obtainable.

SERVING A CHINESE MEAL

Rice is the staple food of the Chinese but it is a mistake to think that the Chinese eat nothing but rice. Rice is the centre, the focal point, but ringed with a dozen different dishes, each blending perfectly with it and with each other. According to Chinese food authority Kenneth C. H. Lo, an average Chinese meal consists of one or two soups – vegetable soup and a chicken or beef-based soup – one or two meat dishes, an egg or fish dish, and one or two vegetable dishes, served in conjunction with the rice. In wealthier families, when up to a dozen separate dishes are served during each meal, rice merely acts as a 'buffer' to the rich and tasty dishes, which may be served course by course or all at the same time.

The one supreme meat for the Chinese is pork. Those Chinese who can afford it eat it almost every day, poorer Chinese dream about it, and even the poorest try to save up a few coins to buy some with which to celebrate the New Year.

Sweet and sour conveys the Orient to our Western palates. Here are two classic recipes for serving pork and lobster balls with this favourite sauce. In our picture, crisp leaves of paper-thin pastry, deep-fried Chinese fashion, form a nest for golden balls of pork or lobster in sweet and sour sauce.

PORK IN SWEET AND SOUR SAUCE

1¼ pounds minced pork
1 small clove garlic, minced
1 level teaspoon salt
1 tablespoon dry sherry
1 tablespoon soy sauce
butter
oil for frying

Combine minced pork and garlic. Season with salt, sherry and soy sauce and form into small balls the size of a walnut. Roll in butter and sauté in hot oil for about five minutes on each side. Remove pork balls to a serving dish and keep hot.

LOBSTER IN SWEET AND SOUR SAUCE

1 pound lobster (or shrimps, prawns or fish)
¼ pound pork, not too lean
1 level dessertspoon cornflour
1 tablespoon dry sherry
1 tablespoon soy sauce
¼ teaspoon salt
1 teaspoon sugar
2 tablespoons water
oil for frying

Shell and clean lobster, shrimps or prawns (or skin and bone fish), and mince finely. Mince pork. Pound fish and meat to a smooth paste in a large mixing bowl with cornflour, sherry, soy sauce, salt, sugar and water. Make the paste into balls the size of large walnuts.

Heat the oil in a thick-bottomed frying pan until very hot. Then reduce heat; dip balls in batter and place in hot oil. Fry for about 5 minutes, turning from time to time so they are cooked to a golden brown on all sides.

This dish is best when served hot from the pan, but may be put into an oven to crisp for 5 minutes before serving.

BATTER

1 egg
8 tablespoons ice-cold water
8 level teaspoons sieved flour

Stir 1 egg in a small bowl, but do not whip or beat. Add ice-cold water and mix well; then sprinkle with sieved flour. Do not beat, just stir lightly to mix the ingredients. Do not worry about lumps in batter. If you stir too much, the batter becomes sticky and will not react properly.

SWEET AND SOUR SAUCE

1 small tin pineapple chunks
2 small carrots
1 green pepper
1 level tablespoon cornflour
1 tablespoon brown sugar
2–3 teaspoons soy sauce
2 tablespoons olive oil
2–3 tablespoons vinegar
3–4 sweet pickles, sliced

Drain the pineapple chunks. Reserve juice. Peel and slice carrots thinly; slice green pepper. Simmer the vegetables gently in pineapple juice for 5 minutes, or until tender. Mix cornflour, brown sugar, soy sauce, oil and vinegar together smoothly and stir into the stock. Cook for 3 minutes. Add pineapple chunks and sliced pickles and add to the sauce. Pour over pork and lobster balls and serve hot.

Jane Grigson
Good Things (1971), *Vegetable Book* (1978)

These recipes (the first from Good Things, *the second from* The Vegetable Book*) typify Grigson's extremely influential approach to food. The aim is elegant simplicity, a celebration of ingredients in their purest state. Yet the simplicity is tempered by a whiff of one-upmanship: this is a rather expensive and exclusive sort of simple life, requiring the best butter, first-class celery, a home in rural France and the leisure to spend a whole day harvesting a rather unpromising vegetable from a wall. The aesthetic is very seductive: this precise form of snobbery was to become so embedded in the foodie culture of the next decades that it now hardly appears as snobbery at all, simply good taste.*

CELERY AND SEA SALT

This is the best way of eating first class celery, but care must be taken with butter and salt. Marks and Spencer now stocks the best, unsalted butter from Normandy (at half the price one pays in France). Unadulterated sea salt is harder to come by, but worth the trouble – and expense. Once you've tasted it, you won't want to return to the free-running varieties. Maldon or Tidman's sea salt can be bought at health food shops and good groceries.

Put on the table two or three heads of celery, outside stalks removed (use these for soup, or in stews), and the inner stalks separated, washed and chilled. Have a dish of unsalted butter at spreading temperature, and some sea salt (a salt mill isn't necessary). Each person puts butter fairly thickly into the channel of his celery sticks, then sprinkles a thin line of sea salt along it. Simple and delicious. Avoid embellishments. A good way to start a meal.

WILD CORN SALAD

In summer in France we pick wild lamb's lettuce, wild corn salad (Valerianella locusta), from the hot flint wall that buttresses our garden. It takes quite a time and the lizards don't like it, vanishing rapidly into the holes between their stones. Then the leaves have to be stripped gently, so as not to tear their softness, from the clusters of tiny white and bluish-white flowers. A holiday occupation, when the hours of the day stretch out slowly in sunshine. We sit round the table under the lime tree, with a bottle of wine, and throw the leaves into a bowl of water, fingers busy as we chatter, and look at the enormous view. Then the leaves have to be swished about thoroughly to remove the dry grit of their preferred habitat.

This simple salad has no need of beetroot, or anything else, only a straightforward olive oil or walnut dressing. Don't spoil its flavours, and the family's work, with one of the tasteless oils or with malt vinegar.

Rose Elliot
Not Just a Load of Old Lentils (1972)

Everything about this recipe is absolutely of its moment and genre –

the pottery crock, staple of so many wholesome, home-spun vegetarian restaurants; the avocado, so newly fashionable an ingredient that it still retains its designatory 'pear'; the dash of chilli the 1970s-way, with tabasco. Even the texture is typical: the 1970s was the decade of the gunged-up and gloopy – taramasalata, houmous, terrines, mousses and pâtés of all sorts were easily whizzed up in the newly acquired blender.

EGG AND AVOCADO PÂTÉ

4 eggs, hardboiled
2 tbs. mayonnaise
2 tbs. whipped cream
2 tbs. lemon juice
1 clove garlic
salt and pepper
1 avocado pear
1 tbs. chopped parsley
few drops tabasco
lemon slices, fresh parsley and lettuce leaves to serve

Liquidise the hardboiled eggs with mayonnaise, cream and 1 tbs. of the lemon juice. Wipe cut clove of garlic round mixing bowl and mix egg in this. Cut avocado in half, peel as thinly as possible and remove stone. Cut into small slices and toss in the remaining lemon juice, then add to the egg mixture; season to taste and add parsley and a drop or two of tabasco. Spoon into a pottery crock and chill, or heap on to lettuce leaves and garnish with lemon twists. Serve with melba toast.

Madhur Jaffrey
An Invitation to Indian Cooking (1976)

Jaffrey's confident wielding of historical and cultural detail, combined with precise, user-friendly instructions, place her in the pantheon of scholar cooks alongside Jane Grigson, with whom she has much in common. Kulfi was just beginning to register on the British culinary map in the mid-1970s, but it was by no means the ubiquitous (mass-produced) Indian-restaurant dessert it was subsequently to become. The domestic freezer was the 'labour-saving' device of the decade, and 1970s cook books included increasing numbers of recipes that made use of this new essential.

Indian sweets tend to be very sweet. They also tend to be made of ingredients like vegetables (carrots, pumpkin), nuts (pistachios, almonds, coconut), flours (plain flour, rice flour, chickpea flour), and sweeteners (sugar, jaggery). But the most important ingredient is milk. Milk forms the base of more than half our sweets, and it is often milk in a form entirely unused in the West. Milk is boiled for hours until it forms a semi-solid dough called *khoya*. Most people do not make *khoya* at home. They go out and buy it. It is simpler. Since *khoya* is unavailable here, I have used several substitutes, powdered milk being one of them. For other desserts, milk is boiled down until it is half or a third of its original quantity. Since I do this in a few of the recipes, let me give you a few tips that may help you.

How to boil milk down

1. Use a very heavy-bottomed pot. Cast-iron or aluminium covered with porcelain is particularly good for this.
2. Since the process is slow and tedious (it may take 1 to 1½ hours), bring a chair and a book to your stove.
3. Bring the milk to an 'almost' boil. Watch it. If you let the milk boil over, you will have a big mess to clean. As soon as it seems that the milk will start to boil and rise, turn the heat down to a medium low.
4. Adjust the heat so that the milk is always bubbling, but will not bubble over.
5. Once the milk has begun its slow boil, settle down with your book. Stir the milk every few minutes.
6. If a creamy crust forms on top, just stir it into the milk. It will taste fine when cold.

KULFI

Serves 6

This is Indian ice cream at its best. Milk is boiled down to a third of its original quantity. Sugar, cardamom, and nuts are added, and the thickened milk is then poured into special containers and frozen. Traditionally, *kulfi* is served with *falooda*, a transparent vermicelli rather like Japanese noodles in a sukiyaki. Since I do not expect you to have the conical containers, you could use empty tins of frozen fruit juice, or individual custard cups or paper cups or even a single bowl.

2½ pints milk	3 tbs sugar
4 whole cardamom pods	1 tbs slivered unsalted pistachios

In a very heavy-bottomed pot, boil milk down to 16 fl. oz. This may take up to 1½ hours. After the first hour, lightly crush two of the cardamom pods and add them to the milk.

When the milk has boiled down to 16 fl. oz turn off heat. Remove and discard cardamom pods. Add sugar and nuts. Stir well.

Grind the seeds from the other 2 cardamom pods and add them to the milk. Leave milk to cool.

When cold, stir once and pour milk equally into six 3-fl. oz or 4-fl. oz paper cups, or similar containers, or a bowl. Cover with aluminium foil and freeze. Stir the *kulfi* every 20 to 30 minutes to help break up the crystals. It will get harder to stir as it thickens. When it becomes too thick to stir, leave to freeze solid. Keep covered.

To serve: Run a warm knife along the inside of each cup or container to remove the *kulfi*. (You may need to pour warm water on the outside to loosen it.) Serve individual portions on small chilled plates.

CHAPTER SIX

From Nouvelle Cuisine to Now

Nouvelle cuisine hit Britain in the late 1970s, and by the beginning of the 1980s it was everywhere. The movement had originated in France a decade earlier, when two food critics, Henri Gault and Christian Millau, wrote an article describing a new sort of cooking being practised by a group of young chefs who challenged the time-honoured conventions of the professional French kitchen.[1] These chefs, who included Paul Bocuse, Roger Vergé, Michel Guérard and the two Troisgros brothers (Jean and Pierre), rejected flour-based sauces, long cooking of meat and what they saw as the overcomplicated, indigestible classics of French haute cuisine.[2] Instead they shortened menus and cooking times, used more fish and less meat, and constructed sauces based on reductions of juices and stocks, essences and spices. This was food redesigned for a health-conscious generation, aware of the dangers of a diet high in fat and cholesterol, body-conscious but physically indolent.[3]

Gault and Millau outlined the principles behind the new cooking in the form of a manifesto, converting the practice of individual chefs into a movement that immediately attracted the attention of the French and then the international press. According to their account, *la nouvelle cuisine* was governed by a set of key principles: avoid unnecessary complication (so use simple cooking methods), shorten cooking times (which necessitated younger, fresher ingredients), shop regularly at the market, reduce choice on the menu (so as not to have a huge stock of ingredients all requiring refrigeration), ban obsolete or boring principles (such as the notion that game must be marinated), banish heavy flour-based sauces, make use of advanced technology (in practice this tended to mean an eager embracing of the food processor and a consequent parade of terrines, mousses and purées), apply knowledge of dietetics (reduced sugar and salt, no frying) and – possibly most crucially – invent constantly. Reflecting in 1996 on the movement he had helped to kick-start, Gault noted that

> this nouvelle cuisine, wishing to be without roots and open to every influence, was the band wagon on to which jumped, along with the authentic cooks, a crowd of

> mountebanks, antiquarians, society women, fantasists and tricksters who did not give the developing movement a good name. Furthermore fashions, mannerisms and trickery attached themselves to this new culinary philosophy: miniscule portions; systematic under-cooking; abuses of techniques in themselves interesting (mousses, turned vegetables, coulis); inopportune marriages of sugar, salt and exotic spices; excessive homage paid to the decoration of dishes and 'painting on the plate'; and ridiculous or dishonest names of dishes.[4]

That just about sums it up. The new method of 'plating-up' in the kitchen rather than allowing the customer to serve himself from dishes brought to the table was seized on by restaurants large and small, good and bad, as the perfect way to institute portion control. Every chef who fancied himself an artist now had licence to swirl his plates with multi-coloured sauces (the food always sat on top, obedient to the principle that nothing must be disguised in the new cooking), serve meat and fish in tiny medallions rather than hefty slabs, and let his imagination run free in the invention of startling combinations of ingredients (duck and pawpaw, lobster and mango). But the vast majority of chefs who embraced the movement with such enthusiasm in fact exhibited a paralysing conformity: every pudding had its flood of fruit coulis (another product of the food processor, invariably oversweetened, with the chemical kick of icing sugar), all vegetables were infants, hand-turned into identical little barrels, and kiwi fruit was the new parsley.

The ubiquity of the kiwi fruit slice perched on British restaurant food of the early 1980s indicates the extent to which most of the adopters of nouvelle cuisine had simply got it wrong: the point was to continue to invent, not to enshrine the inventions of others in a sort of cultural aspic. Pink peppercorns and raspberry vinegar met a similar fate: desperately trendy and overexposed (and actually not very nice), the bottles gathered dust in homes all over the country. Because it was not just restaurateurs who bought nouvelle cuisine: magazines seized on the new culinary style because it made such pretty pictures. And that, of course, was the point about most of the new ingredients – their colours and shapes were much more important than their taste, hence the fondness in these years for the flavourless but graphic star fruit. So delicatessens and even supermarkets began to stock the new ingredients, manufacturers to make the requisite oversized black or white octagonal plates (the shape apparently helped chefs perfect the pattern of the food), and the readers of the magazines to attempt to reproduce the dishes for their dinner parties.

It is hard to imagine that many of those dinner parties were very successful. Nouvelle cuisine was essentially restaurant food, a theatrical performance requiring bustling waiters, gleaming napery, silver cutlery and a succession of surprises issuing forth from the kitchen to 'oohs' and 'aahs' and fanfares. It also helped the effect if the meal cost a lot. It is no accident that this food reached its high point in the Thatcherite 1980s, when a new class of entrepreneurs and city boys was desperate to display its wealth. Spending was good in the 1980s, the more conspicuous the better. In this rampantly consumerist decade, food became one of the key ways of demonstrating wealth and status. And what was more conspicuous than paying a fortune for a beautifully produced meal that left you hungry? This was food as art object rather than as a source of sustenance. It was the era of the specialist food magazine – publications like *A la Carte* and *Taste* presented exotic foods in gorgeous double-page spreads, tweaked by stylists and airbrushed like models. The aesthetic of the new food formed an interesting contrast with the browns and beiges and earthenware platters of the 1970s wholefood movement and with the vibrant hues of Mediterranean dishes. This food was colourful, but with a delicate, almost pastel palette: creamy sauces tinged with pink, green and yellow, the pink of salmon, the fresh greens of pistachios and mange-tout, the soft reds of radicchio and oak-leaf lettuce (almost entirely without flavour or texture, but a very pretty colour). The food looks artistic and tasteful (in the non-culinary sense) – like the perfect lady in her camels and soft pinks, it looks *expensive*.

Nouvelle cuisine produced a response in the British press unheard of for a mere matter of food: analyzed, fêted and fulminated against, it was the wonder of the age. Elizabeth David gave a characteristically measured but ascerbic response to the new cooking in the preface to the 1983 reprint of *French Provincial Cooking*, noting that it was not really so new at all:

> In 1960, when this book was first published, it seemed to me that so called *cuisine classique* with its rigid traditions and immutable rules had already been unrealistic and hopelessly out of date at least since 1939, let alone by fifteen years after the end of the Second World War. Belatedly, then, in the early 70s a group of younger professional chefs began to make rebellious announcements about lighter food and less of it, about vegetables being undercooked in the Chinese style instead of stewed to pulp, about fish being poached or grilled until the flesh just came away from the bone rather than tumbling from it in a shower of flakes. Very laudable aims all these were too, if not perhaps as startling to the ordinary public as they seemed to the young men themselves.[5]

Mocking, as do most other commentators, the finicky presentation of the new chefs ('the five green beans sitting lonely on one side of a huge white plate, three tepid chicken livers *avec ses quelques feuilles de salade* nine inches distant on the opposite edge'), she nonetheless acknowledges the necessity and inevitability of continual culinary evolution. The main problem with nouvelle cuisine, in her opinion, is not its innovations but the attitude its presentational pretensions imply towards the customer:

> The enticement of the wonderful smells of fine cooking, now diffused and muddled by the obligatory plate service, the intense visual stimulus once inseparable from a meal in a good French country restaurant but now destroyed by misguided imitation of Japanese-style presentation, could quite easily be restored to us. In other words, it is not so much the cooking that is wrong, except in the most blatantly arrogant establishments, as a certain coldness and ungenerosity of spirit, an indifference to the customer, now manifest in establishments operated on nouvelle cuisine principles.[6]

Such attitudes are very clearly apparent in the rash of books produced by chefs famous and infamous in the 1980s. As expensive and glossy as art tomes, these books depicted food that was virtually impossible to achieve in a domestic kitchen. They make little pretence of seriously instructing: their purpose was to advertise the chef, enhance his fame and offer the reader a lifestyle to which to aspire. This lifestyle, crucially, was one in which you could dine *chez* Nico or at Raymond Blanc's Manoir, not one in which you laboriously constructed a cack-handed version of one of their famous dishes. And the customer is certainly not king for chefs like Nico Ladenis or Marco Pierre White, both of whom devote considerable space in their books to fulminating over the dining atrocities committed by the public: 'If I came to your house for dinner an hour late, then criticized all your furniture and your wife's haircut and said all your opinions were stupid, how would you feel?' rants Marco Pierre White in his 1990 *White Heat*. 'People still come here and expect a three-course meal in an hour. What do they think I do – pull rabbits out of a fucking hat? I'm not a magician.'[7] The famously irascible Nico Ladenis allows himself a whole chapter in his 1987 *My Gastronomy* to prove that 'The customer is not always right.' He happily lists the insults he has doled out to people enquiring about the sort of restaurant he runs, but is equally contemptuous about the knowledgeable foodies and wine buffs whose remarks he overhears. Above all he insists that customers should always be led in their choices by the wisdom of the chef and waiters: 'In our restaurants it has always been one of our most important rules that customers should be guided, assisted and, if necessary, cajoled into a well balanced meal. My wife is positively meticulous in the pursuit of this golden rule, many times to the dissatisfaction and displeasure of the customer.'[8] They could behave like this because they were the beneficiaries of a dramatic shift in the status of the chef achieved by the publicity and drama surrounding nouvelle cuisine – and the beginning of a cult of personality attached to him. As Nico himself notes:

> Until a few years ago, chefs . . . had no status. They were part of the service and the service meant a lower scale of dignity. The image of the chef was of a simple, humble person, someone with little ambition, a plodding, shuffling body who did the dirty work. But today, things are changing. The chrysalis has burst and the butterflies are beginning to emerge. The clothes they wear in the kitchen are smart, they are sparkling clean, they are brilliant white, they are well-tailored. The great chef is now a star.[9]

The chef-stars of the 1980s in Britain were the Roux brothers (Albert and Michel), with Le Gavroche and The Waterside Inn, Raymond Blanc, with Le Manoir Aux Quat' Saisons, Nico Ladenis with Chez Nico, Anton Mosimann at the Dorchester and Pierre Koffmann at La Tante Claire (a younger generation emerged towards the end of decade that included Simon Hopkinson, Alistair Little, Rowley Leigh and Marco Pierre White). None would have been happy calling their style of cooking nouvelle cuisine, but all inherited the key principles and attitudes of the movement: an intention to 'source' fresh produce daily, a belief in enhancing rather than masking the intrinsic flavour of the main ingredients, an emphasis on rapid cooking of the highest-quality ingredients rather than lengthy cooking to transform poorer, tougher cuts of meat or older vegetables, and above all a commitment to innovation rather than tradition.

Most of the first generation of star chefs produced books, and the styling of those books is remarkably uniform. In *At Home with the Roux Brothers* (1988), *Recipes from Le Manoir Aux Quat' Saisons* (1988) and *My Gastronomy* (1987) we find the same full-page pictures of plated-up dishes, the plates fine bone china (often discreetly decorated to signal that the fashion for plainly coloured massive octagonal affairs is now old hat), the food more plentiful than in the early days of nouvelle cuisine but still artfully arranged, with quenelles, turned vegetables and flooding sauces much in evidence. Recipes are long and elaborate, usually given in point form, with as much attention paid to the garnishes and the niceties of serving as to the dish itself: this is Nico Ladenis on the dressing of a Salade Tiède de Homard au Beurre de Truffes:

On each plate, arrange 3 segments of orange, 1 next to the other, followed by 2 tomato petals, slightly overlapping, the sliced mushroom, 2 slices of avocado, a 'turned' carrot and half an artichoke. Dress the salad leaves with the vinaigrette and then place 2 small leaves of frisée, a radicchio leaf, 4 or 5 mâche leaves and an oak leaf lettuce leaf in the middle of the plate.[10]

And heaven help you if you get your frisée out of place. Significantly, although much space is given to lingering descriptions of the taste of the dishes and the moments of inspiration that led to their perfection, the recipes themselves are closely laid out in much smaller typefaces – and in pale grey in Raymond Blanc's book, which makes them virtually unreadable. In graphic terms these books make it abundantly clear that the reader is not expected to read, let alone cook from, the recipes. Instead the emphasis is on the individual genius of the chef. Invention is a key motif, with each chef eager to highlight his own innovations and concoctions. Raymond Blanc gives his recipe for Chlorophyll (vegetable extract) in his introductory section of basic recipes and techniques: it is an elaborate process that results in a few tablespoons of foam with a mild flavour of the chosen vegetable – either red pepper or spinach. The Roux brothers do something rather similar to produce a green herb essence, while Nico Ladenis gives 'an audacious recipe' for Rognons de Veaux aux Feuilles de Laurier, in which one veal kidney is cooked with ten bay leaves. A product of this spirit of invention is the freedom – or laxity – with which names are given to dishes. Nico Ladenis has a 'spaghetti' of vegetables and a 'panache' of fruit (the term usually refers to a mixture of seafood); the Roux brothers have Salmon Tartare; Raymond Blanc has a 'charlotte' of vegetables in which he lines the mould not with buttered bread or sponge fingers (as in the original versions of the pudding of this name) but with spinach. Such has been the long-standing influence of nouvelle cuisine on the French culinary establishment, incidentally, that recent editions of the *Larousse Gastronomique*, the bible of French culinary practice, have tended to legitimize such inventions by including them within the definitions of classic dishes. In the decades that have followed, this reassigning of culinary names has become more and more typical of the practice of chefs – hence the cappuccinos of soup that did the rounds a few years back.

The new ingredients and methods explored by 1980s chefs percolated fairly rapidly through to the home cook: there was more interest in fish, especially salmon and monkfish (a favourite with nouvelle-cuisine chefs, perhaps because it is easy to cut into medallions), and seafood, particularly scallops (also conveniently portion-controlled). Mangetout, exotic mushrooms, nut oils and flavoured vinegars were experimented with, and the warm salad (salade tiède) of assorted exotic salad leaves (conveniently available packaged and prewashed in supermarkets towards the end of the decade) topped with grilled goat's cheese became a positive craze. The nouvelle-cuisine approach to decorative cookery was simplified for domestic purposes by books such as Natalie Hambro's *Visual Delights* (1985), which presented simple dishes like scrambled eggs with spinach in pictorial forms as elaborate as those of any aspiring chef (in this case the eggs are surrounded with 'deux verdures' – first a ring of purëed spinach, then a fan of the leaves of the same vegetable raw). Hambro shares the freeness with culinary names that characterizes the chefs of the time – her Tarte Tatin sacrilegiously has no pastry and does not caramelize the apples (it is simply sliced apples packed deeply into a cake tin and baked slowly to form a solid 'cake') – but unlike theirs her dishes are pretty easy to achieve: dinner-party food cunningly designed to look much more elaborate than it really is.

By the early 1980s food was taken so seriously by so many people that the phenomenon was awarded its own sobriquet: the devotees of the culture of food for its own sake were christened 'foodies' by Ann Barr and Paul Levy, whose *Official Foodie Handbook* was published in 1984. Barr (who was deputy editor of *Harpers & Queen*) and Levy (a food journalist) anatomized the pretensions, snobberies and preoccupations of those to whom food is of pre-eminent importance, treating them with a tongue-in-cheek mockery that allowed the reader (assumed to be a foodie) to laugh at himself. The approach of the *Foodie Handbook* was very much that established by Ann Barr's earlier best-selling *Official Sloane Ranger Handbook* – social analysis disguised as bluffer's guide disguised as social analysis.[11] The book is really concerned with a new breed of culinary consumers who treat food as a status prop: the natural customers for nouvelle cuisine. 'Foodies are typically an aspiring professional couple to whom food is a fashion,' in contrast to the old-style gourmet, 'a rich male amateur to whom food was a passion'.[12] But with great cunning the term is also applied to the food professionals caricatured in a section on Foodie Types (Dr Barbara Bookish, the squalor scholar cook, who gives papers on yeast doughs under Louis XIV and lives off dyed kippers, tea and biscuits; Nyree Nymph O'Manioc, the popularizer of Asian food in the West) and to the culinary great and good named in the roll-call of the Foodie Who's Who. The reader is greatly flattered by the connection established between himself and these culinary luminaries, while many of those mentioned were not at all amused. Veteran radio food journalist Derek Cooper told Levy he would sue if his name appeared in the book, so it does not, while Elizabeth David, who was frequently mentioned, hit back with a caustic review.[13] Entitled 'Scoff Gaffe', it began by revealing all the mistakes in the *Handbook*'s brief account of her own life and career, then went on to ridicule its infelicities of style, ending with an assertion that the problem is that the writers are unable to attain the detachment necessary for effective satire. But, of course, the *Foodie Handbook*, as its title suggests, was not intending to be satirical. Its aim was to give the thoughtful consumption of food as much recognition and social credibility as its creation, and in this it succeeded beyond all expectations. If the foodie, with his snobberies about brands of olive oil and types of coffee beans, seems to have disappeared, it is only because we are virtually all foodies now, jumping on every culinary bandwagon as it lumbers around the corner, sourcing our miso and Thai fish sauce from the Special Selection section of the supermarket if not from little ethnic grocers, trying out the new Malaysian, Japanese, North African restaurant as soon as it opens. This is not the result of Levy and Barr's book, of course, but in naming the phenomenon they gave it respectability, allowing the eager consumer to see himself as a cultured connoisseur rather than just a greedy guts.

With the economic crash that marked the end of the decade, attitudes to food began to change. Feeling the financial chill, people wanted to hunker down at home instead of blowing their cash in a fashionable restaurant. The cook books that started to sell were those concerned with nesting rather than display. In *Howard and Maschler on Food* (1987), novelist Elizabeth Jane Howard and food critic Fay Maschler relocated food firmly within the domestic context, offering menus for a variety of situations and occasions, including Dull People, Weekend Entertaining, Impressing People, Greedy People, House-Moving Supper and Jane Grigson to Dinner. There is a welcome sense of life-as-it-is-really-lived: the need to entertain people you don't really like, to knock together meals in a rented holiday house, to prepare the food for a funeral. The recipes are simple and pleasant, tending to the hearty, and very much in the tradition of Grigson herself: Kipper Fillet Salad, Fish Pie, Lancashire Hot-Pot, Normandy Pheasant, Curried Parsnips, Kedgeree, Celeriac Remoulade, Brown Bread Ice-Cream and Sussex Pond Pudding. The book seems to represent a reaction for Maschler away from the restaurant food she ate endlessly for her day job, though a few select recipes are borrowed from restaurateurs – Anton Mosimann's Bread and Butter Pudding (a very famous reworking, which turned the dish from a repository for leftovers into something ineffably light and tremendously rich), a Roux brothers' recipe for Oeuf Froid Carême, Pierre Martin's Apple Tarts. In general, though, the book aims to shift home cookery away from attempts to emulate restaurant food and towards an embracing of the sort of food that is much better produced in a domestic environment. So Skate with Browned Butter is 'just what you hope to be fed after hearing that a nouvelle cuisine chef in Altrincham is flavouring his mid-meal sorbets with Chanel No 5', and Perfect Roast Chicken represents the height of pleasure:

> We have noticed that the more involved with food you become, the more you gravitate towards simplicity. A well brought-up chicken, considerately cooked becomes a far more beguiling dish than any nouvelle cuisine flight of fancy, pushed and primped and served in pre-ordained portions, which obviate that pinnacle of eating enjoyment, second helpings.[14]

Roast chicken becomes an emblematic dish in the late 1980s and early 1990s: as free-range, grain-fed, sometimes organic chickens became available, the dish attained a status as a simple luxury – *proper* food, unlike the ubiquitous cling-film-wrapped, water-injected portions of chicken breast from scrawny, unhealthy mass-produced birds, which were piled high on the supermarket cold-shelves. The dish, and the *echt* method of producing it (rubbed with butter, stuffed with lemon, served with watercress and/or potatoes), carried such a freight of cultural meaning that chef Simon Hopkinson called his first book *Roast Chicken and Other Stories*, thereby clearly announcing his allegiances to the simple and traditional. Co-written with Lindsey Bareham and published in 1994 (though apparently having taken five years to write), the book is divided into sections which each focus on a favourite ingredient. These are headed with an essay and then followed by a succession of recipes. This form, which derives from the format of recipe columns in newspapers and magazines, became very popular in the 1990s and denotes a certain sort of cook book – clever, personable, relaxed. From the beginning Hopkinson makes it clear that this is not another chef book and that his subject is not the rarefied inventions of the professional kitchen but the time-honoured pleasures of simple food produced at home:

> We are all drawn to the smell of fish and chips, fried onions, roast beef, Christmas lunch, pizza, fresh coffee, toast and bacon, and other sensory delights. Conversely, to my mind, there is nothing that heralds the bland 'vegetable terrine', the 'cold lobster mousse with star anise and vanilla', or the 'little stew of seven different fish' that has been 'scented' with Jura wine and 'spiked' with tarragon. I feel uncomfortable with this sort of food and don't believe it to be, how shall we say, genuine.[15]

Hopkinson's dishes are drawn from the Mediterranean and southern European repertoire of Elizabeth David and her followers (Grilled Aubergines with Sesame, Salade Niçoise, Saint-Émilion au chocolat), the pre-war traditions of good-quality English and French foods (Eggs Florentine, Cervelles [brains] au Beurre Noir, Roast Grouse with Bread Sauce and Game Chips, Fruit Fool) and what might be called modern classics (Grilled Asparagus with Parmesan, Chocolate Tart, Poached Cod with Lentils and Salsa Verde, Baked New Garlic with Creamed Goat's Cheese, Olive Oil Mash). The dishes in this latter category were mostly the invention of particular restaurateurs but had been widely adopted elsewhere: they are the high-concept tastes of the 1990s. Other dishes in this category (most of which Hopkinson also gives recipes for) would include onion confit; parmesan crisps (grated parmesan baked to form crisp biscuits and used to garnish starters); halved red peppers stuffed with garlic, tomatoes and anchovies, anointed with olive oil and baked; and Mexican-influenced salsas (chunky cold sauces combining sweet, sour, hot and salty tastes). What these dishes have in common is a combination of piquancy and gutsiness – they are a long way from the refined delicacy of flavour that typified the inventions of nouvelle cuisine. Yet that movement is not entirely forgotten: Simon Hopkinson is, after all, one of those chefs who made their reputation in the 1980s on the back of the culinary revolution, and he gives recipes from stars such as Michel Guérard, Frédy Girardet and Pierre Koffmann. It is notable, though, that however well he speaks of these pioneers of nouvelle cuisine, none of them merit one of his 'Fanfares' – the interpolated celebrations of influential cookery figures that are scattered throughout the book. That honour is reserved instead for luminaries such as Elizabeth David and less well-known figures such as Margaret Costa (author of the cultish *Four Seasons' Cook Book* of 1970) and George Perry Smith. The food writers' restaurateur, the latter was the chef-proprietor of the famous Hole-in-the-Wall in Bath and probably the most celebrated food person never to have written a cook book. In paying homage to these figures, Hopkinson is creating for himself a pedigree, and it is very markedly one of scholar cooks rather than experimental chefs. Like many of his fellow food writers in the late 1980s and early 1990s, Hopkinson has moved beyond the nouvelle-cuisine movement. But what is notable is the extent to which he and others like him feel obliged to make a public disavowal of the movement, caricaturing its worst excesses and explicitly disassociating themselves. Yet in the mere fact of their avoidances and mockery they express a distinct anxiety of influence – an awareness that many of their attitudes, and even their careers, are attributable to the changed emphases produced by the phenomenon of nouvelle cuisine.[16]

The preoccupation with the homely and domestic continued throughout the 1990s and beyond. The formal dinner party was shouldered aside in favour of the informal 'kitchen supper', with an emphasis on simple, pleasurable food, produced quickly and served without fuss. Jenny Baker, well known for *The Student's Cookbook*, published *Kitchen Suppers* in 1993, and Claire Macdonald produced *Suppers* the following year. Baker's title implies entertaining, the phrase having already gained social currency as an unstuffy, stylishly bohemian alternative to the dinner party: 'For the last couple of years we all seem to have stopped giving dinner parties and settled instead for this appealing alternative. Just hearing the words, "Come round for a kitchen supper", makes us feel relaxed.'[17] Her dishes are in fact pared-down versions of the dinner parties of the past, with fewer courses and more licence to use ready-made food for starters – crudités and dips feature largely – and cheese and fruit for pudding. Despite this, there is still some attempt to impress with largesse and with technical or visual complication: there are lots of wrapped dishes – Salmon in Vine Leaves, Rabbit in Packets, Trout in Puff Pastry – and exotica like

Mushrooms Stuffed with Snails, and Rose-Scented Peaches. Macdonald's *Suppers* focuses more centrally on the needs of the family, with entertaining a secondary consideration dealt with in chapters such as the one entitled 'More than Just the Family'. An exuberantly jolly work, filled with references to her own life and family, the book concentrates on simple, filling dishes, often all-in-one: Fish and Vegetable Chowder, Baked Creamy Crab, Cheese and Tomato Pudding, Black Pudding with Baked Apples. She places centrally the issue of cooking for children and of persuading them to eat unfamiliar foods:

> Although children can't be expected to like, for instance, the taste of a hot curry, most children will try – and enjoy – just about everything else, with a little encouragement and the odd bribe. I tried to make mine eat a tiny amount of things they didn't like just so that when they were guests in the homes of friends they would be able to eat more or less anything. And it's paid off. Hugo, who loathed peas, carrots and tomatoes, now loves all three. But then from an early age he loved Stilton and squid, so perhaps he isn't an ideal example! But I find that a way to get around fussy eating children is to get them to help in the preparation and cooking wherever possible – they love to eat something if they have had a hand in its making.[18]

This is the gospel of children and food that has emerged in the last two decades: they should be expected to explore as many food tastes as possible as early as possible and on the whole to eat the same diet as adults. The advice throughout the 1980s from experts on infant feeding was to liquidize whatever the family was having for supper for the benefit of infants from the age of six months onwards, as there is thought to be a crucial 'window' of taste receptivity between six and twelve months of age, during which time a lifetime's tastes and distastes can be established. It is a marked contrast to the Victorian practice of rearing children on a diet of farinaceous foods and milk, or the blithe 1970s embracing of processed foods as the ideal quick solution for busy mums. But, in fact, it is not as simple as it seems, because conflicting advice followed a little later from another group of experts, concerned about the possible ill effects of introducing many foods too early – salt is the main worry, but there are also issues with cow's milk, citrus fruits, eggs, liver and nuts. For the middle classes in the last decade children's food has acquired whole new ramifications of guilt and effort. Aware of the decline in families eating together, preoccupied with the dangers posed particularly to the young by foodstuffs and the chemicals with which they are treated, mothers patrol the arena of their children's food and eating with a new intensity. The informed and food-conscious have continually to tread the line between the food advisers for whom every undercooked egg threatens your child and the foodie ideal of being able proudly to brag of a toddler who loves olives (or squid and Stilton).[19]

In recent years the subject of cooking for children has assumed a new prominence in works on general cookery. One of the most lauded features of Nigella Lawson's very well received *How to Eat* (1998) was the chapter on feeding babies and small children, in which she starts from the very beginning, with weaning foods – indeed, she goes back even further, to discuss the tastes a child acquires from its mother's foods when in the womb and via breast milk. Having, like all who enter the vexed arena of children's food, to steer a course between infant nutritionists and foodies, Lawson comes down firmly in the latter camp. She acknowledges the importance of introducing some foods later than others and offers a rather perfunctory version of the weaning timetable included in most baby-care books, but her strongest commitment is towards offering children a wide range of tastes and encouraging them to enjoy rather than fear food. She is contemptuous about the current obsession with food intolerances (as opposed to allergies), stating baldly, 'I don't believe in them.' She warns against 'muesli malnutrition' – 'the term which doctors apply to the low-fat starvation diet on which many well-meaning, affluent parents keep their children', insisting that children need a reasonable amount of fat in their diet.[20] She is unusual in discussing the taste of the infant foods she prepares, something invariably omitted in most books on the subject. This is her on the preparation of the frozen cubes of mush demanded by the modern orthodoxy on weaning:

> After the first month or so of plain fruits and vegetables, I got into the habit of creating certain mixtures, and they're useful ones. The compound I was most pleased with was a mush of spinach and sweetcorn – the spinach, with its metallic almost bitter hit, is sweetened, and somewhat de-slimed by the corn. Another – broccoli and carrot – also works well. Though broccoli has a definite sweetness of its own, it also has a cabbagy mustiness which babies, and adults, can warm to less. Carrots intensify the sweetness and seem to neutralise the otherwise enduring Brassica-family brackishness. You will create a sludge of a particularly unattractive khaki, but your baby will be able to live with that. When my babies were beyond purées, they ate the broccoli florets whole, a small green tree clasped in each fat pink fist.[21]

Such taste notes are typical of Lawson's general style as a food writer, as is the final comment, with its celebration of the pleasures and fleeting moments of ordinary domestic life. The foods Lawson recommends for small children beyond the weaning stage are 'proper' foods – largely a combination of the classics of her own childhood in the 1960s and 1970s (eggy bread, macaroni cheese, shepherd's pie, meatballs) and some of the simpler foreign dishes and ingredients now firmly established in the repertoire of the 1990s cook. Pasta is obvious, but Japanese noodle soup, couscous and garlic mushrooms are more unlikely ideas. She is committed to the notion that children enjoy much stronger tastes than we give them credit for and includes a recipe for chilli con carne (heated with cloves rather than chillis), as well as pesto and a number of garlic-infused dishes. Some of her suggestions are inspired – the miniature pleasures of hard-boiled quails eggs accompanied by little boiled new potatoes (certainly a hit in our house) and individual frittatas cooked in blini pans. There is no sense that food for children should be cheap, and she is acerbic about this prevailing cultural assumption: 'People who would never think of asking how much something costs before they eat it themselves, get twitchy about expensive tastes in their young.' So there are some distinctly lordly suggestions: 'a poussin is about the right size for two children'; Valhrona lacte 'or other really good chocolate' is needed to make Children's Chocolate Mousse.[22] The underlying principle is one of the central tenets of post-war foodie-ism – the idea that our approach to food should be more like that of the southern Europeans:

> Giving children real food, the sort of food we'd eat ourselves, is important. It's why the French eat well, and the Italians: their children are not fobbed off with lesser ingredients and different meals in the erroneous belief that good food or expensive items are wasted on them. I'm not saying that you must bankrupt yourself to provide your angels with little luxuries and *bonnes bouches*, but simply that they should not eat worse than you do. If I grate fresh parmesan on to my pasta, why should I insist that theirs comes ready-grated, bitterly musty, smelling of old trainers and trapped in a plastic-lidded drum?[23]

To encourage children to develop an interest in food, Lawson suggests cooking with them, but argues in favour of involving them with the preparation of everyday meals rather than Rice Krispie cakes.[24]

The subject of cooking with and for children currently has prominence in the field of food writing for the first time since the interwar years, and the reason now is the same as it was then: a prevalent anxiety about the culinary abilities of the population as a whole. The post-war baby boomers were taught at least the culinary rudiments at school, but as home economics was successively downgraded and finally dropped from the core curriculum in the early 1990s, there has been an increasing concern that a whole generation of young people have no cooking experience beyond the operation of the microwave. This concern has been responsible for the main direction taken by food writing in the last fifteen years, as it has moved away from showy, complex foods for special occasions and towards basic guides to cooking from first principles and many and various attempts to woo the young in particular into the kitchen. The most important writer in this respect, and almost certainly the best food writer of his generation, is Nigel Slater. Food editor of *Marie Claire* magazine from its launch in 1988 until 1993, and subsequently playing the same role on the *Observer*, Slater published his first cook book, *Real Fast Food*, in 1992. Its simple concept was to provide recipes for good food that could be prepared and cooked in half an hour, so offering a viable alternative to the increasingly prevalent supermarket ready-meal for people returning home from work tired and hungry. This was not in itself a spectacularly original idea; the book is a belated addition to a long tradition of cook books promising quick and easy food. But the 'real' of the title is crucial – unlike so many earlier guides to convenience foods, Slater's concentrates on fresh ingredients and authentic methods. 'I am always suspicious,' he remarks, 'of recipes that "tart-up" commercial products, remembering the maxim about the uselessness of throwing good after bad.'[25] Equally avoiding the other extreme of offering pared down, rushed versions of complex dishes, he has collected recipes for snacks and fast food from a wide range of culinary traditions both new and old: Croque Monsieur, Scallops with Coriander and Lime Butter, Broad Beans with Ham, Sloppy Joes, a Spanish recipe for a traditional tapas of Kidneys Cooked with Sherry. The book is very much in the tradition of pre-war writers like Ambrose Heath and Nancy Shaw (both of whom Slater refers to), and particularly resembles Edouard de Pomiane's *Cooking in Ten Minutes*, in which the man Elizabeth David called 'the *enfant terrible* of French gastronomy' offered chapters on subjects such as 'Sausages and So On' and 'Some Delicate, If Hasty, Dishes', challenging the most dearly held precepts of classical French cooking by proving that food can be both good and quick.[26] Like Pomiane, who was famed among his adoring French public for his light-hearted, personable style, Slater's writing is probably the most significant factor in his success. Relaxed, amusing, but rarely striving after effect, it draws the reader in. Most notably, it is writing that brings alive the pleasures of food in a remarkably visceral way. Slater's descriptions of food make you salivate, and, curiously enough, this is a rare skill among food writers. Open his books at almost any page and he will make you want to eat the food NOW. He can even make leftover Christmas turkey sound appetizing:

Strip the carcass. No, I don't know why you bought such a big bird. You will be left with lumps of brown and white meat of all sizes and some wonderful jelly. Melt a large knob of butter in a frying pan and gently cook a tablespoon dried tarragon which you have reconstituted with an equal amount of boiling water. Stir in a 100ml/4fl oz pot of double cream. Boil until it starts to thicken. Throw in the turkey scraps and the jelly. Warm through, then taste and add salt and pepper. A drop or two of lemon juice would not go amiss. Serve with hunks of bread and glasses of dry white wine.[27]

Although like all foodies he has his minor predilections and extravagances ('dark, bitter and absurdly expensive chocolate', totteringly aged balsamic vinegar, caviare in the fridge for casual raiding), Slater is the master of the *infra-dig* snack.[28] He writes lyrically of the delights of the bacon sandwich (use factory white bread and dip it in the bacon fat) and of condensed milk as a snack from the fridge (boil it in its can for an hour, chill, then dip in, bearing in mind that 'an index finger is preferable to thin biscuits which break in the thick sweet gunge').[29] And only Nigel Slater would give you rules for a chip butty:

The bread should be white and thick sliced. The 'plastic' type is more suitable than real 'baker's bread' because it absorbs the melting butter more readily

The chips should be fried in dripping, not oil, and sprinkled with salt and malt – yes, I said malt – vinegar

The sandwich should drip with butter

Good eaten when slightly drunk, and the perfect antidote to the char-grilled-with-balsamic-vinegar-and-shaved-Parmesan school of cookery. And so frightfully common.[30]

This is what makes his writing so accessible: he understands greed, the moments when only hot, crisp, greasy, carbohydrate-laden food will do. He also makes food intensely personal, evoking an atmosphere of secret treats and pleasures that is the antithesis of that sense of food as precious social display that characterized the typical 1980s cook book. Take, for example, this virtually pornographic recipe for Purple Figs with Warm Honey:

A snack to share with someone special, in bed, on a cold winter's night.

Split two bulging purple figs per person. They must be seriously ripe. Gently warm a small pot of runny honey, thyme or orange blossom if you have it, in a pan of simmering water. Carefully remove the pan from heat, twist off the lid, using oven gloves or a tea towel, and spoon the warm honey over the ripe figs. Eat with your fingers, sucking the purple-red flesh from the skins.[31]

Slater's books encourage the reluctant and the underskilled to cook by making them want to eat. He leads by the appetite, structuring the book around the types of food you might want to eat at a particular moment (bakery goods, eggs, pasta, cheese), providing lots of brief recipes, then ending each section with a further range of ideas in note form – 'Good things to team up with Eggs in a Sandwich', for instance. The largesse of this approach does much to overcome that deadening sense of repetition that strikes the most food-obsessed of us when we try to think of yet another way to serve pasta. It also seems perfectly adapted to hold the reputedly brief attention spans of the MTV generation. If the recipes in *Real Fast Food* are short, so too are the lists of ingredients. Slater's philosophy is to combine a central one or two fresh ingredients with staples already in the house: 'I like the idea of buying one ingredient that looks particularly good, then mixing it with some storecupboard staples and seeing what happens.'[32] It is a practical solution to the conflicting pulls of the supermarket (convenient and increasingly full of unusual and specialist ingredients) and the small local shops which the food-conscious are loath to see go out of business.

Nigel Slater's food epitomizes the 1990s in its wide and eclectic range of influences: he cites many of the same earlier food writers as Simon Hopkinson – Margaret Costa, Elizabeth David, Jane Grigson, Claudia Roden, as well as historical figures like Eliza Acton and Elizabeth Raffald (author of *The Experienced English Housekeeper* of 1782). Italian food is a staple, with some French dishes and a number of Mediterranean ones, particularly Greek. He has a taste for Oriental foods which becomes more dominant in his later books, where he displays a distinct preoccupation with noodle soups and steamed or stir-fried greens. Though he is very much of his time, there are certain food tastes and combinations that are particularly characteristic of him: for instance, the use of bread and other floury substances with hot food (fried potato with spices stuffed into pitta bread; Oyster Po' Boys; mushrooms cooked in cream and served in crisped, hollowed-out bread rolls; Five-Spiced Pork Buns), and the creation of 'plates' of dessert, as in the following example of An Orange Plate:

Peel and slice 1 blood orange per person, taking care to remove all the pith. Serve the slices in little mounds on plates, arranged with an assortment of sweet and sticky dates, squares of darkest chocolate or little chocolate truffles, strips of crystallised orange and lemon peel and crisp biscuits such as brandy snaps. Set before your guests on your most beautiful plates, as an instant dessert, with hot dark roast coffee.[33]

He perhaps overdoes these arrangements – they predominate in the companion book *Real Fast Puddings* (1993) – but they typify his attitude to food as a pleasure to be celebrated rather than an arduous, socially anxious ordeal. They are generous but not elaborate, elegant but not effete; presentation is important, but it is left entirely to the artistry of the reader. And this is Slater's real importance as a food writer: he convinces the reader of their own competence and taste by the simple expedient of focusing on pleasure rather than process – on the things you love to eat rather than the procedures you have to go through to produce them.

In marked contrast is the work of the other writer who did most in this period to encourage people into their kitchens. Delia Smith's approach to cookery is all process and little pleasure – she famously finds it disgusting when fellow TV chefs taste the food they have prepared on screen.[34] Having been extremely successful as a food writer and television cook throughout the 1970s, Smith – a devout Catholic – concentrated her energies in the 1980s on writing religious books.[35] But in 1990, relieved that nouvelle cuisine, so antipathetic to her own approach, was on the way out, she returned to food writing with *Delia Smith's Christmas*, which sold 300,000 copies within a month. It was followed by two more seasonal cookbooks – *Delia Smith's Summer Collection* (1993) and her *Winter Collection* (1995). Both were publishing phenomena: the *Summer Collection* sold more than a million copies in two years, while the *Winter Collection* reached the same figure within a few days of its launch in October 1995, making publishing history. It also led to a famous food shortage, as the fresh cranberries she mentioned in the book and the accompanying TV series sold out all over the country: in Sainsbury's sales of cranberries increased by 200 per cent.

The success of Delia's books is inseparable from her role as a television cook: her books sell because her television shows are so popular. The Delia phenomenon has tended to infuriate other food writers and sophisticated foodies, who complain that her work is highly derivative, her recipes tested to the point of lifelessness, and her television performances bland and wooden. All true – but that, of course, is why she is so popular. Like Isabella Beeton she is a translator, reworking the ideas of chefs and the dishes scholar cooks have adopted from other lands, making them a bit more homely, a touch more English, and testing them until the recipe is foolproof. She makes exotic food seem safe; and her ineffable ordinariness is one of the most reassuring things about her. This is a fact of which Delia, an extraordinarily successful businesswoman, must be aware, as must her producers. The gaucherie, the shy glances under her fringe that characterized her early television performances in the 1970s were clearly genuine, but in the thirty years in which she has been appearing on our screens she must surely have become entirely comfortable with the medium. The fact that she still seems awkward and ill at ease must be to some extent deliberate policy – this is not a star, her performance shouts, this is an ordinary housewife just like you:

> The sheer lack of charisma is astonishing. Delia is less a performer than a martyr; she is as wet as skimmed milk, as wooden as a board, as awkward as fish bones. She stumbles over her words – no small achievement considering the programme is prerecorded – and the constant use of her pet phrase 'And now I'd like to show you' triggers outbreaks of Delia bingo in sitting-rooms across the land.[36]

But, of course, Delia is far from being an ordinary housewife – or even a housewife at all. Her recent television series have all been filmed at her home in Suffolk, but the kitchen in which we see her working is in fact an elaborately constructed set in her conservatory, which is taken down and then rebuilt for each new series. Out of sight in a large industrial unit around the side of the house her three assistants prepare most of the food needed for the shoots. And then there are her other businesses: *Sainsbury's – The Magazine*, which is edited by her husband Michael Wynne-Jones and in which the couple are the major shareholders, and Norwich City Football Club, in which they also hold most of the shares.

Delia's enormous public and financial success inevitably fuelled resentment in the fairly small world of food writing: when her *Summer Collection* won the Glenfiddich Award in 1993 she was reportedly booed and hissed by some of the audience of fellow food writers, and her fabulously successful *Winter Collection* was contentiously not even shortlisted for the award three years later. Other food writers have often been willing publicly to criticize her, but it is notable that she has been treated with more respect in recent years and has acquired something of the mantle of a grand old lady of the food world. This change in attitude towards her may well be the result of the fact that as the owner and food editor of the country's most successful food magazine she was now in the position of a mentor to other writers, able to exercise benign patronage over those she favoured (these included Simon Hopkinson, Nigel Slater and Ruth Watson). But it may also be attributable to the books she published at the end of the decade, which moved back into a territory that Delia could legitimately call her own. *Delia's How to Cook, Book One* appeared in 1998, and *Book Two* the following year. The simple concept was to go back to basics – to teach people culinary skills from the bottom up. The first volume covered eggs, bread, pastry, cakes, sauces, potatoes, rice and pasta; the second fish, meat, vegetables, salads, dairy products, fruit and chocolate. The books and the accompanying twenty-two-part television series caused an enormous furore in the press, started off by chef Gary Rhodes, who broached the cordon sanitaire around 'Saint Delia' by fulminating (at the press launch of his own new book) that it was patronizing and offensive to teach the public how to boil an egg. Antony Worrall Thompson joined the fray by pronouncing Delia the Volvo of cookery – because 'she prefers safety first'. Delia, incidentally, gave as good as she got: 'Actually, I hate Gary Rhodes's programmes,' she spluttered in an interview with Jan Moir for the *Telegraph*, 'and I think that Antony Worrall Thompson is worse; he is dreadful, just repulsive. I think that *Food and Drink*, the show that he is on, is the most disgusting programme on television. I will never, ever know, as long as I live, how the BBC or the general public can tolerate it.'[37] Leaving aside these publicity-gleaning spats, the fact remains that a back-to-basics approach to cook books and, even more, television programmes was a novelty in this period of personality-driven, entertainment-oriented cookery. As more sober commentators pointed out, it was clearly not the case that most people knew what boiling water looked like; Prue Leith remarked that 'the fact is people DO need to be told when food should go into boiling water, when it should go into simmering water and when it should go into poaching water'.[38] Delia's manner and approach were certainly patronizing – she devoted her second programme to the making of toast and on another occasion brandished a potato masher while intoning 'this is a potato masher' – but what she was really doing was a home-economics class on the screen. Utterly uninspirational, her work was nonetheless a well-intentioned attempt to provide basic skills; and that it was successful to the extent that people actually made her recipes is testified to by the fact that *How to Cook, Book One* and the accompanying series provoked yet another nationwide shortage, this time of that most esoteric of ingredients – eggs.

How to Cook is in the Good Housekeeping Institute tradition of triple-tested recipes, picture cookery and simple scientific explanations of culinary procedures. Delia belongs very much to the cooking-is-a-science side of the arts/science divide; her main animus against nouvelle cuisine is what she sees as its pretentious elevation of a practical skill to an art form. There is nothing artistic about Delia's work. Just like the skirts and jumpers she carefully selects to resemble those she assumes are worn by her target audience, the language of her books is resolutely unthreatening in its eschewal of all literary flourish.[39] Schoolgirlish, slightly old-fashioned, carefully unassuming, her prose has the same slightly off note, the bungled stresses, of her verbal delivery. In *How to Cook, Book One*, in a general essay on the subject of sauces, she headlines a paragraph 'More power to your elbow', then muses, 'I'm not sure if this old cliché came into being through the subject of saucemaking or not, but it does say something wise and that is this: when flour, fat and liquid are combined and heated, they always need extremely vigorous whisking.'[40] Despite her commitment to clarity, her prose is full of genteel circumlocutions and pomposities – 'if I may say', 'I am here to tell you' – and her recipes lengthened by a continual and obsessional marking of time – 'first of all', 'what you need to do now is', 'after that'. Pressure of time is clearly an issue for Delia – she often writes scathingly of those happy simply to potter in the kitchen: 'I am perfectly aware that there are people who simply don't mind standing over things for ages, nurturing them along and whisking till the cows come home (as my Welsh grandmother would say), but not me – I don't want to be confined to the kitchen, missing out on a conversation.'[41] So she muses that three minutes to knead bread dough 'is a long time in a busy life', and, unwilling to stir, contentiously gives a recipe for Oven-Baked Wild Mushroom Risotto in the *Winter Collection* that one critic entertainingly described as tasting 'like an ageing relative just back from the Betty Ford clinic – the alcohol has boiled away but the look is still crinkled, unhealthy, and the aroma lingers'.[42] Hers is not evocative food writing; there is no attempt to conjure flavours and sensations, and her fairly rare descriptive words are largely from the lexicon of girls' school stories – 'yummy', 'brilliant'. There is a hesitancy about enjoyment in Delia's approach to cooking: her response to food is resolutely unsensual, the pleasure always balanced by an awareness of its risks and drawbacks: 'the Spanish also serve tortilla sandwiched between chunks of crusty bread – sounds yummy but very fattening'.[43] In a tongue-in-cheek piece for the *Times Literary Supplement* in March 1996 academic Eric Griffiths compared the lack of sensuality in Delia's cooking to Hegel's theory of the aesthetic, in which the philosopher argued that 'smell, taste, and touch remain excluded from the enjoyment of art'. 'Hegel would, on the whole, have approved of Delia Smith,' thinks Griffiths, 'and settled back after a day of wrestling with the Absolute to watch eagerly what she might think to do next with a cranberry.' It is her sense that abandoned culinary pleasure is not quite nice that makes Delia such a rarity among contemporary food writers; it says almost everything about Delia as a cookery writer that she declares herself 'devoted' to brussels sprouts.[44]

Television has increasingly dominated the cook-book market in the last decades. Food writers who make it on TV are guaranteed sales and status of an utterly different order from their book-bound contemporaries. In the 1980s food was packaged by television companies as entertainment. The staid approach of cooks like Delia in the 1970s was replaced with flamboyant, energetic presenters and high-concept shows. Ken Hom demonstrated stir frying with such energy and panache that the wok rapidly became a standard item of equipment in the British kitchen, and cookery was taken out of the studio with programmes like *Fat Man on a Bicycle* (in which Tom Vernon toured Europe, cooking and eating as he went) and the shows of Keith Floyd. Floyd was the most extravagant performer of his day – he glugged back the wine meant for the stew, getting redder of face and wilder of gesture as filming proceeded, and chatted animatedly to the camera crew rather than decorously ignoring them; the food appeared as if by chance, seemingly the product of his unending loquacity. The innovative programmes in which he starred opened the flood gates for the chef-performers and cooking game shows that were to dominate the television schedules for much of the next decade. The beginning of the 1990s was marked by the appearance of Gary Rhodes – young, spiky-haired, clearly designed to appeal to a youthful audience. And then there was *Ready Steady Cook*, giving a television platform to a horde of fresh-faced 'chefs' eager to become household names. At the more serious end of the spectrum was *Masterchef*, in which non-chefs – usually nicely brought-up women of a certain age – prepared elaborate dinner-party food while being interrogated by the lugubriously vowelled Lloyd Grossman and two visiting experts.[45]

As the 1990s wore on TV executives, in a relentless search to capture more and more of a clearly lucrative market, found talent to fit every possible market niche – fearless large posh ladies, young cheeky chappies, gorgeous pouting totty. Some shows were much better than others – anything with Gary Rhodes, Ainsley Harriot or Antony Worrall Thompson was pretty dire; but the Two Fat Ladies were very entertaining, and Clarissa Dickson Wright, at least, knew what she was talking about. Jamie Oliver is one of the few television chefs to handle food and tools as if he knows what he is doing: turn down the sound and his performances are a masterpiece of physical dexterity and economy of movement. And Nigella Lawson's performance was hypnotic, though one didn't look much at the food.

Television as a medium has certainly infected the language of food. The style of address in almost all contemporary cook books – even those whose authors have not yet appeared on the box – is casual, unaffected, as if spoken, and revealing snippets of personality are sprinkled over the whole. Television chefs have their own linguistic coinages, which have tended to drift into the written medium. The most notable (and infuriating) is the insertion of unnecessary adverbs and prepositions: 'fry it off' is a common instruction, with the 'off' presumably intended to signify a macho speed and skill, a lack of mimsy feminine fussing over details that the unmodified 'fry' would not convey; the tic reached the level of the ridiculous when one chef instructed the viewers to 'bake the potato off for an hour'. Equally prone to general adoption are those curious euphemisms employed on restaurant menus. 'Pan fry' is the most obvious – how else would you fry something?

As TV cookery programmes have become more sophisticated, it has become clear that the real product is not the food but the presenter. What we see increasingly with successful television cooks is an awareness of themselves as commodities, a willingness to package their personalities into neat boxes. So Delia refers to herself in the third person – 'here at last is the Delia paella' – and Clarissa Dickson Wright and Jennifer Paterson, total strangers brought together for the purposes of the *Two Fat Ladies* programme, gamely zoomed around on an antique motorbike, cooked all over the country for bemused groups of people and co-wrote cook books which in fact only serve to emphasize their many differences, as each contributed separate and often conflicting recipes and advice.

In the last decade, cook-book publishing in general has followed the model of television food programmes by commodifying its authors and devoting itself to filling in smaller and smaller niches in the market. There has been a general sense of belatedness, of everything obvious having already been done. So we have a plethora of books on single ingredients: Lindsey Bareham's definitive *In Praise of the Potato* (1989) and *Onions without Tears* (1995), a whole host of books on fish, and Silvija Davidson's *Loaf, Crust and Crumb* (1995), which devotes itself not to the making of bread but simply to buying it and using it as an ingredient. There are constant attempts to mark out new areas, to produce something entirely new or absolutely essential – Hattie Ellis's 1998 *Mood Food*, for example (structured around matching food to occasion or mood), or Ruth Watson's hopefully titled *The Really Helpful Cookbook* (2000), both sound and solid books, but neither as original as their high-concept packaging would suggest.[46]

The clear public appetite for more and more discussion about food signalled by the popularity of discursive cook books led food writing into all sorts of unexpected genres and territories. In John Lanchester's much-praised début novel *The Debt to Pleasure* (1996) his poisonous gourmet narrator Tarquin Winot recalls his decadent, murderous pleasures in what he describes as 'a gastro-historico-psycho-autobiographico-anthropico-philosophic lucubration'. Such hybridity is much in evidence in real-life food publishing, where we suddenly, in the 1990s, find food novels, detective stories, biographies, memoirs, essays, anthologies, histories and political treatises. Works that would have languished on publishers' slush piles in previous decades, for lack of a market, are lavishly produced and heavily promoted. Food memoirs were particularly successful, like Elisabeth Luard's *Family Life: Birth, Death and the Whole Damn Thing* (1996), in which she entwines personal history with recipes, telling of the years spent with her young family in an Andalusian cork forest and offering us instructions for the dishes they ate; describing her eldest daughter's favourite birthday cake so that we feel her death from AIDS in her early twenties with the heightened shock of intimacy. The genre emerged as very gender-specific, with women placing eating and cooking in the context of familial life, while men glossed it with the lure of macho adventuring.[47] The latter tendency is typified by Anthony Bourdain's *Kitchen Confidential: Adventures in the Culinary Underbelly* of 2000, which notoriously revealed the violence, dirt and deceptions of the restaurant kitchen in a swaggering macho-punk style A. A. Gill described as 'Elizabeth David written by Quentin Tarantino'.[48] And then there were the histories. The niche for slim single-topic historical works created by the phenomenal success of Dava Sobel's *Longitude* (1996) was filled by a crop of histories of individual food products such as Larry Zuckerman's 1998 survey of the history of the potato and Mark Kurlansky's award-winning *Cod: A Biography of the Fish that Changed the World* (1997). Big ambitious food histories have followed in their wake, two of the most notable being Felipe Fernández-Armesto's *Food: A History* (2001), a pyrotechnical cultural-culinary history of the world that begins with the origins of cooking, and Colin Spencer's 2002 *British Food: An Extraordinary Thousand Years of History*, which seeks to enrich and complicate our sense of the British culinary heritage by studying its earliest manifestations. All of these books achieved major success both critically and in terms of sales, indicating the emergence in these years of a significant market for food writing that focuses on horizons beyond the recipe.

In the 1990s the look and styling of cook books became as important a factor as their content. The most famous example of this phenomenon is the *River Café Cook Book* and its sequels, the startling success of which is largely attributable to their innovative visual style. The original *River Café Cook Book*, published in 1995, was a large, squarish book, unlike the chefs' books of the last decade in its fat chunkiness. It looked immediately and compellingly modern: very largely a function of the stark yet solid typeface used for the title and the graphic arrangement of its letters to form a rectangle that filled the cover. Similar typographic games were played inside the book, with a very generous layout with acres of blank space, the random insertion of coloured pages and the use of white type over full-page pictures of ingredients. The style is one developed in the 1980s for cutting-edge magazines like *The Face*, but it was unheard of to employ it for a cook book. It summed up the ethos and atmosphere of the River Café – modern, (relatively) youthful, above all trendsetting.[49]

The restaurant had been started in 1987 by Ruth Rogers (wife of the architect Richard) and Rose Gray. The food was Italian – largely Tuscan – farmhouse cooking, or *cucina rustica*, influenced by the direct, simplifying approach to rural cooking developed in the restaurants of California in the previous decades by pioneers like Alice Waters. The governing concept was to serve domestic food in a restaurant environment, with a simple menu that changed daily and a small open kitchen so that diners could watch their food being prepared. Although the food is simple, it is notoriously hard to reproduce. This is partly because Rogers and Gray insist on the necessity of 'sourcing' raw ingredients direct from Italy or from out-of-the-way companies (you must have cavolo nero, Capri rocket, buffalo mozzarella, cultivated dandelion leaves). But it is also because the recipes surprisingly often fail to work. The most notorious is Chocolate Nemesis, which takes 2 lbs of bitter-sweet chocolate, 10 whole eggs, 1 lb 5 oz of caster sugar and 1 lb of butter, and serves 10–12. The authors tag the recipe with the claim that it is 'the best chocolate cake ever', but few people have ever been able to make it successfully, to the extent that some thought its title a cruel jibe at the hapless public's expense. Similarly tricksy are the Farinata al Rosmarino (chickpea pancake with rosemary) from the *River Café Cook Book Green* (2000) and the Zuppa d'Aosta (a baked soup of savoy cabbage, bread, cheese and anchovies) from the first book, both of which I tried because I could not imagine, from the recipe, what they would taste like. Bad, is the answer. The River Café recipes are often oddly unimaginable, even for those who usually find they can 'taste' dishes when reading recipes. It is partly because they use curiously few ingredients and partly because the quantities are so large – suited for a restaurant rather than a home. Or maybe (whisper it) they're just not very good at writing recipes. Many of the recipes already existed in better, more authentic versions elsewhere (in the works of Anna del Conte and Marcella Hazan, for example), but those who bought their books were not looking for originality or authenticity, or even for workable recipes: they were buying a lifestyle – a combination of taste and paradoxically inaccessible rustic chic.

The River Café books represented a new phase in the marketing of food as style, but they were soon to be joined by others. Nigella Lawson's *How to Eat* (1998) also sold itself as minimalist while offering the blueprint for a distinctly ritzy way of life: one critic aptly described it as 'a fantastically glamorous glimpse into A1 Georgian-house luxury-living, packaged as a fashionably utilitarian cook book'.[50] A stark white cover shows a row of artfully artless objects (a stack of cheap plastic beakers, an old tin grater, an egg in a wooden egg cup and a savoy cabbage), while the chapters are divided by similar images of isolated culinary objects (a kitchen timer, a child's cup, a potato) against plain, strongly coloured backgrounds. The styling resembles that of *Elle Deco* magazine, whose hip, urban readers are very much its target audience. The novelty of *How to Eat* is its leisurely discursiveness. Its stated aim, at least in its opening chapter on 'Basics' (which begins with the ubiquitous roast chicken), is to make its recipes redundant: to lure people away from style-conscious dinner-party cooking by encouraging them to learn techniques that they will repeat time after time. So the recipes are not graphically separated – the chat leading into one follows pretty much straight on from the end of the last. There are no pictures of the dishes, because the dishes themselves are not precisely the point – they are indicative of the *sort* of food you will cook if you devote yourself to living well.

Lawson, a very intelligent writer, is well aware of the pitfalls of an overly precise, dictatorial definition of good living – she clearly has no aspirations to make herself into another Martha Stewart and is constantly larding her discourse with qualifications and negations ('a vegetable soup doesn't require a recipe, and I certainly don't want to suggest you get out your scales to make it with mechanical accuracy') and throwing in dashes of self-conscious trashiness like ham baked in Coca-Cola and deep-fried Bounty bars.[51] She also evades accusations of bossiness with a host of little self-abnegations. She is anxious about baking because neither her mother nor her grandmothers ever did it, so she 'didn't acquire early in life that lazy confidence, that instinct'; she too has 'faltered, made mistakes, cooked disasters'.[52] And she insists repeatedly on her own cack-handedness. Such statements and admissions serve the paradoxical dual purpose of creating a sense of near-equality with the reader, while giving the narrative voice that diffident, apologetic, self-mocking note that reads as upper class; because class is certainly an issue in Nigella's books, though it is handled so cleverly that it becomes an asset rather than an impediment. It is there in the throwaway remark that 'my life is improved considerably by the fact that I can go to my greengrocer's and routinely buy stuff I used to have to go to Italy to find', in the spirit that puts grouse and white truffles in a chapter on basics.[53] Yet this lordliness is so cleverly balanced by the kitsch and the general atmosphere of plain speaking that it just gives a zest to the whole. There is a teasing quality in her first books and early television appearances – glimpses of a glamorous, chic, urban existence, with fabulously fashionable guests laughing in the other room, tantalizingly just out of sight. And then there was John Diamond, Nigella's journalist husband, whose fame, which long preceeded hers, was cemented by his decision to reveal all the sordid, boring, painful and tragic details of his throat cancer in his column in *The Times* and subsequently in the astoundingly clear-sighted *C: Because Cowards Get Cancer Too* (1998). There was a certain morbid intrigue in spotting him on the edge of the camera shot in the television series, in the idea of a cookery writer with a husband who couldn't eat her food; a sick glamour that made one shamefacedly but preternaturally aware of her remarks about eating alone, or comfort food. This uncomfortable fascination lies behind much of the media frenzy which greeted Nigella's first book and, even more, her second, and which reached a head with her television series *Nigella Bites*, broadcast in 2000. Very few mentioned John Diamond directly, but the pressure of the knowledge lay behind the fantasy Nigella the press conspired to create: beautiful, womanly, classy-but-accessible, and so *brave* (though no one would say this, since Diamond had mockingly exposed the spurious attachment of this adjective to anyone affected by cancer). With all this going on in the margins and subtext, the food in *How to Eat* often seems beside the point, but it is pretty good. The recipes are typical late-1990s eclectic (lots of Italian, Mediterranean classics, revivalist British, some American, and a pan-Oriental note). There is a surprising amount of meat – she is very fond of a hefty roast or braise – and little concern about fat or other dietary hang-ups of the moment (though there is a chapter on dieting in which she usefully introduces the notion of Temple Food – as in 'my body is a').

As Nigella Lawson became a bigger name, her books became more straightforwardly commercial, with the intriguing mannerisms of *How to Eat* crystallizing into something more formulaic. The styling was notably different: instead of the run-on recipes and prose we get larger typefaces, more space, a new page for each new recipe and glossy full-page photographs of the dishes. The styling suggests something less edgy, focused on a wider market. Such generosity with space and pictures became increasingly *de rigueur* in the cook books of the later 1990s and early 2000s. The effect is that each recipe acquires an iconic, almost fetishized status: like the recipe for Bloody Mary in *Nigella Bites*, in which three lines of directions are bumped up to two pages with artless lifestyle-conjuring chat and two full-colour art-directed photographs (one of the drink itself and one huge close-up of the chilli-spiked vodka Nigella makes specially for the drink). Curiously, this is the reverse of the intention of many of the writers – like Lawson, Nigel Slater and Sophie Grigson – for whose books the format is used and who profess an eagerness to free their readers from the tyranny of the recipe. Similarly, the apparent practicality of the layout, with its large clear type and sharply focused pictures of the finished dishes, is contradicted by the sheer weight of these books and the grease-attracting properties of their glossy pictures and fashionable low-sheen covers. The styling of Nigel Slater's 2002 *Thirst*, which concentrates with a somewhat maverick intensity on juice extraction, seems at first glance to attempt to overcome this problem, with its wipe-clean plastic cover, but inside the coloured type and eccentric layout inhibit reading with an almost wanton perversity. The luxury of space in these books is not at all about usability: their designers focus on graphic novelty and heft (hence the spinning out of thin content into fat books with big type and lots of space) because the publishers, if not the authors, are well aware that the books are bought as lifestyle icons, not manuals. The reason so few people cook from today's cook books is because they are not supposed to do so.

Style-wise, cook books struck out in a new direction with the publication of *Moro: The Cookbook* in 2001. A beautiful book, with a slightly textured plain beige cover resembling undyed linen, with the title in a fine cursive script in old gold, the book made the brash sixties-retro minimalism of the previous few years suddenly look old hat. Inside, slightly soft-focus pictures of food in rustic dishes against dark interiors carried something of the atmosphere of Dutch or Spanish old master paintings – entirely appropriately, as the book and the restaurant that spawned it concentrate on the cooking of Spain and the Muslim Mediterranean with which it is historically linked by the seven hundred years of Moorish occupation. Run by husband and wife team Sam and Sam Clark (Samuel and Samantha), the restaurant had opened in Clerkenwell in 1997 and rapidly earned a major reputation. Expanding the British sense of Spanish food beyond the tapas that had been popular here for the last decade and tapping into a growing interest in North African cuisine, the Clarks offered just what the jaded foodie market was looking for: something rustic and rawly authentic, exotic, yet comfortingly familiar, because many of their dishes belonged to the by now well-known Mediterranean repertoire. One might also speculate that their redrawing of the culinary map to bring together two cuisines more usually considered separately struck a chord with the new geopolitics of the third milliennium: as Europe became more and more aware of the political power of Islam, there was something reassuring in discovering age-old affinities between the two cultures. The Clarks' project brings together several strands that had characterized the British engagement with foreign foods over the past twenty years: a search for the exotic, a balancing of a commitment to authenticity with an impulse towards reinterpretation, and an abiding interest in peasant food.

So diligent were restaurateurs, food writers and publishers in searching out the exotic and undiscovered that by the 1990s virtually all foreign cuisines had been offered to the British public. The next stage was inevitable – the invention of fusion food. Fusion combined the ingredients and methods of one or more distinct national cuisines to produce something new. It is variously claimed to have originated in San Francisco and Sydney, both cities which have substantial Asian populations. Also known as 'Pacific Rim' cookery, it most commonly consisted of European-style dishes given an Asian twist (in the early days most often Thai, hence the preponderance of lemon grass and coconut in fusion dishes). Tandoori-style pizza, chocolate won tons, mango duck bouillabaisse, and the maki roll – a Californian piece of sushi filled with crab and avocado – are typical inventions. The term particularly caught on in America, where it was extended to encompass all sorts of cross-cultural culinary marriages (banana salsa, mango soup, sofrito mashed potatoes). It also gained surprising status in a number of Asian countries; prestigious restaurants in India, Hong Kong and Bangkok reversed the trend to serve Asian food with a European twist (naan bread in the form of a soft roll flavoured with sun-dried tomatoes at Doc Cheng's in Bangkok, for example). In Britain the trend belonged more to restaurants than to cook books; although dedicated fusion cook books were published here, none made a significant splash (probably the most important were those by Peter Gordon, the New Zealand chef of The Sugar Club, the best-known fusion restaurant in London). This is in part to do with the nature of the beast: as with nouvelle cuisine, invention and the shock of the new was all, and few recipes lasted long enough to attain any sort of classic status. But it was a difficult trend to ignore entirely. Its star has now waned, but when I began work on this book seven years ago, I envisaged fusion as the natural end point of the story I wanted to tell. Most cook-book writers in the 1990s saw fusion not as a distinct trend but as a new way of thinking about food, and its influence is obvious in the general licensing of eclecticism we find in their books. Nigel Slater's *Real Cooking* of 1997 includes Roast Fish with Indian Spices and Coconut; Thai Pork Rissoles with Lime Leaves, Chilli and Mint; Roast Chicken Thighs with Lime Juice and Ginger; and many other similar dishes sandwiched between the pastas and fish cakes. The same is true of almost all of his contemporaries, who clasp Thai food in particular to their bosoms but confidently adapt it and other Asian foods to the ingredients and structures of British cooking. They do not invent as freely or bizarrely as chefs, but a general insouciance about adaptation has replaced the meticulous authenticity of the Elizabeth David-influenced generation, a spirit summed up by Nigella Lawson's borrowing from Jonathan Miller to describe her Chinese-inspired dish as 'not quite char siu . . . just char siu-ish'.[54]

It has been suggested that the 'post-modern' form of the 1990s cook book – arranged by ingredients and methods, with chapters on tomatoes, cheese, chocolate, baking and so on, rather than by the stages of a traditional meal – may have played some part in the creation of fusion food:

> This classification encourages fusion experiment by removing the cultural barriers of recipe categories, such as appetizers and soups. By liberating the ingredient (for example, potatoes) or the technique (grilling), these cookbooks open the doors to an infinite diversity of ingredient combinations.[55]

It is certainly the case that both fusion experiments and cook books freed from the categories of the conventional meal are products of a culture that sees the past with an essentially post-modern sensibility as something to be played with rather than revered. And in a world where both people and products move freely and quickly, the notion of indigenous ingredients and local culinary styles had become increasingly artificial. Fusion was the logical product of globalization, the ultimate melting pot. And yet at the same time there was also a manifest anxiety about the ease with which culinary traditions could be reworked and hybridized. Many food critics and commentators expressed concern about (con)fusion food, which was sometimes represented as a form of cultural imperialism by the West. In Britain, as the 1990s wore on, food writers and restaurateurs rethought fusion as 'Modern British' food, a tag that indicated a combination of revived Anglo-French cooking *à la* Jane Grigson and fusion confections. Sybil Kapoor's *Modern British Food* (1995) works hard to suggest that the fusion impulse is one that has always characterized British cooking and that its inventions are therefore somehow authentic as well as exciting. It is an approach that often stretches the notion of Britishness to breaking point, as when she remarks of Squid with Spicy Peanut Sauce that 'this recipe is typical of the modern British (East meets West) Californian-influenced grilled dish'.[56] What she ignores, of course, is the difference between the gradual assimilation of new ingredients and methods that is a feature of all cuisines and the arbitrary and sometimes violent yoking of alien ingredients and methods to each other for the sake of novelty which characterizes fusion experiments.[57]

The most significant foreign influence on British food in the 1990s was the figure of the Mediterranean peasant, who loomed over our diets throughout the decade. It is his spectre that haunts the bread and cabbage soup of the River Café, the bean purées of Moro; it is in his name that we ritually dipped our ciabatta in the dishes of olive oil that replaced the butter in every neighbourhood trattoria. In the early 1990s a series of influential conferences on public health and diet held in America put together evidence that had begun emerging in the 1950s indicating that people living in the Mediterranean basin had significantly lower levels of heart disease compared to other populations. A committee drew up the Mediterranean Food Guide Pyramid, with breads, rice, pasta and other complex carbohydrates at the bottom (as the foods that formed the basis of the diet), fruits, beans and legumes, nuts and vegetables as the next level, followed – most contentiously – by olive oil, then cheese and yoghurt, with fish and poultry to be eaten a few times a week, eggs very occasionally, and red meat only a couple of times a month or more often but in very small amounts. Regular physical exercise was recommended, along with the regular moderate consumption of wine, particularly red. This model was tremendously influential, taken up by nutritionists all over the world and adopted by the World Health Organization. Lots of vegetables and carbohydrates, a strong scent of garlic, pints of olive oil, rough red wine, and meat or fish as garnish rather than central feature of the meal: such a diet, we were assured, is why the peasants of southern Europe had traditionally lived to such advanced old age. Yet what was de-emphasized in most accounts was that this diet reflected a way of life that had disappeared. The original research focused on tiny groups of men in Crete and Sicily in the 1950s and 60s, living in small isolated communities, eating diets that were the product of poverty and hardship. They worked in the fields for up to ten hours a day, took siestas, ate two leisurely meals daily in the presence of their extended families and inhabited a society marked by strong patriarchal structures and extensive support networks between family and neighbours. Any or all of these factors might have been responsible for the very low incidence of heart disease the surveys found, as might the absence of all the stresses of modern urban living that separate their lives fundamentally from those lived by most northern Europeans and Americans today. And the research is very difficult to replicate today because, even in Crete and Sicily, people no longer live like this. As affluence has increased, Crete has no longer been able to boast the lowest incidence of heart disease in Europe.[58]

The Mediterranean diet was essentially a fantasy, one that promised us health and long life while allowing us to indulge in fat and alcohol. Mediterranean foods were nothing new to food writers, of course; the main effect of this new barrage of nutritional advice was to consolidate a taste for these foods that had been developing since the publication of Elizabeth David's first book in 1950. Italian cook books, in particular, enjoyed a surge of popularity on the crest of this nutritional wave, though the best (those by native Italians Marcella Hazan and Anna del Conte, by chef Alastair Little and American food critic Patricia Wells) concerned themselves with more than the newly popular *cucina povera*.[59] Perhaps the most dominant effect was the new ease with which dietetically concerned writers now felt able to splash about the olive oil: it is from the early 1990s that we can date the practice of 'finishing' a dish with a drizzle of extra virgin olive oil (preferably estate bottled – this is one of the foodie snobberies that survived 1980s excess).

A number of restaurateurs got rich on peasant food, but what few seemed to remember was that this was a cuisine with its roots in a profound, sometimes startling, poverty. An exception was Elisabeth

Luard, whose first book, *The Rich Tradition of European Peasant Cookery* (1986), anticipated the revived interest in peasant cooking. She is one of the few writers who, while recognizing the appeal of such food to the modern sophisticate, also acknowledges the social deprivations that had brought it into being. This is her account of the subsistence meal eaten by her Spanish neighbours, as prepared by her housekeeper:

GAZPACHO

Ana's gazpacho, Andalusia's traditional, all-purpose meal, was basically bread soaked with water. For flavouring (rather as one might eat porridge with sugar and milk) there was olive oil, vinegar, and garlic – plus maybe a little chopped hard-boiled egg and diced *jamón serrano*, and a sprinkling of whatever the vegetable patch might offer. In winter, the dish was taken hot. In summer it was eaten cold. The bread, garlic, vinegar, and water are either pounded in a mortar, or merely infused together. Here is our (modern) family version of this ancient bread porridge.[60]

The 1990s interest in peasant foods was in part a reaction to the overblown excesses of the 1980s food scene, a longing to return to a sense of food as honest and simple, something intrinsically linked to basic human needs and rituals. And yet there was also something fanciful in it. It is no coincidence that the notion of peasant cooking became so significant at exactly the moment that the peasant way of life was actually disappearing in western Europe (all those fabulously cheap rural properties snapped up by Brits all over France, Spain and Italy having become available because so many peasant farmers were finding it impossible to continue living off the land). Our taste for the ancient food of these disappearing cultures was not actually simple at all but in itself something oddly sophisticated. M. F. K. Fisher described as 'faintly perverse' the consuming of 'all primitive dishes by too worldly people' – though this was not necessarily a criticism coming from the very worldly and often wilfully perverse Ms Fisher.[61] And there is a sense in which the aping of the cuisine of people whose whole way of life revolves around the production and consumption of their own food is merely another form of that obsession with food that had characterized the 1980s foodie.

There was, though, another major factor behind the 1990s preoccupation with peasant food: a deep sense of our own food as frightening. We are not the first generation to fear what we eat – we might remember the concerns Mrs Beeton expressed about food adulteration, with red lead in the butter, white lead, alum and chalk in the bread. But we have lived in this country through a series of catastrophes that have fundamentally eroded our trust in the food we are sold. The first was the salmonella crisis of 1988, when the hapless Edwina Currie had to warn the nation about the dangers of raw and undercooked eggs. Then there was BSE, the problem that haunted the 1990s, with the EEC ban on British beef only lifted in 1999. As well as the appalling physical results of Creutzfeldt-Jakob disease (or CJD, the human form of BSE), there were the fears of an epidemic of this fatal degenerative condition. And there was the fundamental erosion of public trust in the pronouncements of the government and its health advisers produced by the repeated denials that there was any danger to humans in eating BSE-infected beef.[62] These crises, and the furore over the unannounced introduction of genetically modified foods in the late 1990s, resulted in a dramatically heightened public awareness of the conditions in which livestock were kept and food produced. The fantasy of the peasant's harmonious relationship to the sources of his food was only one of the outcomes. Another was the massive increase in the visibility and popularity of organic food, to the extent that 75 per cent of British households now regularly buy some organic foodstuffs.[63] Recognizing a boom market, supermarkets have dramatically increased their organic lines, but one of the biggest growth areas has been organic box schemes, where small-scale growers provide customers with a selection of seasonal produce. Also increasingly important are farmers' markets, where local farmers can sell directly to the public, cutting out the supermarkets and their punitive pricing policies and fulfilling the Green ideal of transporting food over the smallest possible distances.

Green food politics have become increasingly influential in the last decade, with the publication of a number of significant books making the case for reducing pesticides, keeping livestock in more benign environments and substantially reducing the energy consumed in the production, packaging and transportation of processed foods. Eric Schlosser's *Fast Food Nation* of 2001 anatomized the American – and global – fast-food industry with savage humour, explaining 'what's in the meat' (you don't want to know) and the bizarre reasons 'why the fries taste good'.[64] Another book that combined investigative journalism with proselytizing food politics to dramatic effect was Joanna Blythman's *The Food We Eat* (1996, with a revised edition covering genetically modified foods published in 1998). Part shopping guide, part political tract, Blythman's book exposed issues such as the abuses of hens allowed under the 'free-range' label, the massively polluting effects of prawn farming in parts of Asia and the toxic chemicals employed by salmon farms. She provides the information needed to decode food labels, while also pointing out the good news: the increasing availability of ethically produced food, of organic produce, artisan cheeses and decent breads. The new popularity of organic foods and the revival of interest in traditional British specialities and artisanal products have gone hand in hand. The new foodie-ism concerns itself not with the rarefied and expensive but with the honest and authentic. That much work may be required to 'source' these products seems to be all to the good – there is the added buzz of virtue at having unearthed the best egg producer, the finest maker of a genuine sourdough loaf.

A number of recent books have engaged in a sort of roving food journalism to track down the best, the most traditional, the most authentic British food.[65] *Food Programme* veteran Derek Cooper collected the results of over thirty years of his interviews with food producers and other campaigning journalism from 'the food front' into his 2000 book *Snail Eggs and Samphire*. Cooper differs from many of his peers in the search for good food in campaigning vigorously against the worst food as well as celebrating the best, recognizing that by no means everybody can afford premium food:

> The policy of trying to keep prices as low as possible has created two kinds of food. There is the cheap and nasty stuff – wretched sausages made with mechanically recovered gristle and slurry, non-nutritious packets and tins of highly coloured rubbish and snacks rich only in empty calories – and the expensive foods which attract the words *real, natural, organic, traditional, pure, handmade*. But shouldn't all food be as safe and as pure and as fresh as possible? Why have cheap bad food at all?[66]

Other books have focused more specifically on organic foods, explaining the organic movement's techniques and principles and the regulations which govern it.[67] In 2001 Sophie Grigson and her husband William Black brought out *Organic*, which was divided evenly between explanations of organic practices and recipes. Rose Gray and Ruth Rogers published *River Café Cook Book Green* in 2000, in which they gave recipes for organically-produced vegetables (many of which they grow themselves for the restaurant in their Thames-side garden), arranged month by month. The problem for organic *cook* books, as opposed to books about organic food, is that nothing very much separates organic vegetables from their non-organic counterparts; there is no obvious reason why the former should require different recipes from the latter. Organic vegetables may taste better, but that is usually a function of their greater freshness, if they have been produced locally, and the fact that they may retain a protective layer of soil that supermarket produce has had removed with pressure hoses (the force of which tends to push grains of soil and bacteria beneath the surface of the vegetable). The essential difference, of course, is what is *not* there: an organic carrot of the same variety, age and freshness as a non-organic one will contain no more vitamins and nutrients, but crucially it will be free of the dangerous pesticides with which the latter has been sprayed. The River Café solution to differentiating organic from non-organic cookery is to focus on the issue of seasonality, since home-grown organic vegetables (rather than those expensive supermarket imports flown halfway around the world) appear and then disappear season by season.

Over the last decade the seasonal structure has become increasingly popular, employed by, among many others, Jenny Baker (in both 1993's *Kitchen Suppers* and 1996's *Kettle Broth to Gooseberry Fool*), Lynda Brown in *The Cook's Garden* (1990), Sybil Kapoor in *Modern British Food* (1995) and restaurateur Sally Clarke in *Sally Clarke's Book* (1999). It is about eating foods at their best, but it also reflects a spirit of self-restraint, a sense that things are more pleasurable if enjoyed only occasionally, that it is somehow more *right* to eat asparagus only in May and June and swedes only in the winter.[68] The same sort of wilful reining-in of our limitless consumer choices is reflected in the organic vegetable-box schemes: when you can buy virtually anything from teeming supermarket shelves, there is something perversely pleasurable about being faced with a selection of vegetables you have not chosen and being forced to make something from them. This new way of buying has opened up a niche for a new sort of cook book – one that provides an answer to the conundrum of what you cook for supper when faced with yet more parsnips, a bundle of pak choi and a large bunch of curly kale. *Annie Bell's Vegetable Book* was published in 1997, at a time when box schemes were only just beginning and obtaining organic produce still required a semi-hunter-gatherer approach, but it nonetheless succeeds very well in dealing with this peculiarly contemporary problem, with sections on thirty-six vegetables, including challenges like Swiss chard, kohlrabi and Jerusalem artichokes.[69]

Organic farming in general, and the vegetable box in particular, has enlarged the vegetable canon in cook books: the reason that we find so many recipes in recent books for once rather unpopular vegetables like beetroot and turnip, or for erstwhile rarities like Swiss chard and purple sprouting broccoli, is that these vegetables are relatively easy to grow organically and can be cropped in the winter at a time when little else is available for the growers to put in the boxes. And if they are easy for farmers to produce without employing intensive, chemical methods, then they are also easy for the gardener. The last decade has seen a small-scale return to the 1970s ideal of growing our own food. The most original book in this area is Hugh Fearnley-Whittingstall's *The River Cottage Cookbook* (2001), which won the following year's Glenfiddich trophy. The book and accompanying television series detail his experiments with the self-sufficient life on his eponymous smallholding in Dorset. As well as growing fruit and vegetables, making jams, freezing gluts and picking wild harvests from the hedgerows, Fearnley-Whittingstall fishes, shoots and keeps pigs, sheep and hens. The book gives copious advice (which the author has gleaned himself as he goes along) on lambing, butchering and embarking on massive sessions of sausage and ham production on the day you slaughter your pig. Despite the epithets with which reviewers have responded to his unrepentantly carnivorous bent – 'enthusiastic muncher of small animals' being the most colourful – Fearnley-Whittingstall's project is about treating animals with respect, his preoccupation with offal not so much a macho pose as a concern to use every part of the animal whose life he has taken – 'everything but the oink, as the old butchers like to say'.[70] The horror with which many commentators greeted his eager embracing of the process of livestock-keeping from birth to death may have something to do with the inexorable spread of vegetarianism in the last few decades – though for many ideological vegetarians (myself included) there is something much more honest about this approach than in the grabbing of unidentifiable chunks of animal protein from a supermarket shelf.

Vegetarianism has progressed from a minority dietary fad to something of major significance since the 1970s. The 1980s was the boom decade for the publication of vegetarian cook books, with hundreds of books on the subject appearing every year. These new books were less proselytizing than the vegetarian cook books of the past and also much less strict. They embraced culinary influences from all over the world and tended to reject the worthy wholefoods that earlier vegetarian writers had deemed essential.[71] The most important British vegetarian food writer of the 1990s was undoubtedly Annie Bell, whose *A Feast of Flavours: The New Vegetarian Cuisine* appeared in 1992. Bell managed to translate the new food interests of the early 1990s into vegetarian food so lively that the absence of meat was unnoticeable. The book is arranged around menus for different sorts of meals in different seasons, and in each she achieves an admirable balance between flavours, textures and colours. In a hot buffet for autumn, for example, she offers a largely Spanish menu of a Catalan Casserole with Pear and Caramelized Onion, Spinach with Pine-Nuts, Stoved Potatoes with Rosemary, a selection of Spanish cheeses, and Chocolate Fondant Cake. Her work is noteworthy for having grasped a fundamental truth about the vegetarianism of the late twentieth century: that many people were now calling themselves vegetarian who would not have done so previously. In particular, she acknowledges the large number of vegetarians-who-eat-fish, and consequently includes fish in some of her recipes, though usually as an element that was easy to leave out. Clearly this is not vegetarianism as the Vegetarian Society would understand it, but then Bell is one of that growing band of food refuseniks motivated by factors other than absolute ideological purity. This 'demi-veg' group forms an increasingly significant segment of the market – a fact attested to by Sainsbury's publication of Josceline Dimbleby's *Almost Vegetarian Cookbook* in 1994 (she included chicken as well as fish). The massive publicity given to the Mediterranean diet persuaded many to readjust the place of meat in their diets, if not to give it up altogether. But the major influence on the growth of vegetarianism as a lifestyle choice rather than a virtually religious commitment has been the food scares and revelations of the past decades – the more we learn, the less appetizing meat seems.

In a decade and a half dominated by food fears we have become desperate for a vision of food as something reassuring – something safe. It is this that accounts for the passionate intensity with which recent cook-book writers focus on one particular property of their dishes: their ability to comfort. Nigel Slater sings the virtues of mashed potato as the ultimate comfort food and assures us that custard is 'one of the most soothing, comforting and calming things you can make'. For Tamasin Day-Lewis Quiche Lorraine is 'food to console and please of the highest order', while Delia Smith describes her Pork Sausages Braised in Cider with Apples and Juniper as 'a lovely, comforting, warm, winter supper dish'. And Nigella Lawson gives us a Plum and Pecan Crumble that is 'comfortingly autumnal' and a Steamed Syrup Sponge which she recommends as 'comfortingly, not cloyingly, sweet' in *How to Be a Domestic Goddess*, the book she subtitled 'Baking and the Art of Comfort Cooking'.[72] It is only since the 1990s that food writers have assumed that comfort and reassurance are what their readers are looking for in a dish. Typical adjectives in the cook books of the 1980s would instead include piquant, luxurious, elegant, pretty, perfect, rich (quite a word portrait of that decade's preoccupations). The sense that we are all in need of culinary comfort also provides a compelling explanation for the surprising re-emergence of the baking book.

Baking has never had the status in this country that it has in America, where it forms a dominant element in classic cook books like Fannie Farmer's *Boston Cooking School Cook Book* and Irma Rombauer's *The Joy of Cooking* and is culturally enshrined in kitsch extravaganzas like the Pilsbury Bake-Off. In Britain, baking survives as a traditionally rural skill, as represented by the WI cake stall, but has not been truly fashionable since before the First World War. Even then it was not very high status since cakes were served at tea, a meal that on the whole only women and children ate. It is probably for this reason that baking has acquired a reputation as something that does not concern men, remaining the last culinary bastion to fall before the male cook. It is not because women had traditionally baked that baking has long been seen as unmasculine but because men are not properly supposed to have an interest in its products. Puddings (boiled), yes; cakes (baked), no. A further explanation is offered by Christopher Driver, who suggests that 'a psychologist might be found to explain male amateur cooks' relative lack of interest in baking puddings and cakes not by their want of a sweet tooth . . . but by a latent confusion of the act of baking with the process of gestation' – a bun in the oven being, naturally, a solely female concern.[73]

There's a long cultural history of cakes as emblematizing an exclusively feminine realm of chatter and competition – the phrase 'muffin worry' to denote a gathering of old maids, the genteel one-upmanship over the seed cake in *Cranford*. In the 1950s we borrowed from America, along with so much else, the notion of baking as the highest achievement of the happy homemaker, but cake recipes nonetheless remained largely the preoccupation of worthily dull cook books and mass-market women's magazines. It is only in the last two decades that baking has been taken seriously in the world of food publishing. It started quietly and decorously in the 1980s with the publication of a few seriously researched books on the subject that were entirely without the gushing and tummy patting that had characterized the women's magazine approach. The first was Helge Rubinstein's *The Chocolate Book*, published in hardback in 1981 and then appearing as part of Jill Norman's Penguin stable in the following year. A stylish and fascinating book, it intersperses brief historical essays on the discovery, development and manufacture of chocolate with recipes for savoury dishes, hot and cold desserts, cakes, biscuits and cookies, confectionery and drinks. It contains a delightful 'Old English' chocolate flan with an almond crust, which can be eaten when the crust is crackling and the filling melting or left until the following day, when 'the crust will have become soft and the filling thick and fudgy'.[74] And it also has the best-ever recipe for chocolate brownies.

In 1982 Barbara Maher's *Cakes* appeared (commissioned by Jill Norman, it was to appear in paperback in 1984). Another book to place its subject in a considered historical context, *Cakes* gives definitive instructions for classic dishes in the English, French, German, Swiss and American baking traditions – confections including Sachertorte, Strudels, Marjolaine, Strawberry Shortcake and Bûche de Noël. The recipes are elaborate and meticulous, and the results are invariably excellent. It is a world away from the spirit of exuberant invention that has traditionally dominated the American approach to the subject of baking: we will find no peach-peppermint surprise cake here.

A few more serious examples appeared in the following decade, but the real explosion in baking books came at the start of the new millennium.[75] The year 2000 saw the publication of Adriana Rabinovich's *The Little Red Barn Baking Book*, Nigella Lawson's *How to Be a Domestic Goddess* and Tamasin Day-Lewis's *The Art of the Tart*, all of which achieved significant sales and garnered rave reviews. Day-Lewis rescued the tart from the dubious legacy of the 1970s quiche, with delights such as Potato, Garlic and Parsley Tourte; Tomato and

Oatmeal Tart; and a Brandade Tart. There is also a truly excellent recipe for Almond Cream Tarts, to be made with a choice of stone fruits, in which the almond filling remains marzipan-soft rather than drying to a disappointing cakiness as do the products of virtually all other recipes for frangipane-filled fruit tarts. Rabinovich's book offered recipes for the products that had achieved a degree of cult status through her Little Red Barn mail-order company. Both the mail-order business and the book offer effectively packaged down-home Americana to a British market, with muffins, brownies and pies – Pecan, Apple, Coconut Cream and the like – featuring prominently. The tone is set by nostalgic chat about her American childhood and cemented by images of her family cut from old photos and surreally juxtaposed with shots of the food – a child in 1960s swimming costume and rubber ring emerges from the centre of a cookie, another in a snow suit perches on a lemon-meringue pie. The effect is to conjure up childhood scrapbooks or the high-school yearbooks that have the glamour of unfamiliarity to a British readership.

A similar fascination with American baking and the culture it evokes is to be found in Nigella Lawson's *Domestic Goddess*. The book's entire concept responds to a fantasy that always belonged more to America than to Britain, though it impacted strongly on our sense of ourselves. The kitsch images of glamorous, hostess-pinnied 1950s housewives that decorate the book's inside covers epitomize that cultural borrowing, as do many of the recipes Lawson collects. Boston Cream Pie, Banana Bread (borrowed from a book with the subtitle 'Recipes from an American Childhood'), Snickerdoodles, Maple-Pecan Biscuits, Strawberry Shortcakes – this list takes us hardly any way into the book. Lawson's fascination with American baking clearly has much to do with cultural associations. It carries with it a seemingly inevitable sense of kitsch that allows it to be passed off as not entirely serious. Her book is all about *playing* mother rather than being her – indulging in a fantasy of ourselves as comforting, nurturing, old-fashioned mothers, baking cookies for when the kids come home from school. That it is not about being our *own* mothers is made clear by the cultural transplantation: we are to play at being the suburban moms reflected in Hollywood films. This safe distance allows for a role play that does not threaten the lifestyle choices made by a generation of women who are generally rather glad not to be living the lives of their own mothers. It is also very clear that the nurturing is to be of ourselves rather than our children. Lawson's proudest invention in this book is her idea of serving cupcakes as a finale to an adult dinner party:

> About the time I started getting into top cupcake and fairy-cake mode, ostensibly for children, I noticed that the people who really seemed to get excited by them were the children's parents. I think it's not till you hit 30 that nostalgia is even a remotely comforting option.[76]

Consequently, she gives at least twelve variations, including Cappuccino and Espresso Cupcakes, Chocolate-Cherry Cupcakes, Lavender Cupcakes and Burnt-Butter Brown-Sugar Cupcakes. In *Nigella Bites* (2001) she continues the theme of American baking as the ultimate in comfort food with a recipe for a Chocolate Fudge Cake derived from a book of American diner desserts, of which she announces 'this is the sort of cake you'd want to eat the whole of when you'd been chucked. But even the sight of it, proud and tall and thickly iced on its stand, comforts.'[77]

The notion of mothering ourselves with sweet, sticky comfort food is a poignant one for increasingly stressed, multitasking modern women. The fantasy does not play so well to men (who would prefer, I suppose, to be mothered by someone else). Despite its newly fashionable status, baking has still not really crossed the gender divide.[78] A possible exception is what looks likely to be one of the next high-fashion culinary trends: artisan baking. The perfection of a sour-dough loaf has emerged over the last few years as the holy grail of those seriously preoccupied with food. Beginning with *le pain au levain naturel* produced in the 1980s by Lionel Poilâne at his now world-famous Parisian bakery, the obsession with buying – or better yet, making – the *echt* sour-dough bread has spread around the foodie world. Because the bread is fermented with natural yeasts, which have to be attracted to a home-grown starter before baking can commence, it is notoriously fickle; because it is an ancient practice, pre-dating by millennia the use of brewer's yeast, it is about as authentic as you can get – both qualities which make its mastery the absolute pinnacle of achievement for the foodie of the new millennium. American food-people Jeffrey Steingarten and John Thorne (author of *Outlaw Cook*, whose Simple Cooking website is one of the best and most visited of the many food-related sites) have both written entertaining essays on the pursuit (with Thorne recording the effect of moving house on his temperamental starter); and now that Baker & Spice, one of the best

British artisanal bakeries, has issued its *Baking with Passion* (1999), the practice is sure to spread.[79]

If the new interest in baking emerges from our preoccupation with food that comforts and reassures, so too does the recent turn to the food of our childhood. While there has long been a movement to revive our ancient, pre-industrial food heritage – witness Elizabeth David's later works and the entire career of Jane Grigson – it is only very recently that we have embraced what the French might call *la cuisine mère*, the food that the now culturally dominant baby boomers ate as children. Simon Hopkinson is undoubtedly the king of this revival, which he arguably kick-started with 1997's *The Prawn Cocktail Years* (co-authored with Lindsey Bareham). Although the title suggests an element of post-modern pastiche (akin to the brief-lived, ironic retro-chic fashion for fondue sets), the book is in fact a respectful foray into the restaurant classics of the 1950s, 1960s and 1970s, offering sound recipes for dishes once the height of culinary sophistication but lost to us through decades of commercial debasement. Black Forest Gateau, Quiche Lorraine, Gammon and Pineapple, Wiener Schnitzel and Duck à l'Orange are revisited and made to seem delicious once again. Indeed, culinary nostalgia has formed a significant element in most of the major cook books published in the last seven years. Steak and Kidney Pudding (Ruth Watson, Nigella Lawson), Hotpot (Watson, Sophie Grigson), Parsley Sauce (Watson, Simon Hopkinson, Hugh Fearnley-Whittingstall), Fish Pie (Lawson, Hopkinson, Grigson, Nigel Slater and Tamasin Day-Lewis), Banana Custard (Slater, Lawson, Grigson), Trifle (Lawson, Day-Lewis, Slater), Crumble (Lawson, Slater, Watson, Fearnley-Whittingstall) and Bread-and-Butter Pudding (everyone): the homely classics of the 1950s, 1960s and 1970s are now firmly back on the menu.[80] Simon Hopkinson even makes a case for savoury mince – 'all dark and brown and rich, bejewelled by tiny chunks of carrot and traces of slippery, gently gilded onion'.[81]

As a nation, we have suffered nearly two hundred years of profound culinary self-abasement: always eager to reinvent our cooking, always contemptuous of the food of the recent past. I am under no illusion that this cycle will suddenly stop – there are too many commercial interests invested in keeping us all on the treadmill of constant culinary change. But it is nonetheless worthy of note that for the first time in a very long time 'food like mother used to make it' is no longer assumed to be an insult.

TYPICAL RECIPES 1980–PRESENT

Raymond Blanc
Recipes from Le Manoir Aux Quat' Saisons (1988)

Although not, strictly speaking, first-generation nouvelle cuisine, Raymond Blanc's cooking nonetheless typifies many of the trends of the movement (note the food processor, the raspberry vinegar, the quenelles). This is one of the shortest and simplest of the recipes in the collection. Nonetheless, the layout works to create an air of bemusing complexity – so many different stages, such meticulous timings given for each. The cult of the chef is in clear evidence – the words of the great man himself are given in hallowing quotation marks as an epigraph, while the chef's notes are a separate element, creating the impression of a masterclass; yet it is notable that the one complex procedure involved – the shaping of quenelles – is not explained at all. There are few concessions to the domestic cook: the quantity is given for twelve, regardless of how few readers would actually want a pepper mousse in those amounts; and the recipe, as with the rest in the collection, is laid out in three closely typed columns, printed in a grey ink so pale that it is barely visible.

MOUSSETTE DE POIVRONS ROUGE
Mousse of Red Peppers

'This fresh and tangy mousse is delicious served with a Tomato vinaigrette or Tomato sorbet.'

Serves 12.
Total recipe time: 40 minutes, plus 3 hours chilling.
Special equipment: 24 x 10 cm/10 x 4 in. terrine or a china bowl, food processor

INGREDIENTS

¼ onion, finely chopped
2 tomatoes, deseeded and chopped
3 red peppers, cored, deseeded and chopped
1½ leaves of gelatine, or ½ teaspoon powdered gelatine
2 tablespoons olive oil
½ teaspoon cayenne pepper
2 tablespoons white wine vinegar

1 teaspoon raspberry vinegar
400 ml/14 fl oz whipped cream, chilled
salt and freshly ground white pepper

Planning ahead
As the mousse needs to set, prepare it at least 3 hours in advance and chill. You can shape the mousse into quenelles half an hour before serving, arrange on the plates and keep in a cool place.

1. Preparing the mousse base
(20 minutes)
Soak the gelatine leaves in cold water for a few minutes until supple. In a large saucepan, sweat the chopped onions in the olive oil for 1 minute without colouring. Add the chopped tomatoes and red peppers, 1 teaspoon salt and ½ teaspoon cayenne pepper. Cook for a further 6–7 minutes over a strong heat, stirring to prevent sticking.

Purée, then return the mixture to the saucepan and reduce for about 5 minutes, stirring constantly, to obtain about 200 ml/7 fl oz purée. Add the soaked gelatine and stir until completely dissolved. Force the purée through a sieve into a small bowl and allow to cool slightly.

Meanwhile mix together the white wine and raspberry vinegar and reduce by two-thirds over high heat. Stir into the purée and leave to cool in the fridge.

2. Making the mousse
(10 minutes, plus 3 hours chilling)
Cream: Whip to soft peaks. Using a wooden spoon, mix one-quarter of the whipped cream into the mousse mixture, incorporating it in fast circular movements. Gently fold in the remaining cream with a wooden spatula. Taste and correct seasoning. Transfer the mousse to a terrine or china bowl, smooth the surface with a palette knife, cover with clingfilm and refrigerate for at least 3 hours until set.

3. Serving (10 minutes)
Chill 12 plates.
Using two dessertspoons dipped in hot water, shape the mousse into *quenelles* and place 3 on each plate.

Storing
The mousse can be kept for 2 or 3 days in a covered container in the fridge.

VARIATIONS

You can turn this recipe into a bavarois of red peppers simply by adding 3 more gelatine leaves to the mousse mixture and chilling the mousse in a 2–3 cm/1 in. deep china flan dish. Dip the dish into hot water to unmould the mousse and turn out onto a serving plate. Refrigerate again and mask the surface with a little jelly made with 100 ml/3½ fl oz water, half a finely diced red pepper and 1 gelatine leaf.

Chef's notes
Whipping cream: The cream must not be whipped solid or it will separate when incorporated into the red pepper purée. It should be light and fluffy but still hold together. One-quarter of the whipped cream is mixed in briskly at first to lighten the mixture and make it easier to incorporate the remaining cream. Make sure that the first step is done fast and the second step slowly and gently, lifting and folding to maintain the light delicate texture. The cream must be chilled; butter fats are more likely to separate if they are tepid or at room temperature. Make sure that the red pepper purée is cold before incorporating the cream!

Jeremy Round
The Independent Cook (1988)

Round's writing about food heralds the preoccupations of the next decade: comfort, nostalgia, simplicity, revivalism, with a pan-Asian edge. It is in a relaxed mode, with the scholarship and practical research tempered by wit and informality – his voice and approach had a clear influence on writers such as Nigella Lawson and Nigel Slater.

SWEETENING RICE

For every person put off the food in their childhood for life, there is another left with a deep need for regular fixes. Rice pudding seems a common bête noire, although the luckiest of us remember only succulent beds of creamy rice with a golden skin, flecked black and tasting richly of caramel.

From Greece to India, cold rice pudding is a popular and refreshing treat, made either in a saucepan and poured into individual serving bowls before chilling, or baked separately in the oven so that each helping has its own crust. The texture is much looser than the moulded French rice rings – sometimes just a sweet sauce with a few grains of rice lurking at the bottom.

The quantity of the milk used is one of the most important factors in the regional variety (try using gold-top from the Channel Islands in the following recipes) and each cuisine adds its own flavouring. Greece and Turkey settle for fragrant mastic resin and sometimes cinnamon, an Arab version dribbles honey over the top, and in India raisins are cooked with the rice and the finished dish is decorated with vark (silver or gold leaf beaten so thin as to be edible).

The best rice pudding I've ever eaten was high up in the lushest green meadows of the Pontiac Alps behind Trabzon, ancient Trebizond, in Eastern Turkey. The little village of Hamsiköy, which stands on the main road over the pass onto the Anatolian plateau and the desolate city of Erzurum, is famous throughout the country for its dairy produce. Every passing bus, lorry and car in the know stops at the biggest café in the centre for its passengers to remind themselves to what gastronomic heights a modest rice pudding can ascend.

[The recipe below] is a baked Turkish version; the mastic resin you need for it can be bought in Greek Cypriot and Turkish shops.

TURKISH RICE PUDDING

serves 6

1½ pints milk
8 oz sugar
5 oz cooked short-grain pudding rice
½ teaspoon crystals of mastic resin – pulverised
1½ rounded tablespoons cornflour
2 small egg yolks – beaten

Bring the milk to the boil in a large saucepan. Stir in the sugar and rice. Take the pan off the heat, then, stirring all the time, sprinkle in the mastic powder. The pan should still be steaming hot, but should not come back to the boil after this has been added, or the mastic gets hard and stringy.

Mix the cornflour with a little water to form a thin paste. Whisk this with the egg yolks into the hot milk, then stir – over a low flame if necessary – until the mixture thickens.

Pour into individual oven-proof bowls and let the mixture cool to blood temperature. Arrange the bowls in a deep oven tray, pour a little cold water into the tray, then pack ice-cubes around the bowls. This is to prevent the mixture boiling while the crust browns.

Place the tray towards the top of a pre-heated oven – about Gas 6/200°C/400°F – for half an hour or so until the top is dark golden brown. Chill the puddings before serving.

Rose Gray and Ruth Rogers
The River Café Cook Book (1995)

The extremely influential gospel of Italian peasant food according to the River Café: robust, obscure greens; chewy, rough bread torn and added to soups and salad; the whole swimming in the pepperiest extra virgin olive oil you can source. We can mock, but a decade later many of us continue to make such soup-stews on a weekly basis. Its roots in the cuisine of the poor are still visible (the idea is to use up stale bread, to soften tough but nutritious winter greens), but in the context of 1990s Britain this was food for the wealthy and leisured, requiring bread and cabbage that were expensive and difficult to find (though both became much easier to source in the wake of the book's popularity). The ethos of the River Café has the ingredients as the stars, and this is made very apparent by the layout of the recipes: here there are no columns to squeeze the ingredients into the smallest possible parameter; in fact, each ingredient stands alone, hallowed by the white space around it, while the very brief method is tacked on at the bottom of the page. The brevity of the instructions produces confusion – at what temperature do we cook the vegetables, why is it not possible to give amounts for liquid, for olive oil? Coupled with the industrial quantities, this adds a layer of mystique and complexity to what is actually quite a simple dish.

RIBOLLITA

Cavolo nero is essential for an authentic ribollita. Robust greens such as Swiss chard, the dark green outer leaves of Savoy cabbage, kale, broccoli or rape may be substituted.
Serves 10

250 g (9 oz) cannellini or borlotti beans, cooked

1 large bunch flat-leaf parsley

4 garlic cloves, peeled and chopped

2 whole heads celery, peeled and chopped

450 g (1 lb) carrots, peeled and chopped

4 medium red onions, peeled and chopped

4 tablespoons olive oil

1 x 800 g (1¾ lb) tin peeled plum tomatoes, drained of their juices

2 kg (4½ lb) cavolo nero, stalks removed, leaves coarsely chopped

2 loaves stale ciabatta bread, crusts removed, sliced or torn

sea salt and freshly ground black pepper

extra virgin olive oil

In a large saucepan fry the parsley leaves, garlic, celery, carrot and onion in the oil for about 30 minutes until the flavours combine. Add the tomatoes and continue to cook on a gentle heat for a further 30 minutes, then add the cavolo nero and half the cannellini beans with enough of their liquid to cover. Simmer for 30 minutes.

In a food processor, purée the remaining beans and return to the soup with just enough boiling water to make the soup liquid. Add the bread, a generous amount of extra virgin olive oil, and season with salt and pepper. As exact amounts are not possible, you must balance the amount of liquid to bread so that the soup is very thick.

Nigel Slater
Real Cooking (1997)

The form of this recipe is the reverse of the River Café one that precedes it: the ingredients are discreetly banished to a side column, while the main focus is on the method. An immense enthusiasm for eating is conveyed: for the tastes and textures of the food, the scents and the juices. The approach is casual and inviting; the reader is encouraged to muck in, get his hands dirty, enjoy the process, but not take it too seri-

ously. There is no kowtowing to notions of authenticity here – the fact that the recipe is an adaptation is headlined, with the implication that we too are free to play around, to invent. The rough and ready measures of the flavourings – the ginger the size of your thumb, the handful of mint leaves – issues a similar invitation to culinary exploration. Yet this is food grounded in knowledge and precision; its exuberance does not direct us to the ersatz or industrially produced. Instead Slater aims to lead by the taste buds, encouraging an interest in the 'proper' ingredients and techniques not out of snobbery or a rigid commitment to authenticity but simply because they taste better. His great gift as a food writer is to make you taste that difference on the page.

THAI PORK RISSOLES WITH LIME LEAVES, CHILLIES AND MINT

Sticky, savoury little cakes, hot with chillies and citrus flavours. I cannot deny that these are simply Thai fish cakes in which I have replaced the fish with pork. As with fish cakes, the texture will be more interesting to eat if you loosely shape them into rough-edged patties rather than attempting perfection. Don't be daunted by the length of the recipe; it is simple and quick.

For 3, or 2 very greedy people

- 125 g fatty bacon (such as pancetta)
- 4 spring onions, roughly chopped
- 8 large lime leaves
- a knob of ginger, about the size of your thumb, grated
- a large, hot chilli, chopped
- 4 cloves of garlic, chopped
- a handful of mint leaves, about 12
- 450 g minced pork
- a little oil for frying

For the dipping sauce

- 5 tablespoons rice vinegar

Mince the fat bacon. This is easiest done in a food processor, although it will actually be very finely chopped rather than minced. At a push you could chop it to a mush by hand – but rather you than me. While the bacon is still in the processor, throw in the spring onions, lime leaves (removing any tough stems), the grated ginger, chilli, garlic and mint. Season generously with both black pepper and salt. Whizz until the aromatics and spices are finely incorporated into the bacon.

Mix with the minced pork and set aside in the cool while the mixture stiffens and the aromatics flavour the meat. For the dipping sauce, bring the rice vinegar and the sugar to the boil in a small saucepan and continue boiling till it turns sticky – a bit like thin golden syrup. Remove from the heat, stir in the soy. Cool, then add the chilli and coriander leaves.

4 tablespoons sugar
a tablespoon of soy sauce
a small red chilli, seeded and finely chopped
a small handful of coriander leaves, chopped

Get a little oil hot in a pan – it doesn't really matter what sort, just enough to cover the bottom in a shallow layer. Shape the seasoned pork into about twelve little patties, burgers if you like, and drop them, half a dozen at a time, into the hot fat.

Fry for a total of ten minutes over a low heat, turning once or twice. They should be cooked right through (test one by breaking it open; it should be light brown, not pink inside) and the surface should be reddy-brown and glistening slightly with stickiness from the bacon fat. Eat immediately with the dipping sauce, dunking each hot, citrus-scented burger into the dip as you eat.

Nigella Lawson
How to Eat (1998)

This is food as personal history – a dish adapted for a particular occasion, with accompanying anecdote (which, incidentally, once again manages to establish a patrician background while craftily disavowing its values). The recipe functions as a record of this event – 'this is how I made it' – as well as a transferable set of instructions. The effect is to restore to food its singularity (each time we cook a dish it will be different) and also its transitoriness. This menu demonstrates the focus on comfort food that is such a feature of its historical moment – comfort at all costs, whatever imbalance it produces: so we have one milky, creamy, soft, white, sauce-covered dish followed by another. Lawson's stylistic devotion to the modifier – nutmeggy, creaturely, milkily-sweet, mushroomy – adds life to her writing but at the expense of sometimes striking a somewhat gushing note. One of the reasons for Nigella Lawson's popular success is that she combines the features of a num-

ber of other very successful food writers: here the detailed discussion of what can go wrong and the acknowledgement that the reader may be nervous place her with Delia in the reader-reassurance camp; while the bracing assertion that even imperfect food can be good, the focus on pleasure and the rendering of taste sensations align her with Nigel Slater. The aestheticism represented by the ruby-glinting cherries, along with her representation of food as one element of a highly desirable lifestyle place her with purveyors of the good life like Martha Stewart.

A COMFORTING LUNCH FOR 4

Fish and porcini pie
Ice-cream, cherries, flaked almonds and chocolate sauce

Fish pie is not particularly labour-intensive to cook, but it's hard to get right: if the flour/butter/milk balance is off, the sauce bubbling beneath the blanket of nutmeggy mashed potato can be too runny or too solid. Don't let nervousness make you scrimp on the milk: it's better runny than stodgy and even an imperfect fish pie is a delicious one. What's important is not to make the sauce taste too floury (using 00 flour sees to that) and not to let your desire for something comforting blunt your appetite for seasoning. I added porcini because I'd been given some by my Austrian Aunt Frieda, who was coming for lunch. Perhaps it would be more correct to say Great Aunt; the title is honorific but she's the generation, was the companion, of my grandmother. She was the matron at my mother and aunts' boarding school and my grandmother, not I think extraordinarily maternal, was so dreading the school holidays that she asked Matron to stay during them. Over forty years later, she's still here, an important figure in all our lives. I wanted to use the mushrooms because she'd given them to me. But I also thought they'd add a creaturely muskiness, a depth of tone, to the milkily-sweet fish-scented sauce. They did.

This is how I made it. You can change the fish as you want.

FISH AND PORCINI PIE

10 g dried porcini
300 ml fish stock (I used a tub of Joubère fish stock)
175 g skinned cod
175 g skinned smoked haddock
175 g skinned salmon
250 ml full-fat milk
3 bay leaves

60 g butter
60 g plain, preferably 00, flour
1.25 kg floury potatoes
150 ml double cream (or 150 ml milk, with 60 g butter, melted)
freshly grated nutmeg

Cover the dried porcini with very hot water and leave for 20 minutes or so. Then drain the mushrooms and strain the soaking liquid into the stock. Choose the dish in which you will cook (and serve) the fish pie. I use an old, very battered, oval, enamel cast-iron dish of my mother's, which has a capacity of about 2 litres. Put the fish in a wide, thick-bottomed pan – I use a frying pan, but anything that'll take them in one layer would do – and cover with milk, the stock with its mushroom liquid and the bay leaves. Bring to a simmer and poach for about 3 minutes. Remove the fish to the buttered dish, and fork into chunks. Sieve the cooking liquid into a jug, reserving bay leaves.

Melt the butter in a saucepan and add the dried soaked mushrooms, very finely chopped and any grit removed. Fry gently for 2 minutes, stir in the flour and fry gently for another 2 minutes. Off the heat, very slowly add the liquid from the jug, stirring with a wooden spoon or beating with a whisk (whichever suits) as you go. When all is incorporated, put back on the heat. Add the bay leaves and stir gently until thickened. If you're going to eat it straight away, pour over the fish in the casserole. Otherwise, remove from heat and cover with butter paper (the foil paper the butter is wrapped in), buttered greaseproof, waxed paper or a film of melted butter.

You can boil and mash the potatoes with the cream and seasoning now (you want lots of salt and pepper), or you may have done them in advance. When you're ready to roll, preheat the oven to gas mark 4/180°C. The fish and mushroomy white sauce should be in the casserole, the potato on top, with more nutmeg, pepper and butter (little dots of it here and there) added just before it goes in the oven. Depending on how hot it all is before it goes in the oven, the fish pie should need about 20–40 minutes. Test as you go: this isn't an untouchable work of art you're creating; dig a hole, taste and then patch up with potato.

For pudding, buy the best ice-cream, vanilla if you can, or make your own. Buy a ruby-glinting jar of bottled, sourish cherries and some flaked or slithered almonds, to go with it and make a glossily dark chocolate sauce. [Recipe given below]

- 200 g bitter dark chocolate
- 120 ml strong black coffee, or 1 teaspoon instant coffee made up with 120 ml water
- 90 g caster sugar
- 120 ml double cream

Now the chocolate sauce: place the chocolate, broken up into small pieces, in a thick-bottomed pan with the coffee and sugar and melt over a low heat, stirring occasionally. Then pour in the cream, still stirring, and when it is very hot pour into a warmed sauceboat or a bowl with a ladle.

Jamie Oliver
Happy Days with the Naked Chef (2001)

A recipe very much of its time, in that it highlights the turn to baking at the millennium and the continuing love affair with all things Italian. Coupled with the enthusiasm for bread is a sense of trespass on a feminine terrain: hence the crack about pregnant women, and the reassuring presence of the old mate. Jamie Oliver's characteristic engagingly laddish tone of voice emerges clearly from this recipe; so too does that emphasis on encouraging culinary skills and a taste for good food in the population as a whole that has increasingly dominated his projects.

THE WONDERFUL WORLD OF BREAD. I'm still really mad about bread – I love it. It's so exciting. While me and my mate Bernie, who's a great baker, were trying to perfect our sourdough recipe it was hilarious 'cos we were like a couple of pregnant women on the phone each day seeing how our buns were proving. But that's what bread does to you. It's such a rewarding, therapeutic, tactile thing and you'll be so proud of yourself once you've cracked it.

And even though you can get all deep and cheffy about flours, fermentations and all that, I love the fact that starting from one great simple bread recipe there's a million things you can do.

Anyone can make bread. I got kids to make the bread for the step-by-step photos, because, if they can do it, then surely you can too. It's easy peasy. And just to prove to you that a little fantasy can stretch a bit of plain bread a long way, here's nine fantastic breads that will get you going on a Sunday morning. Get stuck in.

BASIC BREAD RECIPE

1 kg/just over 2 lb strong bread flour · 625 ml/just over 1 pint tepid water · 30g/1 oz fresh yeast or 3 x 7 g/¼ oz sachets dried yeast · 2 tablespoons sugar · 2 level tablespoons 30g/1 oz salt · extra flour for dusting

Stage 1: Making a Well

Pile the flour on to a clean surface and make a large well in the centre. Pour half your water into the well, then add your yeast, sugar and salt and stir well with a fork.

Stage 2: Getting it Together

Slowly, but confidently, bring in the flour from the inside of the well. (You don't want to break the walls of the well, or the water will go everywhere.) Continue to bring the flour in to the centre until you get a stodgy, porridgey consistency – then add the remaining water. Continue to mix until it's stodgy again, then you can be more aggressive, bringing in all the flour, making the mix less sticky. Flour your hands and pat and push the dough together with all the remaining flour. (Certain flours need a little more or less water, so feel free to adjust.)

Stage 3: Kneading!

This is where you get stuck in. With a bit of elbow grease, simply push, fold, slap and roll the dough around, over and over, for 4 or 5 minutes until you have a silky and elastic dough.

Stage 4: First Prove

Flour the top of your dough. Put it in a bowl, cover with clingfilm, and allow it to prove for about half an hour until doubled in size – ideally in a warm, moist, draught-free place. This will improve the flavour and texture of your dough and it's always exciting to know that the old yeast has kicked into action.

Stage 5: Second Prove, Flavouring and Shaping

Once the dough has doubled in size, knock the air out for 30 seconds by bashing it and squashing it. You can now shape it or flavour it as required – folded, filled, tray-baked, whatever – and leave it to prove for a second time for 30 minutes to an hour until it has doubled in size once more. This is the most important part, as the second prove will give it the air that finally ends up being cooked into your bread, giving you the really light, soft texture that we all love in fresh bread. So remember – don't fiddle with it, just let it do its thing.

Stage 6: Cooking Your Bread

Very gently place your bread dough on to a flour-dusted baking tray and into a pre-heated oven. Don't slam the door or you'll lose the air you need. Bake according to the time and temperature given with your chosen recipe. You can tell if it's cooked by tapping its bottom – if it sounds hollow it's done, if it doesn't then pop it back in for a little longer. Once cooked, place on a rack and allow it to cool for at least 30 minutes – fandabidozi. Feel free to freeze any leftover bread.

ROLLED BREAD OF PARMA HAM, NICE CHEESE, EGG AND BASIL

1 x basic bread recipe · 10 slices of Parma ham · 8 large organic eggs, boiled for 8 minutes and shelled · 400 g/14 oz cheese (a mixture of Cheddar, Fontina, Parmesan or any leftovers that need to be used up), grated · 2 handfuls of fresh basil · optional: sun-dried tomatoes or plum tomatoes and olives, halved · extra virgin olive oil · sea salt and freshly ground black pepper

Proceed through the basic bread recipe until Stage 5, dusting the dough with flour as you shape it into a long rectangle about 1 cm/½ inch thick. This should end up being about 1 metre/39 inches long and about 18–20 cm/7 or 8 inches wide.

Along the middle of the bread, lay out your Parma ham, eggs, cheese, basil and tomatoes and olives if you are using them. Drizzle with extra virgin olive oil and season with salt and pepper. Pull the dough over the filling so it forms what looks like a cannelloni shape. Then what you need to do is bring one end round to the other so that they join up. Pinch and pat the two ends together firmly to form a doughnut-shaped loaf. Transfer to a flour-dusted baking tin, allow to prove for 15 minutes, dust with flour and place in your preheated oven at 180°C/350°F/gas 4 for 35 minutes until golden. Allow to cool and then either transport to a picnic and carve it there – if you're lucky it will still be a little warm in the middle – or eat there and then. Fantastic.

Conclusion

We have long been ashamed of our culinary heritage. One particular narrative about British food still dominates all discussions on the subject – the idea that our food has only recently recovered from a dreadful decline. It is an interesting claim, because people have been making it for at least a century, always harking back to a golden age of traditional British cooking that is just out of reach, always condemning the food of the immediate past. The story as it is told today has Elizabeth David as the rescuer, with many claiming that the British simply could not cook until she introduced us to the food of the Mediterranean. This narrative sees our food as having gradually improved as European produce and recipes became available and as more of us travelled abroad and tasted what we had been missing. Yet when we look closely at the cook books produced over the last century, a rather different story emerges. Elizabeth David was by no means the first writer to introduce us to the domestic culinary traditions of Europe; these foods had been made intensely fashionable by a considerable contingent of food writers from the 1920s onwards. Foreign recipes, in fact, were present in sizeable numbers in the books of Mrs Beeton and her Victorian contemporaries. Deference to French cuisine was a feature of British cook books throughout the eighteenth and nineteenth centuries, and a number of writers, including Isabella Beeton, strayed much further afield in their search for recipes, including dishes described as Portuguese, Spanish, Indian, German, Italian, Russian and Turkish, among others. Indeed, the more closely we look at the history of British food writing, the more we realize that it has always been international in its influences, and the notion of it as an insular, unimaginative tradition begins to look like a myth. If anything, it has been our eagerness to incorporate foreign influences, our willingness to tweak recipes, to add a bit of this and a little of the other that led to the debasement of our national cuisine. Really, the history of British cooking as it is told by our cook books is of a long internationalist development suddenly interrupted by the patriotism and food shortages of the Second World War. Our food took a long time to recover from the habits of parsimony and substitution adopted during the years of rationing, and was only in the 1980s again attaining the levels of assurance and sophistication reached in the 1930s. And it is almost certainly no accident that now that we are at last feeling confident about our national culinary standards, the food writers of the new millennium are choosing to revisit the once-reviled traditions of British cookery.

They are a largely unexamined part of our everyday lives, but cook books are not simple things. Even the most apparently straightforward is a veritable salmagundi of history, culture and science, enticingly jumbled together. We read them to learn – to recover skills that our society is rapidly losing. We read them to salivate, to explore new culinary horizons, to feel comforted and mothered. They tell us what we fear and what we desire, about our bodies and our appetites, our domestic politics, our economic circumstances and our fantasies. They tell us who we are, and who we want to be. There is a pleasurable perversity in reading instructions for dishes you have no intention of preparing; in tasting food in the imagination rather than in reality; in finding a story that wasn't meant to be there. For modern women in particular there is also an insidious satisfaction in flirting with the myth of the domestic hearth: a myth that contradicts many of our hard-won freedoms, but nevertheless exerts a powerful pull. And then there are the intense satisfactions of a more active engagement: of comparing recipes, trying them out, bringing the dish that existed only as text and image into physical form. It is a process that has its disappointments too, of course: the large, aching gap between image and reality, the dish that fails to live up to its author's glowing encomium; the mess, crumbs and bloated stomachs that are the only legacy of your culinary engagement. But when the washing-up is done, the kitchen once more restored to order, the dish is still there, in the cook book – delicious, untouched, full of promise. Reading cook books allows us to eat our cake and still have it, and what could be better than that?

Acknowledgements

I had the first glimmerings of an idea for this book twenty years ago, and since then a great many people have helped, encouraged and inspired me. I am very grateful to them all and hope I have remembered them here.

I owe particular debts of thanks to Judith Murray, who was one of the first enthusiasts for this project, to James Davidson, who brought it to the attention of Faber and Faber, and to Walter Donohue, who has been a generous and helpful editor.

The late Alan Davidson was very kind and encouraging at an early stage of my thinking about the cultural history of cook books. Friends including Stephanie Bird, Katrina Chapman, Rachel Cooke, Michael Dobson, Simon Edwards, Matthew Fox, Steve Gentle, Jenny Hartley, Frances Henderson, Linda Holt, Tara Lamont, Susan Matthews, Donna Paananen, Vesna Pistotnik, Kim Reynolds, Marcus du Sautoy, James Taylor, Kate Teltscher, Ann Thompson, Mark Turner, Sarah Turvey, Cathy Wells-Cole and Frances Wilson shared my interest in food, or at least put up with my monologues on the subject.

For extremely helpful discussions of this project, and cook books in general, I have to thank Margaret Beetham, Suzanne Daly, Ross Foreman, Carol Heaton, Sarah Moss and Paul Newland. Laura Marcus and Lindsay Duguid commissioned articles from me, and Judith Luna asked me to edit Mrs Beeton's *Household Management* for Oxford World's Classics – all encouraging me to think that there might be an interest in cook books as a subject. The students on my literature of food courses at Roehampton University helped me greatly with their insights and interest. Paula Thompson and Vicky Petzold were immensely supportive during the time I was writing this book. Joan Addison, John Addison, Dorothy Bacon, Phyllis Cleaver, Irene Grey, Edward Grey, Edith Horne, Audrey Jennett, Marjorie King, Betty Lee, Gladys Meggs and, especially, Rosalind Priestman gave me invaluable information about their experiences of food and cooking during the Second World War. Antiquarian bookseller Tess McKirdy managed to supply virtually every book I needed, no matter how obscure. Ian Bahrami, Lucy Owen, Kate Ward, Jude Young and others at Faber and Faber did a wonderful job on the editing, production and marketing of the book.

My stepchildren Ben and Anna Priestman have been enthusiastic supporters of my interest in food, while my son Luke has patiently endured my lectures on food history and cooking techniques, as long as he gets to lick out the bowl.

My greatest debts are to my mother, Patricia, who taught me to cook, to my father, Brian, who showed me that men can do the cooking, and to my husband, Martin, who keeps that faith alive.

PICTURE ACKNOWLEDGEMENTS

Bob Carlos Clarke: photograph from *White Heat* by Marco Pierre White (Pyramid Books, 1990), © Bob Carlos Clarke, reproduced by permission of Panic on behalf of the photographer; David Gentleman: cover of *Plats du Jour, or Foreign Food* (Penguin Books, 1957), © David Gentleman, reproduced by permission of PFD on behalf of the illustrator; Renato Guttuso: drawings from *Italian Food* by Elizabeth David (Penguin Books, 1954), © DACS 2005, reproduced by permission of DACS; Raymond Hawkey/Continuum 2: cover of *Len Deighton's Cook Book* by Len Deighton (Penguin Books, 1967); Hilary Knight: cover and drawing from *The 'I Hate to Cook' Book* by Peg Bracken (Corgi, 1967), reproduced by permission of Random House Group UK; John Minton: drawing from *A Book of Mediterranean Food* by Elizabeth David (John Lehmann, 1950; rev.ed. Penguin Books, 1955); George Molnar: cover of *Oh, for a French Wife!* (Angus & Robertson, 1964), reproduced by permission of Carol Molnar; Victor Ross: lithograph from *Off the Beeton Track* by Peter Pirbright (Binnacle Books/Golden Galley Press, 1946); Georgia Glynn Smith: photograph from *Real Cooking* by Nigel Slater (Michael Joseph, 1997), reproduced by permission of Georgia Glynn Smith.

Notes

INTRODUCTION

1. Which, according to Margaret Visser, the enthralling 'anthropologist of everyday life', are precisely those that most significantly govern and inform our lives. See *Much Depends on Dinner: The Extraordinary History, Mythology, Allure and Obsessions, Perils and Taboos, of an Ordinary Meal.*
2. The historical study of food has developed significantly in recent decades. Landmarks include Theodore Zeldin's *An Intimate History of Humanity* (1994), in which food and our attitudes to it are considered as one element of a grand emotional history, Sidney W. Mintz's *Sweetness and Power* (1985), with its groundbreaking account of the role played by sugar in modern history, and Colin Spencer's monumental history of vegetarianism in *The Heretic's Feast* (1993). Still more ambitious is Spencer's more recent *British Food – An Extraordinary Thousand Years of History* (2002). Other wide-ranging histories of food are Reay Tannahill's *Food in History* (1973) and Felipe Fernández-Armesto's *Food – A History* (2001), which begins with the origins of cooking and ranges with verve across the globe and the intervening millennia. Anthologists have also made significant contributions to the study of food. Paul Levy's *Penguin Book of Food and Drink* (1996) establishes a canon of good twentieth-century prose writing on food, taking cook books as seriously as essays and journalism, while Joan Smith's quirky *Hungry for You – From Cannibalism to Seduction* (1996) examines some of the big themes associated with food – desire, starvation, obsession and pleasure. Mark Kurlansky, the American author of *Cod* (1997) and *Salt* (2002), studies of the histories of ingredients in the tradition established by Mintz, combined both approaches in his *Choice Cuts* (2002), which travels, as his subtitle declares, Around the World and Throughout History.
3. The dirtiest cook books I have found in many years searching the shelves of second-hand shops are invariably those by Marguerite Patten, the tireless author of over 160 cook books written in the course of a seventy-year career. I longed to tell her this when I met her at a conference, but I was afraid she might think it an insult. It seems to me a tremendous compliment.

CHAPTER ONE

1. Hannah Glasse's *The Art of Cookery Made Plain and Easy* (1747) is actually the source of the hare; the eggs, I think, are apocryphal.
2. Advertisement in the second volume of the twenty-four-volume part-work of *Household Management*, published between 1859 and 1861.
3. Isabella Beeton, *Household Management* (Oxford: Oxford World's Classics, 2000), pp. 249–50.

4. Eliza Acton, *Modern Cookery for Private Families*, p. 283.
5. Though a scholar has recently claimed that this book was actually the work of a French teacher, Adolphe Duhart-Fauvet, who received money for it but no credit. See Michael McKirdy, 'Who Wrote Soyer's Pantropheon?'
6. Alexis Soyer, *The Modern Housewife*, in *The Selected Soyer*, compiled by Andrew Langley, p. 36.
7. So exuberant and self-regarding was Soyer that he found it immensely difficult to remove his personality from his writing. Even in his attempts to describe the success of his nutritional arrangements for the troops in the Crimea in his 1857 *Culinary Campaign* he is constantly pulled off track by the lure of anecdotes illustrating his own cleverness and social success: his account of his arrival at Scutari Hospital to begin his work is lengthily deferred by the elaborate pleasantries exchanged between himself and various assembled aristocrats, and he is much given to impromptu speeches that are received by various audiences of patients, kitchen staff or dignitaries with 'shouts of laughter and rounds of cheers'.
8. Isabella Beeton, *Household Management*, pp. 225–6.
9. *Ibid.*, p. 3.
10. See Graham Nown, *Mrs Beeton: 150 Years of Cookery and Household Management*, p. 60.
11. Isabella Beeton, *Household Management*, pp. 8; 33.
12. *Ibid.*, p. 446.
13. *Ibid.*, pp. 90; 254.
14. Isabella Beeton, *Household Management*, pp. 372–3.
15. Beeton notes that there were 20 million pigs in Britain at this date – or roughly one for each household; thirty years later the domestic rearing of pigs was already the stuff of rural nostalgia, when Thomas Hardy inserted the famous pig-killing scene in his *Jude the Obscure* of 1895.
16. Though she reports with apparent approval that the gentleman in question had anglicized the recipe and therefore, he thought, improved it.
17. Although it sounds comically like a soap powder, Luxette is in fact 'a purée of a dozen natural ingredients of which fish of various kinds forms part'.
18. Auguste Escoffier, *Guide to Modern Cookery*, p. v.
19. *Ibid.*, p. vi.
20. *Ibid.*, p. vii.
21. Colonel Kenney-Herbert, *Culinary Jottings for Madras*, p. 2.
22. *Ibid.*, p. 15.
23. These little dried fish were inexplicably popular with the British in India; David Burton, in his fascinating culinary history *The Raj at Table*, remarks that 'it seems strange that a nation of such conservative eaters as the British should have acquired such a taste for this strong, salty titbit, but perhaps smoked kippers set a precedent' (p. 105).
24. So Sir Henry Thompson in the tenth edition of his *Food and Feeding* in 1898, taking a whistle-stop tour around the globe explaining the rice dishes of each nation, follows half a page of details on risotto with the bald statement that 'the curry of rabbit or of poultry and the kedgeree of fish are further varieties which it is unnecessary to describe'.

25. Isabella Beeton, *Household Management*, p. 88–9.
26. Alexis Soyer, *Shilling Cookery for the People*, in *The Selected Soyer*, compiled by Andrew Langley, p. 57.
27. Charles Elmé Francatelli, *A Plain Cookery Book for the Working Classes*, p. 14.
28. *Ibid.*, pp. 19; 22.
29. Mrs Black, *Household Cookery and Laundry Work*, p. 8.
30. Jennifer Davies, *The Victorian Kitchen*, pp. 23–4.
31. Penguin edition, 1967, pp. 152–4.
32. Thompson, incidentally, was a noted gourmet, who gave famous dinners which he called Octaves: they were served at eight o'clock, to eight men, and consisted of eight courses; King George V, when Prince of Wales, was a guest at the 300th Octave.
33. Mrs Marshall, *Cookery Book*, p. 491.
34. A fundamentalist group influenced by the teachings of Swedenborg – also a great influence on William Blake – who had pledged themselves to abstain from the consumption of flesh.
35. Unsurprisingly, such arguments disappeared pretty much without trace after the revelation of the dietary habits of Adolf Hitler.
36. Mrs Bowdich, *New Vegetarian Dishes*, pp. vi; vii.
37. One of the most interesting features of Lady Algernon Percy's collection is the chapter on invalid cooking and preparations with which it ends. As well as the usual broths and jellies and embrocations for burns and sprains, there are some truly remarkable concoctions, including Restorative Jujubes – 'useful in some forms of heart disease'; a Chelsea Pensioner's Recipe for Rheumatism contributed by the Hon. Ada Trefusis; instructions for dealing with Insects in the Ear, which sensibly ends 'Then send for a doctor'; and two Valuable Recipes for Cancer (one an infusion of figs soaked in milk, the other of violet leaves) with copious testimonials to their effectiveness.
38. Anon., *The Best Way*, p. 17.
39. At least one book – Helen Watkeys Moore's *Camouflage Cookery: A Book of Mock Dishes* of 1918 – was completely devoted to the subject.
40. *Ibid.*, p. 20.
41. Mrs Peel, *The Daily Mail Cookery Book*, p. i.
42. Though Arabella Boxer notes its occasional use for picnics and shooting parties (*Book of English Food*, pp. 192, 194).
43. Marion Neil, *The Thrift Cook Book*, pp. 214; 220.

CHAPTER TWO

1. Agnes, Lady Jekyll, *Kitchen Essays*, p. 14.
2. It was at a weekend house party at Mrs Allhusen's house that Jessica Mitford first met her cousin Esmond Romilly, with whom she very shortly afterwards ran away to fight for the Red Brigade in the Spanish Civil War. In her memoir *Hons and Rebels*, she described Dorothy Allhusen's house:

> Cousin Dorothy's house was deliciously comfortable and pleasant. Unlike most English country houses, the rooms were always glowingly warm. You got the feeling that the fires burned in the fireplace continuously all winter. Being a childless house, it had a

quiet, timeless, clean quality often missing in the houses of other aunts and cousins. There were many old-fashioned touches: oranges stuffed with cloves in the chests of drawers, early morning tea in your bedroom, and savoury at the end of dinner – hot stuffed mushrooms or chicken livers wrapped in bacon. (Jessica Mitford, *Hons and Rebels*, p. 111.)

3. Dorothy Allhusen, *A Book of Scents and Dishes*, pp. 2; 247–8.
4. Ruth Lowinsky, *Lovely Food: A Cookery Notebook*, pp. 12; 32.

   Another fashionable writer was Lady Sysonby, the wife of a courtier, whose eponymous cook book of 1935 was notable for its introduction by Osbert Sitwell and decorations by Oliver Messel. A renowned beauty and fêted hostess, Ria Sysonby and her husband (who was Private Secretary to Queen Victoria and then Edward VII) lived in a grace-and-favour apartment in St James's Palace. Her cook book is far from stuffy and is shot through with quirky detail and opinion: under the Messel illustration for the meat chapter, showing befrilled lamb cutlets surrounding a pile of mashed potatoes and peas, is the bald statement, 'This has been drawn as a warning. Don't ever use paper frills.'
5. Ruth Lowinsky, who only learned to cook after the Second World War, gives a recipe for 'Grenadilla [passion fruit] Ice', which is typical in its imprecision: 'To half a pint of grenadilla pulp add one and a half pints of syrup and juice of three lemons. Leave in the pips. Enough for eight to ten people' (p. 19). There are no instructions for making the syrup or for freezing the ice, and her one detail simply confuses: she presumably means to leave in the grenadilla 'pips' rather than those of the lemon, as the grammar would suggest.
6. Cynthia White, *Women's Magazines 1693–1968*, pp. 314–6.
7. Robert Graves and Alan Hodges, *The Long Week-end: A Social History of Great Britain 1918–1939*, pp. 40–1.
8. Brian Braithwaite, Noëlle Walsh and Glyn Davies (compilers), *Ragtime to Wartime: The Best of Good Housekeeping 1922–1939*, p. 11.
9. Ruth Lowinsky, *Lovely Food*, pp. 2–3.
10. Quoted in Deirdre Beddoes, *Back to Home and Duty*, p. 61.
11. June and Doris Langley Moore, *The Pleasure of Your Company: A Text-book of Hospitality*, pp. 238–9.
12. The same problem arises in the fiction of the period: in Lettice Cooper's *The New House* (1936) the sensitive Rhoda is painfully aware of the position of her family's servants and deals with them in an agony of embarrassment, while her mother 'regarding them at the bottom of her heart as automata . . . handled them with assurance and precision'. Rhoda, who 'was secretly afraid of asking too much . . . got a far more unwilling and inefficient service'. (p. 101.)
13. Lady Jekyll, *Kitchen Essays*, p. 72; June and Doris Langley Moore, *The Pleasure of Your Company*, p. i.
14. Rachel and Margaret Ryan, *Dinners for Beginners: An Economical Cookery Book for the Single-Handed*, p. 9.

   The Ryans' imagining a part of their putative readership as bachelors is an indication of the beginning of an acknowledgement in this period that men might enter the kitchen. Lady Jekyll suggests that in fact men can have a particular affinity with both food and servants:

Those who have been privileged to stay in bachelor households or to dine at restaurants with their men friends, will often admit their superlative capability both in running the domestic machinery with noiseless and well-oiled efficiency and in ordering a better dinner from a chef or maître d'hôtel than most women would be able to achieve. (*Kitchen Essays*, p. 26)

She includes a whole chapter on the subject of bachelors entertaining (called 'For Men Only'), in which she considers the particular problems they encounter, such as not being able to face the thought of ordering dinner at breakfast time (notably, no writer imagines that a similar reluctance might afflict the female reader). There appears to be a new awareness in the 1920s and 1930s that men might also be interested in food. It is notable, for example, just how much of the plot-line in the many novels of P. G. Wodehouse is taken up with food – the luring away of chefs, Jeeves's famous pick-me-ups, the Eggs, Beans and Crumpets who seem to permanently inhabit the Drones club. Menus and even the occasional recipe are given in full in these novels and drooled over by the male characters.

15. Ambrose Heath, *Good Food; Month by Month Recipes*, pp. 14–15.
16. Osbert Lancaster, *Here, of All Places: The Pocket Lamp of Architecture*, p. 152.
17. As René Cutforth remarked, 'The universal game was class judgement and assessment . . . I think it's true to say, though it makes me sad to think of it, that for millions of people in England in the Thirties, to score well at this game was the chief reason for existence.' (*Later than We Thought: A Portrait of the Thirties*, p. 34.
18. For a fuller discussion of the dynamics of middle-class identity during the interwar years, see my account of *The Feminine Middlebrow Novel, 1920s to 1950s: Class, Domesticity and Bohemianism*, pp. 57–107.
19. Elizabeth Craig, *Keeping House with Elizabeth Craig*, pp. v; 64.
20. Winifred Hope Thomson, *Someone to Dinner: Chef Cooking for Little Kitchens*, pp. 9; 11.
21. Barbara Tims (Ed.), *Food in Vogue: Six Decades of Cooking and Entertaining*, p. 55.
22. *The Complete Hostess* (1935), from fashionable restaurant Quaglino's, gave Brave New World, The Fel of Eros, Hollywood, Wake Up and Dream, and Knockout, among many others.
23. Lady Jekyll, *Kitchen Essays*, p. 61.
24. Ruth Lowinsky, *Lovely Food*, p. 54. Sometimes the desire to challenge her readers' bourgeois sensibilities gets the better of her, as when she muses very tastelessly on the cooking skills used on martyrs:

    Painful though it must be for the expert cook to watch a delicious joint being ruined by a novice, his agony cannot compare with that of the victim who is himself the aforesaid joint. Let us hope that Saints Lorenzo of Rome and Juan de Prado, two patron saints of cooking, were lost in admiration of the skill with which they were roasted alive. (pp. 69–70)

25. 'U' meaning 'upper class', as formulated by Nancy Mitford in her 1956 essay 'The English Aristocracy'.
26. Ambrose Heath, *Good Food*, pp. 184–5; 68.
27. Naomi Jacob, *Me – in the Kitchen*, p. 21.

28. 'Whilst slow-eating guests are chewing their last mouthfuls, the hostess can chat with such brilliancy that no one notices anything but her talk, while she wipes soiled silver and knives with a paper serviette, and puts them into a deep-mouthed jar, in which they can afterwards be washed in boiling soapy water . . . A similar lidded jar, in colours that match the dinner service, should ornament the table, and hold the scraps off plates.' Moira Meighn, *The Magic Ring for the Needy and Greedy*, pp. 28–9.
29. *Ibid.*, p. 61.
30. As Margaret Eyles had remarked in her record of working-class life *The Woman in the Little House* (1922), 'The average author knows nothing of the grey, steady hardship of working-class life; he knows plenty about poverty, but it is a gay sort of Bohemian poverty that dresses perfectly for lunch at the Savoy with some important person, and cheerfully pawns its beautiful clothes to buy fish and chips for lunch tomorrow!' (p. 101.)
31. John Burnett, *Plenty and Want: A Social History of Diet in England from 1815 to the Present Day*, pp. 317–9.
32. George Orwell, *The Road to Wigan Pier*, pp. 88–9.
33. See R. J. Hammond, *Food* (*Civil History of the Second World War*), Vol. 2, pp. 65–81.
34. I have in my possession a 1950s edition passed down from my maternal grandmother, which is one of the things that first provoked my interest in cook books: I was very intrigued as a child by its recipe for 'fadge' – which (made as it was with mostly flour and a smidgen of fat) seemed to me a very horrible form of fudge; I now know it to be a corruption of a Northern Irish potato cake.
35. A pamphlet published by the British Medical Association, this was addressed to 'the women who have to get a full pennyworth of food value from every penny of their outlay'. Clear guidance about economical shopping and cooking is given ('if you cannot afford to cook every day, by careful selection you will find it possible to do two days' cooking at a time' [p. 2]), and the dietary needs of children are particularly focused on, all within the context of an unflinching awareness of the economic realities of the lives of its readers:

    Children of school age can usually get extra milk at school. One-third of a pint of milk daily at school costs one half-penny in the school milk service. Please let them have it. If you have to cut down at home to manage this, do so on their bread. (p. 3)

36. In a famous article of 1936 it showed photographs of Parisian hostesses cooking – 'Comtesse Charles de Polignac stirs them up', 'Colette watches the pot', 'Comtesse Alexandre de Castéja handles a crisis'. ('Madame Tries Her Hand', reproduced in Barbara Tims [Ed.], *Food in Vogue: Six Decades of Cooking and Entertaining*, pp. 77–8.)
37. Quaglino, *The Complete Hostess*, p. 9.
38. For a further discussion of the domestic-science movement, see Margaret Horsfield, *Biting the Dust: The Joys of Housework*.
39. In 1925 *Good Housekeeping* magazine gave the kitchen a new status as 'the working centre of the house, the laboratory in which the family meals are prepared'. (Jan Boxshall, *Good Housekeeping: Every Home Should Have One*, p. 21).

40. A typical example is the rather inaptly named *Savour* (1931) by Claire McInerny and Dorothy Roche, who were lecturers on cookery at the Northern Polytechnic and at the Good Housekeeping Institute. The stages of recipes are given in numbered point form ('1. Remove all fat from the meat. 2. Cut the meat into small pieces' . . .), and much use is made of tables to convey the maximum of information in the least discursive manner possible (so directions for nine types of steamed pudding are given in the form of a foundation method and a table of variations taking only two pages of the book).
41. So in 1927 husbands were exhorted to 'Give her Pleasure – Give her Leisure – Give her an ELECTROLUX for Christmas.'
42. First published in 1927, the book had sold over two million copies and gone into forty-seven editions by 1955.
43. Jan Boxshall, *Good Housekeeping: Every Home Should Have One*, p. 25. Housewives may have noticed these new appliances, but they had to wait some time to obtain them: electricity was not laid on in most homes until the 1940s, though it was in place twenty years earlier in the homes of the better-off; the first refrigerators were available in the early 1920s, but even by 1953 only 3.5 per cent of households had a fridge.
44. Of course, we can read these social phenomena differently. Feminist polemicist Barbara Ehrenreich (writing of the American instigators of the scientific housework movement) sees it all as an anti-feminist conspiracy: 'Housework-as-we-know-it . . . was invented . . . around the turn of the century for the precise purpose of giving middle-class women something to do . . . Enter the domestic-science experts, a group of ladies who, if ever there is a feminist hell, will be tortured eternally with feather dusters. These were women who made careers out of telling other women they couldn't have careers, because housework was a big enough job in itself. And they were right, since their standard for a well-kept home was one that revealed no evidence of human occupation.' (*The Snarling Citizen*, p. 26.)
45. See Elizabeth David's entertaining account of his life in 'Having Crossed the Channel: The Work of X. Marcel Boulestin', *An Omelette and a Glass of Wine*, pp. 162–74.
46. X. Marcel Boulestin, *What Shall We Have To-Day? 365 Recipes for All the Days of the Year*, p. 14.
47. *Ibid.*
48. X. Marcel Boulestin, *The Conduct of the Kitchen*, p. 26.

    Other writers were influenced by Boulestin's instructive approach: in their *Dinners for Beginners* sisters-in-law Margaret and Rachel Ryan give scrupulously full instructions, providing a list of the ingredients needed in the larder and the equipment in the kitchen, giving detailed shopping lists for each menu and precisely calculated timings to enable the novice cook to produce a full meal on schedule. They recognize the need for the reader to understand the *reasons* for what she is doing, but, like Boulestin, their interest in the science behind cooking techniques leads them not to the bald, personality-free instructions of the domestic-science textbooks but to a detailed narrative approach in which every possibility is explained. In the recipe for peas *à la Française*, the reader is advised to 'shell two pounds of peas, being careful to let no worm past your eye', and in that for brown potato purée warned that 'if you fail to mash your potatoes absolutely smooth, the smallest lumps will stick in the nozzle of the forcer and block it up, while the potato surges out at the wrong end of the bag'. The Ryans are very much on the side of their harassed and anxious reader, bolstering her with kindly comments and encouragement: 'this is a strenuous dinner to cook', they counsel of one menu, 'so don't start on it unless you are feeling strong and calm' (p. 79), and towards the end of the timetable for said strenuous meal comes the reassurance 'HERE, AT LAST, IS A SMALL INTERVAL IN WHICH YOU CAN DRAW BREATH' (p. 81).

49. Mrs C. F. Leyel, *The Gentle Art of Cookery*, p. 385.
50. Moira Meighn, *The Magic Ring*, pp. 26–7.
51. Truby King's theory of 'Mothercraft' involved a return to breastfeeding (which had been going out of fashion since around the turn of the century), but also an emphasis on leaving infants alone for long stretches of time, preferably out of doors, even in midwinter. The 'Truby King Baby' was imaged as a prodigy of independence, rolling happily around the yard like an exuberant puppy, needing no toys but nature and its own fingers and toes. Even more devoted to the ideal of the independent infant was ex-advertising copywriter Broadus Watson, who advised mothers to refrain from kissing and caressing their babies (especially sons) in order to avoid creating an Oedipus complex. Such advice was highly influential in the years between the wars, and the middle-class ideal of the distanced, briskly competent mother is repeatedly reflected in the films, novels and magazines of the period.
52. Alice Martineau, *Caviar to Candy*, p. 6.
53. X. Marcel Boulestin, *The Conduct of the Kitchen*, p. 7.
54. It is notable how many writers insist that their recommended foods are highly economical: Ambrose Heath prefaces *Good Food* with the claim that he will 'demonstrate that good cooking need not be expensive, as so many seem to think it must be', and Alice Martineau acknowledges that while some of her recipes do use cream, eggs and liqueurs, it is only those 'suitable for great occasions'. (Ambrose Heath, *Good Food*, p. 13; Alice Martineau, *Caviar to Candy*, p. 4.)
55. Lady Jekyll, *Kitchen Essays*, pp. 109–10
56. Lady Sysonby, *Lady Sysonby's Cook Book*, p. 125.
57. *Ibid.*, p. 101; Alice Martineau, *Caviar to Candy*, p. 3.
58. Alice Martineau, *Caviar to Candy*, p. 76.
59. Nancy Shaw, *Food for the Greedy*, p. 9; Mrs Leyel, *The Gentle Art of Cookery*, pp. 31-2.
60. Elizabeth David, 'Survival', *Spectator*, 28 June 1963.
61. Many recipe books included chapters for vegetarian food: there is one covering 'cereals and vegetarian foods' in Mrs Francillon's *Good Cookery* of 1920, and another in *Aunt Kate's Household Annual* (1933). Lady Jekyll has a chapter called 'Meatless Meals', which she opens with a lengthy evocation of 'a certain maigre luncheon on a sunny Friday of an early summer, now far away and long ago' (p. 125). The meal in question was taken with a Jesuit father

and a nun, and Jekyll associates meatless meals with Lenten observance rather than matters of principle or health. For Alice Martineau vegetarians become one more social responsibility, as she talks of her shame 'when, at the end of what I thought was a vegetarian dinner, my guest asked if he might have some bread and cheese' (p. 77). To avoid her readers facing similar embarrassment, she offers a range of suggestions for suitable dishes. Ruth Lowinsky also approaches vegetarianism from the social aspect, offering a menu for a friend who never eats red meat and another for a maigre dinner for a Cardinal 'who is down in his hostess's book as very greedy, without further comment' (p. 44).

62. X. Marcel Boulestin, *Simple French Cooking for English Homes*, pp. 10–11.
63. Alice Martineau, *Caviar to Candy*, p. 1.
64. *Ibid.*, pp. 122–3.
65. Countess Morphy, *Recipes of All Nations*, p. 9.
66. *Ibid.*, p. 7.
67. Countess Morphy, *Recipes of All Nations*, pp. 764; 529; 421. See Elizabeth David, 'Kitchens and their Cooks', in *Is There a Nutmeg in the House?*, pp. 4–5.
68. Countess Morphy, *Recipes of All Nations*, pp. 195; 733. There were other world cook books published in these years: *The World's Best Recipes* by Edith A. Browne and Jessie J. Williams, also of 1935, takes in Chile, Guatemala, Egypt, Burma, Bulgaria, Roumania, Japan and west Africa. They cover fifty-nine regions in all, distinguishing Indian from Anglo-Indian food, and Californian from American. And yet some lingering remnants of the British suspicion of abroad remain at the deepest level of the text: among the regions of origin for the recipes are listed 'Colonial', 'Continental', 'Oriental' and (my favourite) 'Overseas'.
69. Agnes Jekyll, *Kitchen Essays*, p. 35.
70. *Ibid.*, pp. 34; 31.
71. Quaglino, *The Complete Hostess*, p. 14.
72. Ambrose Heath, *Good Food*, pp. 27–8; 49–50.
73. The Bloomsbury set were pioneers in their taste for, and knowledge of, the ordinary food of Italy, France and Spain, gained on their travels. They were particularly influenced in these tastes by Marcel Boulestin, whom they knew as a member of the radical intellectual circles of London between the wars.
74. Rachel and Margaret Ryan, *Dinners for Beginners*, p. 296.
75. For more on Florence White, see Chapter Five, pp. 183–4.
76. X. Marcel Boulestin, *Simple French Food*, p. 1.
77. Nancy Shaw published *Food for the Greedy* in 1936, the Lowinskys dedicated *Lovely Food* 'to each other and our greedier friends', and in his introduction to *Lady Sysonby's Cook Book*, Osbert Sitwell proclaimed that 'to be greedy should carry no slur attached to it'.

CHAPTER THREE

1. The name was changed when Churchill wrote to the Minister of Food, Lord Woolton: 'I hope the term "Communal feeding centres" is not going to be adopted. It is an odious expression, suggestive of Communism and the workhouse. I suggest you call them "British Restaurants". Everyone associates the

word "restaurant" with a good meal, and they may as well have the name if they cannot have anything else' (Minute of 21 March 1941).

2. The Ministry of Food, *The ABC of Cookery*, p. 1.
3. Good Housekeeping Institute, *Book of Fish, Meat, Egg and Cheese Dishes*, frontispiece.
4. Josephine Terry, *Food without Fuss*, p. 11.
5. Previously Sir Fred Marquis, Woolton was raised to the peerage to give him a seat in Parliament.
6. Drummond's work in the Ministry of Food was largely unsung at the time, and he only became widely known in August 1952 when he, his wife and their daughter were savagely murdered by a French farmer near whose land they had camped. (See DNB Supplement 1951–60; also Christopher Driver, *The British at Table 1940–1980*, p. 19.)
7. Jennifer Davies, *The Wartime Kitchen and Garden*, quoting *The Memoirs of the Rt Hon the Earl of Woolton*.
8. The standard ration frequently yielded one egg per person per month.
9. Elizabeth David comments interestingly on the National Loaf in her *English Bread and Yeast Cookery* (1977): 'Good for you as the National loaf may have been it was much disliked, partly because it was often badly baked and lacked volume due to the low gluten content of the flour, and partly because there was no choice. To make things worse there was a long period during which it was an offence to sell a newly baked loaf, so the bread was always dry and stale. Although in retrospect the bread made from National flour seems a great deal more acceptable than today's commercial white loaf, it was no doubt the long years of the dry, uninteresting loaf that helped to confirm the majority of the English people in their taste for bread that is whiter than white, no matter what its taste, texture or content' (pp. 85–6).
10. Some wag coined the slogan 'Pigging for Victory'.
11. Jennifer Davies, *The Wartime Kitchen and Garden*, p. 178.
12. It succeeded to the extent that by 1945 two thirds of the food eaten in Britain was grown here, in comparison with one third in 1939.
13. In his nineteenth Lend–Lease report to Congress in 1945 President Truman remarked that 'Our lend–lease food shipments to Britain in 1944 amounted to about 3% of our total food supply, but it represented to the British about 10% of their requirements . . . the British diet is distinctly inferior to our own, both in quantity and variety.' (Quoted in Susan Foreman, *Loaves and Fishes: An Illustrated History of the Ministry of Agriculture, Fisheries and Food 1889–1989*, p. 44.)
14. Norman Longmate, *How We Lived Then: A History of Everyday Life During the Second World War*, p. 154.
15. Gert and Daisy were played by comediennes Elsie and Doris Waters, while the Buggins family was the brain-child of Mabel Constandurous, who played Mrs Buggins.
16. Amateur speakers would write down their recipes as they gave them to prevent them speaking too quickly.
17. Jennifer Davies, *The Wartime Kitchen and Garden*, p. 46.

18. Marguerite Patten, *We'll Eat Again*, p. 34.
19. These included *Gert and Daisy's Wartime Cookery Book* (1941), with excerpts from their famous 'Feed the Brute' talks, and *The Kitchen Front*, published by Nicolson and Watson in 1942 and containing 122 recipes selected from the programme.
20. Ambrose Heath, *Kitchen Front Recipes and Hints*, pp. 13–15.
21. In the foreword to *The Queen Cookery Book* (1961); a complete list of Heath's publications is given in Michael Bateman, *Cooking People*, pp. 165–6.
22. Ambrose Heath, *Good Food: Month by Month Recipes*, pp. 138–9; *Kitchen Front Recipes and Hints*, pp. 54–5.
23. Ambrose Heath, *More Kitchen Front Recipes*, p. 11.
24. *Ibid.*, p. 30.
25. Alan Davidson, *The Oxford Companion to Food*, p. 457.
26. Irene Veal, *Recipes of the 1940s*, pp. 5; 10; 10.
27. *Ibid.*, p. 144.
28. Norman Longmate, *How We Lived Then*, pp. 154–5.
29. *Ibid.*, p. 155.
30. In surveys I have carried out among people who remember the war the Be-Ro cook books and leaflets are mentioned more frequently than any other.
31. Veteran food writer Marguerite Patten was one of them.
32. Ambrose Heath, *More Kitchen Front Recipes*, pp. 49; 39.
33. Josephine Terry, *Food without Fuss: 200 New Recipes and a Few Thoughts*, p. 11.
34. *Ibid.*, p. 85.
35. *Ibid.*, p. 51.
36. *Ibid.*, p. 55.
37. The Daily Telegraph, *Good Eating: Suggestions for Wartime Dishes*, pp. 56–7.
38. Ambrose Heath, *More Kitchen Front Recipes*, pp. 24; 70.
39. Josephine Terry, *Food without Fuss*, p. 37.
40. *Ibid.*, p. 114.
41. John Miles (Ed.), *A Kitchen Goes to War*, p. 38.
42. Christopher Driver, *The British at Table 1940–1980*, pp. 33–4.
43. Script quoted in Jennifer Davies, *The Wartime Kitchen and Garden*, p. 208.
44. Ambrose Heath, *Kitchen Front Recipes and Hints*, p. 80.
45. In an article on '"Come When You Can" Cooking', *Vogue* gave recipes for Czech Dumplings, Potato Platski, Chicken à la Paprika and Pork Goulash alongside more traditionally British fare.
46. The Daily Telegraph, *Good Eating*, p. 100.
47. Constance Spry, *Come into the Garden, Cook*, p. 1.
48. *Ibid.*, p. 2.
49. *Ibid.*, p. 6.
50. *Ibid.*, p. 16.
51. *Ibid.*, pp. 26; 49.
52. *Ibid.*, p. 36.
53. *Ibid.*, p. 90.
54. Sheila Kaye-Smith, *Kitchen Fugue*, p. 3.

55. *Ibid.*, pp. 61–2.
56. *Ibid.*, p. 68.
57. *Ibid.*, p. 116.
58. *Ibid.*, pp. 108–9.
59. Barbara Griggs, *The Food Factor*, p. 188.

CHAPTER FOUR

1. Marguerite Patten, still busily demonstrating, recalls that she loathed handling it, because 'the raw meat had a strong and very unpleasant smell of fish and stale oil'. (*Post-War Kitchen: Nostalgic Food and Facts from 1945–1954*, p. 34.)
2. The Ministry of Food's *Food and Nutrition* booklet of September 1947, quoted in Patten, *ibid.*, p. 34.
3. Susan Cooper, 'Snoek Piquante', in Michael Sissons and Philip French (Eds), *Age of Austerity 1945–51*, p. 51.
4. *Ibid.*, pp. 51–2.
5. *Ibid.*, p. 53.
6. *Ibid.*, p. 53.
7. Little attention has been paid by historians to the British League of Housewives, but it was a major movement, boasting a million members by its high point in 1948. Hijacked by extremists at this point, it was subsequently dismissed as a tool of the Conservative Party, but, as Christina Hardyment notes, it was among the first groups to identify the new problems that were to face the middle-class housewife in the post-war world:

   > The League's political position is best understood by drawing a parallel with the Green Party today. In conception, it was no more Tory than the Greens are socialist. What the League did stand for was middle-class values. And in this lies the clue to a deeper cause of discontent than food shortages and queues: the humiliation experienced by women who had once been able not only to run attractive homes but to enjoy interesting lives of their own.

   (*Slice of Life: the British Way of Eating Since 1945*, p. 27. See also James Hinton, 'Militant Housewives: The British Housewives League and the Attlee Government', *History Workshop*, Autumn 1994, pp. 129–56.)
8. Christopher Driver, *The British at Table 1940–1980*, p. 39.
9. Rachel and Margaret Ryan, *Quick Dinners for Beginners: A Book of Recipes Taking One Hour or Less to Prepare and Cook*.
10. Ambrose Heath, *Kitchen Table Talk*, pp. 30; 53.
11. Peter Pirbright, *Off the Beeton Track*, p. 13. Pirbright went on to write for *Vogue* in the 1950s.
12. *Ibid.*, pp. 12; 85.
13. *Ibid.*, p. 9.
14. *Ibid.*, p. 9.
15. *Ibid.*, p. 11.
16. Elizabeth David, *Summer Cooking*, p. 21. Constance Spry makes a similar comment in *The Constance Spry Cookery Book*: 'One meets sometimes, in English cookery books, a timorous recommendation to rub garlic round the inside of the salad bowl. I do not deny that if you put your head well over the

bowl you will be able to detect its presence with your sense of smell, but for those who like it this is an inadequate way of using it' (p. 334).

17. Peter Pirbright, *Off the Beeton Track*, p. 9.
18. *Ibid.*, p. 46.
19. *The Oxford Companion to Food*, p. 773.
20. *Ibid.*, pp. 65; 126.
21. *Ibid.*, p. 122. Pirbright appears to use 'macaroni' to refer to some long form of pasta rather than the short curved tubes we know by this name. In applying the term in this way he is part of a long tradition of English muddle: *The Oxford Companion to Food* notes 'the terminological confusion which for long surrounded "vermicelli" and "macaroni", dating back to the seventeenth century, and confusing Mrs Beeton among others' (p. 466).
22. Rachel and Margaret Ryan, *Quick Dinners for Beginners*, p. 1.
23. Ambrose Heath, *Kitchen Table Talk*, pp. 35–6.
24. *Ibid.*, p. 43. See Christina Hardyment, *A Slice of Life*, pp. 76–9.
25. Ambrose Heath, *Kitchen Table Talk*, p. 104. The American cream pie is a pie shell filled with a stiff flour- or cornflour-thickened pastry cream, variously flavoured. It does not contain cream, which was still rationed at this date.
26. Sylvia Lovegren, *Fashionable Food: Seven Decades of Food Fads*, p. 139.
27. Ambrose Heath, *Kitchen Table Talk*, p. 23.
28. Rachel and Margaret Ryan, *Quick Dinners for Beginners*, p. xi.
29. *Ibid.*, p. xiii.
30. In 1948 Dr Alfred Kinsey published his *Sexual Behaviour in the Human Male*, which was followed by *Sexual Behaviour in the Human Female* (1953). The shock waves caused by his revelations about the prevalence of adultery, homosexuality, pre-marital sex and female masturbation reverberated from his native America around the world.
31. Peter Pirbright, *Off the Beeton Track*, pp. 14–15.
32. The similes are, respectively, Michael Bateman's (*Cooking People*, p. 149), Katharine Whitehorn's (in Christina Hardyment, *Slice of Life*, p. 91) and Alan Davidson's (*The Oxford Companion to Food*, p. 245).
33. Both quoted in Christina Hardyment, *Slice of Life*, p. 91.
34. Think, among many others, of Alice Martineau, Marcel Boulestin and Mrs Leyel: Elizabeth David herself wrote essays celebrating the achievements of both Mrs Leyel and Boulestin.
35. Elizabeth David, *A Book of Mediterranean Food* (John Lehmann edition), p. vi.
36. Elizabeth David, *A Book of Mediterranean Food* (Penguin edition), p. xii.
37. Artemis Cooper, *Writing at the Kitchen Table*, p. xiii.
38. *Ibid.*, p. xiii.
39. Michael Bateman, *Cooking People*, p. 154.
40. This is one of the most serious areas of disagreement between David's two biographers: Liza Chaney in her *Elizabeth David: A Mediterranean Passion* takes Gibson Cowan's account to be accurate, while Artemis Cooper goes with David's less dramatic version of events. There seems to be more evidence for the latter reading.

41. Quoted in Rose Prince, 'Elizabeth the First', *Independent on Sunday*, 5 October 1997.
42. Artemis Cooper, *Writing at the Kitchen Table*, p. 65.
43. Elizabeth David was later to write of her experiences cooking on the island and of her attempts to make piccalilli and Christmas pudding to satisfy her Greek neighbours' curiosity about British food. ('Christmas Pudding Is Mediterranean Food', *Spices, Salts and Aromatics*, pp. 208–11.)
44. Artemis Cooper has an account of her tearing a copy of the book to pieces in front of the friend who owned it, hissing, 'Never, ever, let me hear that man's name again!' (*Writing at the Kitchen Table*, p. 204).
45. Elizabeth David, 'John Wesley's Eye', *Spectator*, 1 February 1963, reproduced in *An Omelette and a Glass of Wine*.
46. *Ibid*., p. 21.
47. Elizabeth David, *A Book of Mediterranean Food*, pp. 106–7.
48. Paul Levy, 'Elizabeth David', *Out to Lunch*, p. 199.
49. Elizabeth David, *A Book of Mediterranean Food*, p. 20; *French Country Cooking*, p. 151.
50. Michael Bateman, *Cooking People*, p. 149.
51. Or perhaps the two are related – think of the cult of Nanny.
52. There is also a rather masculine cast to the recipe selection: she has very little interest in cake.
53. W. H. Auden, Introduction to M. F. K. Fisher, *The Art of Eating*, p. xii.
54. *Mediterranean Food*, p. 156, quoting Lawrence Durrell, *Prospero's Cell*.
55. *Ibid*., p. 155.
56. *Ibid*., p. 9.
57. It is significant that when *Vogue*'s food writer Doris Lytton Toye wrote soon after the war of the food readers might encounter on their summer holidays abroad, she wrote of Scandinavia; a few years later it would be absolutely assumed that travellers would head south. (Doris Lytton Toye, *Contemporary Cooking: Receipts from Vogue 1945–1947*, p. 114.)
58. Elizabeth David, *Mediterranean Food*, p. 17; *French Country Cooking*, p. 44.
59. Christina Hardyment, *Slice of Life*, p. 96.
60. Susan Cooper, 'Snoek Piquante', in Michael Sissons and Philip French (Eds), *Age of Austerity 1945–51*.
61. Quoted in Christina Hardyment, *Slice of Life*, p. 39.
62. The nation remained divided between the virtues of the two fuels until the emergence of today's combination cookers – electric ovens for reliability, gas hobs for precise control – which seem to have solved the dilemma.
63. Advertisements for Formica went one better and suggested to husbands that they match the colour of the work surfaces to their wife's eyes.
64. Betty Friedan, *The Feminine Mystique*, p. 181.
65. Christina Hardyment, *Slice of Life*, p. 40.
66. In fact, many did so: 4 million British married women were in paid employment in 1958, compared with 2 million ten years earlier.
67. Christina Hardyment, *Slice of Life*, p. 66.
68. *The Book of Woman's Hour*, pp. 9–12; 152–3.

69. Elizabeth Wilson, *Only Half-Way to Paradise: Women in Post-War Britain 1945–1968*, pp. 3–4.
70. Doris Grant, *Dear Housewives*, pp. 17; 62.
71. *Ibid.*, pp. 19–20.
72. Ethelind Fearon, *The Reluctant Cook*, p. 10.
73. *Ibid.*, pp. 9; 14.
74. *Ibid.*, pp. 25–6.
75. Constance Spry and Rosemary Hume, *The Constance Spry Cookery Book*, p. xi.
76. *Ibid.*, p.1. Though one can imagine that Mrs Spry at least (who disliked alcohol) would have found such occasions fairly excruciating.
77. Ann Barr and Paul Levy, *The Official Foodie Handbook*, p. 132.
78. Not all modern food writers are hostile to Constance Spry – Sybil Kapoor writes generously of her importance, and Prue Leith records that she learnt to cook by working her way steadily through the tome, presenting the results to the firm of solicitors whose lunch she was employed to prepare (they got suet puddings in mid-summer because that was where she was in the book). (Sybil Kapoor, 'A Feast Fit for a Queen', *Independent*, 1 June 2002; Christopher Driver, *The British at Table*, p. 161.)
79. Colin Spencer is fair enough to acknowledge this, conceding that 'over fifty years later it still remains an excellent work of reference and can still be used with perfect results as a cookery book'. (*British Food – An Extraordinary Thousand Years of History*, p. 322.)
80. Christopher Driver, *The British at Table*, p. 10.
81. Fannie Farmer, *The Boston Cooking-School Cook Book* (1896).
82. Constance Spry and Rosemary Hume, *The Constance Spry Cookery Book*, p. 248.
83. *Ibid.*, p. 1,012.
84. Apparently one of the students dropped the contents of a full platter onto the floor, but Rosemary just swept it back on again with a dustpan and brush – scrupulously clean, she later claimed. (Sybil Kapoor, 'A Feast Fit for a Queen', *Independent*, 1 June 2002, quoting Rosemary's niece Griselda Barton.)
85. *Ibid.*, pp. 794; 660.
86. *Ibid.*, p. xi.
87. Hume seems to have been aware of her limitations as a writer since all of her books are co-authored – at first with Dione Lucas, and after Spry's death with Muriel Downes, her second-in-command at the Cordon Bleu Cookery School.
88. *Ibid.*, pp. 1,055; 1,056.
89. *Ibid.*, p. 1,035.
90. Colin Spencer, *British Food*, p. 322.
91. Constance Spry and Rosemary Hume, *The Constance Spry Cookery Book*, p. 1,052.
92. *Ibid.*, p. 250.
93. Her personal life was also far from conventional: she was a rather unenthusiastic mother; left her first husband, who was moody and depressive; and around the end of the First World War began a relationship with a married man, Shav Spry, whom she married once they had divorced their respective spouses. She

had at least one serious lesbian affair, in the early 1930s, with the painter 'Gluck' (Hannah Gluckstein). During this period Constance divided her time between her husband in the country and Gluck in London; encouraging her lover to dress in a markedly androgynous style she squired her around the fashionable drawing rooms of the capital. (Diana Souhami, *Gluck: Her Biography*.)

94. Christina Hardyment, *Slice of Life*, p. 57.
95. Viola Johnstone, *The Hostess Cooks*, inside-cover blurb.
96. Christina Hardyment, *Slice of Life*, p. 52. In fact, he turned out not to have been her husband at the time – they were only married in 1977.
97. Roland Barthes, 'Ornamental Cookery', *Mythologies*, p. 78.
98. *Ibid.*, p. 78.
99. André Simon, *The Gourmet's Week-End Book*, p. 15; Michael Bateman, *Cooking People*, p. 220.
100. Michael Bateman, *ibid.*, pp. 16–17.
101. *Vogue* were sufficiently impressed to run a series of articles by Mrs Chowdhary in 1955.
102. Alice B. Toklas, *The Alice B. Toklas Cook Book*, p. 15.
103. Patience Gray and Primrose Boyd, *Plat du Jour*, p. 42.
104. *Ibid.*, p. 73.
105. *Ibid.*, p. 277.

CHAPTER FIVE

1. Alice Miles, *The Executive Cook Book*, blurb; Carol Wright, *The Liberated Cook's Book*, p. 7; John and Marina Bear, *The Something Went Wrong What Do I Do Now Cookery Book*, subtitle.
2. Michael Bateman, *Cooking People*, pp. 275–6.
3. Elizabeth David, *French Provincial Cooking*, p. ix.
4. Such is the cult of Mrs David that these remarks feel somewhat foolhardy. I know there are many who will claim to have lived their lives according to her precepts and example, but I would suggest that they are the leisured minority – affluent women who don't work and whose children are off their hands for most of the day – or those – male and female – who work from home in jobs undemanding enough to allow for frequent pottering in the kitchen. (I certainly delved deepest into her oeuvre when a graduate student avoiding writing my PhD.)
5. The 1955 *Summer Cooking*, while charming and still very useful, is not one of her major works, as it mostly reworks recipes she has given elsewhere. She herself referred to it as 'a less taxing book' in the Introduction to *Italian Food* (p. 24).
6. Elizabeth David, *French Provincial Cooking*, pp. 206–7.
7. *Ibid.*, p. 204.
8. *Ibid.*, pp. 131–2.
9. Elizabeth David, *Italian Food*, p. 77. The recipe she doubted must have come from Countess Morphy's *Recipes of All Nations*, which includes in the Italian section Olives Ripiene (Ascoli) and gives much the same recipe as Elizabeth David herself.

10. Elizabeth David, *French Provincial Cooking*, p. 234.
11. *Ibid.*, pp. 18–19.
12. Elizabeth David, *Italian Food*, p. 21.
13. Elizabeth David, *Spices, Salt and Aromatics in the English Kitchen*, p. 7.
14. *Ibid.*, p. 20.
15. *Ibid.*, p. 24.
16. *Ibid.*, p. 25.
17. *Ibid.*, p. 43. One might think this is a case of 'do as I say not as I do', since David herself is not averse to the abstruse and long-winded mode, nor to particularity about ingredients.
18. Elizabeth David, *Spices, Salt and Aromatics in the English Kitchen*, p. 60.
19. *Ibid.*, p. 44.
20. *Ibid.*, p. 135.
21. *Ibid.*, p. 174.
22. Elizabeth David, *English Bread and Yeast Cookery*, p. 35
23. *Ibid.*, p. 81.
24. She quotes C. Henry Warren's *Corn Country* (1940): 'it has been left to our own refined age to prefer a bread made of wheat from which the very germ has been extracted – only to be sold again as a patent food without which, as the advertisements unashamedly profess, we may look in vain for a long and healthy life'.
25. Elizabeth David, *English Bread and Yeast Cookery*, pp. 56; 54.
26. *Ibid.*, p. 109.
27. *South Wind Through the Kitchen: The Best of Elizabeth David*, p. 355.
28. Ann Barr and Paul Levy, *The Official Foodie Handbook*, p. 13.
29. It was sent to her by Roger Eland, an old friend from her Cairo days, who was the information officer in the British Embassy in Tunisia. (Artemis Cooper, *Writing at the Kitchen Table*, p. 252.)
30. Alan Davidson died at the end of 2003.
31. When Jane Grigson died in 1990, Elizabeth David wrote about that first reading of her work: 'Now that the book has long since passed into the realm of kitchen classics we take it for granted but, for British readers and cooks in the late 1960s, its content, the clarity of its writing, and the confident knowledge of its subject displayed by this young writer were new treats for us all.' (Hazel Castell and Kathleen Griffin, *Out of the Frying Pan*, p. 56.)
32. Jane Grigson, *Charcuterie and French Pork Cookery*, p. 7.
33. Jane Grigson, *Good Things*, p. 17.
34. *Ibid.*, p. 216.
35. Jane Grigson, *English Food*, p. 156.
36. Hazel Castell and Kathleen Griffin, *Out of the Frying Pan*, pp. 57–8.
37. Jane Grigson, *Fish Cookery*, pp. 59–60.
38. Jane Grigson, *Good Things*, p. 198.
39. Jane Grigson, *Jane Grigson's Vegetable Book*, p. 14.
40. Jane Grigson, *English Food*, p. 3.
41. *Ibid.*, p. 1.
42. *Ibid.*, pp. 1–2.

43. Personally, I think it tastes of primeval swamp.
44. *Ibid.*, p. 61.
45. *Ibid.*, p. 56.
46. *Ibid.*, p. 232.
47. Florence White, *Good Things in England: A Book of Real English Cookery*, p. 189.
48. *Ibid.*, p. 74.
49. Dorothy Hartley, *Food in England*, p. 345.
50. *Ibid.*, p. 121.
51. Uttley had already made the same nostalgic material part of the mental furniture of several generations of children with her 1939 novel *A Traveller in Time*.
52. Elizabeth David, *English Bread and Yeast Cookery*, p. xix.
53. '[Cooper] wears his engagement in food wars on the "Marxist–lentillist" side as a badge of honour' (Fiona Beckett, Joanna Blythmann, Richard Ehrlich, Matthew Fort, Malcolm Gluck and Roger Protz, 'Noshtalgia', *Guardian*, Saturday 29 June 2002).
54. Examples are taken here from the revised edition of 1985, published as *A New Book of Middle Eastern Food*.
55. Claudia Roden, *A New Book of Middle Eastern Food*, p. 23.
56. *Ibid.*, p. 15.
57. *Ibid.*, p. 14. This project was to be more fully realized in her 1997 *Book of Jewish Food*.
58. Hazel Castell and Kathleen Griffin, *Out of the Frying Pan*, p. 81.
59. *Ibid.*, p. 84.
60. Claudia Roden, *A New Book of Middle Eastern Food*, pp. 20–1.
61. It was particularly the appetizers and the street food that were adopted: Baba Ghanoush (the purée of aubergines and tahina described by Roden as 'exciting and vulgarly seductive'), stuffed vine leaves (Roden's is the definitive recipe, much repeated by later food writers and even reprinted on the packaging of the most popular brand of vacuum-packed vine leaves), falafel and grilled haloumi. Some of her most interesting recipes are for the many varieties of savoury pastries – böreck, brik, fila, spanakopittá, pastele and bstilla – that are sold in the street or served as appetizers all over the region. While the Greek and Turkish recipes for spinach- and feta-filled pies (fila and spanakopittá) were seized on by the proprietors of delicatessens and vegetarian restaurants as 'home-made' food that was easy to produce in bulk, most of these pastries have not become part of our national culinary consciousness. Personally, I am waiting for the arrival of the brik, a parcel of deep-fried fila containing among the filling a softly-cooked egg that oozes deliciously into your mouth when a corner of the crisp pastry is broached.
62. Christopher Driver, *The British at Table*, pp. 75–81.
63. *Ibid.*, p. 82. Christina Hardyment adds that 'this was a region from which young men traditionally went to sea for a few years before settling down on the land, but as conditions of crewing deteriorated in the 1950s, they gravitated to Britain, aware of the small communities of seamen who had long ago jumped

ship . . . Many of these earlier settlers had set up restaurants, and the newcomers naturally gravitated into the restaurant business.' (*Slice of Life*, p. 132.)

64. Christina Hardyment, *Slice of Life*, p. 137.
65. E. P. Veerasawmy, *Indian Cookery*, p. 125.
66. Madhur Jaffrey, *An Invitation to Indian Cooking*, p. 11.
67. *Ibid.*, p. 27.
68. Hazel Castell and Kathleen Griffin, *Out of the Frying Pan*, p. 135.
69. *Ibid.*, p. 30.
70. *Ibid.*, p. 15.
71. *Ibid.*, p. 139.
72. Kenneth Lo, *Chinese Food*, blurb.
73. Frank Oliver is typical, mourning his memories of 'Peking in the good days'. *Chinese Cooking*, p. 11.
74. Kenneth Lo, *Chinese Food*, pp. 24; 54.
75. *Ibid.*, p. 72. He does though dismiss chop suey as an American invention, unknown in China and the antithesis of real Chinese food, which keeps flavours separate – it 'is really no more than a savoury mess' (p. 82). Other authorities would concur: in her 1935 *Recipes of All Nations* Countess Morphy gave a fascinating account of the origins of the dish: 'The venerable Viceroy, Li Hung Chang, when in Washington, was pestered by American newspaper reporters. One of these having spied on him during a meal, begged to be told the name of a particular dish in which the ingredients were all chopped in small pieces, and his Excellency, annoyed at this intrusion, snapped out "Chop Suey!" – the literal translation of which is "dirty mixed fragments". American journalists were quick in advertising this as a typical Chinese dish, and Chinese restaurateurs in America at once adopted the name' (p. 713).
76. *Ibid.*, p. 72.
77. *Ibid.*, p. 74.
78. This tallies with the history of the adoption of foreign cuisines in America, where the tendency has invariably been towards assimilation and adaptation rather than the studied attempts at authenticity that have tended to be the British response to their adopted cuisines. America, at least from the 1960s onwards, has tended to produce hybrid cuisines, developing and melding other cuisines to create something new. The food famously developed in California in the 1970s, with its French, Italian and wholefood and vegetarian influences, is just one example.
79. Sylvia Lovegren, *Fashionable Food: Seven Decades of Food Fads*, p. 227.
80. Elizabeth David, *French Provincial Cooking*, p. 474.
81. Sylvia Lovegren, *Fashionable Food*, p. 225.

Another American import was Richard Olney, whose quietly learned yet demystifying approach to French cooking earned him the respect of the food establishment on both sides of the Atlantic. *Simple French Food*, his best-known book, was published in America in 1974 but did not appear in this country until 1981. He popularized mousses, terrines and pâtés, and his recipe for a Vegetable Terrine may well have been the source of the mosaicked, delicately flavoured (some might say bland) confections produced by so many nouvelle cuisine chefs in the 1980s.

82. M. F. K. Fisher, *The Gastronomical Me*, p. 441.
83. Philippa Pullar, *Consuming Passions: A History of British Food and Appetite*, p. 216.
84. Erin Pizzey, *The Slut's Cook Book*, p. 146.
85. Katharine Whitehorn, *Cooking in a Bedsitter*, p. 13.
86. *Ibid.*, pp. 180–1.
87. Delia Smith, *How to Cheat at Cooking*, p. 7.
88. *Ibid.*, pp. 9–10.
89. *Ibid.*, p. 24.
90. *Ibid.*, p. 27.
91. *Ibid.*, p. 45.
92. 'Lucky Dip', reproduced in *An Omelette and A Glass of Wine*, pp. 27–8.
93. A letter from Iain Hamilton to Elizabeth David (2.7.62) and the draft of a letter from Elizabeth David to the management of Walls, quoted in Artemis Cooper, *Writing at the Kitchen Table*, p. 218.
94. *Ibid.*, p. 303.
95. 'Fast and Fresh', 9 December 1960; 'Summer Holidays', 24 August 1962; 'Oules of Sardines', 12 October 1962, all reproduced in *An Omelette and a Glass of Wine*, pp. 24, 33, 275–9; Elizabeth David, *Italian Food*, p. 41 and note.
96. Jane Grigson, *Good Things*, p. 227.
97. Peg Bracken, *I Hate to Cook Book*, pp. 15; 37.
98. *Ibid.*, pp. 9; 79.
99. *Ibid.*, p. 13.
100. *Ibid.*, pp. 62–4.
101. Shirley Conran, *Superwoman*, p. 99.
102. Greer, for example, put great argumentative effort into convincing the reader that men don't rape women simply because they find them attractive.
103. Shirley Conran, *Superwoman*, pp. 21; 153.
104. Carole Wright, *The Liberated Cook's Book*, p. 9.
105. Ted Moloney and Deke Coleman, *Oh, for a French Wife!*, p. 85.
106. Donald Kilbourn, *Pots and Pans: Man's Answer to Women's Lib*, p. 1.
107. *Ibid.*, pp. 4, 11.
108. Michael Bateman, *Cooking People*, p. 68.
109. See Elizabeth David, 'Big Bad Bramleys', 26 October 1962, *An Omelette and a Glass of Wine*, pp. 36–7.
110. Michael Bateman, *Cooking People*, p. 72.
111. *Ibid.*, p. 74.
112. If food writers began to be commodities in this period, so too did the kitchen and everything associated with it. Where the new science of kitchen design in the 1950s had concentrated its energies on minimizing the time the housewife had to spend in the room, the next two decades saw the kitchen reimagined as the centre of the house. It was a change of attitude that was an inevitable concomitant of the culinary philosophy of Elizabeth David and her disciples – if cooking

was the new cultural activity then you wanted the tools and the processes on show. Elizabeth David's own shop (which she founded with friends in 1965 and ran until 1973, when disagreements with her partners led her to sever all connections with the business) sold the 'right' tools and accoutrements – French carbon steel knives, coeur à la crème dishes, earthenware dauberies. In its heyday it had a literally cultist status, with the faithful paying obeisance at the shrine, begging a bit of the vinegar mother started by David herself, hoping for a glimpse of their icon, who was sometimes to be spotted in her cubbyhole under the stairs. A younger generation bought the culinary lifestyle from Terence Conran, whose first Habitat store opened in Fulham in 1964, selling garlic presses (Elizabeth David famously refused to stock them in her shop), Mouli food mills, fish kettles and butchers' blocks. The ultimate dream, endlessly reiterated in the magazines, cook books, advertisements and domestic fiction of the 1970s, was the farmhouse-style kitchen, with a scrubbable pine refectory table at its centre (inevitably 'huge' to accommodate one's hordes of friends) and ideally an Aga for that constant maternal warmth. It is no accident that this earth-mother fantasy gained such a hold over the feminine imagination at precisely the time when women were at last becoming a significant presence in the work place.

CHAPTER SIX

1. 'Vive La Nouvelle Cuisine Française', *Gault-Millau* magazine, October 1973.
2. Most of these chefs had trained with the celebrated Ferdinand Point (1897–1955), later acknowledged as the father of nouvelle cuisine, who insisted that ingredients should be of the highest quality and freshness, and must always taste of themselves and not be disguised. Everything was to be done from scratch – there must be nothing on the stoves in the morning.
3. Michel Guérard invented a diet version of nouvelle cuisine, cuisine minceur, which many foreign interpreters of the new movement confused with nouvelle cuisine: cuisine minceur replaced butter with fromage blanc, rich sauces with foaming confections of a little egg yolk and a lot of air, and sugar with artificial sweeteners.
4. Henri Gault, 'Nouvelle Cuisine', in *Cooks and Other People*.
5. Elizabeth David, *French Provincial Cooking*, p. xvi.
6. *Ibid.*, p. xvii.
7. Marco Pierre White, *White Heat*, p. 32.
8. Nico Ladenis, *My Gastronomy*, p. 215.
9. *Ibid.*, p. 218.
10. *Ibid.*, p. 50.
11. Peter York, who is frequently credited with the authorship of *The Official Sloane Ranger Handbook*, was in fact a contributor, though the co-author of a number of the later projects that emerged from it.
12. Ann Barr and Paul Levy, *The Official Foodie Handbook*, p. 7.
13. See Artemis Cooper, *Writing at the Kitchen Table*, pp. 308–10, for an account of David's reaction and that of Derek Cooper.
14. Elizabeth Jane Howard and Fay Maschler, *Howard and Maschler on Food*, pp. 135; 141.

15. Simon Hopkinson, *Roast Chicken and Other Stories*, p. 1.
16. 'The anxiety of influence' is a concept articulated by literary critic Harold Bloom in his 1973 book of that title to describe the ambivalent father–son relationship that writers feel towards those who have most influenced them, and from whose overbearing presence they struggle to be free. Bloom's primary example is William Blake's response to Milton and his provocative recasting of the theology of *Paradise Lost*, with Satan as the hero.
17. Jenny Baker, *Kitchen Suppers*, p. xi.
18. Clare Macdonald, *Suppers*, p. 97.
19. In the face of these confusions and anxieties it is no accident that the most significant new boom area of food publishing in this decade has been in books on cooking for and with children. Leader of the pack is Annabel Karmel, whose many books on food for babies and toddlers are responsible for the hordes of sleep-deprived new mothers frantically batch-cooking vegetable purées at midnight. In the books of Karmel and her imitators we also find a surprising new ingredient – breast milk. With the aid of a breast pump the mother can extract small quantities of precious bluish milk to be warmed and mixed with powdered baby rice to provide the first weaning food. It is not as universally repellent as the cooking and consuming of a placenta (a practice famously shown on television for the first time on a taboo-busting episode of Hugh Fearnley-Whittingstall's *TV Dinners*, with the recipe given in the book of the series), but it certainly extends the repertoire of the cook book. It is interesting to note that these new departures in the feeding of infants – which are all very much the province of the 1990s equivalent of the earth mother – are highly dependent on technology. Without a freezer and liquidizer, and ideally a microwave, you cannot prepare the multicoloured cubes of veggie mush; without a fridge or freezer, a breast pump – preferably electronic – and elaborate sterilizing equipment you cannot extract breast milk and keep it free of bacteria. The ideal is to encourage a relaxed, natural appreciation of food in our small children; the reality is something else.
20. Nigella Lawson, *How to Eat*, pp. 453; 454.
21. *Ibid.*, p. 458.
22. *Ibid.*, pp. 459; 469; 494.
23. *Ibid.*, p. 460.
24. A writer who has taken further the notion that children should be involved in day-to-day cooking is Heston Blumenthal, chef–proprietor of the Fat Duck restaurant in Bray and darling of the broadsheet food critics. In his restaurant, and in the innovative cookery column he wrote until recently for the Saturday *Guardian*, Blumenthal has adopted a spectacularly experimental approach to food, with inventions such as white chocolate and caviare buttons, crab ice cream, cod with cockscombs and liquorice, snail porridge, and bacon caramel to his name, and it is this spirit that he carries through into his *Family Food: A New Approach to Cooking* of 2002. This promises to be not just another guide to serving your children's food in the form of a clown's face but an attempt to inspire parents to involve their children in the kitchen by turning culinary processes into scientific experiment. Part science manual, part guide

to producing a child chef, the book takes the novel approach of involving children by promising excellence rather than ease: 'you can teach them how to cook the perfect roast chicken, for example, or the principle for blanching green vegetables or making pommes purée as good as you will find anywhere'. Blumenthal is heavily influenced by Harold McGee's ground-breaking work *On Food and Cooking: The Science and Lore of the Kitchen* (1984), in which science is put at the service of the cook and a range of myths and misconceptions exploded. Blumenthal follows McGee's lead, experimenting with low-temperature methods of cooking meat, suggesting the grating of the raw vegetable on top of cooked vegetable soup, constructing a chocolate cream invented by a French molecular chemist from just water and chocolate whisked together. His is not so much a guide to family-friendly meal preparation as a workbook which treats cooking rather like learning the piano: 'what seems to me remarkable is that although we encourage our children to draw, paint, play musical instruments and learn languages we do little to encourage or consciously develop their appreciation of food and flavour'.

25. Nigel Slater, *Real Fast Food*, p. 210.
26. The book was published in 1930 in his native France (as *La Cuisine en Dix Minutes ou L'Adaptation au Rythme Moderne*) and first appeared in an English translation in 1948. Elizabeth David's 1967 article on Pomiane is reproduced in *An Omelette and a Glass of Wine*, as are her later thoughts on Pomiane's unacknowledged influence on the founding figures of nouvelle cuisine.
27. Nigel Slater, *Real Fast Food*, p. 234.
28. *Ibid.*, p. 8.
29. *Ibid.*, p. 312.
30. *Ibid.*, p. 176.
31. *Ibid.*, p. 292.
32. *Ibid.*, p. 8.
33. *Ibid.*, p. 290.
34. Referring to her rivals on the BBC's *Food and Drink* programme she announced that she found it revolting to see TV chefs taste what they had made: 'I can't bear it. It's just everything I hate. I can't bear people eating on TV, it's one thing I will never, ever do: I will never put anything in my mouth and go, "Delicious". That is just the pits, isn't it?' Alison Bowyer, *Delia Smith: The Biography*, p. 240.
35. *A Feast for Lent*, a collection of psalms and prayers, was published in 1983, followed by *A Feast for Advent* and *A Journey into God*.
36. Harriet Lane, *Observer*, 12 December 1999.
37. 'I'm not prim – in fact, I am a bit of a bitch', *Daily Telegraph*, 25 September 2000. Interestingly, *Food and Drink* was subsequently axed – perhaps it really doesn't do to cross Delia.
38. Alison Bowyer, *Delia Smith*, p. 223.
39. In her (unauthorized) biography Alison Bowyer points out that Delia is 'a careful guardian of her own image': 'Two wardrobe assistants accompanied her on a two-day shopping spree to buy suitably inoffensive attire for the *Win-*

ter Collection series. The look they were aiming for was "warm and cosy, nothing too exotic or flamboyant", Frances [Whittaker, executive producer of the series] explains. But it is interesting to note that in searching for her "ordinary housewife" attire Delia chose Harrods in which to do her shopping.' *Delia Smith: The Biography*, pp. 184–5.

40. Delia Smith, *How to Cook, Book One*, p. 146.
41. *Ibid.*, p. 61.
42. *Ibid.*, p. 77. Eric Griffiths, 'Hegel's Winter Collection – Defending Delia: Fairy-Tale Cookery and the Art You Cannot Eat', *Times Literary Supplement*, 8 March 1996.
43. Delia Smith, *How to Cook, Book One*, p. 46.
44. Delia Smith, *How to Cook, Book Two*, p. 120.
45. Typical dishes were things like Roast Sea Bass with Braised Fennel and a Bloody Mary Sauce, and Wild Salmon filled with Spinach Mousse in a Puff Pastry Parcel, and on virtually every programme – why? – someone would make Rosti.
46. Watson's book was most remarkable for having been sold with a choice of jacket colours – perhaps the hope was that people would short-sightedly buy two.
47. Other examples of women's food memoirs are *Tender at the Bone: Growing Up at the Table* (1998) by American food critic Ruth Reichel, and its sequel *Comfort Me with Apples* (2002); Nora Seton's *The Kitchen Congregation: A Memoir* (2000), which celebrates the life of the kitchen for five generations of her family; and Patricia Volk's 2002 book *Stuffed: Growing up in a Restaurant Family*.
48. Another form of machismo is to be found in Jeffrey Steingarten's *The Man Who Ate Everything* (1997), a wittily erudite, fascinating collection of essays by the food critic of American *Vogue* recounting how he trained his palate to accept anything, including anchovies, lard, horse fat and Greek food.
49. It was to prove the training ground for a number of the next generation of innovative chefs, including Sam Clark (of Moro) and Jamie Oliver.
50. Jacques Peretti, 'Too Hot to Handle', *Guardian*, 30 August 2000.
51. Nigella Lawson, *How to Eat*, p. 23. The latter is to be found in *Nigella Bites* (2000), along with Elvis Presley's Fried Peanut-Butter and Banana Sandwich, in a whole chapter on 'Trashy Food'.
52. *Ibid.*, p. 7.
53. *Ibid.*, p. 47.
54. Nigella Lawson, *How to Eat*, p. 443.
55. Barbara Santich, 'Inevitable, Yes, but Desirable?', *Slow: The International Herald of Tastes*, Issue 34, Nov–Dec 2002.
56. Sybil Kapoor, *Modern British Food*, p. 184.
57. The pull back towards authenticity that underlies the somewhat Emperor's-New-Clothes invention of modern British food is to be seen in the fact that the books about foreign food that have made the most significant impact in the last few years are those with a deep sense of tradition. They are books that investigate food embedded in a rich cultural context and manage to find new stories

to tell about it. Elisabeth Luard followed up her *Family Life* with *Still Life* (1998), on one level a sequel to that undomestic story of domestic life, documenting the journeys undertaken by her husband and herself when their children had left home; but more fully an exploration of the intertwining of food and culture in various corners of the world. Eastern Europe, the Hebrides, and the lands above the Arctic Circle are investigated for the insights their food and domestic arrangements can lend to questions about gender roles, relationships, history and the deepest consequences of being human. The pictures she paints are both everyday and curiously affecting, like the scents of the stews wafting from apartments in Belgrade that decisively separate Croatians from Serbs from Montenegrins. Another book to open up an obscure culinary culture was *Sichuan Cookery* (2001) by Fuchsia Dunlop, East Asia specialist for the BBC World Service, which discussed in tantalizing detail that mountain-bound province whose food the West has hardly begun to explore. The first foreigner to undertake a professional training course at the Sichuan Institute of Higher Cuisine, Dunlop gives meticulous recipes for such exotica as Hot-and-Numbing Chicken Slices, Man-and-Wife Meat Slices, Strange-Flavour Peanuts, and Ants Climbing a Tree (bean-thread noodles with minced meat), while painting an intriguing picture of a prized ancient cuisine adapting itself to a changing world. The adaptations of another ancient cuisine under the pressure of historical circumstance are at the heart of Claudia Roden's *The Book of Jewish Food* (1997). The book, which explores the complex history of Jewish food 'from Samarkand and Vilna to the present day', represents the culmination of the project, begun in *A Book of Middle Eastern Food* of 1968, of tracing the food of Roden's own family of displaced Egyptian Jews. Roden follows the model established in her earlier books, weaving stories, legends and quotations with authoritative recipes developed from the many versions she has collected. This book, though, is more concertedly historical than her previous works, with long passages describing the life of Jews in medieval Germany, in the shtetls of eastern Europe in the nineteenth century, in Muslim Spain between 711 and 1492, and in the Ottoman empire, to which many Spanish Jews fled when expelled by Ferdinand and Isabella. The book is brought alive by the many graphic illustrations of the effects of history, religion and culture on culinary traditions. Orange cakes, she explains, are typical of all Mediterranean Jewish communities, even though they are not usually found in the surrounding local cuisines, because Jews have a tradition of citrus cultivation going back to Biblical times, as they needed citron as part of the religious ritual of the Feast of the Tabernacles. These new historically focused cook books charm with their intense sense of the particularity of the lives that produced the recipes, and seem to me likely to be the first of a wave of books that productively intertwine historical, anthropological and culinary stories.

58. Other concerns about the Mediterranean diet are to do with the large quantity of olive oil recommended (between 30 and 40 per cent of the calories in the diet were to come from olive oil), which could lead to weight gain and hence to other risk factors like diabetes and high blood pressure. In concentrating only on reducing the risk of heart disease the diet ignores factors (like alcohol

consumption) that are linked with conditions such as breast cancer. Food writers such as Claudia Roden have also pointed out that the food pyramid is not typical of the diets of many Mediterranean peoples, many of whom eat much more meat and fish than is suggested, as well as pastries dripping with sugar syrup. Nor does the emphasis on alcohol consumption represent the many Muslim peoples who inhabit the Mediterranean basin.

59. The most authoritative books have been those written by Anna del Conte and Marcella Hazan, Italians whose translation of their native foods for a British audience has the meticulous attention to detail of a cookery course. Indeed, cooking courses in the splendour of the Umbrian countryside or Tuscan hills have become a great trend with the affluent middle classes – one of the most prestigious is run by chef Alastair Little, whose *Italian Kitchen* was published in 1996. It begins with the bald assertion that 'there is no real Italian food outside of Italy', which does make one wonder about the point of the whole enterprise. He takes irritated sideswipes at trendy 'Italianate' food in Britain, mocking its predilection for polenta – 'no wonder the diehards of the food world love it; it's tedious to prepare and tastes like grainy wallpaper paste' – and the needless mystique spun around simple dishes like Ribollita – 'much complicated nonsense is talked about this Tuscan soup'. The dishes he typically reproduces are less rarefied than those of the River Café, more domestic in both scale and feel: Pasta e Ceci (pasta with chickpeas), memorably described as 'spicy, oily, mealy and cheesy', Pasta e Patate (pasta and potatoes), Maiale al Latte (pork cooked in milk). His Italy is essentially modern, not the rustic fantasy indulged in by other translators of the Italian culinary dream for a British market. He has a nice sense of the recent trends in restaurants in Italy and the way fashions in Italian foods are adopted and mutated across Europe. He gives one of the first recipes for oven-dried tomatoes, which were to oust the sun-dried variety (ingredient *de non plus* of the early 1990s) in the foodie lexicon. The British sense of Italian food became much more sophisticated in these decades: moving beyond the horizons of spaghetti, lasagne and pizza, we dusted off our hand-cranked pasta machines, prepared platters of antipasti, dutifully stirred our risottos, embraced polenta and discovered crostini.

60. Elisabeth Luard, *Family Life: Birth, Death and the Whole Damn Thing*, p.122.

61. M. F. K. Fisher, *The Art of Eating*, p. 216.

62. Accompanied by the profoundly unedifying spectacle of health minister John Selwyn Gummer illustrating his absolute confidence in beef by feeding his small child a hamburger in front of the massed TV cameras.

63. Fiona Beckett *et al.*, 'Noshtalgia', *Guardian*, 29 June 2002.

64. Because the flavour of the 95 per cent beef tallow in which the major burger suppliers cooked their fries until 1990 (they switched to vegetable oil after a barrage of criticism about high cholesterol levels) is replicated by elaborate flavour compounds produced in high-tech laboratories.

65. Hattie Ellis's *Eating England* of 2001 combined a hunting out of the best small food producers with an analysis of the current state of British food; and Rick Stein covered much the same ground in 2002 in the television programme and

associated book entitled *Rick Stein's Food Heroes*. In *Simply the Best: The Art of Seasonal Cooking* (2001), based on her columns in the Saturday *Telegraph*, Tamasin Day-Lewis combined in-depth features on food producers with recipes to be made using their produce (or much less authentic simulacra if you are too busy to source the best).

66. Derek Cooper, *Snail Eggs and Samphire: Dispatches from the Food Front*, p. 206.
67. The movement had its origins in the work of Lady Eve Balfour, who founded the Soil Association in 1946, which devoted itself to improving the health and fertility of the soil through natural means, and which is still the nation's principal organic certification body.
68. An interest in returning to seasonality in food consumption actually pre-dates the recent huge success of the organic movement and has been a significant feature of cook-book publishing over the last twenty years. Margaret Costa's *Four Seasons Cookery Book* of 1970 was the inspiration for many; its celebratory approach to the seasonal cycles of food and its revival of traditional favourites like Rhubarb and Ginger Jam and Iced Cucumber Soup making it the perfect antidote to the exploding convenience-food culture of her day. The book, which had long gone out of print, was reissued in 1996 amid a flurry of genuflections from the big food names of the day. Another significant influence on other food writers was Jeremy Round, whose *The Independent Cook* of 1988 is subtitled 'Strategies for Seasonal Cooking' and was one of the first books to attempt to reverse the trend of anti-seasonality actively encouraged by the major supermarket chains. Arranged month by month, with tables of seasonal availability and guides to the best varieties of vegetables, this would be a useful book even if the recipes were banal; but in fact they are excellent and still smack of individuality fifteen years on. Like Nigel Slater, who has to some extent followed in his footsteps, Round is resolutely unsnobbish, extolling the pleasures of peanut butter and jam sandwiches, and condensed milk, which he uses for a definitive lemon-meringue pie which knocks the socks off the horrible cornflour-thickened versions given by virtually all other British food writers. His best recipes combine a startling newness with a sense of inevitable rightness. His influences are particularly Turkish and American – informed by travel as much as second-hand garnering of dishes – and he is in the vanguard of that late 1980s turn to traditional homely British and French dishes. Round remains a cookery writers' cookery writer rather than a more public figure, as he sadly died young in 1989 of a heart attack following a banquet in Hong Kong. His work deserves to be much better known.
69. Also useful is Lynda Brown's 1990 *The Cook's Garden*, which deals with the same problem from the point of view of the gardener with her seasonal gluts rather than the veg-box customer with her wilting greens, but covers such likely acquisitions as celeriac, spring greens and spinach beet. Another interesting take on dealing with the unplannned-for vegetable comes from Nina Planck, who was responsible for introducing farmers' markets to this country, following the model established in the early 1980s in her native America. Her *Farmers' Market Cookbook* of 2001 covers such newly available produce as cavolo nero, misome and mizona (the latter both Asian greens), as well as tra-

ditional varieties of apples, plums, squash and tomatoes.

70. Hugh Fearnley-Whittingstall, *The River Cottage Cookbook*, pp. 16; 162.

71. Rose Elliot continued to publish, bringing out what must be close to her seventy-fifth vegetarian cook book in 2003. Some of the other most influential writers were American: Martha Rose Shulman, whose *Vegetarian Feast* (1982) incorporated Mexican, Italian, French, Middle Eastern, Chinese and Japanese dishes; and Anna Thomas, whose 1972 book *Vegetarian Epicure* brought pleasure into American vegetarian cookery in much the same way that Rose Elliot's first book did in this country, followed it up with *The New Vegetarian Epicure* (published in this country in 1991, thirteen years after it first came out in America) and *From Anna's Kitchen* (1996). These books were very much influenced by the West Coast food revolution, as was Deborah Madison's *The Greens Cook Book* (1988), a product of the celebrated vegetarian restaurant on San Francisco Bay, whose typical dishes include Goat Cheese Pizza with Red Onions and Green Olives, Cottage Cheese-Dill Bread and a number of roulades – the dish that became *the* vegetarian dinner-party centrepiece in the 1980s.

72. Nigel Slater, *Appetite*, p. 190; Tamasin Day-Lewis, *The Art of the Tart*, p. 8; Delia Smith, *How to Cook, Book One*, p. 178; Nigella Lawson, *How to Be a Domestic Goddess*, pp. 128; 132.

73. Christopher Driver, *The British at Table*, p. 181.

74. Helge Rubinstein, *The Chocolate Book*, p. 89.

75. One of the best 1990s baking books was Sue Lawrence's *On Baking* (1996), in which the author, who had launched her career as a food writer after winning both the BBC's *Masterchef* and the *Sunday Times* Amateur Chef of the Year award, combines traditional British classics (particularly favourites from her Scottish childhood) with a modern, eclectic selection of baked goods from around the world, including Swedish Saffron Rolls, Greek Easter Bread and the rather dubious Banana Pizza.

76. Nigella Lawson, *Domestic Goddess*, p. 39.

77. Nigella Lawson, *Nigella Bites*, p. 47.

78. One of the few recent male food writers to include cake recipes is Nigel Slater, whose willingness to embrace his feminine side may have something to do with the loss of his mother at a young age.

79. Jeffrey Steingarten, 'Primal Bread', *The Man Who Ate Everything*; John Thorne, 'Natural Leavens: Sorting Out Sourdough', www.outlawcook.com; Dan Lepard and Richard Whittington, *Baker & Spice: Baking with Passion*.

80. The works cited are Simon Hopkinson, *Gammon & Spinach* (1998) and *Roast Chicken and Other Stories: Second Helpings* (2001); Hugh Fearnley-Whittingstall, *The River Cottage Cookbook* (2001); Tamasin Day-Lewis, *Simply the Best* (2001); Nigella Lawson, *How to Eat* (1998); Ruth Watson, *The Really Helpful Cookbook* (2000); Nigel Slater, *Real Food* (1998) and *Appetite* (2000).

81. Simon Hopkinson, *Roast Chicken and Other Stories: Second Helpings*, p. 134.

Bibliography

Acton, Eliza, *Modern Cookery for Private Families*, first published 1845 (Lewes: Southover Press, 1993).

Adams, Samuel and Adams, Sarah, *The Complete Servant*, first published 1825 (Lewes: Southover Press, 1989).

Allhusen, Dorothy, *A Book of Scents and Dishes*, first published 1926 (London: Williams & Norgate, 1934).

Anon., *Aunt Kate's Household Annual* (London: John Leng and Co., 1933).

Anon., *Be-Ro Self-Raising Flour: For Economical Baking* (London: Thomas Bell & Son, 1957).

Anon., *The Best Way: A Book of Household Hints and Recipes* (London: The Amalgamated Press, 1916?).

Anon., *The Book of Woman's Hour* (London: Ariel Productions, 1953).

Anon., *The Doctors' Cookery Book* (London: The British Medical Association, 1938).

Anon., *Every Woman's Book of Home-Making* (London: The Amalgamated Press, 1938).

Anon., *The Kitchen Front* (London: Nicolson and Watson, 1942).

Anon., *The Radiation Cookery Book*, first published 1927 (London: Radiation Group Sales, 1955).

Attar, Dena, *A Bibliography of Household Books Published in Britain 1800–1914* (London: Prospect Books, 1987).

Auden, W. H., Introduction to M. F. K. Fisher, *The Art of Eating* (London: Macmillan, 1990).

Ayrton, Elisabeth, *The Cookery of England*, first published 1974 (Harmondsworth: Penguin, 1977).

Baker, Jenny, *Kettle Broth to Gooseberry Fool: A Celebration of Simple English Cooking* (London: Faber & Faber, 1996).

Baker, Jenny, *Kitchen Suppers* (London: Faber & Faber, 1993).

Bareham, Lindsey, *In Praise of the Potato* (London: Michael Joseph, 1989).

Bareham, Lindsey, *Onions without Tears*, first published 1995 (Harmondsworth: Penguin, 1996).

Barnes, Julian, *The Pedant in the Kitchen* (London: Atlantic Books, 2004).

Barr, Ann and Levy, Paul, *The Official Foodie Handbook* (London: Ebury Press, 1984).

Barthes, Roland, 'Ornamental Cookery', *Mythologies*, first published 1957 (London: Granada, 1973).

Basu, Shrabani, *Curry in the Crown: The Story of Britain's Favourite Dish* (New Delhi: Harper Collins, 1999).

Bateman, Michael, *Cooking People* (London: Leslie Frewin, 1966).
Bear, John and Bear, Marina, *The Something Went Wrong What Do I Do Now Cookery Book* (London: Macdonald, 1973).
Beck, Simone, Bertolle, Louisette and Child, Julia, *Mastering the Art of French Cooking*, first published 1961 (Harmondsworth: Penguin, 1976).
Beckett, Fiona *et al.*, 'Noshtalgia', *Guardian*, 29 June 2002.
Beddoes, Deirdre, *Back to Home and Duty* (London: Pandora, 1989).
Beeton, Isabella, *Beeton's Book of Household Management*, a part-work (London: S. O. Beeton, 1859–61).
Beeton, Isabella, *Beeton's Book of Household Management* (London: S. O. Beeton, 1861).
Beeton, Isabella, *Beeton's Book of Household Management*, facsimile of first edition (London: Chancellor Press, 1989).
Beeton, Isabella, *Mrs Beeton's Book of Household Management*, abridged, Ed. Nicola Humble (Oxford: Oxford World's Classics, 2000).
Beeton, Samuel (Ed.), *Beeton's Dictionary of Universal Information* (London: S. O. Beeton, 1858–62).
Beeton, Samuel (Ed.), *Englishwoman's Domestic Magazine* (1852–65).
Bell, Annie, *Annie Bell's Vegetable Book* (London: Michael Joseph, 1997).
Bell, Annie, *A Feast of Flavours: The New Vegetarian Cuisine* (London: Bantam Press, 1992).
Black, Mrs, *Household Cookery and Laundry Work* (London: Collins, 1882).
Blanc, Raymond, *Recipes from Le Manoir Aux Quat' Saisons* (London: Guild Publishing, 1988).
Blatch, Margaret, *One Hundred and One Practical Non-Flesh Recipes*, first published 1916 (London: Longmans, Green & Co., 1917).
Bloom, Harold, *The Anxiety of Influence* (New York: Oxford University Press, 1973).
Blumenthal, Heston, *Family Food: A New Approach to Cooking* (London: Michael Joseph, 2002).
Blythman, Joanna, *The Food We Eat*, first published 1996 (Harmondsworth: Penguin, 1998; revised edn).
Bon Viveur (Fanny and Johnnie Cradock), *The Sociable Cook's Book* (London: The Daily Telegraph, 1967).
Boulestin, X. Marcel, *The Conduct of the Kitchen* (London: William Heinemann, 1925).
Boulestin, X. Marcel, *Simple French Cooking for English Homes* (London: William Heinemann, 1923).
Boulestin, X. Marcel, *What Shall We Have To-Day? 365 Recipes for All the Days of the Year* (London: William Heinemann, 1931).
Bourdain, Anthony, *Kitchen Confidential: Adventures in the Culinary Underbelly* (London: Bloomsbury, 2000).
Bowdich, Mrs, *New Vegetarian Dishes*, first published 1892 (London: G. Bell & Sons, 1912).
Bowyer, Alison, *Delia Smith: The Biography* (London: Andre Deutsch, 2002).
Boxer, Arabella, *Book of English Food: A Rediscovery of British Food from*

before the War, first published 1991 (Harmondsworth: Penguin, 1993).
Boxer, Arabella, *First Slice Your Cook Book* (London: Nelson, 1964).
Boxshall, Jan, *Good Housekeeping: Every Home Should Have One* (London: Ebury Press, 1997).
Bracken, Peg, *The I Hate to Cook Book*, first published 1960 (London: Corgi, 1978).
Bracken, Peg, *The I Still Hate to Cook Book* (London: Arlington Books, 1967).
Braithwaite, Brian, Walsh, Noëlle and Davies, Glyn (compilers), *The Home Front: The Best of Good Housekeeping 1939–1945* (London: Ebury Press, 1989).
Braithwaite, Brian, Walsh, Noëlle and Davies, Glyn (compilers), *Ragtime to Wartime: The Best of Good Housekeeping 1922–1939* (London: Ebury Press, 1986).
Briggs, Asa, *Victorian Things* (London: Batsford, 1988).
Brillat-Savarin, Jean-Anthelme, *The Philosopher in the Kitchen*, first published 1825 (as *La Physiologie du goût*), trans. Anne Drayton (Harmondsworth: Penguin, 1988).
Brotherton, Mrs, *A New System of Vegetable Cookery*, first published anonymously in 1821.
Brown, Lynda, *The Cook's Garden*, first published 1990 (London: Vermillion, 1992).
Brown, Lynda, *Fresh Thoughts on Food* (London: Dorling Kindersley, 1988).
Browne, Edith A. and Williams, Jessie J., *The World's Best Recipes* (London: George Newnes, 1935).
Buckner, Rose, *Rose Buckner's Book of Homemaking* (London: Odhams Press, 1950).
Bunting, Madeleine, 'Finding Your Inner Cook', *Guardian*, 11 December 2000.
Burnett, John, *Plenty and Want: A Social History of Diet in England from 1815 to the Present Day*, first published 1966 (London: Scolar Press, 1978).
Burton, David, *The Raj at Table: A Culinary History of the British in India* (London: Faber & Faber, 1993).
Cadwallader, Sharon and Ohr, Judi, *The Whole Earth Cookbook* (Harmondsworth: Penguin, 1973).
Carrier, Robert, *Great Dishes of the World* (London: Thomas Nelson & Sons, 1963).
Carrier, Robert, *Robert Carrier's Cookery Cards*, first series (London: Thomas Nelson, 1966).
Carson, Rachel, *Silent Spring* (London: Hamilton, 1963).
Castell, Hazel and Griffin, Kathleen, *Out of the Frying Pan* (London: BBC Books, 1993).
Chaney, Liza, *Elizabeth David: A Mediterranean Passion* (London: Macmillan, 1998).
Chowdhary, Savitri, *Indian Cooking* (London: Andre Deutsch, 1954).
Clark of Tillypronie, Lady, *Cookery Book*, first published 1907 (Lewes: Southover Press, 1994).
Clark, Sam and Clark, Sam, *Moro: The Cookbook* (London: Ebury Press, 2001).
Clarke, Sally, *Sally Clarke's Book* (London: Macmillan, 1999).

Conran, Shirley, *Superwoman: Everywoman's Book of Household Management* (London: Sidgwick and Jackson, 1975).
Cooper, Artemis, *Writing at the Kitchen Table* (Harmondsworth: Penguin, 2000).
Cooper, Derek, *Snail Eggs & Samphire: Dispatches from the Food Front* (London: Macmillan, 2000).
Cooper, Lettice, *The New House*, first published 1936 (London: Virago, 1987).
Cooper, Susan, 'Snoek Piquante', in Michael Sissons and Philip French (Eds), *Age of Austerity 1945–51* (London: Hodder & Stoughton, 1963).
Corbishley, Gill, *Ration Book Recipes: Some Food Facts 1939–1945* (London: English Heritage, 1995).
Costa, Margaret, *Four Seasons Cookery Book*, first published 1970 (London: Grub Street, 1996).
Couffignal, Huguette, *The People's Cookbook*, first published 1970 (as *La Cuisine des Pauvres*) (London: Macmillan, 1979).
Cradock, Fanny and Cradock, Johnnie, *Cook Hostess' Book* (London: Collins, 1970).
Cradock, Fanny and Cradock, Johnnie, *A Dish to Remember: A Cook for All Seasons* (Exeter: Webb & Bower, 1981).
Cradock, Fanny and Cradock, Johnnie (Bon Viveur), *The Sociable Cook's Book* (London: The Daily Telegraph, 1967).
Craig, Elizabeth, *Keeping House with Elizabeth Craig* (London: Collins, 1936).
Craig, Elizabeth, *250 Recipes by Elizabeth Craig for Use with Borwick's Baking Powder* (London: George Borwick & Sons, date unknown).
Cutforth, René, *Later than We Thought: A Portrait of the Thirties* (Newton Abbot: David & Charles, 1976).
Daily Telegraph, *Good Eating: Suggestions for Wartime Dishes* (London: Hutchinson, date unknown).
David, Elizabeth, *A Book of Mediterranean Food* (London: John Lehmann, 1950).
David, Elizabeth, *A Book of Mediterranean Food*, revised edn (Harmondsworth: Penguin, 1955).
David, Elizabeth, *English Bread and Yeast Cookery*, first published 1977 (Harmondsworth: Penguin, 1979).
David, Elizabeth, *French Country Cooking*, first published 1951 (Harmondsworth: Penguin, 1963).
David, Elizabeth, *French Provincial Cooking*, first published 1960 (Harmondsworth: Penguin, 1986).
David, Elizabeth, *Harvest of the Cold Months: The Social History of Ice and Ices*, Ed. Jill Norman (London: Viking, 1994).
David, Elizabeth, *Italian Food*, first published 1954 (Harmondsworth: Penguin, 1987).
David, Elizabeth, *Is There a Nutmeg in the House?* (Harmondsworth: Penguin, 2001).
David, Elizabeth, *An Omelette and a Glass of Wine* (Harmondsworth: Penguin, 1986).
David, Elizabeth, *South Wind through the Kitchen: The Best of Elizabeth David*, compiled by Jill Norman, first published 1997 (Harmondsworth: Penguin, 1998).

David, Elizabeth, *Spices, Salt and Aromatics in the English Kitchen*, first published 1970 (Harmondsworth: London, 1973).
David, Elizabeth, *Summer Cooking*, first published 1955 (London: The Cookery Book Club, 1968).
Davidson, Alan, *Mediterranean Seafood* (Harmondsworth: Penguin, 1972).
Davidson, Alan, *North Atlantic Seafood* (Harmondsworth: Penguin, 1979).
Davidson, Alan, *The Oxford Companion to Food* (Oxford: Oxford University Press, 1999).
Davidson, Silvija, *Loaf, Crust and Crumb* (London: Michael Joseph, 1995).
Davies, Jennifer, *The Victorian Kitchen* (London: BBC Books, 1989).
Davies, Jennifer, *The Wartime Kitchen and Garden* (London: BBC Books, 1995).
Day-Lewis, Tamasin, *The Art of the Tart* (London: Cassell & Co., 2000).
Day-Lewis, Tamasin, *Simply the Best: The Art of Seasonal Cooking* (London: Cassell & Co., 2001).
Deighton, Len, *Len Deighton's Action Cook Book*, first published 1965 (Harmondsworth: Penguin, 1967).
Deighton, Len, *Où Est Le Garlic: Len Deighton's French Cook Book*, first published 1965 (Harmondsworth: Penguin, 1967).
Dickens, Charles, *Bleak House*, first published 1853 (Harmondsworth: Penguin, 1985).
Dickens, Monica, *One Pair of Hands* (London: Michael Joseph, 1939).
Dickson Wright, Clarissa, *Food: What We Eat and How We Eat* (London: Ebury Press, 1999).
Dimbleby, Josceline, *The Almost Vegetarian Cookbook*, first published 1994 (London: Websters International, 1995).
Douglas, Norman, *Venus in the Kitchen* (London: Heinemann, 1952).
Driver, Christopher, *The British at Table 1940–1980* (London: Chatto & Windus and The Hogarth Press, 1983).
Driver, Elizabeth, *A Bibliography of Cookery Books Published in Brtain 1875–1914* (London: Prospect Books, 1989).
Drummond, J. C. and Wilbraham, Anne, *The Englishman's Food: Five Centuries of English Diet*, first published 1939 (London: Pimlico, 1991).
Dunlop, Fuchsia, *Sichuan Cookery* (London: Michael Joseph, 2001).
Durack, Terry, *Hunger* (London: Allen & Unwin, 2000).
Ehrenreich, Barbara, *The Snarling Citizen* (New York: Farrar, Straus & Giroux, 1995).
Ellis, Hattie, *Eating England: Why We Eat What We Eat* (London: Mitchell Beazley, 2001).
Ellis, Hattie, *Mood Food* (London: Headline, 1998).
Elliot, Rose, *The Bean Book*, first published 1979 (London: Fontana, 1985).
Elliot, Rose, *Not Just a Load of Old Lentils*, first published 1972 (London: Fontana, 1986).
Elliot, Rose, *Simply Delicious* (London: White Eagle Publishing Trust, 1967).
Escoffier, Auguste, *Guide to Modern Cookery*, first published 1907 (London: William Heineman, 1952).
Eyles, M. L., *The Woman in the Little House* (London: Grant Richards Ltd., 1922).

Farmer, Fannie, *The 1896 Boston Cooking-School Cook Book*, first published 1896 (as *The Boston Cooking-School Cook Book*) (New York: Gramercy, 1997).
Fearnley-Whittingstall, Hugh, *The Best of TV Dinners* (London: Channel 4 Books, 1999).
Fearnley-Whittingstall, Hugh, *The River Cottage Cookbook* (London: Harper Collins, 2001).
Fearon, Ethelind, *The Reluctant Cook* (London: Herbert Jenkins, 1953).
Fernández-Armesto, Felipe, *Food: A History*, first published 2001 (London: Pan Books, 2002).
Fisher, M. F. K., *The Art of Eating* (London: Macmillan, 1990).
Fisher, M. F. K., *The Gastronomical Me*, first published 1943, collected in *The Art of Eating* (London: Macmillan, 1991).
Fisher, M. F. K., *With Bold Knife and Fork* (London: Chatto & Windus, 1983).
Fisher, Patty, *Vegetarian Cookery* in 500 Recipes series (London: Hamlyn, 1969).
Fliess, Walter and Fliess, Jenny, *Modern Vegetarian Cookery*, first published 1964 (Harmondsworth: Penguin, 1975).
Floyd, Keith, *Floyd in the Soup: My Life and Other Great Escapes* (London: Pan Books, 1988).
Foreman, Susan, *Loaves and Fishes: An Illustrated History of the Ministry of Agriculture, Fisheries and Food 1889–1989* (London: Her Majesty's Stationery Office, 1989).
Fort, Matthew, 'Food', *Guardian*, 4 November 2000.
Francatelli, Charles Elmé, *A Plain Cookery Book for the Working Classes*, first published 1861 (Whitstable: Pryor Publications, 1997).
Francillon, Mrs, *Good Cookery: Simplified and Adapted to Modern Needs* (Gloucester: Minchin & Gibbs, 1920).
Freud, Clement, *Freud on Food* (London: J. M. Dent & Sons, 1978).
Friedan, Betty, *The Feminine Mystique*, first published 1963 (Harmondsworth: Penguin, 1972).
Gaskell, Elizabeth, *Cranford*, first published 1853 (Harmondsworth: Penguin, 1986).
Gaskell, Elizabeth, *North and South*, first published 1854 (Harmondsworth: Penguin, 1986).
Gattey, Charles Neilson, *Foie Gras and Trumpets* (London: Constable, 1984).
Gault, Henri, 'Nouvelle Cuisine', in *Cooks and Other People*, Oxford Symposium on Food History (Totnes: Prospect Books, 1995).
Gault, Henri and Millau, Christian, 'Vive La Nouvelle Cuisine Française', *Gault-Millau* magazine, October 1973.
Glasse, Hannah, *The Art of Cookery Made Plain and Easy* (1747).
Good Housekeeping Institute, *Book of Fish, Meat, Egg and Cheese Dishes* (London: Gramol Publications, 1944).
Grant, Doris, *Dear Housewives* (London: Faber & Faber, 1954).
Grant, Doris, *Your Daily Bread* (London: Faber & Faber, 1944).
Graves, Robert and Hodges, Alan, *The Long Week-end: A Social History of Great Britain 1918–1939*, first published 1940 (Harmondsworth: Penguin, 1971).

Gray, Patience, *Honey from a Weed* (London: Prospect Books, 1986).
Gray, Patience and Boyd, Primrose, *Plat du Jour, or Foreign Food* (Harmondsworth: Penguin, 1957).
Gray, Rose and Rogers, Ruth, *The River Café Cook Book* (London: Ebury Press, 1995).
Gray, Rose and Rogers, Ruth, *The River Café Cook Book Two* (London: Ebury Press, 1997).
Gray, Rose and Rogers, Ruth, *River Cafe Cook Book Green* (London: Ebury Press, 2000).
Greer, Germaine, *The Female Eunuch*, first published 1970 (London: Granada, 1981).
Griffiths, Eric, 'Hegel's Winter Collection – Defending Delia: Fairy-Tale Cookery and the Art You Cannot Eat', *Times Literary Supplement*, 8 March 1996.
Griffiths, Sian and Wallace, Jennifer (Eds), *Consuming Passions: Food in the Age of Anxiety* (Manchester: Manchester University Press, 1998).
Griggs, Barbara, *The Food Factor* (London: Viking, 1986).
Grigson, Jane, *Charcuterie and French Pork Cookery* (London: Michael Joseph, 1967).
Grigson, Jane, *English Food* (London: Purnell Book Services, 1974).
Grigson, Jane, *Fish Cookery*, first published 1973 (Harmondsworth: Penguin, 1985).
Grigson, Jane, *Good Things*, first published 1971 (Harmondsworth: Penguin, 1991).
Grigson, Jane, *Jane Grigson's Fruit Book*, first published 1982 (Harmondsworth: Penguin, 1983).
Grigson, Jane, *Jane Grigson's Vegetable Book*, first published 1978 (Harmondsworth: Penguin, 1980).
Grigson, Jane, *The Mushroom Feast* (London: Michael Joseph, 1975).
Grigson, Sophie and Black, William, *Organic* (London: Headline, 2001).
Guérard, Michel, *Cuisine Minceur*, translated by Caroline Conran, first published 1976 (as *La Grande Cuisine Minceur*) (London: Pan, 1978).
Hambro, Natalie, *Visual Delights* (London: Conran Octopus, 1985).
Hammond, R. J., *Food (Civil History of the Second World War)*, Vol. 2 (London: Her Majesty's Stationery Office and Longmans, Green and Co., 1956).
Hardy, Thomas, *Jude the Obscure*, first published 1895 (Harmondsworth: Penguin, 1979).
Hardyment, Christina, *Slice of Life: the British Way of Eating Since 1945* (London: BBC Books, 1995).
Harrison, Ruth, *Animal Machines* (London: Vincent Stuart, 1964).
Hartley, Dorothy, *Food in England*, first published 1954 (London: Little, Brown, 1996).
Hauser, Gayelord, *Look Younger, Live Longer* (London: Faber & Faber, 1951).
Heath, Ambrose, *Good Food; Month by Month Recipes* (London: Faber & Faber, 1932).
Heath, Ambrose (Ed.), *The International Cookery Book* (London: Frederick Muller, 1953).

Heath, Ambrose, *Kitchen Front Recipes and Hints: Extracts from the First Seven Months' Early Morning Broadcasts by Ambrose Heath* (London: Adam and Charles Black, 1941).

Heath, Ambrose, *Kitchen Table Talk* (London: Victor Gollancz, 1953).

Heath, Ambrose, *More Kitchen Front Recipes* (London: A. & C. Black, 1941).

Heath, Ambrose, *The Queen Cookery Book* (London: Gerald Duckworth & Co., 1961).

Highton, N. B. and Highton, R. B., *The Home Book of Vegetarian Cooking* (London: Faber & Faber, 1964).

Hill Hassall, Arthur, *Food and Its Adulterations*, first published 1855 (London: Longmans, Green and Co., 1876).

Hindlip, Lady, *Minnie, Lady Hindlip's Cookery Book* (London: Thornton Butterworth, 1925).

Hinton, James, 'Militant Housewives: The British Housewives League and the Attlee Government', *History Workshop*, Autumn 1994.

Hogarth, Grace (Ed.), *American Cooking for English Kitchens* (London: Hamish Hamilton, 1957).

Hom, Ken, *The Taste of China*, first published 1990 (London: Bracken Books, 1994).

Hopkinson, Simon, *Gammon & Spinach*, first published 1998 (London: Macmillan, 2001).

Hopkinson, Simon, *Roast Chicken and Other Stories: Second Helpings* (London: Macmillan, 2001).

Hopkinson, Simon and Bareham, Lindsey, *The Prawn Cocktail Years* (London: Macmillan, 1997).

Hopkinson, Simon and Bareham, Lindsey, *Roast Chicken and Other Stories*, first published 1994 (London: Ebury Press, 1995).

Horsfield, Margaret, *Biting the Dust: The Joys of Housework* (London: Fourth Estate, 1997).

Howard, Elizabeth Jane and Maschler, Fay, *Howard and Maschler on Food*, first published 1987 (London: Sphere Books, 1988).

Humble, Nicola (Ed.), *Mrs Beeton's Book of Household Management*, abridged (Oxford: Oxford World's Classics, 2000).

Humble, Nicola, *The Feminine Middlebrow Novel, 1920s to 1950s: Class, Domesticity and Bohemianism* (Oxford: Oxford University Press, 2001).

Humble, Nicola, 'Little Swans with Luxette and Loved Boy Pudding: Changing Fashions in Cookery Books', *Women: A Cultural Review*, 13/3 Winter 2002.

Hume, Rosemary and Downes, Muriel, *Cordon Bleu Cookery*, first published 1963 (as *Penguin Cordon Bleu Cookery*) (London: Book Club Associates, 1978).

Hyde, H. Montgomery, *Mr and Mrs Beeton* (London: George Harrap & Co., 1951).

Innes, Jocasta, *The Pauper's Cookbook* (Harmondsworth: Penguin, 1971).

Ives, Catherine, *The Catherine Ives Cookery Book* (London: Gerald Duckworth & Co., 1951).

Ives, Catherine, *When the Cook Is Away* (London: Gerald Duckworth & Co., 1928).

Jacob, Naomi, *Me – In the Kitchen* (London: Hutchinson & Co., 1935).
Jaffrey, Madhur, *An Invitation to Indian Cooking*, first published 1973 (Harmondsworth: Penguin, 1978).
Jekyll, Lady Agnes, *Kitchen Essays*, first published 1922 (London: Collins, 1969).
Johnstone, Viola, *The Hostess Cooks* (London: Seeley, Service & Co., 1955).
Kapoor, Sybil, 'A Feast Fit for a Queen', *Independent*, 1 June 2002.
Kapoor, Sybil, *Modern British Food*, first published 1995 (Harmondsworth: Penguin, 1996).
Karmel, Annabel, *Feeding Your Baby and Toddler* (London: Dorling Kindersley, 1999).
Kaye-Smith, Sheila, *Kitchen Fugue* (London: Cassell, 1945).
Kenney-Herbert, Colonel, *Culinary Jottings for Madras*, first published 1878 (Madras: Higginbotham & Co., 1883).
Kerr, Graham (The Galloping Gourmet), *The Graham Kerr Cook Book*, first published 1966 (London: W. H. Allen, 1971).
Kilbourn, Donald, *Pots and Pans: Man's Answer to Women's Lib* (London: William Luscombe, 1974).
Kinsey, Alfred, *Sexual Behaviour in the Human Female*, first published 1953 (Bloomington: Indiana University Press, 1998).
Kinsey, Alfred, *Sexual Behaviour in the Human Male*, first published 1948 (Bloomington: Indiana University Press, 1998).
Kurlansky, Mark, *Choice Cuts: A Selection of Food Writing from Around the World and Throughout History* (London: Jonathan Cape, 2002).
Kurlansky, Mark, *Cod: A Biography of the Fish that Changed the World*, first published 1997 (London: Jonathan Cape, 1998).
Kurlansky, Mark, *Salt: A World History* (London: Jonathan Cape, 2002).
Ladenis, Nico, *My Gastronomy* (London: Ebury Press, 1987).
Lake, Nancy, *Menus Made Easy: How to Order Dinner and Give the Dishes Their French Names* (London: Frederick Warne, 1911).
Lancaster, Osbert, *Here, of All Places: The Pocket Lamp of Architecture* (London: John Murray, 1959).
Lanchester, John, *The Debt to Pleasure* (London: Picador, 1996).
Lane, Harriet, 'Twenty Years On, We're Still in Love with Delia', *Observer*, 12 December 1999.
Langley, Andrew, compiler, *The Selected Soyer* (London: Absolute Press, 1987).
Langley Moore, June and Langley Moore, Doris, *The Pleasure of Your Company: A Text-book of Hospitality* (London: Gerald Howe Ltd., 1933).
Lappé, Frances Moore, *Diet for a Small Planet: How to Enjoy a Rich Protein Harvest by Getting Off the Top of the Food Chain*, first published 1971 (New York: Ballantine Books, 1974).
Larousse Gastronomique (London: Hamlyn, 2001).
Lawrence, Sue, *On Baking* (London: Kyle Cathie, 1996).
Lawson, Nigella, *How to Be a Domestic Goddess: Baking and the Art of Comfort Cooking* (London: Chatto & Windus, 2000).
Lawson, Nigella, *How to Eat: The Pleasures and Principles of Good Food* (London: Chatto & Windus, 1998).

Lawson, Nigella, *Nigella Bites* (London: Chatto & Windus, 2001).
Leonardi, Susan J., 'Recipes for Reading: Summer Pasta, Lobster à la Riseholme and Key Lime Pie', *PMLA*, 104/3 May 1989.
Lepard, Dan and Whittington, Richard, *Baker & Spice: Baking with Passion* (London: Quadrille, 1999).
Levy, Paul, *Out to Lunch* (Harmondsworth: Penguin, 1988).
Levy, Paul (Ed.), *The Penguin Book of Food and Drink*, first published 1996 (Harmondsworth: Penguin, 1997).
Leyel, Mrs C. F. and Hartley, Miss Olga, *The Gentle Art of Cookery*, first published 1925 (London: Chatto & Windus, 1935).
Little, Alastair, *Italian Kitchen: Recipes from La Cacciata* (London: Ebury Press, 1996).
Llanover, Lady, *Good Cookery*, first published 1867 (Llanddewi Brefi: Brefi Press, 1867).
Lo, Kenneth, *Chinese Food* (Harmondsworth: Penguin, 1972).
Longmate, Norman, *How We Lived Then: A History of Everyday Life During the Second World War* (London: Arrow, 1973).
Lovegren, Sylvia, *Fashionable Food: Seven Decades of Food Fads* (New York: Macmillan, 1995).
Lowinsky, Ruth, *Lovely Food: A Cookery Notebook* (London: The Nonesuch Press, 1931).
Luard, Elisabeth, *Family Life: Birth, Death and the Whole Damn Thing* (Corgi: London, 1996).
Luard, Elisabeth, *The Princess and the Pheasant* (London: Bantam Press, 1987).
Luard, Elisabeth, *The Rich Tradition of European Peasant Cookery* (London: Bantam Press, 1986).
Luard, Elisabeth, *Still Life* (London: Bantam Press, 1998).
Lucas, Dione and Hume, Rosemary, *Au Petit Cordon Bleu*, first published 1936 (London: J. M. Dent & Sons, 1939).
Mabey, Richard, *Food for Free: A Guide to the Edible Wild Plants of Britain*, first published 1972 (London: Collins, 1974).
MacClancy, Jeremy, *Consuming Culture* (London: Chapmans, 1992).
Macdonald of Macdonald, Claire, *Suppers*, first published 1994 (London: Corgi, 1996).
Madison, Deborah with Brown, Edward Espe, *The Greens Cook Book*, first published 1987 (London: Bantam Press, 1996).
Maher, Barbara, *Cakes*, first published 1982 (Harmondsworth: Penguin, 1984).
Marshall, Agnes, *Mrs A. B. Marshall's Cookery Book* (London: Simpkin, Marshall, Hamilton, Kent & Co., 1888).
Martineau, Mrs Philip (Alice), *Caviar to Candy: Recipes for Small Households from All Parts of the World*, first published 1927 (London: Cobden-Sanderson, 1933).
McGee, Harold, *On Food and Cooking: The Science and Lore of the Kitchen*, first published 1984 (London: George Allen & Unwin, 1987).
McInerny, Claire and Roche, Dorothy, *Savour: A Cookery Book*, first published 1931 (London: Oxford University Press, 1956).

McKirdy, Michael, 'Who wrote Soyer's Pantropheon?', *Petit Propos Culinaire*, 29, 1988.
Meades, Jonathan, *Incest and Morris Dancing* (London: Cassell & Co., 2002).
Meighn, Moira, *The Magic Ring for the Needy and Greedy* (London: Oxford University Press, 1936).
Miles, Alice, *The Executive Cook Book* (London: Frederick Muller, 1965).
Miles, John (Ed.), *A Kitchen Goes to War: A Ration-Time Cookery Book with 150 Recipes Contributed by Famous People* (London: John Miles, 1940).
Ministry of Food, The, *The ABC of Cookery* (London: The Ministry of Food, 1945).
Ministry of Food, The, *Canteen Catering* (London: The Ministry of Food, 1942)
Ministry of Food, The, *Community Feeding in Wartime* (London: The Ministry of Food, 1941).
Ministry of Food, The, *The Manual of Nutrition* (London: The Ministry of Food, 1945).
Ministry of Food, The, *Potato Pete's Recipe Book* (London: The Ministry of Food, date unknown).
Ministry of Food, The, *Wise Eating in Wartime* (London: The Ministry of Food, 1943).
Mintz, Sidney, *Sweetness and Power: The Place of Sugar in Modern History*, first published 1985 (Harmondsworth: Penguin, 1986).
Mitford, Jessica, *Hons and Rebels*, first published 1960 (Harmondsworth: Penguin, 1962).
Moir, Jan, 'I'm Not Prim – In Fact, I Am a Bit of a Bitch', *Daily Telegraph*, 25 September 2000.
Moloney, Ted and Coleman, Deke, *Oh, for a French Wife!*, first published 1952 (London: Angus & Robertson, 1964).
Morphy, Countess, *Recipes of All Nations*, first published 1935 (London: Herbert Joseph for Selfridges & Co., 1949).
Neil, Marion, *The Thrift Cook Book* (London: W. & R. Chambers, date unknown, but shortly after 1918).
Nown, Graham, *Mrs Beeton: 150 Years of Cookery and Household Management* (Ward Lock: London, 1986).
Oliver, Frank, *Chinese Cooking*, first published 1955 (London: The Cookery Book Club, 1967).
Oliver, Jamie, *The Naked Chef* (London: Michael Joseph, 1999).
Oliver, Jamie, *The Return of the Naked Chef* (London: Michael Joseph, 2000).
Olney, Richard, *Simple French Food*, first published 1974 (Harmondsworth: Penguin, 1983).
Orwell, George, *The Road to Wigan Pier*, first published 1937 (Harmondsworth: Penguin, 2001).
Palmer, Arnold, *Movable Feasts: Changes in English Eating Habits*, first published 1952 (Oxford: Oxford University Press, 1984).
Paterson, Jennifer and Dickson Wright, Clarissa, *Two Fat Ladies: Gastronomic Adventures (With Motorbike and Sidecar)* (London: Ebury Press, 1996).
Patten, Marguerite, *Marguerite Patten's Century of British Cooking* (London: Grub Street, 1999).

Patten, Marguerite, *Post-War Kitchen: Nostalgic Food and Facts from 1945–1954* (London: Hamlyn, 1998).

Patten, Marguerite, *We'll Eat Again*, first published 1985 (London: Hamlyn, 2000).

Peacock, Lady, *Beating Austerity in the Kitchen* (London: Faber & Faber, 1952).

Peel, Mrs C. S., *Eat-Less-Meat Book* (London: John Lane, 1917).

Peel, Mrs C. S., *The Daily Mail Cookery Book* (London: Associated Newspapers, 1919).

Percy, Lady Algernon, *Our Grandmothers' Recipes* (London: Simpkin, Marshall, Hamilton, Kent & Co., 1916).

Peretti, Jacques, 'Too Hot to Handle', *Guardian*, 30 August 2000.

Pirbright, Peter, *Off the Beeton Track* (London: Binnacle Books series, Golden Galley Press, 1946).

Pizzey, Erin, *The Slut's Cook Book*, first published 1981 (London: Macdonald, 1982).

Planck, Nina, *The Farmers' Market Cookbook* (London: Hodder & Stoughton, 2001).

de Pomiane, Edouard, *Cooking in Ten Minutes*, first published in 1930 (as *La Cuisine en Dix Minutes ou L'Adaptation au Rythme Moderne*) (London: The Cookery Book Club, 1969)

Prince, Rose, 'Elizabeth the First', *Independent on Sunday*, 5 October 1997.

Pullar, Philippa, *Consuming Passions: A History of British Food and Appetite*, first published 1970 (London: Book Club Associates, 1977).

Quaglino, *The Complete Hostess*, Ed. Charles Graves (London: Hamish Hamilton, 1935).

Rabinovich, Adriana, *The Little Red Barn Baking Book* (London: Ebury Press, 2000).

Raffald, Elizabeth, *The Experienced English Housekeeper* (Manchester: publisher unknown, 1769).

Reichel, Ruth, *Comfort Me with Apples* (London: Century, 2002).

Reichel, Ruth, *Tender at the Bone: Growing Up at the Table* (London: Ebury Press, 1998).

Richardson, Paul, *Cornucopia: A Gastronomic Tour of Britain* (London: Little, Brown & Co., 2000).

Richardson, Tim, *Sweets: A History of Temptation* (London: Bantam Press, 2002).

Roden, Claudia, *A New Book of Middle Eastern Food*, first published as *A Book of Middle Eastern Food* 1968 (Harmondsworth: Penguin, 1986).

Roden, Claudia, *The Book of Jewish Food: An Odyssey from Samarkand and Vilna to the Present Day* (London: Viking, 1997).

Rombauer, Irma, *The Joy of Cooking: A Compilation of Reliable Recipes with an Occasional Culinary Chat*, first published 1931 (London: J. M. Dent & Sons, 1947).

Round, Jeremy, *The Independent Cook: Strategies for Seasonal Cooking* (London: Barrie & Jenkins, 1988).

Roux, Albert and Roux, Michel, *At Home with the Roux Brothers* (London: Guild Publishing, 1988).

Rubinstein, Helge, *The Chocolate Book*, first published 1981 (Harmondsworth: Penguin, 1982).
Ryan, Deborah, *The Ideal Home Through the 20th Century* (London: Hazar, 1997).
Ryan, Rachel and Ryan, Margaret, *Dinners for Beginners: An Economical Cookery Book for the Single-Handed*, first published 1934 (London: Hamish Hamilton, 1936).
Ryan, Rachel and Ryan, Margaret, *Quick Dinners for Beginners: A Book of Recipes Taking One Hour or Less to Prepare and Cook* (London: Hamish Hamilton, 1950).
Santich, Barbara, 'Inevitable, Yes, but Desirable?', *Slow: The International Herald of Tastes*, 34, Nov–Dec 2002.
Schlosser, Eric, *Fast Food Nation: What the American Meal is Doing to the World* (London: Allen Lane, 2001).
Scott-Moncrieff, Joanna, *The Book of Woman's Hour* (London: Ariel Productions, 1953).
Seton, Nora, *The Kitchen Congregation: A Memoir*, first published 2000 (London: Phoenix, 2001).
Sexton, David, 'Pudding's Proof', *Times Literary Supplement*, 27 November 1998.
Shaw, Nancy, *Food for the Greedy*, first published 1936 (Westfield: Florian Press, 1951).
Shulman, Martha Rose, *The Vegetarian Feast*, first published 1982 (Wellingborough: Thorsons, 1985).
Simon, André, *The Gourmet's Week-End Book* (London: Seeley Service & Co, 1952).
Slater, Nigel, *Appetite* (London: Fourth Estate, 2000).
Slater, Nigel, *Real Cooking* (London: Michael Joseph, 1997).
Slater, Nigel, *Real Fast Food*, first published 1992 (Harmondsworth: Penguin, 1993).
Slater, Nigel, *Real Fast Puddings*, first published 1993 (Harmondsworth: Penguin, 1994).
Slater, Nigel, *Real Food*, first published 1998 (London: Fourth Estate, 2000).
Slater, Nigel, *Real Good Food* (London: Fourth Estate, 1995).
Slater, Nigel, *Thirst* (London: Fourth Estate, 2002).
Slater, Nigel, *Toast: The Story of a Boy's Hunger* (London: Fourth Estate, 2003).
Smith, Delia, *Delia Smith's Christmas* (London: BBC Books, 1990).
Smith, Delia, *Delia Smith's Complete Cookery Course*, first published 1978 (London: BBC Books, 1982).
Smith, Delia, *Delia Smith's Summer Collection* (London: BBC Books, 1993).
Smith, Delia, *Delia Smith's Winter Collection* (London: BBC Books, 1995).
Smith, Delia, *How to Cheat at Cooking*, first published 1971 (London: Ebury Press, 1976).
Smith, Delia, *How to Cook, Book One* (London: BBC Worldwide, 1998).
Smith, Delia, *How to Cook, Book Two* (London: BBC Worldwide, 1999).
Smith, Joan, *Hungry for You: From Cannibalism to Seduction: A Book of Food* (London: Chatto & Windus, 1996).

Smollett, Tobias, *The Expedition of Humphry Clinker*, first published 1771 (Harmondsworth: Penguin, 1967).
Sobel, Dava, *Longitude*, first published 1996 (London: Fourth Estate, 1998).
Souhami, Diana, *Gluck: Her Biography* (London: Pandora Press, 1988).
Soyer, Alexis, *A Culinary Campaign*, first published 1857 (Lewes: Southover Press, 1995).
Soyer, Alexis, *The Gastronomic Regenerator* (London: Simpkin, Marshall & Co., 1846).
Soyer, Alexis, *The Modern Housewife* (London: Simpkin, Marshall & Co., 1850).
Soyer, Alexis, *The Pantropheon, or History of Food and Its Preparation, from the Earliest Ages of the World* (London: Simpkin, Marshall & Co., 1853).
Soyer, Alexis, *A Shilling Cookery for the People*, first published 1854 (London: George Routledge & Co., 1855).
Soyer, Alexis, *Soyer's Charitable Cookery or The Poor Man's Regenerator* (London: publisher unknown, 1848).
Spain, Nancy, *Mrs Beeton and Her Husband* (London: Collins, 1948).
Spencer, Colin, *British Food – An Extraordinary Thousand Years of History* (London: Grub Street, 2002).
Spencer, Colin, *The Heretic's Feast: A History of Vegetarianism* (London: Fourth Estate, 1993).
Spry, Constance, *Come into the Garden, Cook* (London: J. M. Dent and Sons, 1942).
Spry, Constance and Hume, Rosemary, *The Constance Spry Cookery Book* (London: J. M. Dent & Sons, 1956).
Spry, Constance and Hume, Rosemary, *Hostess* (London, J. M. Dent & Sons, 1961).
Stein, Rick, *Rick Stein's Food Heroes* (London: BBC Books, 2002).
Steingarten, Jeffrey, *It Must've Been Something I Ate* (London: Review, 2002).
Steingarten, Jeffrey, *The Man Who Ate Everything* (London: Headline Books, 1998).
Stewart, Martha, *The Martha Stewart Cook Book: Collected Recipes for Every Day* (New York: Clarkson Potter, 1995).
Sysonby, Lady, *Lady Sysonby's Cook Book*, first published 1935 (London: Putnam, 1948).
Tannahill, Reay, *Food in History*, first published 1973 (London: Review, 2002).
Terry, Josephine, *Cook Happy* (London: Faber & Faber, 1945).
Terry, Josephine, *Food without Fuss* (London: Faber & Faber, 1944).
Thaw, George (Ed.), *Second Helpings: A Taste of the Glenfiddich Awards* (London: Good Books, 1996).
Thomas, Anna, *From Anna's Kitchen* (Harmondsworth: Penguin, 1996).
Thomas, Anna, *The New Vegetarian Epicure*, first published 1978 (as *The Vegetarian Epicure, Book Two*) (Harmondsworth: Penguin, 1991).
Thomas, Anna, *The Vegetarian Epicure*, first published 1972 (Harmondsworth: Penguin, 1981).
Thompson, Sir Henry, *Food and Feeding*, first published early 1880s (London: Frederick Warne, 1898).

Thomson, Winifred Hope, *Someone to Dinner: Chef Cooking for Little Kitchens* (London: Cobden-Sanderson, 1935).
Thorne, John, 'Natural Leavens: Sorting Out Sourdough' (1996), www.outlaw-cook.com.
Thorne, John, *Outlaw Cook*, first published 1992 (Totnes: Prospect Books, 1999).
Thorne, John, *Serious Pig* (New York: North Point Press, 1996).
Tims, Barbara (Ed.), *Food in Vogue: Six Decades of Cooking and Entertaining* (London: George G. Harrap, 1976).
Toklas, Alice B., *The Alice B. Toklas Cook Book*, first published 1954 (Harmondsworth: Penguin, 1961).
Toye, Doris Lytton, *Contemporary Cooking: Receipts from Vogue 1945–1947* (London: Conde-Nast, 1947).
Tuxford, Mrs, *Cookery for the Middle Classes*, first published 1902 (London: Simpkin, Marshall, date unknown, but before 1907).
Uttley, Alison, *Recipes from an Old Farmhouse* (London: The Cookery Book Club, 1966).
Uttley, Alison, *A Traveller in Time*, first published 1939 (Harmondsworth: Penguin, 1984).
Veal, Irene, *Recipes of the 1940s* (London: John Gifford, 1944).
Veerasawmy, E. P., *Indian Cookery*, first published 1963 (London: Mayflower, 1979).
Visser, Margaret, *Much Depends on Dinner: The Extraordinary History, Mythology, Allure and Obsessions, Perils and Taboos, of an Ordinary Meal*, first published 1986 (Harmondsworth: Penguin, 1989).
Visser, Margaret, *The Rituals of Dinner: The Origins, Evolution, Eccentricities and Meaning of Table Manners* (London: Viking, 1992).
Visser, Margaret, *The Way We Are*, first published 1994 (London: Viking, 1995).
Volk, Patricia, *Stuffed: Growing up in a Restaurant Family*, first published 2002 (London: Bloomsbury, 2003).
Waters, Elsie and Waters, Doris, *Gert and Daisy's Wartime Cookery Book* (Manchester: Withy Grove Press, 1941).
Watkeys Moore, Helen, *Camouflage Cookery: A Book of Mock Dishes* (1918).
Watson, Ruth, *The Really Helpful Cookbook* (London: Ebury Press, 2000).
Webb, Mrs Arthur, *War-Time Cookery*, first published 1939 (London: Dent, 1944).
Wells, Patricia, *Trattoria*, first published 1993 (London: Kyle Cathie, 1995).
White, Cynthia, *Women's Magazines 1693–1968* (London: Michael Joseph, 1970).
White, Florence, *Good Things in England: A Book of Real English Cookery*, first published 1932 (London: Jonathan Cape, 1940).
White, Marco-Pierre, *White Heat* (London: Pyramid Books, 1990).
Whitehorn, Katharine, *Cooking in a Bedsitter*, first published 1961 (as *Kitchen in the Corner*) (Harmondsworth: Penguin, 1963).
Willan, Ann, *Great Cooks and Their Recipes: From Tallevent to Escoffier* (London: Pavilion, 1995).

Wilson, Elizabeth, *Only Half-Way to Paradise: Women in Post-War Britain 1945–1968* (London: Tavistock, 1980).

Woolton, Earl of, *The Memoirs of the Rt Hon the Earl of Woolton* (London: Cassell & Co., 1959).

Wright, Carol, *The Liberated Cook's Book* (London: David & Charles, 1975).

Zeldin, Theodore, *An Intimate History of Humanity* (London: Sinclair-Stevenson, 1994).

Zuckerman, Larry, *The Potato: From the Andes in the Sixteenth Century to Fish and Chips, The Story of How a Vegetable Changed History*, first published 1998 (London: Macmillan, 2000).

Recipe Index

BY AUTHOR

BY CATEGORY

STARTERS

SOUPS

SAUCES

FISH

MEAT

VEGETABLES

VEGETARIAN

CHEESE AND EGGS

PUDDINGS

BREAD AND CAKES

Index

RECIPE SOURCES

Raymond Blanc, from *Recipes from Le Manoir Aux Quat'Saisons* (Guild Publishing, 1988), © Raymond Blanc. Reprinted by permission of Le Manoir Aux Quat'Saisons; **X. Marcel Boulestin**, from *Simple French Cooking for English Homes* (William Heinemann, 1923), © The Estate of X. Marcel Boulestin, 1923. Reprinted by permission of PFD () on behalf of the Estate of X. Marcel Boulestin; **Peg Bracken**, from *The 'I Hate to Cook' Book* (Corgi, 1978); **Robert Carrier**, from *Great Dishes of the World* (Boxtree, 1999). Reprinted by permission of Macmillan, London; **Elizabeth David**, from *A Book of Mediterranean Food* (John Lehmann, 1950; Penguin Books, 1955); *French Provincial Cooking* (1960; Penguin Books, 1986), and *An Omelette and a Glass of Wine* (Penguin Books, 1986). Reprinted by permission of Jill Norman; **Rose Elliot**, from *Not Just a Load of Old Lentils* (Fontana, 1986). Reprinted by permission of The White Eagle Publishing Trust; **Ethelind Fearon**, from *The Reluctant Cook* (Herbert Jenkins, 1923); **Rose Gray** and **Ruth Rogers**, from *The River Café Cook Book* (Ebury Press, 1995). Reprinted by permission of The Random House Group Ltd; **Jane Grigson**, from *Good Things* (Penguin Books, 1991), and *Jane Grigson's Vegetable Book* (Penguin Books, 1980), Reprinted by permission of David Higham Associates; **Ambrose Heath**, from *More Kitchen Front Recipes* (A & C Black, 1941). Reprinted by permission of the publisher; **Madhur Jaffrey**, from *An Invitation to Indian Cooking* (Penguin Books, 1978), © 1973 Madhur Jaffrey. Reprinted by permission of the author c/o Rogers, Coleridge & White Ltd., 20 Powis Mews, London W11 1JN; **Lady Agnes Jekyll**, from *Kitchen Essays* (Collins, 1969); **Sheila Kaye-Smith**, from *Kitchen Fugue* (Cassell, 1945). Reprinted by permission of Mrs B. M. Walthew; **Nigella Lawson**, from *How to Eat: The Pleasures and Principles of Good Food* (Chatto & Windus, 1998); **Mrs C. F. Leyel** and **Miss Olga Hartley**, from *The Gentle Art of Cookery* (Chatto & Windus, 1935). Reprinted by permission of The Random House Group Ltd; **Ruth Lowinsky**, from *Lovely Food: A Cookery Notebook* (The Nonesuch Press, 1931); **Mrs Philip (Alice) Martineau**, from *Caviar to Candy: Recipes for Small Households from All Parts of the World* (Cobden-Sanderson, 1933); **Jamie Oliver**, from *Happy Days With the Naked Chef* (Michael Joseph, 2001); **Jeremy Round**, from *The Independent Cook: Strategies for Seasonal Cooking* (Barrie & Jenkins, 1988), © Jeremy Round, 1988. Reprinted by permission of A M Heath & Co Ltd; **Nigel Slater**, from *Real Cooking* (Michael Joseph, 1997), © Nigel Slater, 1997. Reprinted by permission of Penguin Books Ltd; **Constance Spry** and **Rosemary Hume**, from *The Constance Spry Cookery Book* (J. M. Dent & Sons, 1956); **Josephine Terry**, from *Food Without Fuss* (Faber & Faber, 1944); **Alice B. Toklas**, from *The Alice B. Toklas Cook Book* (Michael Joseph, 1954), © Alice B. Toklas, 1954. Reprinted by permission of Penguin Books Ltd; **Katharine Whitehorn**, from *Cooking in a Bedsitter* (Penguin Books, 1963). Reprinted by permission of PFD on behalf of the author.

Although every effort has been made to establish copyright and contact copyright holders prior to printing this has not always been possible. If contacted, the publisher will be pleased to rectify any errors or omissions at the earliest opportunity.